Management for Professionals

For further volumes:
http://www.springer.com/series/10101

Akram Al Ariss
Editor

Global Talent Management

Challenges, Strategies, and Opportunities

 Springer

Editor
Akram Al Ariss
Toulouse Business School
Université de Toulouse
Toulouse
France

ISSN 2192-8096   ISSN 2192-810X (electronic)
ISBN 978-3-319-34300-6   ISBN 978-3-319-05125-3 (eBook)
DOI 10.1007/978-3-319-05125-3
Springer Cham Heidelberg New York Dordrecht London

Springer is part of Springer Science+Business Media (www.springer.com)

Acknowledgements

The making of this book was achieved at the hands of many, without whose hard work, cooperation, skills and talent it would never reached publication.

My sincere thanks therefore to each of the contributing authors, all of whom have not only shared their rich and diverse expertise and perspective on global talent management, but who have remained supportive and cooperative over the long weeks of preparation, editing, and publication. Thanks to you all for your patience and collaboration.

I thank also the Springer team Dr. Prashanth Mahagaonkar and Mrs. Ruth Milewski for all of your help in rendering what was a mere concept for this book a concrete project and for your ongoing assistance throughout the editorial process.

For her much appreciated assistance in the editing, proofreading, and finalizing the work as a whole, I thank Miss Arabella Lawson, and Mr. Adam Hoteit whose help in the initial phase in his capacity as a management consultant was fundamental.

Lastly, I would like to make a special dedication to my parents, Chirine and Abdel-Salam, and to my wife, Christine, for their continuous support. Thank you.

Contents

Part I

Meaning and Processes of Global Talent Management

Global Talent Management: An Introduction and a Review

Akram Al Ariss

1   What Is Global Talent Management?

Talent management (TM) has now become a fashion trend in modern organizations. While businesses and consulting firms have been plowing ahead with the practice and discourse of TM (Nijs et al. 2013), there remains a lack of knowledge as to the meanings, challenges, and future vision of global talent management (GTM). Moreover, focus has predominantly been on GTM in Western contexts (Cooke et al. 2013). This confusion over what GTM signifies and should signify in practice, together with the Western bias of research to date leads to uncertainty over where GTM could be taken in the future. This book hopes to go some way in addressing this absence of clarity by outlining the fundamental GTM challenges, strategies, and opportunities in an international context. It bridges theoretical and practical conceptions of GTM, and indicates possible paths to be taken by future research and practice in investigating this topic further. Each chapter offers a table presenting five key learning points on understanding Global Talent Management challenges, five key learning points regarding strategies to overcome these challenges, and five key learning points on future opportunities in Global Talent Management.

Table 1 identifies some key definitions/meanings covered by the term GTM and used in the literature. GTM has also seen the manifestation of a number of different ways of translating the concept into practice, including firstly, old international human resource (HR) practices rebranded and used in a more systematic and efficient way. GTM in this case often refers to the management of all employees, i.e. the inclusive approach; secondly, international succession planning practices. This involves using various means such as technology, virtual, and physical networks, in order to secure talent pools into jobs throughout the organizations, internationally; and thirdly, the management of talented (or best) employees globally. This exclusive approach refers to the management of high-achieving

Professor A. Al Ariss, Ph.D. (✉)
Université de Toulouse, Toulouse Business School, Toulouse, France
e-mail: info@akramalariss.com

A. Al Ariss (ed.), *Global Talent Management*, Management for Professionals,
DOI 10.1007/978-3-319-05125-3_1, © Springer International Publishing Switzerland 2014

Table 1 Meanings of global talent management

References (non-exhaustive list)	Meanings of global talent management
Scullion et al. (2010) Vaiman et al. (2012) McDonnell et al. (2010) Farndale et al. (2010)	GTM involves organizational activities for attracting, selecting, developing, and retaining the best employees in the most strategic roles to achieve organizational strategic business priorities internationally. This takes into account differences across countries in how talent should be managed
Al Ariss et al. (2013) Sidani and Al Ariss (2013)	Very similar to the above but with continued commitment to the perceptions of employees, to organizational benefits, and to the wellbeing of societies, while taking local and international contexts into account
Farndale et al. (2010)	GTM involves global competition for talent, managing new forms of international mobility, improving organizational capability to manage talents in emerging markets, elaborating new corporate HR roles
Tarique and Schuler (2010)	GTM includes systematically utilizing international human resource management (IHRM) activities to attract, develop, and retain individuals with high levels of human capital in consistency with the strategic directions of the multinational enterprise in a dynamic, highly competitive, and global environment"
Schuler et al. (2011)	GTM refers to using HR policies and practices to manage the several global talent challenges that a company confronts: location and relocation management; planning and forecasting; staffing, training, and developing; and evaluating employees consistent with a firm's strategic objectives while taking into account regulatory requirements
Stahl et al. (2011)	Various possible conceptualizations acknowledged. From the research made, two distinct understandings of TM are identified: the differentiated approach, and the inclusive approach. The paper also presents a diagram called the Talent Management Wheel in which are depicted the practices and guiding principles. There are six of these latter and they are: internal consistency, management involvement, employer branding through differentiation, balancing global and local needs, cultural embeddedness, and alignment strategy
Mellahi and Collings (2010)	GTM involves the systematic identification of major positions which differentially contribute to the organization's long-term competitive benefit on a global scale, the development of a talent pool of high potential and high performing executives to fill these roles which reflect the international scope of the multinational enterprise, and the development of a differentiated human resource architecture to help filling these positions
Shen and Hall (2009)	GTM should be conducted in the light of the best outcome for the company as well as the individual in a way to appropriately manage the needs and issues of talents, wherever they are in the world
Dries (2013)	Talent (rather than GTM) as capital; talent as individual difference; talent as giftedness; talent as identity; talent as strength; and talent as the perception of talent
Gallardo-Gallardo et al. (2013)	Talent (rather than GTM) as 'object' i.e., talent as natural ability; talent as mastery; talent as commitment; talent as fit; versus 'subject' i.e., talent as all people; talent as some people

employees (Iles et al. 2010; Meyers and van Woerkom 2013). Most of these meanings agree that an optimization of talent potentials will lead to better organizational performance.

With data collected from 33 multinational corporations headquartered across 11 countries, Stahl et al. (2011) suggest two distinct conceptions of TM: the differentiated approach, and the inclusive approach. They concluded that firms should avoid attempting to replicate the practices of top-performing companies and instead incorporate TM practices into their own needs. The various readings of the term 'Global Talent Management', as shown in Table 1, have led to a lack of clear understanding of its scope and purpose (Al Ariss et al. 2013).

The meaning of GTM is therefore multifold (Lewis and Heckman 2006). In this book, it is understood in at least three major ways. Firstly, it includes identifying, selecting, recruiting, developing, and retaining talents in a way that meets the global strategic goals of companies. This entails taking into account the business interests of parent companies as well as of their subsidiaries and, when appropriate, their other forms of inter- and intra-linkages. Secondly, GTM is also about identifying, selecting, recruiting, developing, and retaining talents in international contexts. This includes organizations in developing countries that have been so far under-researched. One of this book's objectives is therefore to shift GTM away from the Western-centric focus, to include more diverse and indigenous perspectives from other international contexts. This is reflected in the variety of countries covered by the chapters of this book as well as the diversity of the authors' perspectives on GTM. Thirdly and finally, GTM is also associated with managing expatriation (Cerdin and Brewster 2014), a critical element of strategic IHRM. As businesses have grown to be more and more globalized, so the conception of GTM has come to heavily incorporate the management of selecting, recruiting, and retaining talents to be expatriated. Given this broad scope of GTM, the next section presents the chapters in this book.

2 Chapters in this Book

Chapters in this book are centered on two key topics: Part 1, comprising Chapters One to Eight, focuses on the "Meaning and Processes of Global Talent Management"; and, Part 2, which includes Chapters 10 to 18, is about "Global Talent Management across Geographical Contexts."

Chapter 2: HR Directors' Understanding of 'Talent': A Cross-Cultural Study This chapter intends to develop a greater understanding of the multiple definitions attributed to 'talent' by HR directors worldwide (N = 410) along with an appreciation of the direct relation between 'talent mindset' and the identification and management of talent within their respective firms. From a variety of cultural clusters, respondents recognized ability, knowledge, skills, and potential as all being highly connected with talent. They also appeared to concur that talent can be cultivated. Cultural differences surfaced at the issues of 'inclusivity' in organizational TM and the reliability of first impressions in talent assessment. On both questions, the cluster with the highest-scoring organizations was the Anglo cluster, which is notable considering the Anglo-Saxon bias of TM literature (as a result of being mostly produced in the US and the UK). Precise implications for both future research and GTM in practice are clearly set out.

Chapter 3: Smart Global Talent Management: A Promising Hybrid Knowledge management and TM are two distinct lines of applied research, which, in this chapter, are brought together to attempt a more effective approach in the face of the problems arising in an ever more international workplace. Combining these two conceptual orientations into a hybrid by which to move global business practice in new directions, known as 'smart global talent management', unites the stronger elements of both while the fusion itself opens the possibility of overcoming the weaknesses in each. The chapter assesses both approaches separately in respect of the strengths and limitations of each, before arguing for the significance of this new model that merges both in one, benefitting future research and practice in global HRM.

Chapter 4: Coaching of Key Talents in Multinational Companies This chapter aims to improve understanding of how executive coaching is used in GTM, the reasons for its use, and the experiences of HR personnel who have known it implemented. The approach taken was a qualitative one based on multiple case studies, and to identify various characteristics at the different stages, the Coaching Continuum Stage Model was applied. While coaching was used by all the multinational corporations to serve leadership development, its implementation was never dictated solely by the needs of the companies' strategic TM. Coaching was used to support key talents in transition situations, and this coaching varied significantly in quality and length, according to the qualifications and competency of the coach. Key talents also received training in coaching skills, though managerial coaching presented difficulties. Once coaching reached a more developed stage in its execution, the organizations managed it more systematically. For its success, it was essential that coaching be recognized as a long-term process, that the idea behind it be clearly explained, and that the coaching be firmly aligned with GTM strategies. This subject is especially significant given the huge investments in coaching talents by organizations. The study enhances our appreciation of the use and objectives of coaching as used by MNCs and offers an important contribution to research on the subject by presenting, as has never before been done, the empirical results obtained via the Coaching Continuum Stage Model. It also has practical implications useful for HR professionals intending to use coaching in their organizations, by describing the characteristics at the various stages.

Chapter 5: Cultural Intelligence as a Key Construct for Global Talent Management In this chapter, focus is on what skills and abilities are required for achieving effective GMT, as per the four main elements in the concept of cultural intelligence (CQ). The chapter presents a framework of CQ in the GTM context by defining and illustrating the CQ concept in its four elements, their precursory forms, and their intermediate and outcome variables with practical examples and interview excerpts with actors in this field. Such a framework enables HR and line managers to advance the development of cross-cultural skills within their own talents, making it possible to increase and better the global activity of their organization.

Chapter 6: Inpatriation as a Key Component of Global Talent Management Lack of sufficient talent is cited as being detrimental to many organizations today. Without enough talent, multinational companies in particular find themselves unable to effectively carry out their work internationally. The following chapter argues that employees known as 'inpatriates', selected from subsidiary offices to work at headquarters, could significantly lessen the GTM problems faced by MNCs, moving away from the more traditional means of addressing TM using expatriates. While substantial research remains to be done into the benefits of inpatriation, it has the potential to significantly increase the successfulness of GTM strategies within an organization. Recognizing that the competitive advantage of one organization over another requires capitalization on every possible source of talent, the gains that distinguish inpatriation from other TM means are outlined. The significance of inpatriation as a core element of GTM is highlighted, while some of the problems arising from its usage are brought to light through the case study of a multinational corporation with headquarters in France. Through the discussion and analysis of inpatriate experiences on assignment, problems with which such employees are confronted are examined while also searching for means to resolve them.

Chapter 7: The Global Talent Challenge of Self-Initiated Expatriates The discussions initiated and developed in this chapter aim to contribute to the literature on GTM specifically on the topic of self-initiated expatriate (SIE) experience: the challenges faced, strategies used, and opportunities available. The importance of SIEs in satisfying the demand for talent internationally has been widely recognized. Any frameworks for developing GTM should therefore take account of the particular traits that characterize SIEs. When formulating GTM systems for SIEs, it is argued the advantages of a multilevel approach so as to comprehend how the macro-country, meso-organizational, and micro-individual inter-relate. Such a perspective is in line with what Al Ariss and Crowley-Henry (2013) have suggested and allows appreciating the diverse nature of SIEs as a group, while encouraging GTM policies and practices to be designed and implemented accordingly. It would also assist in the capitalization on global talent for its social and economic value on the meso-organizational level as a strategic resource, and within the talent pool on the macro-country level.

Chapter 8: Opportunities and Challenges for Organizations and Highly Skilled Migrant Professionals The talent market remains hugely competitive, and organizations must be able to seize hold of the highly talented workers with international mobility. However, sometimes, organizations lose out entirely on this wealth of talent since they lack the systems that would be necessary to secure global talent. Many international workers seeking employment are selected for job posts unequal to their qualifications and experience in which they find themselves overqualified and unable to put to use their complete set of skills. This chapter is based on the results of interviews conducted in eight different nation states. Respondents were all drawn from a pool of talent of people with a high level of education and all enjoyed the right of freedom to move about the EU. The focus group for this research was therefore made up of professionals whose high-level talent and mobility would suggest their ability to acquire top positions within the global workplace. The research indicated, however, that more needs to be done by organizations in order to attract and retain talent given the competition in the international business context.

Chapter 9: Global Talent Management in Brazil: Jeitinho as a Managerial Talent This chapter examines 'jeitinho', a concept originating in Brazil. It is demonstrated how it can be a means of facilitating the integration of teams located internationally, and a managerial talent. The jeitinho is a characteristic typical of Brazil and a social mechanism pushing a view focused on short-term outcomes and especially crisis solutions. Based on data drawn from a case study of Volvo 3P, it is revealed how the jeitinho is both a characteristic deriving from the Brazilian culture and also a talent that comprises flexibility when managing relations between members within a team, thus enhancing both integration and level of performance. This chapter features elements of jeitinho as a Brazilian cultural characteristic and its impact on cultural adaptation and integration. Implications for practice are discussed.

Chapter 10: Talent Management in China China is the world's biggest transitional economy. This chapter describes how TM has developed in China, in both policy and practice, and how it exists today, referring to a number of frameworks, including labor economics, labor migration, HRM, cross-cultural management, and strategic management. The author seeks to establish a specific model of TM accounting for both the Chinese government and Chinese culture as significant actors. The field of TM in China is changing rapidly, though most firms continue to see HRM as a support function. A few of the larger state-owned companies and the multinational corporations in particular include strategic considerations in their HR and TM practices. The chapter underlines the challenges particularly faced by Chinese managers and foreign entrepreneurs and then indicates future GTM opportunities in China and internationally.

Chapter 11: Global Talent Management in Japanese Multinational Companies: The Case of Nissan Motor Company Following a series of in-depth interviews with the company managers of Nissan Motor Company, this chapter presents a report of GTM within this particular organization. In the past, Nissan conducted IHRM almost identically to its management of Japanese expatriates. As a result of three 'glass ceilings', Nissan faced the challenge of being able to attract and to retain talented local employees in their subsidiaries abroad, and were therefore failing to maximize their use of human resources at a global level. To address these difficulties, in 1999 Nissan appointed President Carlos Ghosn to lead their GTM initiative. They began by establishing the "NAC", a personnel committee so as to build a pipeline of international talent, and then went on to lay down their own global corporate values, known as the "Nissan Way". This serves to achieve "normative integration". They have also disseminated their personnel evaluation system to be referred to by managers across the world for the sake of "systems integration" in IHRM. By sharing the Nissan Way, international networks and mutual trust between leaders in important global positions have been built up, irrespective of nationality or the location of assignment. In order to optimize utilization of human resources at a global level, and to attract and retain talented employees, the company has affected multi-directional personnel transfers. Then, through international collaborations outside the home country borders, a new process of innovation has been born. Key practical implications are drawn from this case study.

Chapter 12: Talent Management in ASEAN: A Study of Thailand The goal of this chapter is to examine how Thai executives put TM into practice, and to understand which factors are those that determine the commitment and performance of talented individuals within the securities industry in Thailand. The featured case study targets a financial and investment brokerage company, which for eight consecutive years managed to retain the top position in Thailand with the highest market share. It is the largest Thai company that has been able to do so. In-depth interviews were conducted with three top executives, 25 branch managers, and 75 high performing employees. The results indicate that executives who are open, approachable, and trustworthy have the most significant effect on the commitment and performance of already high performing employees.

Chapter 13: Global Talent Management in Knowledge Intensive Firms in Europe and India This chapter is intended to suggest directions for future research, concentrating on both theoretical and empirical research on TM in knowledge intensive organizations particularly in Western Europe and India and focuses on the business process offshore industry. Initially, authors give a detailed description of the strategies of TM used in Western Europe before then examining those that are beginning to appear in India, hoping to draw attention to specificities between both areas. Beyond this, authors offer a description and analysis of the patterns of talent flow from Western Europe to India and the difficulties faced in India by those European expatriates. Indications helpful both to future research and practice are indicated.

Chapter 14: Talent Management in the MENA and GCC Regions: Challenges and Opportunities While in general, research into the challenges and opportunities that talent management puts to private and public organizations is increasing internationally, there is a significant lack of literature covering the Middle East and North Africa (MENA) region (Al Ariss 2014). The following chapter seeks to redress this oversight and offers advice on how to best understand and approach the topic of talent management in the MENA region. Focusing on the region in general and specifically on the Gulf countries, the chapter closely studies the challenges faced in attempting to achieve optimal talent management. Crucially, it highlights the disjunction between how the subject of talent management is conceived and realized in a global context and how this is done in the MENA region. In the latter, there are a number of factors, socioeconomic and educational, which remain as obstacles not only to the management but also the training and development of talent in readiness for and within the job market. Within its particular physical setting, notably that of the Gulf Corporation Council (GCC), the definition of talent management comprises the local governmental policy, processes, apparatuses, and practices of HRM enforced for the sake of educating, attracting, retaining, and developing talent. Through this chapter, the author endeavors to assess how these factors affect local pools of talent, going on to envisage the steps needed to fully capacitate this talent and successfully incorporate it within the job market.

Chapter 15: Talent Management in Poland: Challenges, Strategies, and Opportunities This chapter aims to elucidate the point to which theory and practice of TM has developed in Poland. While it is limited and cannot be understood to cover TM in Poland in general, this study draws an outline of the challenges, strategies to dealing with such challenges, and opportunities within TM in Polish companies and in businesses at a global level. The chapter offers a definition of 'talent' as well as a number of TM models and a depiction of how TM is practiced in Poland.

Chapter 16: How to Attract and Retain Global Careerists: Evidence from Finland There is increasing international demand for professionals with the will and capacities to take on positions overseas, wherever the need might be. However, it remains a huge strategic challenge for global organizations to successfully identify individuals who have the abilities required to achieve the objectives of an international assignment and have an interest in being relocated overseas. This chapter addresses the difficulties met by TM in the face of global careerists, that is to say global managers boasting great experience and pursuing long-term international careers with diverse assignments overseas. From a series of studies conducted with professionals such as these from Finland, the authors present an evaluation and cross-analysis of the observations drawn. The means by which multinational corporations might entice, encourage, and secure commitment from global careerists who are most capable of ensuring the achievement of these companies' HR internationalization strategies are examined.

Chapter 17: Global Talent Management in French Multinationals In the aim of international expansion, many employees are expatriated to countries overseas by their companies. For the sake of an organization's global mobility, it is crucial that this expatriation is managed with efficiency in order that both the organization and the global talents are able to achieve their respective objectives. This leads then to the fundamental question: How should global talent international assignments be efficiently managed? Using a bibliographic review as well as interviews conducted with HR professionals, the authors distinguish what possible developments could be effected and which improvements could be necessary in respect of the process of international assignment. A model with very practical implications is suggested for such international assignment of global talents. Combining the fields of GTM and management of international assignments also opens up new approaches that might be taken in future research.

Chapter 18: Global Talent Management and the American Female Executive In this chapter, GTM, understood as the management of top-level talent beyond national borders, is reviewed as it manifests in the context of some of the biggest organizations in the United States. Transnational Corporations (TNCs) is the name given to such organizations acting at a global level. Internal organization is decentralized, authority being transferred down to the individual level.

Conclusions

Building on Al Ariss et al. (2013), six suggestions can be offered here that would ensure that GTM is better understood and practiced. Firstly it is integral that organizational leaders and researchers perceive TM as a relational construct, in that one cannot ignore the significance of the relationships between individuals in organizational, industry/occupational, institutional, and national/international contexts (Al Ariss and Crowley-Henry 2013). This starts with organizations taking into account the perceptions of their employees regarding the management of the talents conducted by HR departments (Sonnenberg et al. 2013). Mismatch between GTM policies offered by HR departments and their perceived value by employees can only devastate organizations. Second, one must not neglect to appreciate the intermediary role of the operational groups and teams in organizations where GTM policy and practice takes place. Third, business leaders and researchers should always consider the local/international contexts, taking into account specific social norms, cultural values, and work regulations and legislations that will affect the transferability of the GTM process across business sectors and national boundaries. Fourth, GTM needs to be open to diversity by, for example, giving the opportunity to international migrants and minority groups to develop within the company and reach leadership positions. Fifth, extending GTM understandings beyond Western contexts of HR and looking at emerging economies such as China, India, South American countries, Russia, and the Middle East among other under-researched contexts can open new avenues for GTM. Finally, GTM and, more broadly, TM should not simply be viewed in terms of success optimization, but also in terms of commitment shown to individuals, organizations, and the wellbeing of societies.

References

Al Ariss, A. (2014). Voicing experiences and perceptions of local managers: Expatriation in the Arab Gulf. *The International Journal of Human Resource Management*. doi: 10.1080/09585192.2013.870288.

Al Ariss, A., & Crowley-Henry, M. (2013). Self-initiated expatriation and migration in the management literature: Present theorizations and future research directions. *Career Development International, 18*(1), 78–96.

Al Ariss, A., Cascio, W., & Paauwe, J. (2013). Talent management: Current theories and future research directions. *Journal of World Business*. http://dx.doi.org/10.1016/j.jwb.2013.11.001

Cerdin, J. -L., & Brewster, C. (2014). Talent management and expatriation: Bridging two streams of research and practice. *Journal of World Business, 49*(2), 245–252.

Cooke, F. L., Saini, D. S., & Wang, J. (2013). Talent management in China and India: A comparison of management perceptions and human resource practices. *Journal of World Business*. http://dx.doi.org/10.1016/j.jwb.2013.11.006

Dries, N. (2013). The psychology of talent management: A review and research agenda. *Human Resource Management Review, 23*(4), 272–285.

Farndale, E., Scullion, H., & Sparrow, P. (2010). The role of the corporate HR function in global talent management. *Journal of World Business, 45*(2), 161–168.

Gallardo-Gallardo, E., Dries, N., & González-Cruz, T. F. (2013). What is the meaning of 'talent' in the world of work? *Human Resource Management Review, 23*.

Iles, P., Preece, D., & Chuai, X. (2010). Talent management as a management fashion in HRD: Towards a research agenda. *Human Resource Development International, 13*(2), 125–145.

Lewis, R. E., & Heckman, R. J. (2006). Talent management: A critical review. *Human Resource Management Review, 16*(2), 139–154.

McDonnell, A., Lamare, R., Gunnigle, P., & Lavelle, J. (2010). Developing tomorrow's leaders: Evidence of global talent management in multinational enterprises. *Journal of World Business, 45*(2), 150–160.

Mellahi, K., & Collings, D. G. (2010). The barriers to effective global talent management: The example of corporate Elites in MNEs. *Journal of World Business, 45*(2), 143–149.

Meyers, M. C., & van Woerkom, M. (2013). The influence of underlying philosophies on talent management: theory, implications for practice, and research agenda. *Journal of World Business*. http://dx.doi.org/10.1016/j.jwb.2013.11.003

Nijs, S., Gallardo-Gallardo, E., Dries, N., & Sels, L. (2013). A multidisciplinary review into the definition, operationalization, and measurement of talent. *Journal of World Business*. http://dx.doi.org/10.1016/j.jwb.2013.11.002

Schuler, R. S., Jackson, S. E., & Tarique, I. (2011). Global talent management and global talent challenges: Strategic opportunities for IHRM. *Journal of World Business, 46*(4), 506–516.

Scullion, H., Collings, D. G., & Caligiuri, P. (2010). Global talent management. *Journal of World Business, 45*(2), 105–108.

Shen, Y., & Hall, D. T. (2009). When expatriates explore other options: Retaining talent through greater job embeddedness and repatriation adjustment. *Human Resource Management, 48*(5), 793–816.

Sidani, Y., & Al Ariss, A. (2013). Institutional and corporate drivers of global talent management: Evidence from the Arab Gulf Region. *Journal of World Business.* http://dx.doi.org/10.1016/j.jwb.2013.11.005.

Sonnenberg, M., Zijderveld, V., & Brinks, M. (2013). The role of talent-perception incongruence in effective talent management. *Journal of World Business.* http://dx.doi.org/10.1016/j.jwb.2013.11.011

Stahl, G. K., et al. (2011). Six principles of effective global talent management. *MIT Sloan Management Review.* Retrieved December 21, 2011, from http://sloanreview.mit.edu/issue/winter-2012/ and http://sloanreview.mit.edu/?content_type=research-feature

Tarique, I., & Schuler, R. S. (2010). Global talent management: Literature review, integrative framework, and suggestions for further research. *Journal of World Business, 45*(2), 122–133.

Vaiman, V., Scullion, H., & Collings, D. (2012). Talent management decision making. *Management Decision, 50*(5), 925–941.

HR Directors' Understanding of 'Talent': A Cross-Cultural Study

Nicky Dries, Richard D. Cotton, Silvia Bagdadli, and Manoela Ziebell de Oliveira

1   Introduction

As no currently available theory has enough scope to capture its different elements or cause-and-effect relationships, and no methodological approach is considered superior to others, talent management fits the criteria of a 'phenomenon' (Hambrick 2007). Looking at the bibliometrics of the field, we see that although there currently still is a huge discrepancy between practitioner and academic interest in talent management—over 7,000 articles in Human Resource (HR) practitioner journals since 1990 compared to only around 100 'real' academic publications—this gap is closing slowly but surely (Dries 2013). Academic interest in talent management has grown exponentially since 2008—especially in global talent management.

Interestingly, talent management and global talent management seem to be evolving into two separate literature streams. Where the global talent management literature borrows heavily from the international HRM literature (e.g., Farndale et al. 2010; Schuler et al. 2011), the talent management literature has its roots mainly in the strategic HRM literature (e.g., Boudreau and Ramstad 2005), typically adopting human capital and resource-based view (RBV)-type frameworks (e.g., Cappelli 2008). A major aim of our chapter is to contribute to the discussions

N. Dries (✉)
Faculty of Business and Economics, Research Centre for Organisation Studies, KU Leuven, Naamsestraat 69, 3000 Leuven, Belgium
e-mail: Nicky.Dries@econ.kuleuven.be

R.D. Cotton
Department of Management, Walker College of Business, Appalachian State University, NC, USA

S. Bagdadli
Department of Management and Technology, Bocconi University, Milan, Italy

M.Z. de Oliveira
Laboratório de Fenomenologia Experimental e Cognição, Programa de Pós-Graduação em Psicologia, Universidade Federal do Rio Grande do Sul, Porto Alegre – Rio Grande do Sul, Brazil

A. Al Ariss (ed.), *Global Talent Management*, Management for Professionals,
DOI 10.1007/978-3-319-05125-3_2, © Springer International Publishing Switzerland 2014

in the global talent management literature by building on what we know from the talent management literature whilst placing our findings within a cross-cultural framework.

Specifically, we aim to advance understanding of the meanings attributed to 'talent' by HR directors across the world, and how their talent mindsets translate into the ways in which talent is identified and managed in their organizations. To date, hardly any data seems to be available about the different meanings attributed to 'talent' across cultures and how these might affect talent management in multinational corporations (MNCs). Considering the increasing international expansion of many large enterprises, it seems important to fully grasp how organizational decision makers (i.e., HR directors, line managers, CEOs), especially from subsidiaries of the same corporation in different cultures, see talent. MNCs need to understand cross-cultural differences in terms of shared mental models about talent before they can formulate a viable global talent management strategy (Farndale et al. 2010). As a response to this gap in the literature, in this chapter we examine the extent to which HR directors from different countries: (a) believe that everyone has talent (vs. believe that talent is a rare commodity); (b) believe that talent is innate (vs. believe that it can be developed); and (c) believe that they recognize talent when they see it (vs. rely on standardized assessment). These three 'tensions' were derived from a recent literature review on talent management (see Dries 2013), and are further discussed below.

1.1 Inclusive vs. Exclusive Approach to Talent Management

Talent management is typically defined in two major ways. 'Exclusive' definitions of talent management refer to the differential management of employee groups with differential value, for example: "Activities and processes that involve the systematic identification of key positions which differentially contribute to the organization's sustainable competitive advantage, the development of a talent pool of high potentials and high-performing incumbents to fill these roles, and the development of a differentiated human resource architecture to facilitate filling these positions with competent incumbents and to ensure their continued commitment to the organization" (Collings and Mellahi 2009, p. 304). On the other hand, we find definitions that are more 'inclusive', for instance that of Buckingham and Vosburgh (2001): "Talent management refers to the art of recognizing where each employee's areas of natural talent lie, and figuring out how to help each employee develop the job-specific skills and knowledge to turn those talents into real performance [...] elevating each person's performance to its highest possible levels, given the individual's natural talents" (p. 22).

Although strong opinions are held on either end, to date it remains unclear which definition of talent management offers the most accurate representation of how the phenomenon plays out in the field. While an inclusive approach to talent management is believed to lead to a more pleasant working environment characterized by openness, trust, and overall employee wellbeing (Warren 2006), the exclusive approach is assumed to generate higher return on investment in terms of profit and productivity, brought about by increases in the achievement motivation of pivotal employees (Boudreau and Ramstad 2005). In this chapter, we will argue that rather than being an 'either-or' story, talent management can actually be implemented in different ways depending on the culture and mission of an organization—and possibly even the national culture in which it resides. Rather than prescribing as academics 'what talent management is (or should be)' it might be more useful to research the different approaches to talent management found in organizations worldwide, systematically mapping beliefs and mindsets about talent held in specific contexts, and examining why these beliefs and mindsets persist. An intended contribution of our chapter is thus that it offers a cross-cultural perspective on this 'best fit' approach to talent management (Garrow and Hirsch 2008).

1.2   Selection vs. Development Approach to Talent Management

This second 'tension' refers to the important discussion about the extent to which talent can be taught and learned (Meyers et al. 2013). Innate perspectives on talent imply a focus on the selection, assessment, and identification of talent. In an era of increasing talent scarcity, this means aggressively searching, recruiting, and selecting highly sought-after profiles—which is expected to become more and more challenging as scarcities become even more tangible (Cappelli 2008). Acquired perspectives on talent, on the other hand, imply a focus on education, training, experience, and learning as tools for talent development (McCall 1998). Although this latter perspective seems particularly attractive considering the changing demand-supply dynamics in labor markets worldwide (cf. the discussion on 'making or buying' talent), research has shown that most organizational decision makers tend to believe that talent is, for the largest part, inborn (e.g., Tsay and Banaji 2011).

Beliefs about talent being innate or not are influenced by a number of factors. A first factor is the implicit person theory that prevails in the organization. Whereas some organizational decision makers will believe that people 'are who they are', and that the odds of people changing over time are low (i.e., 'fixed' or 'entity' mindset), others will believe that people are determined primarily by the lessons they learn from experience, and that people can change even at a later age (i.e., 'growth' or 'incremental' mindset) (Heslin et al. 2005). Whether a manager, or a group or managers, believes in one or the other will affect the extent to which an organization's (or a department's) talent management practices focus more on selection, or development of talented employees. It also has 'path dependency' implications, in that an entity theorist who does not see the potential of a particular employee at one point in time, is not likely to change his mind at a later time (Heslin et al. 2005). A second factor is culture. In her philological analysis of the word 'talent' from both a historical and a linguistic-comparative point of view, Tansley (2011) found that while European languages such as English, German and French stress the innate nature of talent, in Eastern languages such as Japanese talent is seen as the product of many years of hard work and striving to attain perfection.

1.3 Standardized vs. Subjective Approach to Talent Identification

Research indicates that a surprising amount of HR practitioners believe that valid identification of talented employees does not require formal assessment policies or even a formal definition of talent—i.e. "I know talent when I see it" (e.g., Tulgan 2001). The main reason for this type of assumption (also referred to as 'X-factor' or 'right stuff' thinking; see McCall 1998) is the fact that organizational decision makers commonly overestimate the validity of intuitive judgment, whilst simultaneously underestimating the validity of paper-and-pencil tests, structured interviews, and assessment centers. These pervasive beliefs lie at the heart of what Highhouse (2008) calls a "stubborn reliance on intuition and subjectivity" (p. 333). The idea that personal judgment can be more valid than formal testing as long as the assessor is experienced enough is referred to as 'the myth of experience'. That is because different sources of rater bias limit the validity of subjective judgment (Highhouse 2008)—e.g., anchoring (i.e. the general tendency of people to interpret new data in light of an existing impression), halo bias (i.e., a form of bias whereby raters do not distinguish their evaluations of candidates among relevant dimensions but rather, attribute either a positive or a negative global score to candidates), and similar-to-me bias (i.e., a preference for candidates more similar to oneself). In the current chapter, we will examine the extent to which HR directors around the world have a preference for standardized assessment or subjective judgment, and how this relates to their beliefs about the inclusive-exclusive and the selection-development divide.

2 Methods

2.1 Sample and Procedure

An online survey was launched through the authors' global network of corporate contacts, using snowball sampling. Multinational companies were asked to have the survey completed by their HR director, and to forward the survey to other potential respondents. The final sample size was 410, with each response being unique to an organization for that local subsidiary.

To obtain a cross-cultural sample, we aimed to collect data for each of the cultural clusters described in the GLOBE [Global Leadership and Organizational Behavior Effectiveness] study, commonly recognized as one of the most important cross-cultural research projects in the management field to date. The GLOBE study was founded in 1993 by Robert J. House and studies leadership across 62 societies. To allow meaningful interpretation of its findings, 'cultural clusters' have been identified as a meaningful level of analysis beyond the individual country level (for more information, see House et al. 2004). In our study, sufficient data was collected from the Anglo, Eastern European, Germanic, Latin American, and Latin European GLOBE clusters to warrant statistical analysis—unfortunately, we did not end up with enough data for the African, Confucian, Nordic, and Southern Asian clusters. The majority of respondents overall came from the US, Belgium, Brazil, and Italy—the home countries of the authors. We clustered our data based on the location where the HR directors were based, rather than their nationality or ethnicity.

Most respondents came from privately owned companies (81 %), from industries such as finance (9.5 %), manufacturing (15.4 %), and professional services (10.2 %). The remaining 19 % of respondents worked for government-owned organizations, mostly from the educational (8.3 %) and scientific sector (11.2 %). The participating organizations were mostly hierarchically structured (with an average of 12.88 hierarchical levels at the subsidiary level), with a moderate degree of formalization, centralization, and performance orientation on average (see Table 1). The majority of the participating organizations (36.6 %) were large organizations, with a global headcount of over 10,000 employees. Most respondents were women (65.6 %) and their average age was 55.59 ($SD = 13.66$), of which 11.36 years ($SD = 8.97$) spent in an HR management function.

2.2 Measures

2.2.1 Associations with 'Talent'

After completing a list of demographic questions about themselves and their employing organizations, respondents were asked to list 10 spontaneous associations evoked by the word 'talent'. They were instructed not to overthink their list, and to keep in mind there are no right and wrong answers. After completing the association exercise, they were asked to rank order their list of ten so that the first association would be the most salient one for them, and so on.

2.2.2 Growth (Incremental) vs. Fixed (Entity) Mindset About Talent

In order to measure whether respondents had a growth (incremental) versus a fixed (entity) mindset, we used Levy and Dweck's (1997) eight-item 'Beliefs about Human Nature' scale. The scale includes four items that measure entity beliefs (sample item: "Everyone is a certain kind of person and there is not much they can really change about that") and four items that measure incremental beliefs (sample item: "People can substantially change the kind of person they are"), on a 6-point Likert scale ranging from 1 = Strongly disagree to 6 = Strongly agree. The four 'incremental' items were reversed so that a higher score on the scale indicates a more fixed (entity) mindset. Internal consistency (α) for the scale—and for all other scales in the survey—is indicated on the diagonal of Table 1.

Table 1 Means, standard deviations, intercorrelations, and scale reliabilities

Study variables	M (SD)	1	2	3	4	5	6	7	8	9	10	11
Organizational characteristics												
1. Ownership (0 = public, 1 = private)[a]	—	—										
2. Number of hierarchical levels[a]	12.88 (17.90)	-.05	—									
3. Degree of formalization[b]	3.43 (.79)	-.19**	.15**	(.72)								
4. Degree of centralization[b]	2.45 (.93)	-.12*	.11	.13*	(.90)							
5. Degree of performance orientation[c]	4.73 (.99)	.31**	-.06	-.01	-.46**	(.62)						
Talent 'mindset' variables												
6. Fixed (entity) mindset about talent[d]	3.64 (.94)	.06	.01	-.07	.07	.02	(.88)					
7. Belief that talent is innate[a]	57.03 (22.64)	-.08	.04	.06	.07	.02	.22**	—				
8. Belief that everyone has talent[a]	52.79 (32.59)	-.09	-.07	-.01	-.17**	.20**	-.04	.04	—			
9. Exclusiveness of TM approach[b]	2.66 (.64)	-.02	.09	.07	.35**	-.36**	-.07	-.08	-.41**	(.67)		
10. Reliance on personal judgment[b]	2.84 (.74)	-.05	-.03	.04	-.12*	.01	-.05	.03	.00	.02	(.60)	
11. Reliance on first impressions[b]	2.35 (.78)	-.01	.13*	.06	.20**	-.10	.23**	.15**	-.34**	.20**	-.10	(.61)

Notes. *p < .05; **p < .01; Cronbach's alphas are listed between brackets on the main diagonal
[a]Sliding scale from 0 to 100
[b]Five-point Likert scale
[c]Seven-point Likert scale
[d]Six-point Likert scale

2.2.3 Belief that Talent Is Innate

In addition to the 'Beliefs about Human Nature scale', which is about the malleability of human nature more generally, we also added an item more specifically about talent. The exact item read: "To what extent do you believe that talent is something people are born with? Please indicate the extent to which you believe talent is innate, on a scale of 0 to 100". Responses were given by sliding a bar to indicate a certain percentage.

2.2.4 Belief that Everyone Has Talent

Similarly, we constructed an item asking about the extent to which the HR directors believed that everyone has talent, i.e. "What percentage of the employees within your organization do you, personally, consider 'talented'?". Again, respondents were asked to indicate their response on a sliding scale from 0 to 100.

2.2.5 Inclusive vs. Exclusive TM Approach

In order to measure whether respondents' organizations had adopted an inclusive versus an exclusive approach to talent management, we developed a six-item scale based on the descriptions of the exclusive versus the inclusive approach found in Iles et al. (2010). Sample items are: "A talent is not something that everyone possesses, but just the lucky few" and "Everybody has a certain talent" (R). All items were scored on a 5-point Likert scale ranging from 1 = Not at all the viewpoint of my organization to 5 = Completely the viewpoint of my organization.

2.2.6 Reliance on Personal Judgment Rather than Standardized Assessment

Reliance on personal judgment in the identification of talent was measured using a self-developed scale based on the work of Highhouse (2008). The scale consisted of 3 items, i.e. "In evaluating the talent of employees, personal judgment is the best standard"; "Standardized tests are better to evaluate the talent of employees than personal judgments" (R); and "In evaluating the talent of employees, more and better information can be obtained from an unstructured interview than from a battery of standardized tests" (R). Respondents were instructed to reply on a 5-point Likert scale ranging from 1 = Do not agree at all to 5 = Completely agree.

2.2.7 Reliance on First Impressions

Reliance on first impressions in the identification of talent was also measured using a self-developed scale, again based on the work of Highhouse (2008). This scale consisted of 4 items, also scored on a 5-point Likert scale ranging from 1 = Do not agree at all to 5 = Completely agree. A sample item is: "If I don't consider a person talented at a first evaluation, the odds of me considering him or her talented at a next evaluation are low".

2.2.8 Organizational Characteristics

In order to rule out alternative explanations, a range of organizational-level variables were included in the analyses (see Table 1): Company ownership

(0 = Government-owned, 1 = Privately owned); Number of hierarchical levels (at the level of the subsidiary for which the HR director works) on a sliding scale from 0 to 100; Degree of formalization of HR practices within the organization [6 items developed by Ferris et al. (1992), e.g. "The organization keeps a written record of nearly everyone's job performance", rated on a scale from 1 = Totally disagree to 5 = Totally agree]; Degree of centralization in decision making within the organization [5 items developed by Ferris et al. (1992), e.g. "In this company even small matters have to be referred to someone higher up for a final answer", rated on a scale from 1 = Totally disagree to 5 = Totally agree]; and performance orientation climate within the organization [4 items developed by House et al. (2004) for the GLOBE study, e.g. "In this organization, employees are encouraged to strive for continuously improved performance" rated on a 7-point scale from 1 = Strongly disagree to 7 = Strongly agree].

3   Results

Table 1 provides an overview of the means, standard deviations, and intercorrelations for the study variables.

In Table 2, we present an overview of the outcomes of our qualitative analyses on the 'associations' data. As can be seen in the Table, we found meanings of talent that were universal (i.e., dominant in all cultures in our sample) and prototypical (i.e., consistently high-ranking), and meanings that were more culture-specific (i.e., only occurring in some cultural clusters but not others) and peripheral (i.e., consistently lower-ranking).

One-way ANOVAs were conducted in order to determine whether HR directors from different cultural clusters hold different mindsets about talent (see Fig. 1 for the means plots). Significant differences were only found for the variables 'belief that everyone has talent' $(F(4, 287) = 11.54, p = .00)$, 'exclusiveness of talent management approach' $(F(4, 289) = 4.25, p = .00)$, and 'reliance on first impressions' $(F(4, 287) = 3.94, p = .00)$. We discuss our findings in more detail below. In Fig. 1, we grouped together the variables that were found to be highly correlated in Table 1.

4   Discussion

The present chapter set out to advance understanding of the meanings attributed to 'talent' by HR directors across the world, and how their talent mindsets translate into the ways in which talent is identified and managed in their organizations. In so doing, we aimed to contribute to the global talent management in two major ways: (1) by integrating knowledge from the general talent management literature into the global talent management debate; and (2) by offering a cross-cultural perspective on the 'best fit' approach to talent management.

Table 2 Associations with 'talent' categorized according to GLOBE cultural cluster

Universal/ Prototypical	Culture-specific/peripheral				
	Anglo	Eastern European	Germanic	Latin American	Latin European
Ability	Performance	Hardworking	Innate	Calling/ Vocation	Innovation
Skills	High potentials	Strong-minded	Giftedness	Career	Creativity
Knowledge	Exceptional	Learning ability	Excellence	Success	Artistic
Potential	Human resources		Passion	Ease	Learning

4.1 Key Findings

Unsurprisingly, respondents from all cultural clusters mentioned ability, skills, knowledge, and potential as high-ranking associations with talent. In fact, our qualitative analyses revealed that the differences between the different clusters were not too great—in that there seems to be a high number of associations with talent that are universal and prototypical. As Table 2 shows, we did find a number of meanings associated with talent that were more culture-specific and less consistent across the countries in our sample. Where respondents from the Anglo cluster stressed the exceptional nature of talent, and take a more 'instrumental' approach in that they associate it with performance, potential, and talent being a resource to the organization, Eastern European respondents emphasized components of talent relation to effort and willpower (i.e., hardworking, strong-minded, and willingness and ability to learn); Germanic respondents related talent to inborn giftedness of abilities that lead to excellence, but also mentioned passion; Latin Americans stressed the fact that talent reflects a person's calling or vocation, and that it leads to career success, but also, that it manifests in a certain ease with which certain activities are undertaken; and respondents from the Latin European cluster associated talent with innovation, creativity, and art, as well as learning.

Surprisingly, in our quantitative analyses we found no significant differences between cultures as concerns having a fixed (entity) versus a growth (incremental) mindset about talent, nor for percentage to which HR directors believe talent is innate. In fact, on average, respondents from each cultural cluster indicated that they believe that talent can be developed for over 50 %. Post-hoc tests revealed that respondents from the Anglo and the Germanic cultural cluster believed to a significantly higher extent that everyone has talent than respondents from the Latin American and the Latin European cluster (with the Eastern European cluster 'somewhere in the middle'). As for the exclusiveness of an organization's talent management approach, this was significantly lower in Germanic countries than in the other countries of study. This finding stands in stark contrast to the qualitative data, where the Anglo and the Germanic clusters were the two clusters in which most HR directors wrote down associations related to 'excellence' and 'exceptional performance'.

Fig. 1 Cultural differences between the GLOBE clusters as concerns beliefs about (how) talent (should be identified) (*Note*: All variables were standardized into a five-point scale prior to plotting the graphs)

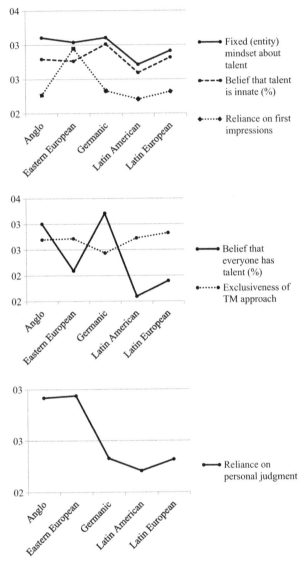

Possibly, this finding indicates that using exceptional performance as a criterion for talent identification does not necessarily imply that only a very small proportion of the workforce is to be considered talented. Two alternative explanations are conceivable. First, that Anglo and Germanic countries engage more in 'topgrading'—i.e., the practice of hiring only the very best performers for every single job in the organization (Smart and Smart 1997)—and therefore that the beliefs that talent is something exceptional versus omnipresent in one's organization, are not necessarily mutually exclusive. Second, that Anglo and Germanic respondents may have more multidimensional conceptions of talent—talent domains that have been identified in the literature include academics, arts, business, leisure, social action, sports, and technology (Gagné 2004)—which heightens the odds of 'everyone being talented at something'. These are just hypotheses, however—further research is necessary to back these claims.

Finally, as for reliance on first impressions, our findings indicate that HR directors from the Anglo and the Eastern European cluster scored higher than respondents from the other cultural clusters, implying that they have a lower preference for continuous assessment (and potentially, a higher belief that "either you have it or you don't") than HR directors from Germanic, Latin American, and Latin European countries.

4.2 Limitations and Suggestions for Further Research

Our study had some limitations, from which avenues for further research can be deduced. First of all, the majority of our respondents came from the US, Belgium, Brazil, and Italy—the home countries of the authors. Future research might do well to strive for a more balanced representation of countries within each GLOBE cluster. The GLOBE clusters in themselves are also not undisputed, however. Countries such as Israel, Malta, Turkey, and South Africa, due to their cultural complexity, have proven difficult to cluster. In addition, the practice of cultural clustering in itself implies making generalizations—for instance, the Anglo cluster includes the US, the UK, Australia and New-Zealand, which makes sense in some respects but does not imply that these countries have identical cultures. Cultural clusters remain 'rough measures' of culture (House et al. 2004). Future studies might focus on more specific cultural contexts (i.e., countries or regions) to counter this specific limitation.

A second limitation is that the survey was only administered at the HR director level. Although HR directors can be expected to play a central role in the talent management strategy of their organizations, they are not necessarily the key decision makers (Boudreau and Ramstad 2005). Moreover, chances are they have different 'talent mindsets' than the line management and top management within their own organization. It is conceivable, for instance, that HR directors have a stronger belief in the malleability of talent because employee development is one of the core functions of HR (Meyers et al. 2013). Further research might adopt multilevel designs, where not only HR but also line management, top management, and individual employees are surveyed about their talent mindsets as well as the talent management climate within their organizations (Garrow and Hirsch 2008). Such designs might reveal differences in terms of intended, enacted, and perceived talent management practices (Dries 2013). In addition, the data of our study could be coupled to other international databases to come to more solid conclusions as to differences in talent management practices between countries. The CRANET [Cranfield Network on International Human Resource Management] database, for instance, might be a useful source of information to expand on our study's findings.

Table 3 Five key GTM challenges, strategies, and future opportunities

Five key points regarding global talent management challenges	Five key points regarding strategies to overcome these challenges	Five key points regarding future opportunities in global talent management
1 Normative positions taken in the GTM literature (e.g, inclusive versus exclusive approaches) may not be most conducive to do 'good' TM research and distill adequate implications for practice	More 'phenomenon-driven' research is necessary to lay theoretical foundations for further GTM research; inductive research first, deductive research should follow later	There is a significant need and opportunity for more theory building and hypothesis development about GTM. Promise might lie in integrating what we know from other literature streams (e.g., the giftedness literature, the strengths literature, the assessment center literature)
2 Little is known about mental models of talent across cultures, although such knowledge might help MNCs to formulate their GTM strategy	We need more research and more knowledge exchange among international HR practitioners about how talent is conceptualized across cultures, and whether or not this implies that an 'ethnocentric' approach to GTM, with decision making centralized in headquarters, is (im)possible and (un)desirable	If we can dissect the mindsets underlying important talent management decisions (such as the allocation of resources across employees), we can help HR practitioners make better (or at least more advised) GTM decisions
3 Little is known about talent mindsets and TM approaches of choice in non-Western regions such as Africa, Confucian Asia, and Southern Asia	We need more research and more knowledge exchange among international HR practitioners about how talent and TM are perceived in non-Western regions, and the extent to which this differs from beliefs held in the West	Learning more about talent mindsets and TM approaches in non-Western regions can provide inspiration for TM in Western countries. In a truly global world, knowledge and expertise about management practices should not only travel from West to East, but also the other way around
4 Most writings about GTM are from the US or the UK; it is unclear to what extent an 'Anglo-Saxon bias' is present in the literature and to what extent Anglo-Saxon TM models can be generalized across cultures	We need more research and more knowledge exchange among international HR practitioners to examine the extent to which Anglo-Saxon beliefs about talent and TM can be 'exported' to other countries, especially other subsidiaries within the same MNC	Knowing which aspects of TM are more 'universal' and which are not can help MNCs decide which of their GTM processes should be governed centrally and which are best left up to the local level

(continued)

Table 3 (continued)

Five key points regarding global talent management challenges	Five key points regarding strategies to overcome these challenges	Five key points regarding future opportunities in global talent management
5 GTM may not be a matter of best practices, but of best fit. To date, we do not know much about which approach to TM fits better with which type of organization	We need more research and more knowledge exchange among international HR practitioners measuring the effects of GTM interventions to desired outcomes over time, taking into account the specific organizational context. What works for one organization, may not work for another	The 'best fit' approach, combined with a stronger focus on measurement (i.e., baseline measures, follow-up measures, and outcome measures—all depending on an organization's specific strategy), offers much promise in the way of making the outcomes of GTM measurable, so that HR practitioners worldwide can demonstrate the return on investment in TM to their boards

Notes. TM talent management, *GTM* global talent management

Finally, further research might examine the relative effects of 'culture' on talent management strategy at different levels—i.e., national culture, organizational culture, occupational culture. It is conceivable, for instance, that strong occupational cultures (e.g., marketing, consulting) may 'override' cross-cultural differences, and thus represent a more meaningful level of analysis (Table 3).

4.3   Practical Implications

How can organizational decision makers make sense out of our findings? It is important to understand that, when it comes to talent management, no single perspective on talent is objectively better than another. As Garrow and Hirsch (2008) assert, talent management is not a matter of best practices, but rather, of best fit—i.e. fit with strategic objectives, fit with organizational and national culture, fit with other HR practices and policies, and fit with organizational capacity. Consequently, the different approaches to talent management described in this chapter may all be equally viable and can subsist in a myriad of configurations, each with its own merits and drawbacks. For example, an exclusive and highly standardized approach to talent management is more likely to fit well in an organization with a meritocratic, competitive culture and an up-or-out promotion system than in an organization that promotes egalitarianism, diversity and teamwork.

As for individual employees, they are often oddly unaware of the talent management dynamics operating within their employing organizations—even though these are likely to have crucial implications for the further course of their career (Dries 2013). Part of the explanation is that talent management procedures are often quite intransparent, with crucial information being withheld from employees (e.g., not being identified as talented). In addition, employees (even 'high-potential' ones) are often naïve, and somewhat reactive, when it comes to managing their own careers (McCall 1998). Advances in the academic literature may help both organizations and individual employees make more sense of how strategic talent management decisions may or may not affect them.

References

Boudreau, J. W., & Ramstad, P. (2005). Talentship and the evolution of human resource management: From professional practices to strategic talent decision science. *Human Resource Planning Journal, 28*(2), 17–26.

Buckingham, M., & Vosburgh, R. M. (2001). The 21st century human resources function: It's the talent, stupid! *Human Resource Planning, 24*(4), 17–23.

Cappelli, P. (2008). *Talent on demand: Managing talent in an age of uncertainty*. Boston, MA: Harvard Business School Press.

Collings, D. G., & Mellahi, K. (2009). Strategic talent management: A review and research agenda. *Human Resource Management Review, 19*(4), 304–313.

Dries, N. (2013). The psychology of talent management: A review and research agenda. *Human Resource Management Journal, 23*(4), 272–285.

Farndale, E., Scullion, H., & Sparrow, P. (2010). The role of the corporate HR function in global talent management. *Journal of World Business, 45*(2), 161–168.

Ferris, G. R., Buckley, M. R., & Allen, G. M. (1992). Promotion systems in organizations. *Human Resource Planning, 15*(3), 47–68.

Gagné, F. (2004). Transforming gifts into talents: The DMGT as a developmental theory. *High Ability Studies, 15*(2), 119–147.

Garrow, V., & Hirsch, W. (2008). Talent management: Issues of focus and fit. *Public Personnel Management, 37*(4), 389–402.

Hambrick, D. C. (2007). The field of management's devotion to theory: Too much of a good thing? *Academy of Management Journal, 50*(6), 1346–1352.

Heslin, P. A., Latham, G. P., & Vandewalle, D. (2005). The effect of implicit person theory on performance appraisals. *Journal of Applied Psychology, 90*(5), 842–856.

Highhouse, S. (2008). Stubborn reliance on intuition and subjectivity in employee selection. *Industrial and Organizational Psychology, 1*, 333–342.

House, R. J., Hanges, P. W., Javidan, M., Dorfman, P., & Gupta, V. (Eds.). (2004). *Culture, leadership, and organizations: The GLOBE study of 62 societies*. Thousand Oaks, CA: Sage.

Iles, P., Chuai, X., & Preece, D. (2010). Talent management and HRM in multinational companies in Beijing: Definitions, differences and drivers. *Journal of World Business, 45*, 179–189.

Levy, S., & Dweck, C. S. (1997). *Implicit theory measures: Reliability and validity data for adults and children*. Unpublished manuscript, Columbia University, New York.

McCall, M. W. (1998). *High flyers: Developing the next generation of leaders*. Boston, MA: Harvard Business School Press.

Meyers, M. C., van Woerkom, M., & Dries, N. (2013). Talent—innate or acquired? Theoretical considerations and their implications for talent management. *Human Resource Management Review, 23*(4), 305–321.

Schuler, R. S., Jackson, S. E., & Tarique, I. (2011). Global talent management and global talent challenges: Strategic opportunities for IHRM. *Journal of World Business, 46*(4), 506–516.

Smart, B. D., & Smart, G. H. (1997, Spring). Topgrading the organization. Directors and Boards.

Tansley, C. (2011). What do we mean by the term "talent" in talent management? *Industrial and Commercial Training, 43*(5), 266–274.

Tsay, C., & Banaji, M. R. (2011). Naturals and strivers: Preferences and beliefs about sources of achievement. *Journal of Experimental Social Psychology, 47*, 460–465.

Tulgan, B. (2001). Winning the talent wars. *Employment Relations Today, 23*(1–2), 37–51.

Warren, C. (2006, March 24–29). Curtain call: Talent management. *People Management*.

Smart Global Talent Management: A Promising Hybrid

Charles M. Vance, Vlad Vaiman, Ana Cosic, Mursal Abedi, and Raquel Sena

1 Introduction

Within our increasingly global business environment, global knowledge management (GKM) represents a critical capability for multinational enterprises (MNEs) for gaining and sustaining competitive advantage (Zaied 2012). MNE GKM is of strategic importance in such key areas for as global integration and coordination, transfer of headquarter knowledge to local subsidiaries, and acquisition and transfer of generalizable, applicable knowledge and innovation from individual foreign subsidiaries back to headquarters and throughout the MNE's global operations (Ryan et al. 2010).

There is increasing recognition that since humans play a central role as recipients and conduits of knowledge within organizations, MNE GKM capability can be greatly influenced by existing human resource management (HRM) policies and practices (Minbaeva et al. 2009). Talent management is a current and popular term representing the traditional human resource management field that appears to resonate well with mainline management since its association with the declaration of a global "war for talent" (Minbaeva and Collings 2013; Coulson-Thomas 2012). We consider global talent management (GTM) as a significant extension of domestic TM, involving the acquisition, development, utilization, and retention of human resources—irrespective of national passport—involving transnational and global applications (Vance et al. 2013; Schuler et al. 2011). And given the critical importance of GKM for MNEs, policies and practices of GTM in turn have a huge influence and can play a strategic role.

C.M. Vance (✉) • A. Cosic • M. Abedi • R. Sena
Loyola Marymount University, Los Angeles, CA, USA
e-mail: cvance@lmu.edu; Anamal50@yahoo.com; mabedi@lion.lmu.edu; raquel_sena@hotmail.com

V. Vaiman
California Lutheran University, Thousand Oaks, CA, USA
e-mail: vvaiman@callutheran.edu

A. Al Ariss (ed.), *Global Talent Management*, Management for Professionals,
DOI 10.1007/978-3-319-05125-3_3, © Springer International Publishing Switzerland 2014

We believe that the key disciplines of GTM and GKM can be combined into a powerful conceptual synergy contributing to organizational success in our competitive global marketplace. We call this powerful combination "smart global talent management," which integrates GKM (i.e., managing key processes involving human competence or "smarts"—whether cognitive, affective, or physical skill-based in nature) with the global human resource function (GTM). Thus "smart global talent management" can be considered as the effective management of all human resources throughout the global enterprise, who represent and embody to a great extent an organization's knowledge capital and capacity to generate, acquire, store, transfer, and apply knowledge and information in support of multinational company goals and objectives.

With their predominantly theoretical perspective, scholars generally have overlooked the fact that productive knowledge management is significantly affected by talent management policies and practices related to recruitment, training, knowledge sharing, performance management, succession planning, global workforce alignment, etc. According to Illegems and Verbeke (2004), HRM (aka talent management) research commonly fails to take into account new challenges in knowledge-intensive and knowledge-competitive organizations. With our new hybrid of smart global talent management, we believe that it is critical for today's global organizations to understand how the utilization of specific global HRM practices may best facilitate knowledge creation and acquisition, transformation from tacit to explicit forms, transfer and sharing across national boundaries and organizational units, and effective local application.

On the other hand, a majority of current work in talent management is primarily practitioner-oriented without a convincing conceptual foundation offered by the discipline of knowledge management. Talent management practitioners tend to focus on specific practices in attracting, selecting, engaging, developing, and retaining employees, while neglecting to sufficiently identify human talent as sources and carriers of valuable knowledge—both tacit and explicit. A good example of this lack of awareness or full appreciation in GTM practices of the key role of human talent in carrying valuable knowledge, including tacitly embodied in experience, is represented by the continuing poor record of repatriate retention, where considerable vital knowledge gained through expatriate experience is frequently lost to the MNE (Tania and McLean 2012).

In this chapter we will present this potentially valuable fusion of the disciplines of GKM and GTM represented by smart global talent management (SGTM). This novel conceptual admixture of SGTM takes a fresh new look at the human talent within organizations, with all employees—at headquarters and abroad—at all organizational levels representing potentially important agents of GKM processes in acquiring, transferring, and applying vital knowledge for achieving competitive advantage. We first will examine strengths and limitations of the traditional GTM model, followed by an analysis of strengths and limitations posed by GKM. We then will examine in greater detail the value of our new GTM/GKM conceptual hybrid, along with important implications for MNE success in the global marketplace.

2   GTM Strengths and Limitations

As with "human capital" and the more generic "human resource management," talent management is perceived as of strategic importance according to resource-based theory of organizations (Barney 2001), in which organizations can obtain a competitive advantage to the degree that their assets and resources (including human) with which they compete and operate are rare, valuable, and difficult to imitate. Organizations that regularly succeed in attracting strong human talent, facilitating the ongoing development of their competencies, assigning them where needed, obtaining their full commitment to organization goals, eliciting their ideas for ongoing innovation and improvement, and retaining this talent will compete well in the long run in the global marketplace compared to other organizations that hold a lower priority on attention to human talent.

We consider the term "talent management" to be an improvement upon the older common terms including "human resources" and "human capital." Although both of these terms represent improvements upon the antiquated "personnel" in presenting a positive picture of employees as valuable resources or assets for the organization, they still represent a degree of human objectification from a humanistic perspective. Much more than the terms "resources" and "capital," "talent" connotes a sense of the important resource-based view characteristics of inimitability, rarity, and value in a positive, humanistic way contributing to an organization's competitive advantage. Talent management projects a potent image and serves as an influential term that can reorient managers' productive management thinking beyond the terms "human capital" and "human resources" in prizing, investing in, and utilizing employees for competitive advantage—wherever they are located in our global marketplace.

Some discussions of human talent in global organizations restrict the term "talent" to a natural or learned capability that is beneficial to an organization. Accordingly, those who are considered the "talent" of the organization are limited to those seen as possessing highly valued skills (Vaiman et al. 2012). This bias favoring identified high-potentials as the elite, true talent of the organization inevitably results in neglect and oversight of other employees within the global workforce whose insights and inputs contributing to innovation and vigilance could have strategically valuable consequence for the organization. This limiting bias in considering who is the talent can be noted by those who consider global talent management as involving the development of a talent pool of high-potential or presently high-performing employees to fill strategic roles within the multinational organization (e.g., see Minbaeva and Collings 2013). However, in this chapter we hold a much more inclusive view of talent, and consider the talent of an organization as all employees, despite their wide variations in levels of ability and knowledge, that can be utilized by the organization. Particularly related to the processes of knowledge management, we believe that an organization's employees (talent) at all levels represent potential present or future sources and points of application of valuable knowledge. Through their many opportunities of external knowledge access and opportunities for insight acquisition, as well as internal knowledge and idea generation, knowledge transfer, and workplace application, all employees represent talent to be prized and valued.

According to the Sapir-Whorf Theory from cultural anthropology, the language and terminology that we use significantly influence our attitudes, thoughts, decisions, and subsequent behavior. New terminology can therefore serve to help us break out of old patterns of thought and redirect us toward productive changes and new managerial approaches contributing to performance improvement. In fact, we believe there at least five important semantic and symbolic benefits in using the term "talent management" rather than "human resource," "human capital," or "personnel" management. First, from the parlance of the entertainment industry, the term "talent" can represent a powerful metaphor that conjures up an image of one or more actors whose valued performance is essential to the production of a play, television program, or motion picture. These talent or actors are essential, without which the show cannot go on. Managers and supervisors, as "directors" of human talent in their organizations, are presented with the same challenge of recruiting and selecting the human talent within the broader labor force, and in developing, rewarding, and managing this talent toward desired performance and achievement of organization goals. But these managers and supervisors must first appreciate and respect the immense value, whether current or potential, of this human talent to their planned workplace performance "productions."

Second, "talent" represents a form of prized capability encased within the human form and manageable through HR practices. This human capability of talent is holistic in nature; it can extend far beyond the intellectual or cognitive dimension to also include physical skill or sensitivity to and management of feelings and emotions. For example, although expatriate selection has traditionally been based on expertise in technical cognitive knowledge, it is increasingly evident that more affect-based personality characteristics and associated behaviors such as personal flexibility, inquisitiveness, openness to new ideas and experiences, and emotional intelligence play a stronger role in international adjustment and expatriate assignment success.

Third, and consistent with the above entertainment metaphor where actors come and go as needed, the concept of talent management is very aligned with our increasingly flexible trend in today's global marketplace in attracting and utilizing human talent on a contingent basis—as the work need arises. There continues to be considerable growth worldwide in contingent employee staffing for utilizing contracted, part-time, temporary, or leased employee services. From the above entertainment metaphor, in a major movie production actors typically are available only for the hours or days in which scenes are scheduled to be filmed—not for the filming of the entire movie. In fact, perhaps an accurate way of looking at actors today is as high profile and popular contracted workers or "temps." Thus, as we find with our organizational boundaries increasingly open to diverse kinds of workers beyond the standard or regular "full-time" employee, organization talent also can also come from the ranks of suppliers, vendors, outsourced (onshore or offshore) work providers, and other contingent working arrangements (e.g., temps) that contribute to organizational performance and productivity. Although we typically speak of our human talent as internal to the organization, organizations should consider the importance and welfare of all working talent who contribute to the success of their operations. In fact, organizations that have considered their outsourced human talent who manufacture and assemble their products as beyond the border of their social responsibility have received a rude awakening in the crucible of global publicity (Arrigo 2013).

Fourth, the term "human resources" or "HR" often brings to many managers' mind a function administered by staff professionals who only add cost to the organization while impeding management's free reign by pointing out legal restrictions, potential liabilities, and generally what management can't or should not do. Rarely do general managers see themselves as HR managers or having central responsibilities in working with company human resources. On the other hand, we often have noted in workshops with general managers and business professionals that a "talent manager" is commonly seen as a general supervisor or manager who regularly works closely with his or her employees or "talent" to achieve organizational performance objectives. The term "talent management" emphasizes in our minds what all managers, committed to organizational perfor-mance success, must to be greatly concerned about and actively involved in—the identification, recruitment, selection, development, and ongoing engagement of human talent. HR professionals and functional specialists can provide helpful input and guidance, but supervisors and managers at all levels play a central, essential role in ultimately implementing the organization strategy through the effective management of their human talent. Thus, by fully committing to a comprehensive effort of effective talent management, all supervisors and managers of an organization's human resources adopt the general role of HR practitioners (not HR professionals or HR specialists), who are directly and regularly dealing with people opportunities and challenges in carrying out organizational objectives.

Finally, the term "talent" contributes an additional meaning of distinct worth to an employee or human resource that should be highly valued, cared for, and developed—and definitely not squandered or taken for granted. The care and investment of this human talent, which can play a central role in organizational productivity, innovation, and the maintenance within the external marketplace of a positive organizational image, requires as much or more thoughtful investment as other forms of organizational capital. A minimal level of respect and appreciation for an organization's human talent typically results in inadequate attention to the development and effective organization-wide utilization of key human resource management practices linked with organization performance success. The neglect of human talent investment only serves to deter efforts to build and sustain a long-term strategy of competitive advantage for surviving and thriving in our global marketplace.

Notwithstanding the above important benefits and advantages of using the term "talent management" rather than the more traditional "human resource manage-ment," or even the formerly common "personnel," much of the current practitioner and scholarly literature on talent management seems only to be "reprocessed" old HRM, only packaged within a more attractive moniker. Much of this published work is very similar to the previous generation of publications under the labels of HRM or the management of human capital. As Lewis and Heckman (2006: 140) indicate in their thoughtful critique of recently published works reflecting the growing interest in talent management,

> It is apparent from the above that the term "talent management" has no clear meaning. It is used in too many ways and is often a means to highlight the "strategic" importance of a HR specialty (recruiting, selection, development, etc.) without adding to the theory or practice of that specialty...Perhaps it serves the purpose of re-branding HR practices to keep them seemingly new and fresh, but it does not advance our understanding of the strategic and effective management of talent.

Certainly a new take on an old familiar concept can provide an opportunity for renewal and refocus, as well as an occasion to redirect and recommit managerial priorities and efforts for organizational improvement. But if GTM is to provide a significantly new contribution to the success of organizations within the global arena, it must reach beyond being simply a "new and improved" label that covers essentially the same old HR product.

3   Knowledge Management: Strengths and Limitations

Besides our rather unconventional ways that we are looking at the term "talent" in this chapter, our merging this term with the conceptual discipline of knowledge management raises talent management to a more strategic level, where employees (including contingent) at all levels represent important points for receiving, analyzing, transferring, and implementing knowledge that can serve organizational performance objectives. As with the saying, "knowledge is power," the global organizational competitive advantages of organizations are based upon their core competencies, knowledge, capabilities, and collective organizational "know-how" that they develop over time (Prahalad and Hamel 1990). On an explicit level, this organizational knowledge is deposited and held within the total set of documented practices, procedures, policies, strategic plans, etc. On an implicit or tacit level, this organizational knowledge is encased within emerging patterns and routines of organizational behavior, and developed through the experiences of employees at all levels and locations of the global enterprise (Nonaka and Takeuchi 1995).

To a major degree, employees are the carriers of an organization's knowledge and skill assets. According to the knowledge-based view of the firm described by Grant (1996), this employee-held knowledge and competence that contribute greatly to an organization's capability and core competencies potentially provides a significant strategic resource to assist the organization in adapting and competing throughout its global market environments. When all employees—both regular and contingent—are seen as current and potential sources and conduits of knowledge and expertise for useful application within the organization, the perceived responsibility of HR functional policies and practices in attracting, developing, motivating, and retaining this talent grows dramatically in strategic importance.

Unfortunately, in many large multinational organizations this strategic importance is not adequately appreciated, and there is a lack of coordination and consistency across national borders and especially among such HR functions as staffing, training, performance management/appraisal, and compensation, which interferes with the potential benefit of effective knowledge management. For example, information shared in the course of a performance appraisal process about an employee's cultural/language appropriate skill and strong interest in having an expatriate assignment in a given country or geographic region may not be shared in a timely manner, or even at all, with others in the HR staffing function who are planning for expatriate deployment in that country or region. When HR policies and practices are seen to have an important impact on effective knowledge management in the organization, this can increase the perceived importance of HR dramatically. In addition, with this recognition knowledge management also may provide a common purpose for more effectively integrating and coordinating knowledge management-related policies and practices within the various HR functions.

Nevertheless, without a clear connection with HR policies and practices, knowledge management alone has potential shortcomings that limit its promise for improving organizational performance. For example, many efforts in have focused on the development of hardware and software data-base applications (e.g., expert systems) with little regard for human and social characteristics and variables affecting both data entry and retrieval of more tacit, experience-based knowledge and information. This neglect of the human dimensions can become especially problematic when cultural differences are involved, as Accenture has experienced in trying to implement its GKM system that deals primarily with formal, explicit knowledge and has experienced significant resistance from Asian employees who are reluctant, apparently unlike their Western counterparts, to convert and enter their informal, tacit knowledge into this global company system (Paik and Choi 2005). And much work that does deal with global human "talent" organizational issues in GKM remains at a rather theoretical, abstract level, such as examining knowledge flows between and among multinational headquarters and subsidiary units, with no clear reference to specific HR practices, procedures, or policies for guiding optimal GKM (e.g., Gupta and Govindarajan 2000).

The useful concept of the "knowledge spiral" as presented by Nonaka and Takeuchi (1995) deals with four modes of knowledge transformation between tacit or implicit knowledge (such as individual know-how or experience-generated knowledge that is difficult explain or formally document) and explicit knowledge (i.e., more easily articulated, documented, and shared). These modes encompass both knowledge creation and transfer between individuals and at different levels within the organization. Hansen and colleagues (1999) provide an easier way of considering connections between knowledge management and human talent in their distinction between the "personalization" and "codification" of knowledge. In the personalization approach, informal experience-based or tacit knowledge is closely tied to the individuals who discover or create it from interaction with external sources, such as through informal networking and other professional sources. They then transfer this knowledge primarily through person-to-person (including virtual) transmissions. In contrast, the codification approach in GKM works to make knowledge more conscious and explicit, facilitating its transfer through data base entry and company operations manual documentation, as well as input into employee training for wider company dissemination. The personalization GKM approach appears to work most effectively in novel, unique situations, such as in international business where local taste and custom adaptation is essential, while the codification approach works best where standardization in support of globalized strategy is desirable, involving fairly predictable applications, conditions, and routine organizational practices (e.g., DHL mail shipment, McDonald's fast food, and Michelin tires). However, these theoretical knowledge management efforts still fail to make a close connection to specific HR functional practices and various communications efforts and activities for creating and transmitting both tacit and explicit knowledge throughout the global organization.

Another limitation of knowledge management and the related management of knowledge workers is an inordinate "intellectualization," or excessive focus on processes of the rational, cognitive domain. There appears to be little attention in much of this research directed at learning and skill development within the affective domain (e.g., emotions, feelings, attitudes) in areas critical for individual, group, and organizational performance. On the other hand, culture, as a human societal and organizational phenomenon consisting of collectively-held beliefs, rules, values, tastes, priorities, and assumptions can be largely characterized as affective in nature.

Considerable work within the affective domain in emotional intelligence, creativity, and nonlinear thinking also points to the need to look beyond strictly cognitive dimensions of rational data gathering and logical analysis of knowledge and information for achieving and maintaining high levels of performance (Vance et al. 2007). In a departure from the nearly complete focus on the cognitive domain, past work analyzing the learning benefits of knowledge sharing groups and communities of practice (both within and across organizations) has identified important forms of learning in the affective domain, such as increased confidence in problem solving, reduced anxiety caused by feelings of isolation, or an increased awareness of and accompanying sense of urgency in addressing a potential future problem (Vance et al. 1991).

4 Important Contributions of the GTM/GKM Hybridization

In our hybrid conceptualization of GTM and GKM to form SGTM considers that which employees can bring of value to the organization as extending far beyond only the cognitive domain. The power of the concept of "talent" includes its relevance to other essential domains of human development and performance besides an individual's store of rational information and cerebral knowledge. The conceptualization of talent held by an experienced employee provides a more vivid picture and strengthens the meaning of deep, tacit knowledge, directing it closer to the influence of specific HR practices in identifying, surfacing and capturing, and spreading this tacit knowledge talent within the organization. The concept of talent also reaches into the affective domain, such as with emotional intelligence, cross-cultural sensitivity, and the ability to read and manage one's own feelings in a constructive fashion, as well as to influence others in doing the same.

This hybrid model of SGTM provides a more productive lens for evaluating current practices and trends associated with our global labor force. For example, related to the pervasive global phenomenon of migration, skilled migrants may be viewed in a much more favorable light as possessing valuable skills to offer to their new national labor talent pool (Al Ariss and Crowley-Henry 2013). Governments would do well to follow this enlightened perspective to avoid the loss of this potential source of valuable talent, as well as associated new jobs and business growth, due to excessively restrictive immigration policies, as happened when Microsoft decided to move new software development operations to Canada in the face of ongoing quota challenges for obtaining visas in the US. Beyond the cognitive level associated with the marketable skills possessed by migrants, it also should be acknowledged that migrants often carry within them productive attitudes, expectations, ambitions, and general values at the affective level that can contribute much vitality to the new national talent pool. A perspective valuing both the cognitive and affective talents of migrants is reflected in the recent comment by a Canadian government official when he stated, "Our employers value the strong work ethic and high literacy skills of Filipino workers, and we will need them to meet the ambitious targets we have outlined in our Growth Plan" (Asia News Monitor 2013).

We can see very successful global organizations today operating with the combined GTM/GKM model of GSTM. One good example is igus, GmbH of Germany, a leading manufacturer of energy chain systems supporting industrial robotics and automation. Managers at all levels are centrally involved in HR activities and practices that combine GTM and GKM, which is quickly apparent when one visits the manufacturing headquarters in Cologne. Consistent with the lower case letters in its name, igus promotes a strong egalitarian culture also characterized by humility, continuous learning, and empowerment. This culture is reflected on their website (http://www.igus.de) that describes, "And nearly every team member acts as an independent manager from the start." This multinational company invests heavily in talent development and training throughout its world-wide operations. The company's furniture design and open office space also supports an egalitarian climate that promotes the sharing of knowledge and infor-mation. Each employee is empowered to directly contact anyone else in the company. A good illustration of igus' SGTM hybrid model in action, which here combines an employee relations empowerment approach with knowledge manage-ment, is the common maxim, "First decide, then inform."

Bayer, the large chemical and pharmaceutical multinational firm also headquartered in Germany, has been very active for many years in encouraging "inpatriate" assignments, which involve bringing to headquarters for 2 or 3-year visits employees from its various subsidiaries located in approximately 150 countries—both developed and developing. Bayer is firmly convinced that these headquarter-based assignments as part of HR staffing policy not only provide valuable experiential learning for these inpatriates—human capability assets that they will use for strategically leveraging headquarter influence when they return to their home countries—but these assignments also inevitably provide valuable spillover benefits to company knowledge about foreign markets, as well as the development of a broader, global perspective.

The global giant, Proctor and Gamble, has been extremely successful in attracting, selecting, developing, and retaining its managerial talent throughout its global operations. P&G's combined GTM/GKM effectiveness in disseminating key knowledge, skills, and abilities throughout its worldwide operations has resulted in the distinct competitive advantage of decision makers who share a common mindset and alignment, which in turn supports an integrated and coordinated global business strategy that thrives on quality and efficiency. This GTM/GKM merger affecting specific HR practice is noted in the work of P&G's East Asia regional senior HR executive, Hide Aida, in what he refers to as "knowledge-based leadership." In this GTM-GKM interaction employees participate in various forms of training and development to master their three critical forms of knowledge within their "PVP" model: Purposes (e.g., company mission), Values (e.g., core values and priorities), and Principles (e.g., P&G strategies and approaches for competing successfully). Once employees demonstrate acceptable mastery of PVP knowledge, they are completely empowered to make their own decisions in carrying out their work performance objectives.

JDA Software serves as a prime example of how GKM processes have been integrated with important GTM practices to promote internal leadership development. Headquartered in Scottsdale, Arizona, JDA Software delivers best-in-class supply chain management solutions that help businesses operate in a more sustainable, efficient manner to increase revenue and profits. JDA serves approximately 6,000 clients in 60 countries, and employs over 3,000 full-time knowledge workers. JDA Software operates various leadership development centers around the world to provide consistent experiences in knowledge acquisition, as well as to provide increased visibility and networking opportunities for its high-performing employees rising in the leadership ranks. One particular example of how JDA Software employees gain exposure to company-wide executive interaction that generates common knowledge and perceptual alignment is through its regular global leadership training conferences. JDA Software executives within each global region have the opportunity to identify and select employees to attend these conferences, convened both virtually and in person. During these meetings external consultants are contracted to share knowledge about different aspects of leadership and multinational organizations. Conference participants also are provided common training in financial management and other important managerial tools, contributing to a consistent skill and performance picture within the firm. These employees are exposed first-hand to the leadership initiatives that JDA Software implements, and they are able to bring the skills, knowledge, and new attitudes that they obtain in these seminars back to their regional offices. As part of ongoing internal training and professional development, JDA Software also are encouraged

Table 1 Five key GTM challenges, strategies, and future opportunities

Five key points regarding global talent management challenges	Five key points regarding strategies to overcome these challenges	Five key points regarding future opportunities in global talent management
1 Recent research on global and domestic talent management appears to present little more than traditional HR in a new package	The combination of the disciplines of GTM with GKM to form "Smart Global Talent Management" (SGTM) provides a fresh new perspective of strategic value to global business	There is great opportunity for developing new research and practice to enhance our understanding of beneficial applications of SGTM in various HR functions of global business
2 Much work on knowledge management is very theoretical, with little clear direction for specific application and practice	Merged with specific practices of GTM within the SGTM hybrid, GKM can be beneficially utilized to competitive advantage in the global marketplace	Potentially beneficial applications should be examined of how SGTM practices can serve as useful conduits of global knowledge acquisition, transfer, and application
3 At present, the term "talent" in talent management is rather superficial and lacks significant substance	SGTM, which applies the talent metaphor from the entertainment industry, emphasizes the vital role of employees as holders of valuable skills, knowledge, and abilities (KSAs)	More research and training should expand upon and promote the power of the entertainment talent metaphor within SGTM for raising the perceived importance among managers of all employees as valued human assets within the global organization
4 Organizations today continue to underestimate and even overlook the value of employees within their contingent workforce	Under SGTM, all employees, at home or abroad, regular or contingent, represent potentially valuable talent with KSAs that can benefit global business	Following the SGTM imperative, organizations can enhance their HR planning efforts to invest in, care for, and more demonstrably value their contingent global workforce
5 Knowledge management research tends to focus primarily upon the cognitive domain, with minimal attention to human capability assets within the affective and psycho-motor (skill) domains	SGTM presents global organizational human talent in a holistic perspective, where human capability "smarts" are comprised of knowledge, affective, and skill-based assets	Within the SGTM framework, more research, both theoretical and applied, should examine approaches for involving the affective and psycho-motor domains as part of the process of GKM

to regularly share best practices and insights with each other on project-based assignments. This integrative practice ensures that JDA Software leaders from all regions are coordinated in their efforts and committed to working toward the same global goals.

Conclusion

The global talent management/global knowledge management conceptual hybrid of smart global talent management merges the strengths of each separate approach, and in combination also is able to overcome the limitations of each individual approach. The matrix presented in Table 1 summarizes five key challenges in SGTM related to our discussion of GTM and GKM, as well as five key strategies for overcoming these challenges and corresponding opportunities future. Based on the above analysis, the distinct strengths of our recommended hybrid concept of SGTM can be summarized as follows:

1. GTM, with its merger with GKM, becomes much more than just a trendy phrase. As SGTM, the functions involved with managing an organization's human assets are now positioned more clearly to a strategic level of major consequence to the organization.
2. GKM provides a common purpose and focus to help coordinate and integrate HR functional efforts and activities, and link them with organizational strategy.
3. The positive term "talent" has a potent meaning that conveys the current or potential value of each employee associated with the achievement of organizational objectives—including contingent employees.
4. The SGTM hybrid has sound theoretical grounding within GKM, yet is positioned within the realm of specific HR functional practices, where all managers and supervisors also have a key, central role.
5. With SGTM, the view of talent extends our view of GKM beyond a primarily cognitive dimension.

This chapter has endeavored to depict the GTM/GKM conceptual hybrid of SGTM as a valuable new perspective for directing managerial action in GTM and its various functional disciplines, leading to more effective GKM practices and, ultimately, organizational improvement and enhanced competitiveness. However, the concept of building a stronger connection between GKM and key HR practices within GTM is still in its early stages. Future applied research is needed to build upon our understanding of this promising new synergy presented by SGTM.

References

Al Ariss, A., & Crowley-Henry, M. (2013). Self-initiated expatriation and migration in the management literature: Present theorizations and future research directions. *Career Development International, 18*(1), 78–96.

Arrigo, E. (2013). Corporate responsibility management in fast fashion companies: The Gap Inc. case. *Journal of Fashion Marketing and Management, 17*(2), 175–189.

Asia News Monitor (2013, October 10) Philippines: Job opportunities await Filipinos after MOU signing by DOLE and Canadian government. *ProQuest*. Web

Barney, J. B. (2001). Is the resource-based theory a useful perspective for strategic management research? Yes. *Academy of Management Review, 26*(1), 41–56.

Coulson-Thomas, C. (2012). Talent management and building high performance organisations. *Industrial and Commercial Training, 44*(7), 429–436.

Grant, R. M. (1996). Toward a knowledge-based theory of the firm. *Strategic Management Journal, 17*(7), 109–122.

Gupta, A. K., & Govindarajan, V. (2000). Knowledge flows within multinational corporations. *Strategic Management Journal, 21*, 473–496.

Hansen, M. T., Nohria, N., & Tierny, T. (1999). What's your strategy for managing knowledge? *Harvard Business Review, 77*, 106–116.

Illegems, V., & Verbeke, A. (2004). Telework: What does it mean for management? *Long Range Planning, 37*, 319–334.

Lewis, R. E., & Heckman, R. J. (2006). Talent management: A critical review. *Human Resources Management Review, 16*, 139–54.

Minbaeva, D., & Collings, D. G. (2013). Seven myths of global talent management. *International Journal of Human Resource Management, 24*(9), 1762–1776.

Minbaeva, D., Foss, N., & Snell, S. (2009). Bringing the knowledge perspective into HRM. *Human Resource Management, 48*, 477–483.

Nonaka, I., & Takeuchi, H. (1995). *The knowledge-creating company*. New York: Oxford University Press.

Paik, Y., & Choi, D. Y. (2005). The shortcomings of a standardized global knowledge management system: The case study of Accenture. *Academy of Management Executive, 19*(2), 81–84.

Prahalad, C. K., & Hamel, G. (1990). The core competence of the corporation. *Harvard Business Review, 68*(3), 79–91.

Ryan, S. D., Windsor, J. C., Ibragimova, B., & Prybutok, V. R. (2010). Organizational practices that foster knowledge sharing: Validation across distinct national cultures. *Informing Science: The International Journal of an Emerging Transdiscipline, 13*, 139–164.

Schuler, R. S., Jackson, S. E., & Tarique, I. (2011). Frameworks for global talent management: Hr actions for dealing with global talent challenges. In D. Collings & H. Scullion (Eds.), *Global talent management* (pp. 17–36). New York: Routledge.

Tania, N., & McLean, G. N. (2012). Repatriation of expatriate employees, knowledge transfer, and organizational learning: What do we know? *European Journal of Training and Development, 36*(6), 614–629.

Vaiman, V., Collings, D., & Scullion, H. (2012). Global talent management: Trends, challenges, and opportunities. *Management Decision, 50*(5), 925–941.

Vance, C. M., Boje, D., Mendenhall, M., & Kropp, H. R. (1991). A taxonomy of learning benefits from external knowledge sharing meetings. *Human Resource Development Quarterly, 2*(1), 37–52.

Vance, C. M., Chow, I. H., Paik, Y., & Shin, K. Y. (2013). Analysis of Korean expatriate congruence with Chinese labor perceptions on training method importance: Implications for global talent management. *International Journal of Human Resource Management, 24*(5), 985–1005.

Vance, C. M., Groves, K. S., Paik, Y., & Kindler, H. (2007). Understanding and measuring linear/nonlinear thinking style for enhanced management education and professional practice. *Academy of Management Learning and Education, 6*(2), 167–185.

Zaied, A. N. H. (2012). An integrated knowledge management capabilities framework for assessing organizational performance. *International Journal of Information Technology and Computer Science, 4*(2), 1–10.

Coaching of Key Talents in Multinational Companies

Raija Salomaa

1 Introduction

This chapter reviews the existing research on Global Talent Management (GTM) and international coaching, and presents the findings of a research study which explored the use of coaching as one of the current interventions used to develop key talents, specifically managers in multinational companies (MNCs).

Over the last decade, workplace and executive coaching has become a mainstream developmental activity, with an estimated annual revenue of two billion USD, according to the International Coach Federation's 2012 Global Coaching Study. Approximately 48 % of all coaching activity is now estimated to be devoted to talents (Coutu et al. 2009). The 2013 Prospects Report of the Chartered Institute of Personnel and Development reveals that coaching is most commonly rated among the most effective talent management activities. The survey suggests that larger organisations support their managers in new roles with key international responsibilities by using coaching and mentoring programmes. At the same time, it is claimed that both talent management (Collings 2009) and coaching are under-researched in the global context (Abbott et al. 2013). For example, Garavan et al. (2011) note that talent development represents an important component of the talent management process, but that here is surprisingly little published research on global talent development issues. Further, most of the coaching interventions in studies reporting on the coaching of talents have taken place in a domestic setting. Coaching is frequently recommended for international managers, but it is listed as just one of a number of other development interventions, and the studies lack definitions and empirical evidence. Several critical reviewers of the coaching literature argue that the coaching industry rests on a limited research and evidence-base.

R. Salomaa (✉)
Department of Management, Vaasa University, Vaasa, Finland
e-mail: raija.salomaa@kolumbus.fi

A. Al Ariss (ed.), *Global Talent Management*, Management for Professionals,
DOI 10.1007/978-3-319-05125-3_4, © Springer International Publishing Switzerland 2014

Even if organisations are using coaching widely, relatively few organisations derive the full benefits of executive coaching by implementing coaching in a systematic way (McDermott et al. 2007). Among the concerns are a lack of clarity and consistency in how coaching is used, a lack of cumulative organisational learning about how to manage coaching, an inconsistent quality of coaching, and a lack of systematic goal setting and outcome evaluation (Peterson 2011). Different kinds of stage models have been developed to describe the implementation of coaching within organisations. Peterson and Little (2008, cited in Peterson 2011) and Peterson (2011) claim that there is a growing use of systematic coaching within organisations—a strategic, programmatic use of coaching to develop talent pools— and have developed the Coaching Continuum Stage Model to describe different stages of implementation (Peterson 2011). The research study described later in this chapter used this model in order to identify the characteristics of the different stages of implementation of coaching within MNCs.

The study aimed to shed light on the following research questions:

- How and why is executive coaching used in GTM?
- What are the experiences of HR professionals in implementing coaching in GTM programmes?

This research is important, since the use of coaching in talent management programmes is increasing and coaching research in the international context is scarce.

The next section briefly reviews the existing literature on GTM. Coaching in general and the Coaching Continuum Stage Model (Peterson 2011) are then described, followed by a discussion of international coaching. Finally, the research study and empirical findings are presented and future research topics and some practical implications are discussed.

2   Global Talent Management

Since the late 1990s, one of the most significant developments in people management has been a focus on effectively identifying and managing the individuals who are the most important to the strategic success of organisations (Schuler and Tarique 2012); and the systematic management of global talent by means of GTM programmes has become increasingly important. There is no consensus regarding the exact meaning of GTM, but there is a growing understanding that it is an emerging field. In this study GTM is defined broadly as:

… systemically utilising International Human Resource Management (IHRM) activities to attract, develop and retain individuals with high levels of human capital (i.e. competency, personality, motivation), consistent with the strategic direction of the multinational enterprise in a dynamic, highly competitive, and global environment. (Schuler and Tarique 2012).

Among the global talent challenges is a shortage of talented leaders who are able to manage in uncertain situations and who possess the organisational and business savvy, and the cross-cultural skills, needed to run global businesses (Evans et al. 2010). Evans et al. point out that leadership development in MNCs involves first selecting those who have the potential to master transitions to more senior roles and then developing the required skills through the provision of appropriate challenges, mobility, coaching and training. Individuals develop skills as they transition to more senior roles and international assignments are regarded as one of the key development methods through which cross-cultural competencies can be developed. However, these transitions demand a significant change in the individual, which can be supported by coaching. Mendenhall (2006) recommends coaching for international managers because the traditional development programmes cannot anticipate the multitude and variety of cross-cultural challenges. He argues that coaching is (1) highly individualized, (2) focused on the present, and (3) confidential and provides a process in which the individual is free to learn. Garavan et al. (2011) posit that talent development must be increasingly work-based, adaptable and flexible. They also suggest that talent development architecture is not a one-size-fits-all approach but that it should be differentiated, with an emphasis on customising talent development strategies to meet the needs of individuals. Self-directed talent development activities, such as coaching, highlight the need for learner insight, self-awareness and self-confidence.

3   Coaching

This section focuses briefly on what is known about coaching, defines it, and presents the Coaching Continuum Stage Model.

Coaching can be seen as a collaborative and non-directive relationship between coach and coachee for the purpose of professional or personal development. The major of leadership and executive coaching is primarily developmental in nature. Coaching is a cross-disciplinary approach that has its roots in psychology, management, learning theory, theories of human and organisational development, philosophy, and sports. In this chapter coaching is defined as 'as a human development process that involves structured, focused interaction and the use of appropriate strategies, tools and techniques to promote desirable and sustainable change for the benefit of the coachee and potentially for other stakeholders'. (Bachkirova et al. 2010, p. 1)

The ambiguity of the concept of coaching has led to discourses in which coaching has been contrasted with other developmental approaches in an attempt to gain greater clarity. Coaching has been compared with mentoring, counselling, consulting, training and therapy. The literature on executive coaching differentiates it from these other interventions and some conceptual distinctiveness can be observed. In contrast to consultants, executive coaches do not provide recommendations on specific business issues, nor do they act as technical experts. Coaching also differs from mentoring in that coaching is more structured and formal in nature and is based on an equal relationship between coach and coachee.

Very little has been documented about the specific coaching needs of executive clients and why coaching is used. The reasons for executive coaching that have been identified have tended to be broad in nature, such as for the development of leadership skills and managerial effectiveness (Feldman and Lankau 2005). An HBR survey (Coutu et al. 2009) suggests that coaching is used for developing talents and for facilitating a transition in or up, for acting as a sounding board, and for addressing a derailing behaviour. Burrus (2010) has described the special characteristics and coaching needs of managers who have lived in numerous countries and currently travel, live, and work all over the world. These managers possess attributes that many MNCs seek—innate intercultural instincts, mobility, and adaptability—and have special coaching needs based on, for example, their rootlessness and lack of support structures. Some evidence from coaching research suggests that it is a valuable tool for managerial development in terms of enhancing the transfer of learning from the classroom to the workplace, and in terms of developing and enhancing skills, self-awareness, motivation, personal confidence and impacting well being (Passmore 2009b).

3.1   The Coaching Continuum Stage Model

Today, organisations tend to focus on the coaching of key groups. These initiatives are usually referred to as 'coaching culture programmes' and are described as stage models. While the literature on the subject is growing, much of it takes a normative approach and lacks empirical evidence. As in the case of GTM, most of the authors share the opinion that the implementation of coaching ought to be supported by top management, and be aligned with the overall business and development strategy of the organisation.

Peterson and Little (2008, cited in Peterson 2011), and Peterson (2011) have developed a conceptual model for presenting the stages of implementation of coaching. In this model, organisations move through four stages along a continuum, from relatively ad hoc uses of coaching to more systemic and strategic applications, as follows:

In the first 'ad hoc' stage most organisations begin to use executive coaching when one individual requests coaching. The request may come from a manager, an HR professional or the potential coachee him/herself. Coaching is reactive and is not implemented in a coordinated manner across the organisation. At the organisational level there is no awareness of who is receiving coaching and what the process involves, nor is there an awareness of the costs and value of the coaching.

The second 'managed coaching' stage is driven by a coaching champion. The role of the champion is to manage all of the coaches working in the organisation. Organisations move to this stage either when they notice that they are spending significant amounts of money on coaching, or when they realise that coaching has significant potential value, which they wish to harness in a more structured way. The coaching champion establishes coach selection criteria, screens and keeps track of coaches, and defines the coaching process. This process may include evaluating coachees' reactions although organisations rarely define who receives coaching nor measure coaching outcomes at this stage.

At the third 'proactive' stage organisations begin to use coaching for groups, such as for onboarding new executives or accelerating the development of talents. This is driven by a business need. The aim is to generate clear organisational value by using coaching to develop talent pools. Organisations start to think more strategically about who provides coaching and who receives it. At this stage, some organisations try to create a 'coaching culture' by enhancing their internal coaching capabilities and limiting the use of external coaches in order to reduce costs. Some organisations define coaching roles for specific needs, e.g. external executive coaching for senior executives, and internal coaching for new hires and middle managers.

At the fourth matured stage coaching is driven by the organisational talent management strategy. Companies at this stage have identified their most critical talent. They have also prioritised where development will make the biggest difference. Stage four organisations have a clear understanding of their talent and their development needs, and have an array of development tools. The solution decided upon may rest on factors such as cost, effectiveness of the method, and the potential business impact of the need. The following section discusses coaching from international perspectives.

3.2   International Coaching

It has been argued that a rapidly changing global business environment accelerates the use of coaching, because traditional management approaches are unable to handle today's faster-paced business processes. Over the last decade, some coaching researchers have started to explore coaching from an international perspective. These approaches to coaching are influenced by international management theories and intercultural research (for a recent literature review see Abbott et al. 2013). Many authors argue that an understanding of culture and cultural differences is of great importance in international coaching. The impact of culture and diversity in coaching has also been discussed from the perspectives of generational, cultural, national and racial difference (Passmore 2009a). Surveys conducted by Bresser Consulting on, for example, coaching within a European context, suggest that there is a great diversity of coaching approaches (cited in Passmore 2009a). There are a number of published papers that discuss coaching in the Asian context and suggest that coaches need to moderate their techniques with Asian coachees (Nangalia and Nanagalia 2010; Sood; Choudhury; Tanaka, cited in Passmore 2009a).

The complexity of the international business environment demands that executive coaches who work with international clientele possess business acumen, combined with organisational and psychological knowledge (Peterson 2011). As distinct from domestic coaches, coaches working with international managers need to be familiar with expatriate experiences, international management and cultural theories.

Coaching is widely used to develop talents, but most of the research reports lack the international perspective. There is a need for empirical evidence on coaching used in GTM. The criteria of the different stages of the Coaching Continuum Stage Model, presented above, are on a rather general level and could be further developed by utilising the model empirically. Further, surprisingly little is known about talent development issues and the reasons behind the choice of coaching as a development tool. The next section describes and presents the results of a research study that aimed to shed light on these issues.

4   The Research Study

An empirical multiple-case study was conducted with three MNCs, in order to explore how and why these global organisations used executive coaching as a tool for the development of talents and to explore how the implementation of coaching was experienced by HR professionals. This section describes the methodological approach adopted.

4.1   Methodology

As previously mentioned, coaching research in the global context is scarce; consequently, this study is exploratory in nature. A qualitative multiple-case study approach was chosen because the case study approach enabled a deep exploration of the experiences of key HR professionals responsible for coaching. Case studies are well suited to new research areas, and may be preferred when 'how' or 'why' questions need to be answered and when the focus is on a current real-life context (Yin 1994).

Three case companies for this study were selected on the basis of the fact that all of these international companies used coaching for developing key groups of managers. In order to prevent the study from being too broad in scope, the research boundaries were set by time and activity, meaning that examination of the coaching activities of these case companies was restricted to include coaching conducted only between 2000 and 2013.

After selection of the case companies, data was gathered. The sources of data included interviews, corporate presentations on GTM and coaching, published and unpublished reports on the case companies, one internal company journal article, web pages, and emails. For reasons of confidentiality the case companies are not named but are instead referred to as Cases A, B, and C.

The interview participants (N = 8) consisted of several nationalities located in five countries on three continents. The interviewees included seven HR professionals and one line manager who had previously worked in an HR key role. The interviewees were chosen because they had been in important roles with

Table 1 Demographics of the interview participants

Case company	Position	Location	Age group and gender	Nationality
Case A	HR Director, coaching internal global coachees	Finland	40–55, female	Finnish
	Senior HR Director, coaching internal global coachees	USA	40–55, female	American
Case B	Director Learning and Development, global responsibility	Finland	40–55, male	Finnish
	Manager Learning and Development, coaching champion, global responsibility	Netherlands	40–55, female	Dutch
	HR Director Asia & Pacific	Singapore	40–55, male	Finnish
Case C	Senior Leadership Consultant, coaching champion, global responsibility	Finland	25–40, female	Finnish
	Senior Manager, ex. Senior Leadership Consultant, coaching internal coachees	Finland	40–55, female	Finnish
	Senior Leadership Consultant, coaching champion, global responsibility	Denmark	25–40, male	Danish

regard to the implementation of coaching within their organisations. The companies included in the study are described below:

Case A company provides medical healthcare solutions and operates in 38 countries, employing some 50,000 people worldwide.

Case B company is a global leader in mechanical engineering with operations in nearly 170 locations and with 19,000 employees in 70 countries.

Case C company operates in the financial sector in nine home markets and has 31,500 employees.

The demographics of the interview participants are described in Table 1 below:

The semi-structured interviews were conducted in Finnish or in English, face-to-face or virtually. Open-ended questions were used in order to allow relevant topics to emerge. In some cases, follow-up questions were sent by email to the interviewee after the interview in order to gain a deeper insight into the issues that arose. The same issues were discussed further with one other representative of the same company.

The interviews were transcribed verbatim. In order to ensure quality, the interview documents were sent back to the interviewees for approval after being transcribed. The collected material was read several times and the emerging observations were marked in the margins of the documents. The data were loaded into QSR NVivo software for the purpose of analysis. Corporate presentations and other unpublished and published reports were used as background material, and for triangulation purposes. One internal journal article, where representatives of HR and coached international managers were interviewed, was also used for analysis. The cases were then compared, and differences and similarities were identified from the observations. When analysing the findings on how coaching was used by MNCs in terms of where they were positioned along the Coaching Continuum, the key characteristics which differentiated the cases were identified. Besides differentiating the cases, these characteristics described those areas of development which the companies had experienced as important in their progress toward well-performing coaching activity.

4.2   Findings

4.2.1   Case A
How Was Coaching Used in Case A?
At the time of the interviews, coaching was offered in development programmes for international managers, including talents, but not in a structured way. The company's HR department launched a one-day global coaching skills training programme for 7,000 managers in 2010, and expected their managers to coach their direct reports. HR representatives were also required to provide coaching services to global, internal coachees. Depending on the geographic area of responsibility, a Finnish HR director may have had internal coachees in, for example, India or the USA. The company had not prohibited the use of external coaches but, because of the investment in the internal coaching programme, it tended not to use external coaching professionals. Most of the coaching could be characterised as a one-time discussion. Here, the interviewed Finnish HR Director described the length of the coaching discussion:

> . . . I guess 80 – 90 % of coaching is a one-time discussion about various challenges.

In some cases, such as in the development programmes for General Managers, coaching consisted of several sessions. Coaching was usually conducted in English.

Why Was Coaching Used?
The company was aiming to integrate coaching into standard managerial practice, and provided coach training to support the initiative. The Finnish HR Director explained:

> We expect our managers to adopt a coaching style in their day to day managerial practice.

She went on to say:

> We have leadership programmes and talent programmes, and coaching is often one element in them.

Executive coaching was being used to support individual talents who were in career transition to a more senior level or, to support managers who, for example, were being transferred to the USA or who were moving from the USA to other countries. During the interview, the Senior HR Director in the USA described her own work as an internal coach:

> I do a lot of my own coaching now with people about the focus of transitions and a lot of the transitions are global. . .leaders who are leading an organisation for the first time so that has

been a theme. Then with the HR work I have done a lot of work in terms of global movement and global talent as well.

What Were the Outcomes and Challenges?

According to those interviewed, no particular outcomes had yet been achieved. With regard to coach training and experience, there were huge differences between different internal coaching providers. For example, the HR manager in the USA interviewed had studied coaching, was credentialled at a professional level by the International Coach Federation (ICF), and had an extensive expatriate working background. Compared with her colleagues in Finland, who had gone through the same one-day coaching skills training as the line managers, and who had no foreign assignment experience, the US HR manager's ability to coach key talents was on a completely different level. In the Finnish subsidiary, HR personnel found it challenging to coach their global coachees virtually and felt that the coaching was not at a professional level. Virtual coaching in general, coping with different time zones and building trust over the phone were mentioned as problems. The HR director interviewed spoke about her experiences:

> Well, let's say that when you are not very experienced in coaching, it makes coaching over the phone very challenging. You have never met your coachee and you do not know him or her. ...different time zones, coaching over the phone are the challenges.

When asked about the challenges in implementing coaching, it was felt that the transition to a more coaching-based management style was difficult for managers. Instead of asking questions, managers typically acted as problem solvers and told their direct reports what to do. The HR Director in the USA spoke about the challenge:

> ...I would say that a part of it is a cultural shift. We are an organisation that is known for being very results orientated and very execution focused and it is much more of a tell rather than ask culture.

Furthermore, coaching was not evaluated or measured. Aside from the one-day coach training, there were no support structures in place and coaching was not integrated with the HR processes. HR tried to keep records of how many subordinates were coached by line-managers, but there was no follow-up. However, the biggest challenge within this company was that the definition of coaching was unclear; it had never been explicitly defined. Here is an excerpt from an interview with a Finnish HR director, talking about the challenge:

> I get a message from my boss: you need to give them some coaching, meaning that I have to tell them what they are supposed to do and not to do. Or then coaching is mixed with some kind of teaching. It is a problem... I think that there is a problem around the concept, what it is and what the expectations are from it.

Case A was positioned in the ad hoc stage on the Coaching Continuum, because coaching was not managed in a systematic manner, it was not integrated in the HR processes, and the concept of coaching and coaching processes had not been defined. The quality and length of internal coaching also varied considerably depending on the professional background of the coach.

4.2.2   Case B
How Was Coaching Used?

The company started to implement coaching by defining what coaching is, and by identifying the optimal coaching infrastructure for the company. It also promoted the positive coaching experiences of key talents, who were located in different business units that had already used coaching. Coaching was supported by the company culture, in which a sharing best-practices attitude prevailed, and was promoted by the CEO and other executives. International leadership programmes, in which coaching was an integral component, were business-driven and co-designed with business representatives. They were offered to different managerial levels and created a learning continuum. The Leadership and Development Director of the company clarified:

> We take people from the business units and from different levels to co-design these programmes. We do not want them to be something invented by HR only.

Coach training was not mandatory. When asked about the best practices of the implementation, the Director of Learning and Development recommended that the concept and infrastructure of coaching should be developed before anything else.

Case B offered individual executive coaching to senior managers, conducted by external professionals. The coaching champion in the Netherlands explained the reasons for using external coaches:

> It is a quite intensive process and I would say quite a long term process to really get internal people to the stage where they would be able to professionally coach more senior people.

The individual coaching process was defined and consisted of: (1) expectations and target setting, discussed and agreed by the coachee, manager and coach; (2) between four and eight coaching sessions; and (3) a triangle evaluation session between the coachee, coach and supervisor. The participants were asked to keep a learning diary. The role of HR was to discuss the individual's needs with the line manager, find suitable coaches, and match a coach with the coachee. The process was recorded as a learning event in the HR system. In addition to the evaluation of the individual coaching processes, the company used coaching-based assessments, a questionnaire, and a 360-feedback tool. Coaching had been defined as one of the leadership competencies of the company. At the time of the research study, coaching was being incorporated into the Key Performance Indicator (KPIs) process. Overall, coaching was integrated within HR processes.

Coaching was offered in either the mother-tongue language of the coachee or in English. The company tried to find a coach who had a similar cultural background to the coachee and, for example, would not hire a Chinese coach for a Finnish coachee. In addition, the coach was required to have experience of the language, culture and business life of the assignment country of the coachee, and to be credentialled by the International Coach Federation (ICF). References were also considered and checked. Coaching was conducted in face-to-face or in virtual sessions, or a mixture of both.

Why Was Coaching Used?

Case B's aim was to create a high-performing company culture in order to increase employee engagement and to help to both source and retain talent. The wider implementation of coaching began because of positive reports from some of the business units about their coaching experiences. In parallel, HR started to benchmark and learn about coaching because they had noticed that the use of coaching was a rising trend in the talent development arena. Here the Learning and Development Director speaks about the reasons behind designing different international development programmes for different managerial levels where executive coaching was included:

> The content and objectives of these development programmes correlate with the challenges of a certain managerial level. On higher levels the challenges change to more strategic ones...

As well as the different development programmes that included coaching, the company had begun to support individual managers in transition using coaching. It was also used for leadership skills development. Here a HR Director explained why he has been using coaching:

> When a person has not had the skills required for a position, he or she has not been able to perform well, or from is a more positive starting point, a person has got new challenges, and we have been supporting him or her by coaching.

He further stated that one of the reasons that he uses coaching is because of ability, through the coaching process to turn learned skills into action:

> I would say that the success rate of coaching is much higher than in other interventions such as classroom style learning events...I prefer coaching if the person involved needs to learn leadership skills...in a classroom style event you get theoretical frameworks, but if you want to turn it to action, you need coaching to support it.

In a corporate presentation of the coaching offering within the company, the manager of Leadership and Development stated that:

> ... senior managers are guided to the next level of performance by coaching.

What Were the Outcomes and Challenges?

Both the interviews and an internal journal article, for which HR professionals responsible for coaching and coached internationally working managers had been interviewed, confirmed that managers found coaching helpful. They stated that coaching had helped coachees to get better positions and to convert plans into action. Coaching had given them a safe place to reflect on who they were as leaders. It had challenged their thinking. Coaching had also helped them to communicate more effectively and had been a positive experience, after which they had easily been able to share best practices with younger employees.

At the time of the interviews, the company was in a 'honeymoon phase' of the implementation; the people responsible for coaching had not encountered any major challenges. However, in those rare cases when coaching was not successful, the reason was regarded as being related to the level of commitment of the coachee, as suggested by the HR Director:

> The biggest challenge is always when a coachee says, OK, I will start a coaching process, but he goes into it by saying it only, and is not committed with his head or with his heart.

There had been many different individual coaching efforts in different countries. The company had begun to formalise its coaching processes. They had tried to identify some global coaching providers, with whom they could enter into a partnership. At the same time, different business units had needed to act in a timely manner and find coaches locally who matched their requirements in the absence of a corporate-wide global network of coaches. The HR Director in Asia spoke about the challenge:

> … we lack a network of coaches, so it means that when I have lunch meetings with representatives of other companies, I ask for references…

Case B was located on the proactive stage (stage 3) of the Coaching Continuum. They had hired a coaching champion who coordinated and developed coaching within the company. Executive coaching and the concept of coaching had been defined. The systematic integration of coaching into the HR processes was in progress. They had also defined to whom coaching was offered and what it comprised. Their global talent development offering consisted of different kind of programmes into which coaching had been integrated, and it formed part of a learning continuum.

4.2.3   Case C
How Was Coaching Used?

The coaching infrastructure within the company had been developed in a very systematic way. Coaching was integrated into all HR processes, and the owner of the coaching initiative was a Senior Leadership Consultant with a coach training background. The next quotation reveals the importance of the international integration of coaching:

> All we do here where I am sitting, we are doing in an international context…Development should be aligned through the company internationally…

The coaching champion and the person responsible for GTM worked together in the Leadership and Talent Management Department, under the same manager, who ensured that the two were aligned. The company required that the ICF certify all of the internal leadership consultants. Talents were identified through Annual Personnel Reviews, which included Performance and Development Discussions between the employee and the supervisor; the results were discussed together with HR Partners and entered into the HR system. In order to identify the most skilled high potentials within the company, a ranking of 1–4 was awarded. A person ranked as talent (4) was supported by an individual development plan, which included mentoring, coaching, career counselling and leadership development programmes. Talents could use also external executive coaches, certified by the ICF.

At the beginning of the coaching implementation process, all the leadership consultants responsible for coaching had to travel abroad to learn what coaching was and how coaching could be implemented. After this phase, the Coaching International Support Team defined coaching and created a coaching infrastructure. Coaching started with pilot groups of middle management, comprising managers ranked as talented leaders. The executive coaching programme was designed at a later stage. The company hired two PhD candidates who researched the coaching processes and outcomes within the company. The research results were also used for employer branding purposes.

The coaching process, and the coaching skills training provided by the company internally, was divided into basic and advanced levels. The training was founded on learning theories with a very practical focus. It consisted of several modules and lasted 2 years. The managers trained in coaching skills were assessed based on the quantity and quality of the coaching discussions and they needed to reach a certain level before they could move to the next module. Both the coaching training and coaching were evaluated. Coaching training was mandatory for all managers.

Why Was Coaching Used?

The implementation of coaching began when a senior HRD director at the headquarters of the company saw an opportunity to use coaching to unite the company after several international mergers and to develop its managers. This initiative was strongly supported by the top management at the headquarters of the company. Coaching was used to support the company's transformation process, for team building, and for achieving business goals. The company also used coaching to improve communication and to meet the individual development needs of its talents. When asked why coaching was used in the talent management programmes, a HR consultant answered by email:

> We use it as a leadership approach... In some programmes we use coaching as a learning activity.

The line manager spoke about one of her coaching assignments concerning a young talent that joined the company recently:

> She is like a bull in a china shop.....many people have told her that she has been acting in a very tough way, she has also said some things that do not fit with the company culture. She came from another company and said that she did not even understand what she was doing wrong.

In this case coaching was used for awareness building on how to be more efficient in communication and for adaption to a new company culture.

What Were the Outcomes and Challenges?

This company had over 10 years' experience in implementing coaching. The Senior Manager, who had been in a key HR role during the implementation phase stated:

> Coaching is part of all our development programmes...it is part of our everyday life and tied to our backbone.

Those interviewed felt that while the organisation had already achieved a great deal by adopting a coaching approach, the journey was still continuing. Even though it was hard to measure the actual return on investment, those interviewed believed that coaching had been a critical element in the company's success. However, the company did not separately document the outcomes of their talent development initiatives. They highlighted that the company had received a lot of positive attention for its coaching initiative in the press (over 30 articles internationally), and that representatives and researchers of the company had been invited to speak at different coaching conferences about their coaching initiative. Aside from coaching's positive influence on the corporate employer brand, they had also achieved good business results. The senior manager stated:

> We can be proud of our business results...We are able to keep the business in the growth area and the turnovers positive...When we started to implement coaching, we did not imagine that it would be so powerful. Of course I am not saying that the results only depend on coaching, but it plays a big role. If asked, everybody thinks so.

She noted that the company had been ranked as the best service provider of their industry internationally. Further, she stated that employee retention was high and that the employee satisfaction index was rising and, at the time of interview, stood at the highest level ever.

Although the implementation of coaching was perceived as successful, the company had also encountered challenges in global integration. Although coaching was supported by the top management at the headquarters of the company in Denmark, it took a while before the Finnish organisation's management team showed any interest in it. At first, they refused to meet with the leadership consultants responsible for coaching. A senior line manager noted that:

> In this phase, our management in Finland did not buy into it - they were of the opinion that it was just HR mumbo-jumbo.

When pressure came from middle management, and HR could show some positive results, the attitude towards coaching changed. The Finnish management team then insisted that an executive-level coaching programme be developed.

A further challenge was that some of the managers had left the company or were transferred to non-managerial positions during the implementation phase. Coaching was included as an important element of the managerial job description, which some managers had difficulties in accepting. At the time of the interviews, managers were not coaching their subordinates as often as they should have been. The Senior Leadership Consultant in Denmark commented:

It is not used all the time. There is a difference in knowing about and using, as you know, so I have trained people who have said they know a lot about coaching, but when it comes to the actual skills and the group part, a lot of people are struggling.

He went on to say that some managers did not understand in which situations they should coach, nor how to integrate coaching into the business environment. The managers felt that they did not have time for it and they found asking the right coaching questions demanding.

Due to budget constraints, coaching and training had recently been cut, and the leadership consultants interviewed felt that much more could be done to develop coaching further. One of the Leadership Consultants interviewed, who had left the company, but worked as an external coach in a talent management programme noted:

> During my time half of the personnel in the leadership and development unit were given notice. The resources were so tight that we had to consider very carefully where to put them. I felt that the development of coaching was not a priority...which was a personal disappointment for me.

She further noted that although coaching and GTM were aligned, the integration could have been tighter. In addition, those interviewed believed that best practices need to be implemented on a long-term basis, and that there was a danger of coaching becoming business as usual and of its continuous development not being a priority. The Senior Manager talked about the concerns:

> The basics are now ok, but there is always the danger when coaching becomes business as usual that we do not repeat good practices on a long-term basis. And what I mean by a long-term basis is 7-10 years.

Case C was positioned in the matured stage of the Coaching Continuum. They had a long-term integration and implementation strategy for coaching. GTM and coaching were aligned. They had a coaching champion and coaching was integrated in all HR systems. Coaching was evaluated and measured. This company used both external and internal professionals, and coaching and the processes of coaching had been defined.

Summary and Conclusions

The aim of this study was to answer the questions of how and why coaching was used in GTM by the case MNCs and to examine how of HR professionals experienced the implementation of coaching. When analysing the findings on how coaching was used by MNCs in terms of where they were positioned along the Coaching Continuum, key characteristics which differentiated the cases were identified (see Table 2). Besides differentiating the cases, these characteristics described those areas of development which the companies had experienced as important in their progress toward well-performing coaching activity. Table 2 describes the characteristics identified and the existing situation of each case company in terms of each of these characteristics.

Table 2 Key differences characterising the different stages of the Coaching Continuum exhibited by the case MNCs

Characteristic	Ad Hoc Case A	Proactive stage Case B	Mature stage Case C
1. Long-term global integration and implementation strategy for coaching	No	In progress	Yes
2. Global coaching policy	No	Yes	Yes
3. Concept of coaching defined	No	Yes	Yes
4. The coaching process defined	No	Yes	Yes
5. GTM and coaching aligned	No	No	Yes
6. Integration of coaching in HR processes	No	In progress	Yes
7. Research-based approach to coaching	No	No	Yes
8. Measurement and evaluation of coaching	No	Yes	Yes
9. A Coaching Champion	No	Yes	Yes
10. A learning continuum created in which coaching is integrated	No	Yes (different programmes for different managerial levels)	Yes (different programmes for different managerial levels)
11. Organised coaching skills training	Yes (one day's mandatory training)	Yes (voluntary training)	Yes (mandatory training, length of total coaching training process 4 modules over 2 years)
12. Requirements for external and internal coaches	No	Yes	Yes
13. Use of external coaches	Yes (permitted, but not used)	Yes (external professionals used for executives and talents)	Yes (external professionals used for executives and talents)
14. Use of internal coaches	Yes (as a managerial approach)	Yes (as a managerial approach)	Yes (as a managerial approach+ certified internal coaches)
15. International coach pool	No	In progress	In progress

The research findings indicated that in more developed stages the MNCs had formulated a long-term integration and implementation strategy, which was connected to business needs and supported by top management. The need to link the development of coaching with business strategy is supported by several authors (cited e.g. in Peterson 2011). Walker-Fraser (2011) also recommends that the way in which coaching is to be integrated into the strategic planning process be clarified at the outset.

The MNCs at the Proactive and Mature stages of the implementation (cases B and C) had a global coaching policy that included a definition of coaching and the coaching process, and defined when, what kind of coaching, to whom and by whom it was offered. The study showed that it was seen as critical to successful implementation that the concept of coaching was clarified and defined at the very beginning, before the development of the coaching infrastructure within the organisation.

The need for alignment of GTM and coaching was also raised up by the interviewees as important to successful implementation. However, only case C demonstrated this alignment clearly. Given that the organisation's mission and business strategy ought to impact the organisation's people development strategy, it would be of benefit, if GTM and coaching are aligned (e.g. Hawkins 2012). At more mature stages the MNCs had also integrated coaching with other HR processes. The integration is important if coaching is managed systematically. In cases B and C coaching processes were recorded as a learning event in their HR systems, they were integrated, for example, with KPIs, and coaching was included in managerial job descriptions.

It was also seen as beneficial to support coaching through adopting a research-based approach to its implementation. In particular, case C had found it necessary to hire researchers who provided HR with arguments in favour of coaching. Measurement and evaluation of coaching on a practical level was found to be important. Cases B and C used coaching based assessments, and, for example, practical evaluation discussions of coaching processes. McDermott et al.'s (2007) study confirms that organisations that coordinate coaching centrally and evaluate its effectiveness report better results. Moreover, the MNCs at more mature stages had hired a coaching champion with a coach training background and whose primary responsibility was the coordination and development of coaching within the MNC. Furthermore, in case C the coaching support team consisted of several people who were, for example, certified by ICF. Also Hawkins (2012) suggests that the coaching support team ought to be broad in nature, since reliance on one person is risky.

Cases B and C had created a learning continuum for coaching. Coaching was integrated into different talent and leadership development programmes for different managerial levels, and it was not regarded as a one-time event. Since all the studied MNCs studied were aiming to create a coaching based managerial practice, a long-term approach was crucial. All the MNCs studied offered coaching skills training, but at the mature stage of implementation this training formed part of a long- term approach, in which the coaching skills of managers were evaluated and measured. For quality assurance case B used one external global provider who was able to offer the training globally, while case C organised the training internally. This meant that key talents were trained in coaching skills, along with other managers, and it was expected that they then coach their subordinates.

As demonstrated by the MNCs at more mature stages, it was also crucial to assure the value and quality of coaching by stipulating global requirements for external and internal coaches. All the MNCs permitted the usage of external coaches for executives and talents, but at the 'Ad Hoc' stage external coaches were not hired in practice, because the company had invested in a one day coaching skills training for managers and this was deemed sufficient. Case B used external coaches, because they found that their internal coaching skills were insufficient for the coaching of more senior managers. Case C also used external coaches for their executives and key talents. Internal coaching practices varied considerably between the cases. In case A, coachees received internal coaching, whose quality varied considerably depending on the professional and international experience of the coach. Case B understood coaching as a managerial approach, but used external coaches to coach their executives and talents, whereas case C, with a cadre of certified internal coaches used both and had defined in which situations internal coaching was to be used. Even if organisations wish to reduce spending on external coaching and to rely only on internal coaches, it is beneficial for them to clearly separate professionally-conducted, executive coaching from 'regular' managerial coaching and to set strict quality requirements for their coaches. This is important since Kombarakaran et al. (2008) argue that managers transfer and model their own positive coaching experiences when coaching their subordinates and peers. They also suggest that investment in well-designed and implemented coaching programmes can contribute to the retention of talent.

None of the studied MNCs had a well-established international coach pool in place, although this was seen as important by the MNCs at the more developed stages of the Coaching Continuum. In support of this, several authors have given advice (e.g. Hawkins 2012) on how to develop an effective cadre of coaches. However, all of the criteria mentioned in Table 2, such as having a long-term global integration and implementation strategy for coaching, defining clear quality requirements and so on, need to be in place before an international coach pool can be established.

Having discussed how coaching was implemented in GTM within the MNCs studied, we next focus on why coaching was used.

In none of the case companies examined was coaching driven purely by the GTM strategy. In all of the MNCs studied, executive coaching was offered as one of the development tools in GTM and the process was tailored to the needs of the coachee. The MNCs used coaching to enable a transformation of their leadership culture. It was used also as a tool to help unify a company after several mergers, to develop managers in leadership and talent management programmes, for better organisational performance, and to support people in career transitions, which could be global in nature (to a more senior role and/or into a new culture). Coaching was also used to turn learned leadership skills into action, for awareness building, for supporting underperforming managers and to enable better communication.

Generally, HR had received positive feedback from global talents, who had received coaching, but no further outcomes of coaching in GTM could be observed. In case C, those interviewed believed that coaching had had an important impact on the overall performance of the company. This study confirmed the earlier observations of McDermott et al. (2007), as evidenced by case A, that most organisations are in the early stages of learning to use coaching in a systematic way. The challenges faced by some of the MNCs in this study were caused because these organisations lacked a long-term integration and implementation strategy for coaching, a clear definition of coaching, any integration between coaching and HR processes, defined requirements and quality assurance of internal and external coaches, a global coach pool, measurement of outcomes and HR personnel experienced in foreign assignments and international coaching.

Overall, this study supports the view that there has been a upward trend in terms of the implementation of coaching within key groups and whole organisations, which has been largely driven by HR in the case of the MNCs studied. Neither the industry sector of the organisation nor the duration of the implementation of coaching played a large role in where these companies were located along the continuum. Case B demonstrated that an organisation can move quickly to a fairly mature stage when the coaching infrastructure is created and managed in a systematic manner.

This study is not without its limitations. The number of interview participants in this study was small; further studies to include members of top management, global talents and coaches working internationally would enrich our understanding of coaching within GTM. Furthermore, some of the interviews were conducted over Skype, which may have influenced the results. Larger-scale multiple case studies including a larger number of interview participants would reveal characteristics of all the stages of the Coaching Continuum and deepen our understanding of the stages. Longitudinal research on the effectiveness and challenges of the processes involved in the coaching of key talents in MNCs is important, such as the influence of the complex global environment, and of utilising virtual technology. Although managerial coaching was not included in the scope of this paper, all the case companies were committed to developing managerial coaching, and it is reasonable to assume that managers working internationally require different kinds of coaching skills than managers working only with domestic teams. This area of managerial coaching is currently under-researched. Since little is known why coaching is used and what are the coaching needs of global talents, it would be important to research it further.

Based on the findings discussed above, some best practices can be summarised as follows:

- Develop a long term integration and implementation strategy for coaching which is aligned with the overall strategy and organisational goals and which is supported by top management
- Define coaching and coaching processes at the beginning of the implementation

- Create a support team for coaching consisting of members experienced in international business and in living and working abroad, and which includes a coaching champion(s) with a professional coach training background
- Align GTM and coaching
- Integrate coaching into all HR processes
- Ensure that the design of coaching programmes and offerings are business-driven
- Specify clear quality requirements for internal and external coaches
- Measure and evaluate coaching
- Clearly differentiate managerial coaching and executive coaching
- Create a continuous learning continuum for coaching consisting of different programmes for different managerial levels
- Cooperate with academia in order to develop the processes and practices and to measure the outcomes of coaching

References

Abbott, G. N., Gilbert, K., & Rosinski, P. (2013). Cross-cultural working in coaching and mentoring. In J. Passmore, D. B. Peterson, & T. Freire (Eds.), *The Wiley-Blackwell handbook of the psychology of coaching and mentoring* (pp. 483–500). Chichester: Wiley.

Bachkirova, T., Cox, E., & Clutterbuck, D. (2010). Introduction. In E. Cox, T. Bachkirova, & D. Clutterbuck (Eds.), *The complete handbook of coaching*. London: Sage Publications Ltd.

Burrus, K. (2010). Coaching managers in multinational companies. Myths and realities of the Global Nomadic Leader. In M. Moral & G. Abbott (Eds.), *The Routledge companion to international business coaching* (pp. 230–238). Oxon: Routledge.

Collings, D. G. (2009). Global talent management: The law of the few. *Poznan University of Economics Review, 9*(2), 5–18.

Coutu, D., Kauffman, C., Charan, R., Peterson, D. P., Maccoby, M., Scoular, P. A., et al. (2009). What can coaches do for you? *Harvard Business Review, 87*, 91–97.

Evans, P., Smale, A., Björkman, I., & Pucik, V. (2010). Leadership development in multinational firms. In J. Storey (Ed.), *Leadership in organizations: Current issues and key trends* (2nd ed., pp. 207–222). New York: Routledge.

Feldman, D. C., & Lankau, M. J. (2005) Executive coaching: A review and agenda for future research. *Journal of Management,* 829–848. doi: 10.1177/0149206305279599.

Garavan, T. N., Carberry, R., & Rock, A. (2011). Mapping talent development: definition, scope and architecture. *European Journal of Training and Development, 36*(1), 5–24.

Hawkins, P. (2012). *Creating a coaching culture*. New York: McGrawHill.

Kombarakaran, F. A., Yang, J. A., Baker, M. N., & Fernandes, P. B. (2008). Executive coaching: it works! *Consulting Psychology Journal: Practice and Research, 60*(1), 78–90.

McDermott, M., Levenson, A., & Newton, S. (2007). What coaching can and cannot do for your organization. *Human Resource Planning, 30*(2), 30–37.

Mendenhall, M. E. (2006). The elusive, yet critical challenge of developing global leaders. *European Management Journal, 24*(6), 422–429.

Nangalia, L., & Nanagalia, A. (2010). The coach in Asian society: Impact of social hierarchy on the coaching relationship. *International Journal of Evidence Based Coaching and Mentoring, 8* (1), 51–66.

Passmore, J. (Ed.). (2009a). *Diversity in coaching: Working with Gender, Culture, Race and Age*. London: Kogan Page.

Passmore, J. (Ed.). (2009b). *Leadership coaching: Working with leaders to develop elite performance*. London: Kogan Page.

Peterson, D. B. (2011). Executive coaching: A critical review and recommendations for advancing the practice. In S. Zedeck (Ed.), *APA handbook of industrial and organizational psychology* (pp. 527–566). Washington: American Psychological Association.

Schuler, R., & Tarique, I. (2012). Global talent management: Theoretical perspectives, systems, and challenges. In I. Björkman & G. Stahl (Eds.), *Handbook of research in IHRM*. London: Edwar Elgar Publishing.

Walker-Fraser, A. (2011). An HR perspective on executive coaching for organizational learning. *International Journal of Evidence Based Coaching and Mentoring, 9*(2), 67–79.

Yin, R. K. (1994). *Case study research: Design and method* (2nd ed.). Thousand Oaks, CA: Sage.

Cultural Intelligence as a Key Construct for Global Talent Management

Joost Bücker

1   Introduction

Global talent management (GTM) is a broad term, used to describe the need to manage corporate talent on a worldwide scale. But this broadness also can create confusion, especially because the three words that constitute the term can be combined in so many different ways. When we refer to talent management, we are generally implying the need to find, nurture, support, and retain talented employees. Adding "global" expands these finding, nurturing, supporting, and retaining tasks to the global scale, across multinational enterprises with subsidiaries all over the world. Yet whereas GTM mainly has appealed to multinational enterprises (MNEs) thus far, small and medium-sized enterprises increasingly are spreading their operations to an international scale, as particularly manifested by the new category of "born global" firms (Knight and Cavusgil 2004).

A prevalent definition of GTM suggests it is

> the HR actions to ensure access to needed talent by multinational enterprises competing in a global environment; it includes HR policies and practices related to planning and forecasting, obtaining, selecting, and motivating, developing, evaluating, retaining, and removing employees consistent with a firm's strategic directions while taking into account the evolving concerns of the workforce and regulatory requirements (Schuler et al. 2011: 18).

This chapter seeks to extend our definition of GTM through a focus on the relatively new concept of cultural intelligence (CQ), which helps specify the competencies that global managers need to communicate and manage both themselves and other employees in a multicultural context. (Note that for the purposes of this chapter, we use similar terms—such as international, global, multinational, or transnational—interchangeably.) That is, to describe the competencies that global

J. Bücker (✉)
Institute of Management Research, Radboud University Nijmegen, Thomas van Aquinostraat 3106, 9800 HK Nijmegen, The Netherlands
e-mail: J.Bucker@fm.ru.nl

A. Al Ariss (ed.), *Global Talent Management*, Management for Professionals,
DOI 10.1007/978-3-319-05125-3_5, © Springer International Publishing Switzerland 2014

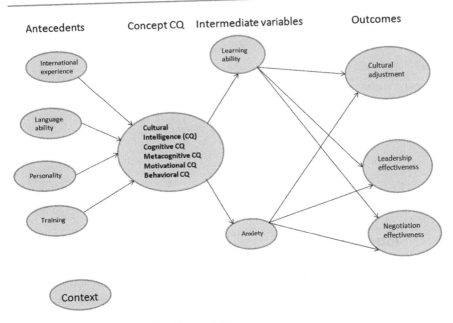

Fig. 1 Framework for cultural intelligence (CQ)

talents need to operate effectively, we turn to insights gained from interviews with (Dutch and Chinese) managers, working in Dutch multinationals in Asia and illustrate the CQ concept with real-life work examples. Asia offers an important setting for such an investigation, because of its massive economic growth and the increasing cooperation between Asia and Europe. Yet the vast cultural distance between these two national or regional settings demands that managers exert additional effort to cope with the complexity of their interactions and makes their use of CQ more visible than it might be in contexts with minimal cultural distances.

This chapter focuses mainly on the "talent" aspect of GTM, offering new insights into the competencies needed to communicate and manage effectively across cultures. Ongoing globalization will continue to require a growing group of talented, culturally intelligent individuals who can accomplish new and ever-changing tasks. As global trade keeps increasing, the stock of talented persons with excellent cross-cultural competences is poised to become a scarce resource. Accordingly, we start off this chapter by defining both GTM and CQ more fully, then relate CQ to the unique experiences of cross-cultural managers. To flesh out our proposed framework, we introduce antecedents of CQ, factors that contribute to its development, and several outcomes, along with a few insightful intermediate variables. Figure 1 at the top of this page shows an overview of this CQ framework. With this framework global managers and human resource departments can better recognize and encourage the key competencies needed by their global talent. Table 1 at the end of this chapter describes the challenges, strategies, and opportunities following from this chapter with regard to GTM.

2 The Need for GTM

The idea of GTM emerged in the 1990s, when worldwide increases in global trade made access to relatively scarce talent more difficult, prompting what some observers called a "global talent war" (Beechler and Woodward 2009). The global economic crisis seemingly should have brought about a truce, but instead the battle for talent rages on, with even greater urgency than before. Both practitioners (Hewitt Associates 2008) and academic literature (Sparrow et al. 2011) acknowledge the lasting, powerful competition for global talent, such that even "in the middle of a global economic slowdown, there are major structural conditions in place to ensure that competition for talent worldwide will continue to be a significant challenge" (Tarique and Schuler 2010: 123). The reason is likely that organizations seeking lasting, sustainable growth (Tarique and Schuler 2010) must have employees with exploitable skills. In particular, skills related to knowledge gathering and knowledge sharing are of crucial importance. Moreover, massive growth in emerging economies, such as the BRIC (Brazil, Russia, India, China) nations, Turkey, Nigeria, and South Africa, places organizations in these countries in direct competition with traditional MNEs as they search for local talent who can meet global standards. In some contexts, insufficient universities and business schools exist to deliver talented graduates who can fill hiring gaps; in more developed nations, dual-career households often limit young talents' global mobility (Collings et al. 2007). These various effects combine to make getting the right people with the right skills to the right places a critical, ongoing challenge for firms.

One way to address this challenge is by carefully defining the knowledge and skills that talented individuals must have if they are to function effectively across cultures, as exemplified by cultural intelligence (CQ). Various terms refer to such skills and knowledge (e.g., global mindset, cultural competence); we prefer the more in-depth notion of CQ (Bücker and Poutsma 2010). In this sense, we consider GTM from a competency-based perspective: The CQ concept serves to specify the required competencies and how organizations and their human resource departments can ensure their talent develop them.

3 Cultural Intelligence

Cultural intelligence builds on the intelligence concept and describes one of the important abilities people use to solve complex organizational problems. Organizations sought to determine why some of their members solved problems better than others; intelligence emerged as a central cause. Employees with greater intelligence solve complex problems well, and intelligence tests, designed to measure rational intelligence (IQ), became important organizational tools for selecting high performing talent. Yet inappropriate uses of IQ tests led to widespread discrimination against underrepresented minority populations. Although some companies continue to use these tests today, many organizations recognized that IQ could not fully explain performance in problem-solving tasks, because emotions have substantial influences, such that managers who could detect and understand others' emotions were better able to achieve effective cooperation. Goleman (1995) and Mayer et al. (2000) in turn introduced emotional intelligence; soon instruments to measure emotional intelligence were developed. Thus organizations could measure both rational and emotional intelligence to predict the performance of (talented) individuals.

Even together though, these measures suffered a major shortcoming: They were context dependent. A person who showed excellent rational and emotional intelligence in the Netherlands would not necessarily perform well in France, especially if he or she could not adapt to the new context. In the early 2000s, a new concept emerged to express an ability to work effectively across cultures. Earley (2002) and Earley and Ang (2003) called it cultural intelligence, and by 2007, a cultural intelligence scale had been developed (Ang et al. 2007). This wider ranging spectrum of intelligences (rational, emotional, and cultural) can describe the main abilities needed for individual talent to be effective in global organizations.

In discussing the current state of CQ, we refer to extant literature as well as interviews with seven Dutch managers working for Dutch multinationals in Asia, predominantly in China; seven Chinese managers working in China for a Dutch multinational; and six experts with extensive knowledge of cross-cultural communication and competencies. Accordingly, we define CQ as an ability to adjust to and understand other cultures (Thomas 2006), which is similar to Earley's (2002) definition of CQ as the capacity to adapt to new cultural settings. As a concept to explain and predict effectiveness in cross-cultural interactions, CQ comprises four dimensions (Ang et al. 2007).

First, metacognitive CQ expresses an ability to reflect on our own knowledge, emotions, attitudes, and motives, which creates alertness and activated senses, able to react appropriately to the new cultural environment. As an example, consider the experience of a French manager, sent to negotiate a joint venture with a Japanese firm. Using his or her metacognitive CQ, this French manager reflects on his or her cultural values and recognizes that they create a possible barrier to effective interaction. He or she also senses the implicitly hierarchical structure that exists in the Japanese firm, which makes it difficult to determine exactly who is in charge of decision making within the Japanese firm's negotiation team. By promoting active thinking about the situation that defines the cross-cultural interaction, as well as the values and motives of all participating actors, the French manager's metacognitive CQ helps him keep alert and open to signals. In contrast, according to one of our interviewed expatriates, "There is a big chance to fail, you may start from the wrong assumptions." Working internationally needs to "challenge your thinking, your beliefs," because "you can do nothing on automated pilot." According to at least one expert we interviewed, metacognitive CQ is the most important component of the overall model.

Second, cognitive CQ refers to knowledge we have about other cultures, including factual information related to geographical issues, climate, the population, demographics, or cultural features. Thus a foreign negotiator might have learned about the invisible hierarchical structures in Japanese firms, such that no single individual makes any decision but instead decision making is left to the team or group. Knowledge about the importance of age in Japanese organizations and the decisive role of the older managers also is part of cognitive CQ. With such knowledge of cultural similarities and differences, cognitive CQ enables more effective cross-cultural interactions; it also can help create tools to describe, measure, and compare cultures to achieve faster understanding and adjustment. Thus another French manager travelling from Japan to the United States to enter into another negotiation adjusts or her behavior, in accordance with his or her knowledge of U.S. management practices: This manager knows he or she will be able to determine quickly who is in charge of the decision. One of our experts recommended, "you need to develop awareness based on Hofstede's [2001] or Trompenaars and Hampden-Turner's [1998] models"—two models that attempt to describe and compare national cultures across the world—"to reconcile differences of cultures." As one of our expatriate managers explained cognitive CQ: "Concerning your hard skills, you are more independent, you require more tools and need to learn them."

Third, motivational CQ refers to the effort needed to dive into unknown cultures, try to understand them, and develop self-efficacy to act appropriately, which reflects a person's interest in functioning and learning in cross-cultural situations. Motivation helps people continue to explore situations that are often stressful and ambiguous. Without motivation, people are likely to exit the cross-cultural environment, overwhelmed by feelings of alienation and unfamiliarity; as one expatriate explained, working and living abroad, "You can feel pretty lonely... You sleep for four hours a couple of nights a week," and furthermore, "I do not like to live out of my suitcase all the time." Expatriates who exhibited far more motivation instead focused on the positive aspects: "I like to work with people with different backgrounds," "Working internationally is professionally challenging," "I enjoy travel," and though "It's hard work ... I have a more intensive life." Motivated talent tends to enjoy exotic lifestyles and travel that allows them to experience storied regions all over the world, but they also express satisfaction with the work itself, as long as it is not monotonous: "I was offered a job in Japan, but it was more of the same ... and you want to do that new thing." Talent with truly strong motivational CQ takes the perspective of one of our interviewees, who noted happily, "In general you directly become 'end-responsible' ... that will never happen at head office."

Fourth, behavioral CQ is the ability to engage in appropriate verbal and nonverbal behavior in cross-cultural interactions (Ang et al. 2006)—as well as to avoid engaging in inappropriate behaviors. The dimension is often immediately relevant in international greeting rituals; handshaking, bowing, and kissing guests on the cheek once, twice, or three times (as in the Netherlands) can be difficult for people to adapt, because of the powerful routinization of these behaviors. A Swedish manager who visits a Brazilian subsidiary, receiving a warm welcome with a lot of kissing and physical touching by Brazilian colleagues, may feel overwhelmed and uncomfortable. In a reverse visit, for a Brazilian salesperson who checks in with Swedish headquarters, the polite but reserved welcome likely feels cold and distant. Yet an interviewed expatriate claimed, "my ideal is to be able to communicate with anybody in the world," so that "I [could] develop the freedom to belong everywhere. ... I like to connect to anyone ... it gives you the possibility to connect as far as you want." Effective learning of behavioral repertoires can enable talent to survive anywhere, in any culture. Behavioral CQ thus is critical as the most visible CQ dimension; both language and an ability to read non-verbal signals are central to every cross-cultural interaction.

Together, the four dimensions represent a set of dynamic competencies, in that they are malleable and can be learned. Thus for GTM, human resources managers have a central role in supporting the development of CQ among new hires. When MNEs engage in global recruitment, their latest hires inevitably will function in an international context, so they must expand and enhance their CQ, which is possible because CQ is an ability. In contrast, static competencies are harder to learn and even might be determined by the person's heritage or personality. For our purposes then, GTM implies managing a learning process that increases the dynamic competencies of newly recruited talent.

4   Antecedents of CQ

Various activities can help talent develop CQ. From a GTM perspective, global firms need to define ways to develop the CQ of their employees in general, and particularly for their new hires, such as through management development and trainee programs. Among the multiple factors that can lead to CQ, we focus on four that are central for modern organizations: international experience, personality, foreign language, and training.

4.1   International Experience

When a person has prior international experience, it has a significant impact on her or his development of cross-cultural competencies (Caligiuri and Tarique 2009). We can distinguish various forms of experience and their effects on cultural understanding. For example, Crowne (2008) refers to cultural exposure to describe experiences related to a certain geographical area that grant the person familiarity with the norms, values, and beliefs that prevail in that area. Such familiarity supports the development of CQ. Exposure can encompass anything that brings the person in closer contact with another culture, such as seeing films, reading novels, visiting (even as a child), studying there, or working in that country previously. The different activities represent varying contact intensity with the other culture: With films and novels, we come in passive, indirect contact with the new culture, but an international education or work experience implies direct, active exposure. When people live abroad for an extended period, whether for work or education, they become more fully immersed into the local culture and must achieve specific goals, usually with their colleagues or fellow students.

Although all forms of exposure can enhance familiarity, the active forms, which involve direct, interpersonal interactions, contribute more to cultural learning than more passive or indirect forms. Yet as noted, even childhood experiences can be influential, as our interviewees revealed: "My first flight to Portugal when I lived at home made me extremely excited" or "The father of my girlfriend traveled a lot ... he always came home with interesting stories, always something to tell." When university students study abroad, they come in direct contact with students from a range of cultures, while living on campus or participating in lectures. If they live together, students confront various cooking and eating rituals, as well as alternative rhythms for scheduling work and leisure time. Nordic students often are surprised when their Spanish roommates only start to prepare their evening meal long after the Nordic students have finished eating for the day. The experience that prompts talent to pursue an international career can be varied, but "Someone has to offer you that opportunity ... [for me it was] my first boss at KLM."

Therefore, when human resource managers look to hire new talent for global positions, they should search for early international experiences and exposures to different cultures. Then experiences in additional international assignments (e.g., leading a cross-cultural project team) can further develop existing employees' CQ. That is, GTM requires the realization that international experience, in any stage, offers an important contribution. If they have the luxury of selecting among candidates though, organizations should prefer those with earlier international experience.

4.2 Personality

People who exhibit an open mind and are open to new experiences tend to pick up more signals and gain a better understanding of cross-cultural situations more readily. Ang et al. (2006) consider the relationship between personality dimensions and CQ, using the Big Five personality model, which integrates extraversion, agreeableness, conscientiousness, emotional stability (versus neuroticism), and openness to experience (Goldberg 1993). They show that, for example, an account manager who is more open to experience absorbs signals from a foreign client earlier than less open-minded colleagues. Openness to experience has a positive impact on all the CQ dimensions (Ang et al. 2006), because as one of our informants explained, "If you are open, you extend the horizons of your subordinates." Ang et al. (2006) also propose that conscientiousness relates more to metacognitive CQ, whereas emotional stability correlates negatively with behavioral CQ. For example, an expatriate who admitted, "I have a kind of an impatient character," wanted to get things done, which pushed him to take initiatives, even in the unfamiliar environment. Extraversion influences both motivational and behavioral CQ dimensions positively; for an expatriate in a foreign country, out of necessity, "You tend to be a much more outgoing person." In terms of agreeableness, a manager who can claim "I [am] much more flexible than most Dutch in what I find acceptable" likely has greater CQ.

However, personality is a relatively stable personal factor (Caligiuri 2006), such that it is difficult to change or develop. Thus it mostly benefits GTM in the recruitment and selection or hiring stages. Selecting a candidate with a promising personality and then developing more dynamic CQ features likely increases organizational efficiency in preparing new talent to work in international environments. Accordingly, one of our expatriates explained that his company selects "global managers who want to learn ... not power hungry people," which means the new hires "bring some good things from [their] own background and you combine that with some of the great things that you get from here." This example of GTM, combining background characteristics with new skills and knowledge, spans the tasks of selection, development, and retention but focuses on personality factors, especially in the selection phase.

4.3 Language Ability

Language and culture are closely interrelated; language even has been equated with culture. As Ting-Toomey (2010) points out, a true understanding of a culture demands fluency in its language. Thus foreign language skills offer an important predictor of communication effectiveness (Caligiuri et al. 2009), not just as a means of communication but also because "an individual's ability and willingness to communicate through linguistic boundaries is related to his or her foreign-language proficiency" (Peltokorpi 2010: 177). Western visitors to Asian cultures who have not learned the local language often find themselves misreading the force and volume of speech patterns: Japanese and Korean employees talk to each other loudly and powerfully, but it does not necessarily imply conflict. The highest echelon of management in Japanese companies often speaks in very low tones, which Western visitors might mistake for reticence or fear. An ability to master even some rudiments of another language instead can help reduce feelings of confusion and ambiguity. For example, "we think we speak English reasonably good [sic] and we do, but for us, Asians and whoever, English is a 'communication vehicle.' It is not your language, but it is an instrument to communicate with each other.... But even [though] we all speak English, we all speak a different language."

4.4 Training

Training and development of cultural competencies is a central priority in global leadership programs (Stroh and Caligiuri 1998), though the types of training vary as much as their implications, such that factual knowledge transfer related to appropriate modes of greeting in certain countries might contribute to higher behavioral CQ, and studying cross-cultural models to compare cultures might enhance cognitive CQ. Role playing and cross-cultural simulation games likely help people reflect on their cultural assumptions, to develop metacognitive CQ. More background knowledge about cultural artifacts may enhance the level of motivational

CQ. Training that focuses on skills and knowledge related to CQ can be part of development programs for both trainees and management in GTM settings.

5   Linking CQ to Performance

Intermediate variables can help explain how CQ leads to preferred outcomes, such as effective communication across borders and leadership. In this chapter, we focus on two such variables: learning and uncertainty. First, when developing their understanding of other cultures, talent proceeds through a learning curve that defines the outcomes. Second, working in a global anxiety environment creates high levels of anxiety and uncertainty that can interfere with the talent's concentration and hinder performance.

5.1   Learning

Learning produces new knowledge, new skills, and, ultimately, new mindsets and behaviors related to unfamiliar global environments. In relation to cultural sensitivity in business settings, Shapiro et al. (2008) suggest a four-phase learning process, in which people start as romantic sojourners, then become foreign workers and then skilled workers, before finally reaching a partner level. Romantic sojourners participate in business activities but are not aware of how others interpret their activities; their lack of experience forces them to rely heavily on their home culture to give meaning to certain events. Foreign workers develop a more realistic understanding of the local culture, mainly through observation. As they become more active participants in the local culture, they become skilled workers, who enjoy a deeper understanding of and more intensive relationships with representatives of the local culture. Finally, partners, with their high level of cultural sensitivity, can distinguish subcultures within the local culture and their related behavioral patterns. Bhawuk et al. (2008) similarly describe a model of cross-cultural competence development (Howell 1982), in which people move from unconscious incompetence to conscious incompetence to conscious competence and finally to unconscious competence.

Another relevant model comes from Kolb's (1984) proposed learning cycle, which consists of concrete experience, critical reflection, abstract conceptualization, and active experimentation. When people experience an unfamiliar, unexpected behavior, they suffer a disconfirmed expectation, which represents a concrete experience. From this experience, two reactions may emerge: Ignore the unexpected behavior, out of an inability to position the experience, or initiate a learning process through reflection and start to conceptualize abstract theories, which support active experimentation with the new behavior. The critical space is the point at which the decision to learn (or not) gets made.

We can also relate CQ to single, double, and triple loop learning (Argyris and Schön 1978). In single loop learning, the mind collects information, compares it against its operating norms or baseline culture, and decides on an action if they conflict. Thus, when confronted with an unfamiliar culture, a person's response follows a single loop that likely leads to disconfirmed expectations and cognitive dissonance. To avoid such dissonance, the person might attempt to adapt the cultural baseline, which constitutes double loop learning. Thus for example, "working abroad means you improve as a person, development takes place; you are out of your comfort zone," or "I re-invented myself over the last two years … now I have much more respect, I have a much more positive view on the world, less controlling." Such learning allows talent to enhance their CQ, as exemplified by two quotes: "People do not tell you when you are wrong" and "I learned more about people's behavior and my own behavior." Such double loop learning is a more intensive process than single loop learning, which demands more energy from the learner. Finally, triple loop learning implies that two people cannot determine whose cultural baseline to prioritize and instead establish a third new cultural baseline, comprised of mutually created operating norms adopted from both existing cultural baselines.

5.2 Anxiety

Exposure to unknown cultures creates some degree of ambiguity, because through this exposure, the global talent experiences different responses to his or her own actions than they would spark in domestic settings. Gudykunst and Nishida (2001) describe ambiguity in terms of *uncertainty*, which results from a lack of appropriate information to predict the near future, and *anxiety*, or feelings that encompass this uncertainty. Another common term to describe ambiguity is stress, though CQ can reduce stress levels. As Kim (2001: 227) acknowledges, "life in an unfamiliar milieu entails some of the most stressful experiences we may ever face." To deal with or avoid such stress, people often seek to identify its source and escape that source, which is not easy for global talent, who might be unaware of the exact source or unable to avoid it. Furthermore, if they find a means to escape, they miss any opportunity to learn from their exposure, such that "Each time we withdraw, we pass up new opportunities for new cultural learning and instead engage in fearful clinging to the past" (Kim 2001: 228). Learning takes time, and the learning process is different for each individual. Another, more effective response to stress is relaxation techniques, which increase people's ability to manage stress and stimulates self-reflection, leading to greater opportunities to engage in self-dialogue, self-learning, and self-integration. That is,

> Particularly in times of crisis, self-reflection helps us to understand how we are doing, how we are feeling, and in what direction we need to move. New perspectives arise, new feelings that awake us to new insights into ourselves and our milieu (Kim 2001: 229).

Through this process of individual development and growth, associated with entering willingly into unfamiliar, often frustrating situations, talent can reduce their anxiety and increase their cultural learning. If they regard such growth as a means for self-development, they should recognize that overcoming challenging moments helps them increase their tolerance for such unpleasant feelings. Cultural intelligence in general increases the tolerance level for stress related to unfamiliar cross-cultural situations, thereby reducing anxiety and indirectly improving performance.

6   CQ Outcomes

As we have suggested, CQ influences several pertinent outcomes, including cultural adjustment, leadership effectiveness, and negotiations, which in turn can encourage better financial performance, market growth, more intensive knowledge sharing, or other forms of organizational effectiveness. Lee and Sukoco (2010) cite an important positive effect of CQ on cultural adjustment and cultural effectiveness; other studies highlight positive relations of CQ with the use of cooperative negotiation (Imai and Gelfand 2010) and leadership effectiveness (Rockstuhl et al. 2011).

As an example, consider the CQ levels of different CEOs and their impacts on leadership effectiveness. Carlos Ghosn, a Brazilian–Lebanese–French CEO of the successful Renault-Nissan alliance, used his strong cross-cultural competencies to innovate a strategic partnership that could oversee both companies through a unique, cross-shareholding agreement. In contrast, Jürgen Schrempp, the architect of the failed Daimler-Chrysler merger, exhibited a distinct lack of cross-cultural competencies in offending the American engineers and salespersons working for the merged company, as well as the U.S. CEO. Thus after years losses, of both dollars and Euros, the merged firm split again. As these two examples reveal, CQ can have a clear positive influence on leadership performance, cross-cultural adjustment, and company performance. In a GTM context, CQ is essential for ensuring that talented people, recruited to work in global environments, possess enough relevant competencies to be effective.

7   Context

The final component of our proposed model is the environment in which CQ develops. Outside influences inevitably affect the development of CQ, as we learned when we showed a preliminary model, without the context, to our informants. One expert responded quickly, "my environment has influenced my forming what you would maybe call into a global manager.... I would probably never have been in this particular job or role, this kind of job really came in from my kind of close friends or circles." For this chapter, we consider a broad view of context, consisting of influences from society, economic developments, political shifts, sociocultural trends, technological changes, and demographic adjustments.

Figure 1 provides an overview of all these components: the four CQ elements; the antecedents of personality, international experience, and language ability; learning and anxiety as intermediate variables; the firm-related outcomes; and the

Table 1 Global talent management challenges, strategies, and opportunities

GTM challenges	Strategies to overcome challenges	Opportunities for GTM
1 Lack of cultural competences among managers with global responsibility	Training and learning in the form of cultural role playing and international developmental assignments should be part of career management	Achieving competitive advantages through highly cross-cultural competent staff. Better understanding across cultures
2 Developing cultural intelligence among employees in a global firm	Human resources should distinguish between dynamic and stable capabilities, then make hiring decisions on the basis of stable characteristics, such as personality. Development then can focus on dynamic capabilities, such as CQ	Appropriate combinations of selection and development mechanisms to attract employees with the potential to develop further cross-cultural competencies later, when needed
3 Effectively including home country, host country, and third country nationals in the GTM process	International human resource management must be truly global in scale, equally present in developing and developed countries	Greatly reduced expatriate costs; more diverse groups of country representatives
4 Reducing anxiety and creating a learning culture in a global firm	Line managers and human resources should collaborate to develop a corporate culture that creates feelings of safety and trust (low anxiety), encouraging talent to leave their comfort zones and develop learning	Develop a corporate strategy that reconciles cross-cultural differences, leading to creative solutions in product and process development
5 Developing a corporate culture of inclusion	The top management teams of MNEs should consist of culturally diverse corporate board members and highlight inclusion and diversity in their corporate vision and mission statements	Further develop diversity policies to include age, gender, disability, and ethnic diversity goals, with the aim of increasing knowledge sharing and creativity

overall context. With this integrative framework of cultural intelligence dimensions, antecedents, intermediates, outcomes, and context, we offer organizations and managers in charge of GTM a template for how to develop their global talent to attain optimal outcomes.

Table 1 provides an overview of the challenges, strategies, and opportunities with regard to GTM from a Cross-Cultural Competence perspective.

References

Ang, S., van Dyne, L., & Koh, C. (2006). Personality correlates of the four-factor model of cultural intelligence. *Group and Organization Management, 31*(1), 100–123.

Ang, S., Van Dyne, L., Koh, C., Ng, K. Y., Templer, K. J., Tay, C., et al. (2007). Cultural intelligence: Its measurement and effects on cultural judgment and decision making, cultural adaptation and task performance. *Management and Organization Review, 3*(3), 335–371.

Argyris, C., & Schön, D. (1978). *Organizational learning*. Reading, MA: Addison-Wesley.

Beechler, S., & Woodward, I. C. (2009). The global "war for talent". *Journal of International Management, 15*, 273–285.

Bhawuk, D. P. S., Sakuda, K. H., & Munusamy, V. P. (2008). Intercultural competence development and triple-loop cultural learning: Toward a theory of intercultural sensitivity. In S. Ang & L. Van Dyne (Eds.), *Handbook of cultural intelligence: Theory, measurement, and applications*. Armonk, NY: M.E. Sharpe.

Bücker, J., & Poutsma, E. (2010). Global management competencies: A theoretical foundation. *Journal of Managerial Psychology, 25*(8), 829–844.

Caligiuri, P. (2006). Developing global leaders. *Human Resource Management Review, 16*, 219–228.

Caligiuri, P., & Tarique, I. (2009). Predicting effectiveness in global leadership activities. *Journal of World Business, 44*, 336–346.

Caligiuri, P., Tarique, I., & Jacobs, R. (2009). Selection for international assignments. *Human Resource Management Review, 19*, 251–262.

Collings, D. G., Scullion, H., & Morley, M. J. (2007). Changing patterns of global staffing in the multinational enterprise: Challenges to the conventional expatriate assignment and emerging alternatives. *Journal of World Business, 42*, 198–213.

Crowne, K. A. (2008). What leads to cultural intelligence? *Business Horizons, 15*(5), 391–399.

Earley, P. C. (2002). Redefining interactions across cultures and organizations: Moving forward with cultural intelligence. *Research in Organizational Behavior, 24*, 271–299.

Earley, P. C., & Ang, S. (2003). *Cultural intelligence: Individual interactions across cultures*. Palo Alto, CA: Stanford Press University.

Goldberg, L. R. (1993). The structure of phenotypic personality traits. *American Psychologist, 48*(1), 26–34.

Goleman, D. (1995). *Emotional intelligence*. New York: Bantam Books.

Gudykunst, W. B., & Nishida, T. (2001). Anxiety, uncertainty, and perceived effectiveness of communication across relationships and cultures. *International Journal of Intercultural Relations, 25*(1), 55–71.

Hewitt Associates. (2008). *Reveal local responses to the global downturn*. http://www.hewittassociates.com

Hofstede, G. (2001). *Culture's consequences, comparing values, behaviors, institutions, and organizations across nations*. Thousand Oaks, CA: Sage.

Howell, W. S. (1982). *The empathic communicator*. Prospect Heights, IL: Waveland Press.

Imai, L., & Gelfand, M. J. (2010). The cultural intelligent negotiator: The impact of cultural intelligence (CQ) on negotiation sequences and outcomes. *Organizational Behavior and Human Decision Processes, 112*, 83–98.

Kim, Y. Y. (2001). *Becoming intercultural: An integrative theory of communication and cross-cultural adaptation*. Thousand Oaks, CA: Sage.

Knight, G. A., & Cavusgil, S. T. (2004). Innovation, organizational capabilities, and the born-global firm. *Journal of International Business Studies, 35*(2), 124–141.

Kolb, D. A. (1984). *Experiential learning: Experience as the source of learning and development*. Englewood Cliffs, NJ: Prentice-Hall.

Lee, L.-Y., & Sukoco, B. M. (2010). The effect of cultural intelligence on expatriate performance: The moderating effects of international experience. *The International Journal of Human Resource Management, 21*(7), 963–981.

Mayer, J. D., Salovey, P., & Caruso, D. R. (2000). Models of emotional intelligence. In R. J. Sternberg (Ed.), *Handbook of intelligence*. Cambridge: Cambridge University Press.

Peltokorpi, V. (2010). Intercultural communication in foreign subsidiaries: The influence of expatriates' language and cultural competencies. *Scandinavian Journal of Management, 26*, 176–188.

Rockstuhl, T., Seiler, S., Ang, S., Van Dyne, L., & Annen, A. (2011). Beyond general intelligence (IQ) and emotional intelligence (EQ): The role of cultural intelligence (CQ) on cross-border leadership effectiveness in a globalized world. *Journal of Social Issues, 67*(4), 825–840.

Schuler, R. S., Jackson, S. E., & Tarique, I. (2011). Framework for global talent management: HR actions for dealing with global talent challenges. In H. Scullion & D. Collings (Eds.), *Global talent management*. New York: Routledge.

Shapiro, J. M., Ozanne, J. L., & Saatcioglu, B. (2008). An interpretive examination of the development of cultural sensitivity in international business. *Journal of International Business Studies, 39*(1), 71–87.

Sparrow, P., Scullion, H., & Farndale, E. (2011). Global talent management: New roles for the corporate HR function. In H. Scullion & D. G. Collings (Eds.), *Global talent management*. New York: Routledge.

Stroh, M. K., & Caligiuri, P. M. (1998). Increasing global competitiveness through effective people management. *Journal of World Business, 33*(1), 1–16.

Tarique, I., & Schuler, R. S. (2010). Global talent management: Literature review, integrative framework, and suggestions for further research. *Journal of World Business, 45*(2), 122–133.

Thomas, D. C. (2006). Domain and development of cultural intelligence: The importance of mindfulness. *Group and Organization Management, 31*, 78–99.

Ting-Toomey, S. (2010). Applying dimensional values in understanding intercultural communication. *Communication Monographs, 77*(2), 169–180.

Trompenaars, F., & Hampden-Turner, C. (1998). *Riding the waves of culture: Understanding cultural diversity in global business*. New York: McGraw Hill.

Inpatriation as a Key Component of Global Talent Management

Jean-Luc Cerdin and Kushal Sharma

Two very important activities in Global Talent Management (GTM) are (a) to identify and attract individuals interested in international work (Tarique and Schuler 2010); and (b) to motivate and retain individuals with international executive talent (Harvey et al. 2001). However, multinational companies (MNCs) are plagued by the weaknesses of their talent management systems to supply them with international management talent. Such talent shortages constrain MNCs from implementing their global strategies (Farndale et al. 2010) since they are unable to utilize the strengths of talented managers with appropriate international experience in the global business environment (Collings et al. 2007). Yet different MNCs utilize a variety of strategies in the management of their global talent (Baruch and Altman 2002).

One such strategy is juxtaposing expatriates with headquarter-trained inpatriates. Inpatriation is the practice of developing host country or third country managers via a transfer to the corporate headquarters (Harvey et al. 2000). For MNCs, this approach presents an ideal opportunity to manage their global talent effectively. For individuals, inpatriation to the company headquarters presents not only the opportunity of learning new skills but also the prospect of building networks. Although we realize that such an arrangement does not completely solve all GTM problems of MNCs, we believe that it serves to address a large chunk of the problem.

Although scholars have argued that inpatriates act as knowledge-transferors and boundary-spanners to facilitate exchanges between different units of MNCs (Reiche 2011); and bring diversity to bolster MNCs' globalization efforts by being a part of multicultural management teams (Harvey et al. 2011), research in this field is still in its infancy. It is not clear what kind of advantages can be derived from inpatriation. Research on international mobility does not explicitly establish a

J.-L. Cerdin (✉) • K. Sharma
Management Department, ESSEC Business School, Avenue Bernard Hirsch – B.P. 105, 95021 Cergy-Cergy-Pontoise Cedex, France
e-mail: cerdin@essec.fr; kushal.sharma@essec.fr

A. Al Ariss (ed.), *Global Talent Management*, Management for Professionals,
DOI 10.1007/978-3-319-05125-3_6, © Springer International Publishing Switzerland 2014

clear link between expatriation and talent management (Cerdin and Brewster 2014) and even less between inpatriation and GTM. Scholars have not examined the role of inpatriates in the broader context of GTM of MNCs (Reiche 2011). In this chapter, we discuss (a) to what extent inpatriation contributes to the development of a talent pool and (b) what unique advantages it provides as compared to other forms of staffing.

The theoretical framework of our study is built upon the length of the 'intelligent career approach' (Arthur et al. 1995; Parker et al. 2009)—in the context of the boundaryless career (DeFillippi and Arthur 1994). Intelligent career approach takes into account three types of knowledge: (1) knowing-why: referring to values and interests of inpatriates, (2) knowing-whom: referring to networking, particularly in the inpatriation country, and (3) knowing-how: referring to the skills and competencies inpatriates are expected to develop during their inpatriation. Boundaryless career approach puts employees learning at its crux. We present case study research approach in one MNC headquartered in France to explore various aspects of inpatriation. Through our case study, we explore the extent to which inpatriation can contribute to MNCs' efforts of managing talents globally. We also examine how effectively individuals utilize inpatriation opportunity for building their networks.

Our study allows us to gain insights into the mindsets of inpatriates from diverse backgrounds and geographic locations. Such insights are essential because an important factor that hinders GTM success is the ethnocentric Western understanding of subsidiaries. Through this study of inpatriates from different cultures, we identify the roots of the challenges related to inpatriation. From our analysis we have a clearer understanding of the global challenges that MNCs face while managing inpatriates. Since our study positions the inpatriate at the center of the phenomenon, we extend knowledge about how inpatriates—the recipients of MNCs' GTM practices—perceive their employers' efforts to integrate them into the organization's broader talent pool. By studying the practices of a real MNC, we also uncover issues that inpatriates consider to be of practical importance during their assignments.

Some researchers suggest that inpatriates might feel overwhelmed in the new setting of the company headquarter due to lack of familiarity with the setting; and lack of credibility and trust from headquarter members (e.g., Harvey et al. 2011; Reiche 2011). We propose some strategies to overcome such challenges. We also discuss current as well as future opportunities while managing inpatriates in the global context of multinationals.

The chapter is structured as follows to address our main research question: how does inpatriation contribute to global talent management? First, we define what we mean by GTM. We then discuss how expatriates have always been at the center of MNCs' GTM activities and why this practice needs revision in the face of new GTM challenges. We outline the advantages that inpatriates offer to MNCs and propose that inpatriation can be an alternative source of staffing for meeting MNCs' GTM requirements. We then present the case study of a French MNC and discuss our findings. Finally, we forward some recommendations regarding how organizations can manage inpatriates most effectively in the present situation as well as in the future. We are confident that our recommendations will be useful to practitioners and researchers alike.

1 Types of International Mobility and Global Talent Management

This section defines what GTM is and shows all the mechanisms involved therein (including various forms of international mobility). It points out that inpatriation can be an essential component of GTM along other types of international mobility.

Broadly defined, GTM comprises of organizational efforts for attracting, selecting, developing and retaining talented employees on a global scale (Scullion et al. 2010). The need for a global focus stems from the fact that competition between employers for attracting superior talent has become more generic and thus the scope has widened from country level to regional and global levels (Farndale et al. 2010). An established assumption in management literature is that proper exploitation of talent spread across subsidiaries contributes towards an MNC's competitive advantage (Mellahi and Collings 2010). Organizations increasingly perceive the need to find and retain talented individuals who can act as boundary spanners in order to exchange knowledge as well as ensure uniformity in application of policies and practices across geographically disperse subsidiaries. Usually, MNCs regard GTM as a critical formal development program intended for grooming their high-potential employees who are expected to occupy important strategic positions in the future (McDonnell et al. 2010). Cerdin and Brewster (2014) define GTM as a focused effort for the development of employees. They identify two approaches: one that focuses on a few selected individuals and the other that is broader in scope, including all employees. High-potentials development, the first of these two approaches, is a combination of two related approaches to talent management—a segmentation approach focused on the development of employees with high potential, and a strategic approach focused on expatriation management. Global-careers development, the second approach, is accessible to all employees and integrates international work experiences as progressive steps in the course of individuals' overall careers.

For several reasons such as trust, greater control and standardization across units, expatriation is the traditionally chosen option for managing talents globally. Expatriation can involve several types of employees such as parent country nationals (PCNs)—employees who are nationals of the country where the headquarters is located, or third country nationals (TCNs)—employees who are nationals of a third country (not nationals of either the host country where the subsidiary is located or of the parent country where the headquarter is located). For training, development, and building networks of their employees, MNCs can invite host country nationals (HCNs)—employees who are nationals of the country where the subsidiary is located—to the headquarters, thus making them inpatriates or can transfer them to another subsidiary, making them TCNs from the perspective of the subsidiary they are sent to. However, these are not the only options for GTM. In addition to assigned expatriates, organizations can also recruit self-initiated expatriates (SIEs)—those who are not sent by any organization but have chosen to relocate themselves of their own will—within their GTM approach (see Andresen et al. 2012; Vaiman and Haslberger 2013). Additionally, migrants—particularly skilled ones—(e.g. Al Ariss and Crowley-Henry 2013; Al Ariss et al. 2013; Cerdin et al. 2014; Zikic et al. 2010) as well as short-terms assignees and flexpatriates (e.g. Collings et al. 2007; Mayerhofer et al. 2004) can also contribute to GTM.

However, as our case study presented below illustrates, inpatriation is an excellent albeit underexplored alternative available to organizations in their GTM efforts. While each of the above mentioned type of employees has the potential to contribute towards GTM efforts of an organization, there are problems associated with each type. The chief ones appear to be lack of control in the case of HCNs (Harvey et al. 2011), lack of local acceptance as well as understanding of the host environment in case of TCNs, and the lack of training regarding corporate culture in case of SIEs. Hence, MNCs are at an advantage in utilizing inpatriates as they do not experience loss of control when they make use of this type of employees. It is because inpatriates have social capital as well as political understanding of how business is conducted at the company headquarters (Harvey et al. 2011).

Since multinationals operate in culturally diverse environments, it is likely that an organization's priorities differ across national boundaries. Indeed, GTM practices seek to be in alignment with global strategic priorities as well as accommodate for differences across national contexts (Scullion et al. 2010). Some also argue that an MNC might appoint citizens of the country where its subsidiary is located into its top management team regardless of such employees' competence so that it can overcome hostilities associated with foreignness and gain increased local acceptance (see Mellahi and Collings 2010). From an institutional perspective, MNCs would not be able to access resources vital to their survival without such legitimacy (Mellahi and Collings 2010). Hence, proper management of local employees of a subsidiary is an important aspect of an MNC's GTM efforts. This is even more important in light of the fact that traditional in-house training approaches such as management training programs are unable to deliver sufficient supply of managerial talent (Farndale et al. 2010) to accommodate increasing global demand for talent. In the next section, we highlight the shortcomings associated with expatriation and focus explicitly on the benefits that inpatriation provides as a flexible alternative to expatriation.

2 How Does Inpatriation Contribute to GTM?

Owing to the relatively novel approach of this staffing alternative, MNCs do not have adequate systems in place to tap into this potential source of talent. Additionally, inpatriation efficacy depends largely on the objectives pursued by MNCs through inpatriation. We suspect that not all inpatriation assignments are developmental in nature and thus inpatriation may not always be a part of GTM. In this chapter, we explore whether MNCs intend all inpatriation assignments to be a component of their GTM plans.

Traditionally, expatriates have been at the forefront of MNCs' GTM plans, largely by virtue of being closer to and thus being more visible to corporate decision makers as compared to subsidiary talents (Mellahi and Collings 2010). Unfortunately, the failure rate of expatriates is high (Brookfield Global Relocation Trends 2012), resulting in increased costs of managing talent. Given the costs involved, MNCs attempt to estimate such costs with measures such as expatriate return on investment (ROI), even though this is not easy to gauge (McNulty et al. 2009). Some authors such as Welch et al. (2009) argue that for both the individual and the organization, intellectual capital with its three components—human capital, structural capital and social capital—better captures the true worth of expatriation than ROI. Irrespective of how the cost is measured, the important fact to note is that expatriation is a costly endeavor for an organization.

Additionally, a setback for MNCs in their GTM efforts is the increasing unwillingness of expatriates to accept foreign assignments (e.g. Baruch and Altman 2002). Expatriates often feel that engaging in expatriation undermines their future career prospects. For example, French expatriates perceive international assignments as risky because they consider that being away from the headquarter results in disadvantages in terms of information and networking (Stahl and Cerdin 2004). Given the severity of problems, MNCs would benefit immensely if the problems associated with expatritaes can be resolved.

Inpatriation is a flexible alternative to expatriation. It helps MNCs to solve their global staffing problems by inpatriating Host Country Nationals and Third Country Nationals into corporate headquarters (Farndale et al. 2010). Inpatriation also contributes towards retaining and improving the morale of subsidiary talents. According to Mellahi and Collings (2010: 147), subsidiary talents feel marginalized because they have limited access to "the circle of power" at the corporate headquarter and thus are deprived of the direct knowledge of activities at the center. Given an opportunity to engage in assignments at the MNC headquarter, they feel motivated and are encouraged to stay (Mellahi and Collings 2010). In his study, Reiche (2011) found that MNCs encouraged inpatriation so that subsidiary talents can build relationships with headquarter staff; learn the corporate culture; improve communication and exchange between the subsidiary and the headquarter; gain technical training; and acquire and transfer market-related as well as technical knowledge. Such exchange can facilitate change, strategic integration, and learning across the organization (Harvey et al. 2011). Due to such benefits, inpatriation can contribute towards the GTM efforts of MNCs.

MNCs seek to develop the competencies of their inpatriates during the assignment so that upon return to their subsidiary, inpatriates can work with increased competence and efficiency. There is also an expectation that learning firm-specific knowledge impacts retention of inpatriates (Reiche et al. 2011). For this, MNCs need to ensure that inpatriates successfully complete their assignments at the company headquarter. Although inpatriation assignments might be different depending upon the objectives (set by the MNC and inpatriates) and might thus necessiate the use of various measures, a generic measure appears to be 'development success' as proposed by Cerdin and Le Pargneux (2009). Individual international assignment success can be effectively captured by the two components of development success—'knowledge, skills, and abilities (KSA) acquisition'; and 'network and relationship building'. Development success ultimately contributes to organizational success in two ways: first, inpatriates transfer their expertise locally upon their return; second, subsidiaries can benefit from the networks of inpatriates who serve as boundary-spanners to create connections between individuals working at previously unconnected units of the MNC (Reiche 2011). Through their boundary-spanning role, inpatriates not only convey corporate goals to the subsidiaries but also provide insider information to the headquarters regarding the subsidiary context as well as expectations of subsidiary staff (Reiche 2011).

In the following section we present our case study that examines the extent to which inpatriation contributes to GTM in the context of an MNC.

3   Case Study

Our case study focuses on Latotte Inc. ('Latotte Inc' is a fictional name used for concealing the company's identity and protecting its privacy), an MNC with headquarters in France. In 2013, the MNC had several hundred inpatriates in France, which made it an interesting case to study. Inpatriation is a requirement of GTM for Latotte Inc. This MNC adopts a 'local content' approach for its business abroad, which regroups all the activities that promote the host country industrial network and improve the competencies of its inhabitants. This translates into HRM with a focus on the recruitment and development of local talent. From the organization's point of view, inpatriation is an important step in developing these local talents.

Latotte Inc considers inpatriates as strategic ressources because they return to their subsidiary aware of the strategic issues of the company. During their inpatriation, inpatriates are expected to have developed an international vision of the company and a network that enables them to turn to the headquarters when needed. This case study focuses on a unique MNC and adopts a double source of informants—HR professionals in charge of inpatriate management, and the inpatriates themselves—to have a deep understanding of inpatriate management (Yin 2009).

Our sample consists of 15 HR professionals and 17 inpatriates. Within the HR professional sample population, 3 are aged 35–40, 9 are 41–45, 2 are 46–50 and the remaining person is above 50. There are 10 men and 5 women. Most of them are French. Within the inpatriate sample population, 6 are aged 35–40, 5 are 41–45, another 5 are 46–50 and the remaining person is above 50. There are 15 men and 2 women. Table 1 describes the inpatriate sample in terms of gender, age, nationality, organizational tenure and inpatriation length. We interviewed HR professionals for 90 min on average, while inpatriate interviews lasted 60 min on average.

Table 1 Description of the inpatriates sample

Inpatriates	Gender	Age range	Nationality	Organizational tenure (years)	Inpatriation length (years)
No. 1	Male	35–40	Nigerian	3	3
No. 2	Male	41–45	Indonesian	18	3
No. 3	Male	46–50	Italian	9	3
No. 4	Male	46–50	Ethiopian	29	3
No. 5	Female	35–40	Syrian	5	4
No. 6	Male	50+	Belgium	32	5.5
No. 7	Male	46–50	Argentinian	5	3.5
No. 8	Male	41–45	Nigerian	15	2.8
No. 9	Male	35–40	Russian	8	6
No. 10	Male	41–45	Burkinabé	19	2
No. 11	Male	46–50	Nigerian	23	4
No. 12	Male	41–45	Indonesian	22	5
No. 13	Female	41–45	Senegalese	11	.5
No. 14	Male	46–50	Burkinabé	26	2
No. 15	Male	35–40	Nigerian	7	1
No. 16	Male	35–40	Syrian	5	1.5
No. 17	Male	35–40	Nigerian	6	2.5

For the overwhelming majority (15 out of 17 inpatriates), inpatriation was undertaken at the initiative of the organization. Amongst inpatriates who initiated their mobility themselves, reasons vary. One of the reasons is career development, as one Senegalese inpatriate states:

I asked to come to France in order to improve my technical expertise, further complete my training, gain more experience and a global vision.

Some employees self-initiated inpatriation for personal reasons such as those brought up by one Argentinian inpatriate, who says:

In order to follow my wife who was transferred to France by another firm, I asked to be able to go with her.

As for the inpatriates who do not themselves initiate their inpatriation, we identified various motivations which led them to accept this mobility. It can be the anticipation of a career promotion, as is the case of this engineer:

I am used to being assigned to projects and I've been asked to come to France in order to gain a wider view, to broaden my spectrum.

It can also be the result of wanting to respond to a subsidiary's needs, as a Syrian inpatriate explained:

I was sent to headquarters as part of a strategy to respond to the subsidiary's goals, which has chosen young high level employees and sent them to be trained in the headquarters so that they will grow accustomed to the way things are done, the processes, the decision-making mecahnism, and later return.

When professionals or inpatriates return from international mobility, they commonly sense that the objectives of their skill acquisition have not been made clear to them prior to their departure, as this HR executive noted:

The objectives of the mobility are not stated clearly, but rather subtly.

According to HR professionals at Latotte Inc, inpatriation and expatriation have identical objectives. The head of the HR department at one of the company divisions stated:

Inpatriation and expatriation aim at the same objectives, inpatriation for local employees while expatriation is particularly for French employees.

A Regional HR Director pointed out that there are benefits to be had from inpatriation for the whole corporation as well as for the employee:

It is highly recommended, because it is a moment of reckoning. It improves your knowledge of the profession; it brings out your adaptive capacity and allows you to acquire legitimacy. It is a change of trajectory which allows you to encounter many different situations. As an inpatriate, you gain expertise, as you will see things through the prism of headquarters instead of your own cultural prism. You will share the norms and the risks, because you will understand the corporation's politics and know its codes, and you will be able to have recourse to its expertise after the inpatriation. A better internationalization provides better international managers with a corporate culture, who can execute their roles in their local subsidiaries. It gives a good image to the corporation in the subsidiaries. The inpatriate will also not hesitate to open up to others. The inpatriation favors fidelity and loyalty.

The head of the International Human Resource Management Department indicated that alternatives to inpatriation may be adopted for family or tax reasons:

In general, we can use short-term assignment instead of inpatriation if the employee's family has to stay in his or her home country, in particular for personal reasons. This concerns mainly the Dutch, Italians and Belgians.

HR professionals and inpatriates alike stressed that the objectives for skill acquisition during inpatriation are not clarified beforehand. A Career Manager from Latotte Inc. explained that:

The skills which are to be acquired should be formalized at the moment of departure. An individual skill profile should be established for the inpatriate as well as a training and action plan that he or she will follow.

Around a third of the inpatriates assume that one of the reasons for their inpatriation was technical skill development. Around two thirds believe that their inpatriation could be due to the need for networking. A very strong majority (15 inpatriates) believe that the chief reason is getting to know how headquarters works. If skill development as a result of inpatriation, besides technical skills, is not actually measured or monitored by Latotte Inc, inpatriates do express the feeling that this kind of assignment enables them to develop managerial competencies and to broaden their network. One of them explained:

Yes, I can develop my soft skills, and this even while trying to long distance manage my team which is on another continent. But I pass on my knowledge to young employees and I develop my network in my area of activity.

Moreover, they can develop their technical skills, as an Indonesian engineer pointed out:

I broaden my network and improve my technical skills, and I will use them because later on I will know whom to contact about any specific issue.

Another possible reason for accepting the inpatriation assignment is to better understand the headquarters' culture. A Belgian inpatriate stated:

I am learning the processes at headquarters and how to develop my relations with French administrations.

Inpatriates are not always clear about how the skills they gain will be useful for their next assignment, since they are not always aware what the assignment will be. However, a Nigerian inpatriate—who knew what his next job position would be—clarified:

I know what job I will have upon my return, so all the skills I am building now as well as my network will be used when I go back to the subsidiary.

Sometimes the inpatriate is not certain of being able to return to his home country and does not know what position he will be assigned to. This can create some confusion as to the skills which should be emphasized during the inpatriation, as this inpatriate explained:

It is hard to know what to work on, I don't know if I wil be going back to the subsidiary or if I will be sent to another country.

Sometimes, the inpatriate can be informed of the location of his next assignment, but not the nature of the work, which also creates uncertainty as to which skills he or she should develop, as this female inpatriate pointed out:

I know I will go back to the subsidiary, but I have no visibility as to my career, therefore I don't really know what kind of knowledge and/or network I should work on the most.

In extreme cases, upon return to the home subsidiary, the inpatriate may be assigned to a position that requires completely different skills than those he or she acquired during the inpatriation, as this engineer inpatriate recounted:

I was able to develop my technical skills and my network, but once I returned to the subsidiary, my position there did not allow me to apply the skills I learned, since now I am working in an entirely different area. In addition, I don't need to contact headquarters, since 100% of my current work is local.

Overall, when inpatriates manage to gain the skills required by the MNC, they bring up the difficulty of foreseeing what their next position will be after the inpatriation, which further complicates the capitalization of skills gained during their mobility.

Another difficulty that arises when inpatriates return to their subsidiaries is the evaluation of the skills they acquired at the HQ during inpatriation. Subsidiaries evaluate only technical competences that are easy to measure. They do not generally evaluate increased knowledge of corporate culture and social capital development.

For social capital development and skill acquisitions, it appears crucial that the inpatriate be successfully integrated in the headquarters. Yet, this process is not always a swift one, as this Nigerian engineer explained:

> Interactions with other colleagues are difficult, except those who've been expatriated, who have more open mindsets, they really help you, they can put themselves in your shoes because they have gone through the same thing.

An Indonesian inpatriate shared:

> It is hard to communicate, because you have to know all the codes. I was used to going straight for the goal, but here I have to learn the ways things are done at headquarters.

However, even if French culture can seem difficult in terms of integration, short-term assignments to France prior to inpatriation make the integration process easier, as this inpatriate from Burkina-Faso indicates:

> Thankfully, I had already been to France on short term assignments, since culturally, it's a bit difficult at the start. In Africa, when people have nothing more to do, they come and tell you and they ask you if you need help. You can speak to your colleagues in complete honesty. What is missing in France is human warmth!

According to the Director of the Leadership Development Program at Latotte Inc, of all the inpatriates in the organization,

- 90 % have been inpatriated for development objectives (without having been identified as High Potentials).
- 3 % of inpatriates are High Potentials, who are being tested by this assignment for advancing their positions in the subsidairies.
- 7 % are inpatriated because of their connections in the subsidiary to facilitate the development of good relations between the HQ and the subsidiary. We label this type of inpatriation "diplomatic inpatriation".

Inpatriate turnover is very high at Latotte Inc. The MNC estimates that nearly half of the inpatriates quit the organization after returning to their home country, mostly because of a lack of career advancement opportunities following inpatriation. As it is the subsidiary that decides in most cases who to send for inpatriation, the headquarter usually does not follow the progress of the inpatriate upon return to his or her home country. Since decisions are not centralized at the headquarters, there is a lack of real vision for managing talents.

In the case of Latotte Inc., inpatriation seems to fit more in the rationale of diversity than talent management. This MNC is a signatory of the UN Global Compact, and diversity is one of the requirements therein. Inpatriation enables the MNC to have a good score in this area and gain credibility for good corporate social responsibility. Therefore, while HR professionals proclaim that GTM rationale guides inpatriate management, in reality, GTM is not always the primary motivating force for inpatriation.

Discussion and Conclusion

This chapter contributes to the literature of both inpatriation and GTM by examining the extent to which they can be combined. Our case study shows that the career capital investment related to inpatriation does not include all the three ways of knowing based on the intelligent carreer approach, namely knowing why, how and whom (DeFillippi and Arthur 1994). Inpatriation essentially contributes to knowing how, with acquisitions of skills, and knowing whom with network and relationship building, which is in line with the objectives pursued though inpatriation (e.g. Reiche 2011). Knowing why, which reflects personal development, does not appear to be on the agenda.

Inpatriation is a key component of GTM, both in terms of high-potentials development and global-careers development (see Cerdin and Brewster 2014). Cerdin and Brewster (2014) propose that inpatriation and expatriation are two forms of international mobility that provide more learning than other forms of international mobility such as short-term assignment, international commuter assignment, and international teamwork. According to these authors, even though inpatriation and expatriation have a greater impact on careers than other international mobility forms, inpatriation seems to provide more career capital development.

This chapter also emphasized difficulties to be overcome so that inpatriation can reach its full potential in terms of talent management. As our case study shows, inpatriation did not always bring expected outcomes in terms of skills acquisitions and network and relationship building, in particular when GTM is not its primary driving force. Surprisingly, 'diplomatic inpatriation' could prevail over the objectives of inpatriation, particularly when diversity is the primary objective pursued through inpatriation. Based on the findings of our case study, we propose that contrary to the suggestions of management scholars (see Cerdin and Brewster 2014; Reiche 2011) and organizations, development objectives might not be the only objectives associated to inpatriation. Orgranizations might be pursuing hidden agendas through inpatriation.

Based on a case study, this chapter stressed how inpatriation can contribute to GTM and identified key issues related to inpatriation. This is a first attempt to link inpatriation with GTM with all the limitations related to this type of approach. Among these limitations are our focus on only one MNC and on the single context of France. However, this enabled us to do an indepth study of inpatriation that can be completed by future research. Such research can adopt a quantitative approach to examine inpatriation in multiple organizations on a bigger sample to capture on a broader scope to examine how inpatriation contributes to GTM. Table 2 summarizes key points of inpatriation as a mechanism of GTM that deserves further research.

Our findings lead to several practical implications. To derive the best benefits out of inpatriation, MNCs might need to centralize inpatriation management at

Table 2 Key points of inpatriation as a mechanism of global talent management

Five key points regarding Global Talent Management challenges	Key points regarding strategies to overcome these challenges	Key points regarding future opportunities in Global Talent Management
1 Development of high-potential inpatriates	Provide international experience to inpatriates in the headquarters Tailor assignments to develop their skills and network for their future positions	Repatriate headquarter-trained high-potentials for a couple of years in their subsidiary of origin before sending them abroad again on another assignment
2 Development of Global-careers inpatriates	Ensure that all inpatriates acquire skills/competencies and develop their network during their inpatriation	Repatriate these global-careers inpatriates in positions in which they can develop new skills as well as implement the skills they acquired during inpatriation
3 Creation of a context favorable to Global talent management at the headquarters (HQ)	Train employees at the HQ to facilitate the adjustment and performance of inpatriates	Global talent management needs employees aware of their cultural intelligence (CQ) level, Therefore, CQ should be assessed at the HQ, particularly on employees in contact with inpatriates
4 Collaboration between the subsidiaries and the HQ to manage inpatriates within a global talent management approach.	Involving the subsidiaries in the process but the HQs must lead and control the full process, in particular to monitor what occurs once the inpatriates come back to their original subsidiary	Create a global talent management mindset both at the HQ and in all the subsidiaries to ensure that inpatriates are managed as key resources to create positive results for both the subsidiary and the whole organization
5 Use of inpatriation in conjunction with other forms of international mobility	Depending upon the skills to be acquired and network and relationship to be built, it may be useful to supplement inpatriation with other types of international mobility	Using inpatriation as the main mechanism of global talent management to develop host country nationals but complete this scheme by other forms of international mobility to fully develop talented HCNs

their headquarters. Moreover, communication between the subsidiaries and the headquarters also appears to be of utmost importance. Inpatriation, when it is a full component of GTM, brings positive outcomes both for the inpatriate and for the organization.

To achieve positive inpatriate outcomes, organizations also need to create a context favorable to GTM at the headquarters. This will help to facilitate the adjustment of inpatriates. As a result, inpatriates will perform adequately during their internatioanl assignment to learn expected skills and build their network at the HQ. Assessing cultural intelligence (CQ) of HQ's employees would help them to be aware of their intercultural competences and better interact with the inpatriates. Too often intercultural training and assessment of intercultural skills is devoted to employees who are moving internationally without including in the process employees who are interacting with mobile employees without being mobile themselves.

At the organizational level, a GTM mindset appears to be a prerequisite to ensure that inpatriates are managed as talented individuals for the development of both the individuals and the organization. It means that even though the organization is not only pursuing GTM objectives through inpatriation, other objectives such as satisfying diversity criteria would appear as supplementary to GTM. The supplementary objectives would not replace GTM ones.

References

Al Ariss, A., & Crowley-Henry, M. (2013). Self-initiated expatriation and migration in the management literature: Present theorizations and future research directions. *Career Development International, 18*(1), 78–96.

Al Ariss, A., Vassilopoulou, J., Ozbilgin, M., & Game, A. (2013). Understanding career experiences of skilled minority ethnic workers in France and Germany. *The International Journal of Human Resource Management, 24*(6), 1236–1256.

Andresen, M., Al Ariss, A., & Walther, M. (Eds.). (2012). *Self-initiated expatriation: Individual, organizational, and national perspectives.* New York: Routledge.

Arthur, M. B., Claman, P. H., & DeFillippi, R. J. (1995). Intelligent enterprise, intelligent careers. *Academy of Management Executive, 9*(4), 7–20.

Baruch, Y., & Altman, Y. (2002). Expatriation and repatriation in MNC: A taxonomy. *Human Resource Management, 41*(2), 239–259.

Brookfield Global Relocation Services. (2012). *Global relocation trends.* 2012 Survey Report, USA.

Cerdin, J.-L., Abdeljalil Diné, M., & Brewster, C. (2014). Qualified Immigrants' Success: Exploring the motivation to migrate and to integrate. *Journal of International Business Studies, 45*(2), 151–168.

Cerdin, J.-L., & Brewster, C. (2014). Talent Management and Expatriation: Bridging two streams of research and practice. *Journal of World Business, 49*(2), 245–252.

Cerdin, J.-L., & Le Pargneux, M. (2009). Career and international assignment fit: Toward an integrative model of success. *Human Resource Management, 48*(1), 5–25.

Collings, D. G., Scullion, H., & Morley, M. J. (2007). Changing patterns of global staffing in the multinational enterprise: Challenges to the conventional expatriate assignment and emerging alternatives. *Journal of World Business, 42*(2), 198–213.

DeFillippi, R., & Arthur, M. (1994). The boundaryless career: A competency-based perspective. *Journal of Organizational Behavior, 15*, 307–324.

Farndale, E., Scullion, H., & Sparrow, P. (2010). The role of the corporate HR function in global talent management. *Journal of World Business, 45*(2), 161–168.

Harvey, M., Ralston, D., & Napier, N. (2000). International relocation of inpatriate managers: Assessing and facilitating acceptance in the headquarters' organization. *International Journal of Intercultural Relations, 24*, 825–846.

Harvey, M., Reiche, B. S., & Moeller, M. (2011). Developing effective global relationships through staffing with inpatriate managers: The role of interpersonal trust. *Journal of International Management, 17*(2), 150–161.

Harvey, M., Speier, C., & Novecevic, M. (2001). A theory-based framework for strategic global human resource staffing policies and practices. *International Journal of Human Resource Management, 12*(6), 898–915.

Mayerhofer, H., Hartmann, L. C., Michelitsch-Riedl, G., & Kollinger, I. (2004). Flexpatriate assignments: A neglected issue in global staffing. *The International Journal of Human Resource Management, 15*(8), 1371–1389.

McDonnell, A., Lamare, R., Gunnigle, P., & Lavelle, J. (2010). Developing tomorrow's leaders—Evidence of global talent management in multinational enterprises. *Journal of World Business, 45*(2), 150–160.

McNulty, Y., De Cieri, H., & Hutchings, K. (2009). Do global firms measure expatriate return on investment? An empirical examination of measures, barriers and variables influencing global staffing practices. *The International Journal of Human Resource Management, 20*(6), 1309–1326.

Mellahi, K., & Collings, D. G. (2010). The barriers to effective global talent management: The example of corporate élites in MNEs. *Journal of World Business, 45*(2), 143–149.

Parker, P., Khapova, S., & Arthur, M. (2009). The intelligent career framework as a basis for interdisciplinary inquiry. *Journal of Vocational Behavior, 75*, 291–302.

Reiche, B. (2011). Knowledge transfer in multinationals: The role of inpatriates' boundary spanning. *Human Resource Management, 50*(3), 365–389.

Reiche, B. S., Kraimer, M. L., & Harzing, A. W. (2011). Why do international assignees stay? An organizational embeddedness perspective. *Journal of International Business Studies, 42*(4), 521–544.

Scullion, H., Collings, D. G., & Caligiuri, P. (2010). Global talent management. *Journal of World Business, 45*(2), 105–108.

Stahl, G. K., & Cerdin, J.-L. (2004). Global careers in French and German multinational corporations. *Journal of Management Development, 23*(9), 885–902.

Tarique, I., & Schuler, R. S. (2010). Global talent management: Literature review, integrative framework, and suggestions for further research. *Journal of World Business, 45*(2), 122–133.

Vaiman, V., & Haslberger, H. (Eds.). (2013). *Talent management of self-initiated expatriates.* London: Palgrave Macmillan.

Welch, D., Steen, A., & Tahvanainen, M. (2009). All pain, little gain? Reframing the value of international assignments. *The International Journal of Human Resource Management, 20*(6), 1327–1343.

Yin, R. K. (2009). *Case study research design and methods* (4th ed.). London: Sage Publications.

Zikic, J., Bonache, J., & Cerdin, J.-L. (2010). Crossing national boundaries: A typology of qualified immigrants' career orientations. *Journal of Organizational Behavior, 31*(5), 667–686.

The Global Talent Challenge of Self-initiated Expatriates

Jenny K. Rodriguez and Tracy Scurry

1 Introduction

In this chapter, we examine global talent management (GTM) in relation to self-initiated expatriates (SIEs). We position this chapter within discussions that call for a consideration of the wider contextual influences on the policies and practices of human resource management (HRM) in the global business environment (Budhwar and Sparrow 2002). The chapter has two aims: (1) to develop the discussion of 'Global Talent Management' (GTM) in relation to self-initiated expatriates (SIEs); and (2) to develop a multi-level perspective that adds a theoretical and practical contribution to the articulation of GTM for SIEs. We begin by discussing existing approaches and understandings of GTM and the challenges they pose in relation to the characteristics of SIEs. We then propose a multi-level perspective that would support the development of strategies for organisations to successfully manage the global talent of SIEs. Finally, we conclude by identifying opportunities, strategies and opportunities pertaining to the GTM of SIEs. This will help to develop further the research and practice agenda in this area.

2 Global Talent Management

Recent years have seen fundamental shifts in the nature and experience of global work and workers, leading to calls for a reconsideration of international resourcing in organisations (Schuler and Tarique 2012). In this context, there has been increased attention on the experiences of self-initiated expatriates: individuals who pursue employment opportunities away from their home country without the support of an employer (Richardson 2006). This group epitomises both the positive as well as the challenging aspects of work and employment in contemporary global

J.K. Rodriguez (✉) • T. Scurry
Newcastle University Business School, England, United Kingdom
e-mail: jenny.rodriguez@ncl.ac.uk; tracy.scurry@ncl.ac.uk

A. Al Ariss (ed.), *Global Talent Management*, Management for Professionals,
DOI 10.1007/978-3-319-05125-3_7, © Springer International Publishing Switzerland 2014

settings. On the one hand, SIEs are seen to possess the skills and competencies that allow them to navigate the complex circuits of globalisation—they are driven, motivated by new experiences and contexts, and have increased global capital as a result of their high mobility (Biemann and Andresen 2010; Scurry et al. 2013b). On the other hand, it is suggested that SIEs are transient with fragile commitment to organisations (Al Ariss et al. 2013).

Increasingly, discussions have focused on the efforts and actions of individuals, hinting that international mobility facilitates the pursuit of self-initiated global careers. However, there is scarcity of literature focusing on the challenges that these dynamics pose to organisations in relation to identifying, deploying and engaging this pool of global talent. This raises important questions about how organisations adapt their human resource management practices to navigate the changing nature of global labour markets. It also emphasises the need for further understanding of relational and contextual dimensions of international human resource management (IHRM) (Al Ariss and Crowley-Henry 2013; Doherty 2013).

With the emergence of the knowledge economy, the management of global talent has become a central feature of HRM (Scullion and Collings 2006). Tarique and Schuler (2010: 124) define global talent management (GTM) as "systematically utilising IHRM activities (complementary HRM policies and policies) to attract, develop, and retain individuals with high levels of human capital (e.g., competency, personality, motivation) consistent with the strategic directions of the multinational enterprise in a dynamic, highly competitive, and global environment". This definition aligns well with the idea of talent management as a three-dimensional function that includes activities and processes oriented to (a) systematically identify key posts which differentially contribute to the organisation's sustainable competitive advantage, (b) develop a talent pool of high potential and high performing individuals to fill them, and (c) develop a differentiated HR architecture to facilitate filling the posts with competent individuals and to ensure their continued commitment to the organisation (Collings and Mellahi 2009).

Overall, there seems to be a general agreement of the fundamental role of talent management in shaping differential features of competitive advantage in contemporary organisations. However, the way in which this is grounded in the practicalities of organisational decision making pertaining to IHRM functions, such as resourcing and retention, is problematic as groups other than company assigned expatriates represent increasingly significant proportions of global talent pools (Haslberger and Vaiman 2013). Furthermore, the ambiguity of cross-cultural skills, such as cultural intelligence, only adds to the complexity of understanding the key features of 'global talent'.

We therefore argue that understandings of GTM need to consider context, and the analysis of GTM needs to be related to the forces that shape employment regimes and HRM in different settings. This is of salient importance given the contradiction presented by globalisation, where on the one hand differences are said to bring complementarities and synergies but at the same time, there is a trend toward homogenisation and standardisation. Therefore, context will always play a part in the identification and value of GTM. In the interest of clearly framing the conceptual terms of this chapter, we refer to managing global talent of SIEs as the systematic use of human resource management activities and processes oriented to attract, manage and develop, and retain individuals with high levels of global capital (human, social and intellectual). In the next section we discuss the challenges of GTM in relation to SIEs.

3 Challenges of Global Talent Management of Self-initiated Expatriates

In addition to the failure to consider the relevance of context on GTM, current conceptions of GTM do not adequately acknowledge or explore the different groups of international workers within organisations—in particular SIEs. This is important for organisations to consider in their search for global talent, given the increasing numbers of individuals independently pursuing careers who represent a potentially rich source of global talent (Haslberger and Vaiman 2013). Furthermore, there is increasing acknowledgement of the potential for this group to contribute at both macro-country and meso-organisational levels and the subsequent need for countries and organisations to develop policies to attract, reward and retain SIEs in order to maximise their contributions (Doherty et al. 2013; Thorn and Inkson 2012).

We shall now go onto discuss how the characteristics of SIEs can result in barriers and challenges that may prevent the effective talent management of SIEs. These can be seen as operating in three interconnected levels: micro-individual, meso-organisational and macro-country.

3.1 Challenges at Micro-individual Level

At the micro-individual level the challenges for GTM mainly relate to the need to acknowledge the diversity of SIEs as a group, in terms of their backgrounds (e.g. nationality, culture) and experiences (e.g. education, work experiences). It is important that organisations seek to understand this diversity as it influences how individuals make sense of whom they are as SIEs and has the potential to influence individuals' relationships and performance in new organisational contexts (Dokko et al. 2009). This diversity present challenges for the GTM of SIEs as it is difficult for organisations to understand how to deploy and develop this group. We identify two main challenges; recognising the human capital of SIEs and understanding needs and expectations of SIEs. We shall now go on to discuss these challenges in more detail.

3.1.1 Recognition of SIEs' Human Capital

There is recognition that the transfer of human capital across borders is problematic (Scurry et al. 2013a) primarily because there is no one single standard way to assign value to human capital. Different settings will prioritise particular elements as a result of a combination of political economy and its impact on labour, work and employment, as well as value systems that shape life and work dynamics. As a result, issues such as the so-called 'brain waste' (Carr et al. 2005) that arises from the failure to recognise education, qualifications and experiences accumulated in different contexts or the potential underutilisation of talent through underemployment and deskilling (Lee 2005; Rodriguez and Mearns 2012), pose a number of challenges for GTM.

First, organisations could 'miss out' on talent if they do not develop a sophisticated understanding of different international qualifications and experience. Second, if individuals have knowledge, skills and abilities that they are unable to utilise, their potential contribution to the organisation is not being maximised. Third, individuals who are underemployed can experience high levels of frustration, display low levels of commitment and experience ill health (c.f. Scurry and Blenkinsopp 2011), all of which have a negative impact on performance.

3.1.2   Understanding Needs and Expectations of SIEs

Existing research suggests that SIEs are driven by a desire to 'be global' regardless of the organisational context. This suggests that SIEs are attracted to work in specific locations rather than specific organisations because their primary interest is in pursuing global experiences. This exacerbates assumptions of transiency and creates tensions underpinned by the idea that SIEs are "wanderers by nature" (Thorn and Inkson, 2012: 85). Given the centrality of personal motives to SIEs' decisions to pursue global work experiences (Doherty 2013) it is unsurprising that this transiency is perceived as a defining feature of this group. However, we must acknowledge the complex array of motivations that underpin SIEs' decision making, and question the notion of this group as perpetual international nomads.

Research continues to highlight that SIEs can remain in organisations for significant time periods (Tharenou and Caulfield 2010). Furthermore, temporariness is being questioned as researchers explore its link with migration (Al Ariss 2010). Therefore, organisations need to understand more comprehensively the motives of SIEs to pursue expatriation and how this relates to career preferences (Schein 1996). Carr et al. (2005) argues that organisations can seek to harness these preferences in order to develop attractive employment opportunities for SIEs; for example, global managers have shown to have a high preference for balancing career with lifestyle (Suutari and Taka 2004) so organisations could seek to develop policies and practices which facilitate work-life balance.

Needs and understanding are central to shaping the expectations that individuals have of their employment experiences. The psychological contract, which are the beliefs individuals have about a reciprocal relationship with organizations and involves both parties subscribing positively to the terms and conditions of the employment relationship and seeking to maintain it, is of fundamental importance in the case of SIEs, in particular due to the emotional and material sacrifices made by SIEs in order to pursue expatriation. Given the centrality of employee behaviour as a mediating variable in talent management systems (Collings and Mellahi 2009) it is important that organisations recognise that the expectations of this group may differ given their experiences of mobility and their motivations. We shall discuss this in more depth when we consider the meso-organisational level challenges.

3.2 Challenges at Meso-organisational Level

The main challenges at the meso-organisational level relate to how and whether SIEs are managed by organisations and the need to account for internal (e.g., management systems, policies and practices) and external elements (e.g., cultural and institutional contexts) that affect the organisation. We identify three main challenges arising at the meso-organisational level; understanding the nature of the employment relationship and the psychological contract, identifying and deploying knowledge and skills, capitalising on cross-cultural synergies. We will discuss this in detail in the following sections.

3.2.1 Understanding the Nature of the Employment Relationship and the Psychological Contract

The conception of SIEs as 'temporary' has potential negative consequences for the articulation and understanding of the employment relationship and the psychological contract. This because perceptions of temporariness reinforce the perception that this group has tenuous organisational commitment owing to the seemingly temporary nature, short-term orientation and potentially 'fragile' transactional psychological contracts traditionally associated with SIEs. This group is often considered individualistic, unpredictable and less committed than company-assigned expatriates (Mayrhofer et al. 2008) and as a consequence organisations still fail to strategically manage SIEs (Howe-Walsh and Schyns 2010). Ultimately, it is not clear whether organisations understand the implications of these features in relation to managing SIEs, identifying career development needs and providing support to increase their career capital (Rodriguez and Scurry 2013).

3.2.2 Identifying and Deploying Knowledge and Skills

Ability (knowledge and skills) is identified as a key element of any talent management system (Collings and Mellahi 2009). We have already discussed the potential for 'brain waste' and underutilisation as a consequence of failing to recognise or value education or experiences at the point of entry to an organisation. However, as Collings and Mellahi (2009) argue, successful talent management systems need to facilitate motive and opportunity for individuals to utilise the ability that they possess. This raises questions not only about the value and recognitions of knowledge and skills but also about the way in which organisations can practically identify and adequately deploy them. One of the main challenges organisations face at the local level is making sense of the variations in human capability (Tarique and Schuler 2010). In the context of global talent, the challenge is to reconcile a localised understanding of knowledge and skills with the global offering of SIEs by developing mechanisms to facilitate global skill transferability.

3.2.3   Capitalising on Cross-Cultural Synergies

The presence of SIEs in organisations poses challenges to manage diversity and facilitate work environments where cross-cultural differences, knowledge and expectations are valued and capitalised. This is not only about organisations articulating culturally responsive strategies, but it is also about acknowledging complex cross-cultural differences and backgrounds. For instance, SIEs might be third-country nationals who bring cultural knowledge and experience of more than one cultural context.

Central to the success of GTM is the development of mechanisms to create and nurture cultural synergies that capture the diverse information, experience, perspectives and cognitive styles brought by SIEs. Organisations might struggle with facilitating organisational learning that accounts for this diversity but this is a fundamental feature of a culturally diverse environment, given the link between leveraged multiculturalism and inclusiveness with organisational success (Holvino et al. 2004).

3.3   Challenges at Macro-country Level

National contexts vary significantly and present significant challenges for the GTM of SIEs. Constraints posed by regulatory frameworks (e.g., migration, work and employment) and the characteristics of local labour markets mean organisations need to develop GTM policies and practices to navigate the tensions between locally situated policies and the GTM of SIEs. We identify challenges in recognising the influence of regulation, institutional and societal arrangements on the attraction, deployment and retention of SIEs.

3.3.1   Navigating the Polysemic Nature of Borders and Regulatory Regimes

Contemporary discourses of global work and experience are often underpinned by assumptions of unfettered global mobility in an open and accessible world where borders are easy to cross. This perspective fails to acknowledge the constraints of regulatory regimes that govern international mobility; for instance, government policies on immigration that regulate state borders, which determine the opportunities that SIEs are able to pursue (c.f. Cooper and Rumford 2011). A central challenge for GTM relates to equalising and differentiating capital through state policies that affect organisations by defining the types of SIEs organisations can attract and employ. For example, discussions about the relationship between migration and credentialism (the overemphasis on formal education and qualifications) (c.f. Singh and Sochan 2010) have noted that migration policies at the macro-country level impose control mechanisms that result in differentiation of capital. Consequently, borders are becoming increasingly polysemic, which means that they are experienced differently by different people (Balibar 2002). For example, Batnitzky et al. (2008: 55) note that whilst migrants from high-income countries work in professional and managerial occupations, migrants from low-income countries tend to be overrepresented in service sector jobs. These polysemic experiences are also linked to the impact of gender, ethnicity and nationality on patterns of and access to mobility, which ultimately determines the main features of global labour markets (Favell et al. 2007; Kofman 2013). This was exemplified by Loveband (2004) in her study of Indonesian migrant women working as carers in Taiwan, where she noted that there are "nationality-based stereotypes that tend to channel migrant workers of different nationalities into different segments of the labour market" (p. 336).

3.3.2 Negotiating Socio-cultural-political Arrangements and Structures to Manage Talent Flow

Labour mobility is a direct response to country needs and migration regulatory regimes, so attracting and retaining SIEs depends on the degree to which migration is regulated. In addition, factors such as location, reputation, opportunities, and how multicultural a place is seen to be, play a role in attracting SIEs to specific destinations and organisations (Thorn and Inkson 2012). Societal responses also affect the presence of SIEs; Doherty and Dickmann (2012) have argued that national and supranational structures can influence perceptions of and attitudes towards SIEs. They use the example of the European Union, whereby efforts to increase mobility have resulted in more positive organisational and societal perceptions of SIEs.

Conversely, policies of localisation can result in negative portrayals of non-native workers as "job snatchers" and can make it challenging for organisations to manage SIEs. By restricting the number of non-native workers in a specific economy in order to facilitate the employment and development of the local workforce, these policies place restrictions to organisations wanting to attract global talent. Research conducted in the Gulf Cooperation Council highlights the potentially negative impact of localisation policies on the management of SIEs (Harry 2007). As Rodriguez and Scurry (2013) have highlighted in their study of Qatar, the potential contributions of SIEs are not fully utilised at both the meso-organisational and macro-country levels as SIEs are positioned as experts and outsiders with no need for, or not worthy of, support and development.

---

4   GTM of SIEs: A Multi-level Perspective

Recognising that global talent is experienced at a localised level is fundamental to understand the scope of GTM in light of the inherent diversity of SIEs. As the previous discussions highlight, organisations need to consider the interactions between the macro-country, meso-organisational and micro-individual to understand the connections between the three main stakeholders: SIEs, organisations and states.

At the individual level, both awareness of the main features of SIEs and adoption of adequate diversity management strategies are needed to capitalise on individual talent as a strategic differentiator (Buckingham and Vosburgh 2001). At the meso-

Table 1 GTM of SIEs: a multilevel perspective

Stage	Analytical level	Considerations for GTM of SIEs	Key challenges
1	Macro-country	Structural dimensions 　Regional and national legislation 　Migration regulation Business systems 　Work and employment legislation 　Types of organisations Labour market characteristics 　Education 　Skill availability 　Diversity 　Unemployment rates	1. Navigating the polysemic nature of borders and regulatory regimes 2. Negotiating socio-cultural political arrangments and structures
2	Meso-organisational	Organisational culture 　Management and leadership styles 　Symbolic and physical manifestations 　Values and justifications HRM 　Policies and practices 　Diversity management 　Career management and development	1. Understanding the nature of the employment relationship and the psychological contract 2. Identifying and deploying knowledge and skills 3. Capitalising on cross-cultural synergies
3	Micro-individual	Individual characteristics 　Socio-cultural background 　Skills and qualifications Career expectations and orientations 　Motive 　Experience 　Future plans	1. Recognition of human capital Understanding needs and expectations

organisational level, there is a symbiotic relationship between SIEs and HRM. The former play an important role in shaping organisational cultures and the latter promote specific dynamics of employment and engagement, reaping the benefits of an increasingly global workforce. Ultimately, identifying, developing and facilitating the implementation of processes that account for individual characteristics of SIEs would serve three purposes for GTM:

1. Attracting and retaining SIEs.
2. Fulfilling SIEs' career needs and expectations.
3. Utilising global capital of SIEs.

We propose a multi-level perspective to inform the GTM of SIEs which focuses on three distinct levels: macro-country, meso-organisational and micro-individual (Table 1). The rationale for our proposed stages and levels responds to the analysis of forces that regulate the attraction, deployment and retention of SIEs. These stages do not work in isolation and the recognising the interaction between the levels is essential to appreciate relevant interconnections, interdependence and tensions. These interactions account for the social/processual and contextual influences that shape the GTM of SIEs (Skirbis et al. 2004).

Stage 1: Macro-country Level When looking at how organisations articulate policies and practices to manage global talent, the macro-country level has a direct impact given the importance of countries engaging with the 'global' discourse (i.e., the idea of a single global political and economic system) in order to participate and benefit from the opportunities it brings such as trade, foreign direct investment and mobility of capital, people and information. On the one hand, there is the assumption that actors are inherently international within the global market: this is; the understanding that global talent is "out there" to be captured by organisations. Ultimately, the use of the 'global' prefix hints at the unrestricted mobility of capital, human and material resources.

On the other hand, local regimes provide a ground-check in relation to what is possible and desirable. In the case of SIEs, forces at macro-country level determine the organisational scope and ways to make use of this global talent. A fundamental analysis central to the GTM of SIEs is the interaction of markets, societies and institutions. The GTM of SIEs is a representation of the acceptance of the discourse of the new global order (Castles 2005) yet at the macro-country level; structural constraints rooted on localised regulatory frameworks emerge as a safeguard from institutions that look beyond organisations and into the perceived interests of society.

Stage 2: Meso-organisational Level At the meso-organisational level, the impact of organisational cultures and HRM practices is fundamental to understand the space given to SIEs in organizations. Assessing the contribution of SIEs using traditional views of the psychological contract renders them potentially 'risky' for developmental investment. However, this does not capitalise on their positive influence on work environments: adding dynamicity, flexibility, and new insights based on diverse experiences of management and leadership. Analytically, this level would explore ways to embed diversity management strategies in the design and organisation of work, supported by HRM policies and practices.

Stage 3: Micro-individual Level SIEs have been portrayed as a disengaged group: belonging anywhere hence belonging nowhere. This assumed psychosocial dislocation (Nava 2002) raises questions about their level of organisational commitment and merit for developmental investment. Yet traditional organisational and HRM logics do not necessarily apply to this group. We indicated at the start of this chapter that SIEs can be seen to represent the main typology of workers in global times. As such, the focus on whether they subscribe to organisational narratives (i.e., organisational culture) neglects the opportunity to see the type of narratives of work they articulate and how these can be used effectively by organisations. Whilst SIEs' expectations of organisational commitment are not 'orthodox', their alternative ways of understanding commitment can be capitalised by organisations.

GTM strategies need to be expanded to account for and capitalise on the pool of knowledge and experience of this group, paying particular attention to fluid notions of commitment and the psychological contract. At this level, the focus is on understanding individual characteristics of SIEs, and mapping out how these characteristics can add to/complement existing human capital in organisations. This mapping would be useful not only to manage SIEs' contribution and potential but to support their career development. Ultimately, the heterogeneity of SIEs needs to be unpacked so that their skills and agentic ability becomes tangible and are capitalised by organisations. The effectiveness of this analytical perspective is linked to working with clear principles that underpin the three central dimensions of the GTM of SIEs: attraction, management and development, and retention. We propose three guiding principles:

Principle 1: GTM of SIEs should recognise that talent is diverse, fluid, and relational. This requires not only positively acknowledging that SIEs bring different skills and competencies, but also articulating policies and practices that account for the different nature of the employment relationship for SIEs. Commitment, engagement and the psychological contract cannot assume that either SIEs or organisations are only pursuing their own interests or focus solely on the long-term. As actors with particular needs and expectations, both their interests and features need to be reconciled by seeking for flexible strategies that are tailored to SIEs as a group to support their commitment and development, and capitalise on their contribution for the benefit of the organisation.

Principle 2: GTM of SIEs should understand individual needs and expectations of SIEs and how these add to/complement existing human capital in the organisation. This means mapping the organisation's external and internal labour market and identifying gaps in global capital that SIEs bring to the organisation. It is of salient importance to establish concrete ways in which the contribution of SIEs to the organisation is recognised and valued.

Principle 3: GTM of SIEs should place special attention to the short term. Given the increasing mobility of this group, organisations should embed diversity management strategies that strongly rely on knowledge sharing to capitalise on what SIEs bring to the organisation from the start of the employment relationship. Investment in the development and career support for SIEs should be a central concern on entry. Rodrigues et al. (2013) note that objective benchmarks of career success are no longer useful in the contemporary world and propose moving from anchors to orientations as the combination of elements such as individual identity, family and social background, work experiences and labour market conditions, which are diverse and vary across time, reflects more accurately and usefully what shapes career preferences. In the case of SIEs, for example, high mobility means knowledge of different labour markets and changing identities developed based on influences from different contexts. Ultimately, the status of SIEs as global commodities makes them competitive and demands a dynamic approach to retention.

Table 2 Five key challenges, strategies, and future opportunities for GTM of SIEs

Five key points regarding GTM challenges	Five key points regarding strategies to overcome these challenges	Five key points regarding future opportunities in GTM
Understanding the talent of SIEs	Acknowledge the factors that influence the talent management of SIEs	Utilise a dynamic multi-level perspective to explore factors at the macro-country level, meso-organisational level, and micro-individual level
Overcoming negative ideas about SIEs	Counteract notions of SIEs' disengagement and lack of organisational commitment	Develop retention strategies that account for diversity in terms of individual characteristics, and career orientations and expectations
Developing inclusive organisational cultures that help to retain SIEs	Integrate SIEs into organisations	Develop internal and external networks that support organisational and social ties
Adequate deployment of SIEs to overcome underemployment and deskilling	Maximise the performance of SIEs through recognition and utilisation of skills and competencies	Articulate policies and practices to facilitate adjustment, development and engagement of SIEs
Managing the institutional and structural factors that impact SIE attraction, deployment and retention	Mediate contextual influences on the employment relationship with SIEs	Manage the interaction between different levels

Conclusion

In this chapter, we examined GTM of SIEs. The chapter aimed to add insight into the challenges associated with the GTM of SIEs and propose a multi-level perspective to enhance the conceptual scope of the GTM of SIEs and support the practical implementation of GTM of SIEs in organisations. The key message from the chapter is the importance of analysing GTM of SIEs from a multi-level perspective that accounts for influences at macro-country, meso-organisational and micro-individual level. This perspective highlights the interplay between individual characteristics, organisational needs and national/supranational regulatory regimes. Models of global talent management have mainly focused on HRM policies and practices, somewhat neglecting the relevance of regulatory regimes that shape, restrict and hinder what is possible and desirable in terms of migration and mobility, and their resulting impact on the influx of talent to local economies. Furthermore, we have highlighted the distinct characteristics of SIEs and the need for organisations to articulate policies and practices that account for the different nature of the employment relationship with this group. In particular, we argue that in developing a strategic approach to the GTM of SIEs, organisations need to challenge prevailing assumptions about them.

Based on the discussions developed in this chapter, Table 2 summarises the five key challenges, strategies and future opportunities for the GTM of SIEs. There are clear implications for researchers and practitioners in particular there is a need to explore further and account for the career orientations of this group and their understandings and expectations of the organisations.

References

Al Ariss, A. (2010). Modes of engagement: Migration, self-initiated expatriation, and career development. *Career Development International, 15*(4), 338–358.

Al Ariss, A., & Crowley-Henry, M. (2013). Self-initiated expatriation and migration in the management literature: Present theorizations and future research directions. *Career Development International, 18*(1), 78–96.

Al Ariss, A., Koall, I., Özbilgin, M., & Suutari, V. (2013). Careers of skilled migrants. *Journal of Management Development, 32*(2), 148–151.

Balibar, E. (2002). *Politics and the other scene*. London: Verso.

Batnitzky, A., McDowell, L., & Dyer, S. (2008). A middle-class global mobility? The working lives of Indian men in a west London hotel. *Global Networks, 8*(1), 51–70.

Biemann, T., & Andresen, M. (2010). Self-initiated foreign expatriates versus assigned expatriates: Two distinct types of international careers? *Journal of Managerial Psychology, 25*(4), 430–448.

Buckingham, M., & Vosburgh, R. M. (2001). The 21st century human resources function: It's the talent, stupid! *Human Resource Planning, 24*(4), 17–23.

Budhwar, P. S., & Sparrow, P. R. (2002). An integrative framework for understanding cross-national human resource management practices. *Human Resource Management Review, 12*(3), 377–403.

Carr, S. C., Inkson, K., & Thorn, K. (2005). From global careers to talent flow: Reinterpreting 'brain drain'. *Journal of World Business, 40*(4), 386–398.

Castles, S. (2005). Nation and empire: Hierarchies of citizenship in the new global order. *International Politics, 42*(2), 203–224.

Collings, D. G., & Mellahi, K. (2009). Strategic talent management: A review and research agenda. *Human Resource Management Review, 19*(4), 304–313.

Cooper, A., & Rumford, C. (2011). Cosmopolitan borders: Bordering as connectivity. In M. Nowicka & M. Rovisco (Eds.), *Ashgate companion to cosmopolitanism* (pp. 261–276). Farnham: Ashgate.

Doherty, N. (2013). Understanding the self-initiated expatriate: A review and directions for future research. *International Journal of Management Reviews, 15*(4), 447–469.

Doherty, N., & Dickmann, M. (2012). Self-initiated expatriation: Drivers, employment experience and career outcomes. In M. Andresen, A. Al Ariss, M. Walther, & K. Wolff (Eds.), *Self-initiated expatriation: Individual, organisational and national perspectives* (pp. 122–143). London: Routledge.

Doherty, N., Richardson, J., & Thorn, K. (2013). Self-initiated expatriation and self-initiated expatriates: Clarification of the research stream. *Career Development International, 18*(1), 97–112.

Dokko, G., Wilk, S. L., & Rothbard, N. P. (2009). Unpacking prior experience: How career history affects job performance. *Organization Science, 20*(1), 51–68.

Farndale, E., Scullion, H., & Sparrow, P. (2010). The role of the corporate HR function in global talent management. *Journal of World Business, 45*(2), 161–168.

Favell, A., Feldblum, M., & Smith, M. P. (2007). The human face of global mobility: A research agenda. *Society, 44*(2), 15–25.

Harry, W. (2007). Employment creation and localization: The crucial human resource issues for the GCC. *The International Journal of Human Resource Management, 18*(1), 132–146.

Haslberger, A., & Vaiman, V. (2013). Self-initiated expatriates: A neglected source of global talent flow. In V. Vaiman & A. Haslberger (Eds.), *Talent management of self-initiated expatriates – A neglected source of global talent* (pp. 1–18). Basingstoke: Palgrave Macmillan.

Holvino, E., Ferdman, B. M., & Merrill-Sands, D. (2004). Creating and sustaining diversity and inclusion in organizations: Strategies and approaches. In M. S. Stockdale & F. J. Crosby (Eds.),

The psychology and management of workplace diversity (pp. 245–276). Malden, MA: Blackwell.

Howe-Walsh, L., & Schyns, B. (2010). Self-initiated expatriation: Implications for HRM. *International Journal of Human Resources Management, 21*(2), 260–273.

Kofman, E. (2013). Gendered labour migrations in Europe and emblematic migratory figures. *Journal of Ethnic and Migration Studies, 39*(4), 579–600.

Lee, C. H. (2005). A study of underemployment among self-initiated expatriates. *Journal of World Business, 40*(2), 172–187.

Lewis, R. E., & Heckman, R. J. (2006). Talent management: A critical review. *Human Resource Management Review, 16*(2), 139–154.

Loveband, A. (2004). Positioning the product: Indonesian migrant women workers in Taiwan. *Journal of Contemporary Asia, 34*(3), 336–348.

Mayrhofer, W., Sparrow, P., & Zimmermann, A. (2008). Modern forms of international working. In M. Dickmann, C. Brewster, & P. Sparrow (Eds.), *International human resource management – A European perspective* (pp. 219–239). London: Routledge.

McLean Parks, J., Kidder, D. L., & Gallagher, D. G. (1998). Fitting square pegs into round holes: Mapping the domain of contingent work arrangements onto the psychological contract. *Journal of Organizational Behaviour, 19*(S1), 697–730.

Nava, M. (2002). Cosmopolitan modernity: Everyday imaginaries and the register of difference. *Theory, Culture and Society, 19*(1–2), 81–99.

Richardson, J. (2006). Self-directed expatriation: Family matters. *Personnel Review, 35*(4), 469–486.

Rodrigues, R., Guest, D., & Budjanovcanin, A. (2013). From anchors to orientations: Towards a contemporary theory of career preferences. *Journal of Vocational Behaviour, 83*(2), 142–152.

Rodriguez, J. K., & Mearns, L. (2012). Problematising the interplay between employment relations, migration and mobility. *Employee Relations, 34*(6), 580–593.

Rodriguez, J. K., & Scurry, T. (2013). Career capital development of self-initiated expatriates in Qatar: Cosmopolitan globetrotters, experts and outsiders. *International Journal of Human Resource Management.* doi:10.1080/09585192.2013.815254.

Schein, E. G. (1996). Career anchors revised: Implications for career development in the 21st Century. *Academy of Management Executive, 10*(4), 80–88.

Schuler, R. S., & Tarique, I. (2012). Global talent management: theoretical perspectives, systems, and challenges. In G. Stahl, I. Bjorkman, & S. Morris (Eds.), *Handbook of research in international human resource management* (2nd ed., pp. 205–219). Cheltenham: Edward Elgar.

Scullion, H., & Collings, D. (2006). International talent management. In H. Scullion & D. Collings (Eds.), *Global staffing* (pp. 87–116). New York: Routledge.

Scurry, T., & Blenkinsopp, J. (2011). Under-employment among recent graduates: A review of the literature. *Personnel Review, 40*(5), 643–659.

Scurry, T., Blenkinsopp, J., & Hay, A. (2013a). Global careers: Perspectives from the United Kingdom. In C. Reis & Y. Baruch (Eds.), *Careers without borders: Critical perspectives* (pp. 31–54). Abingdon: Routledge.

Scurry, T., Rodriguez, J. K., & Bailouni, S. (2013b). Narratives of identity of self-initiated expatriates in Qatar. *Career Development International, 18*(1), 12–33.

Singh, M. D., & Sochan, A. (2010). Voices of internationally educated nurses: Policy recommendations for credentialing. *International Nursing Review, 57*(1), 56–63.

Skirbis, Z., Kendall, G., & Woodward, I. (2004). Locating cosmopolitanism: Between humanist ideal and grounded social category. *Theory, Culture and Society, 21*(6), 115–136.

Suutari, V., & Taka, M. (2004). Career anchors of managers with global careers. *Journal of Management Development, 23*(9), 833–847.

Tarique, I., & Schuler, R. S. (2010). Global talent management: Literature review, integrative framework, and suggestions for further research. *Journal of World Business, 45*(2), 122–133.

Tharenou, P., & Caulfield, N. (2010). Will I stay or will I go? Explaining repatriation by self-initiated expatriates. *Academy of Management Journal, 53*(5), 1009–1028.

Thorn, K., & Inkson, K. (2012). Self-initiated expatriation and talent flow. In M. Andresen, A. Al Ariss, M. Walther, & K. Wolff (Eds.), *Self-initiated expatriation: Individual, organisational and national perspectives* (pp. 75–89). London: Routledge.

Opportunities and Challenges for Organisations and Highly Skilled Migrant Professionals

Bradley Saunders and Michael Nieto

1   Introduction

This chapter offers a critical evaluation of the issues relating to Global Talent Management with specific reference to the implications this has for employment mobility. The expansion of global business is creating new opportunities for migration, but also challenges for organisations in retaining employees (Al Ariss et al. 2013). This applies to both qualified professionals and lower skilled workers. According to Nieto (2013) there has been a significant shift in the orientation of employment distribution during the first quarter of the twenty-first century, as evidenced by increasing global employment mobility and the realignments of where work is located.

We contribute to the GTM literature in two important ways: firstly, we identify the underutilization of highly skilled migrant professionals, and secondly, we add to the body of qualitative literature of this relatively young and growing field of academic enquiry.

We begin with a brief discussion of Global Talent Management and the increasing demand for, and mobility of highly skilled workers. We then focus on the European Union and the implications that the freedom of movement which it confers on its citizens has on EU labour mobility. We then discuss the global talent challenges facing employers and migrant workers before examining our methodology and findings. Finally, we conclude by highlighting the waste of human capital of migrant workers and the negative impacts this has on the European Community.

B. Saunders (✉)
University of Derby, Derby, United Kingdom
e-mail: b.saunders@derby.ac.uk

M. Nieto
Regent's University, London, United Kingdom
e-mail: nietom@regents.ac.uk

A. Al Ariss (ed.), *Global Talent Management*, Management for Professionals,
DOI 10.1007/978-3-319-05125-3_8, © Springer International Publishing Switzerland 2014

2   The Growing Demand for Global Talent

The term 'Global Talent Management' has been defined in several ways. Core to these various definitions are the twin concepts of individuals with high levels of talent which could be of benefit to an organisation and the systems that the organisation puts in place to manage such employees. Tarique and Schuler (2010: 124 italics added), for example, define Global Talent Management as

> ... systematically utilizing IHRM activities (complementary HRM policies and policies) to attract, develop, and retain individuals with high levels of human capital (e.g., competency, personality, motivation) consistent with the strategic directions of the multinational enterprise in a dynamic, highly competitive, and global environment.

The emerging economies are expanding their commercial and industrial sectors and thereby creating a new and growing requirement for global talent. Concomitantly, there has been an increasing demand for highly-skilled workers as a result of the internationalization of professional labour markets (Mellahi and Collings 2010). It is estimated that 100 million global migrant workers now account for about three per cent of the global workforce (UNFPA 2005). The outcome of these changes in labour market demand is that people with professional knowledge and skills have the opportunity to enjoy greater employability and global mobility.

In practice this means that people are moving to where there is work. Furthermore, some parts of the global workforce are more likely to regard moving to another country as part of a one-job stay. This is significantly different from more traditional immigrations whereby people have sought a permanent change of residency, as was the tendency in the twentieth century. Such 'one-off' movements leading to permanent resettlement have given way to more fluid practices of international mobility involving alternating residence in different countries (Penninx et al. 2008).

3   EU Labour Mobility

Since the Treaty of Rome was signed in 1957, the right of freedom of movement throughout the EU for EU citizens and their families has been one of the core 'acquis' of the European Communities. In 2006, designated the European Year of Workers' Mobility, Vladimír Špidla, the EU Commissioner for Employment, Social Affairs and Equal Opportunities, put forth an impassioned call for a more mobile workforce, equipped to learn new skills and adapt to new environments in order to meet the EU's growth and jobs strategy. (Vandenbrande et al. 2006: 1) stressed the importance of greater mobility within the EU in order to increase the community's competitive ability in the face of "the growing challenges of globalisation, rapid technological change and a developing knowledge society". Such objectives imply an efficient and constructive community-wide utilisation of human capital.

According to the research for this chapter, a number of highly-skilled migrants have found themselves unable to use their human capital and other attributes to obtain work commensurate with their experience and qualifications. The respondents reported that employment agencies had not taken into consideration their skills, qualifications or experience, opting instead to place them into manual/low-skilled occupations.

Such practice has negative effects not only on the workers themselves, but also on the host nation, the sending nation and organisations. The sending nation's failure to exploit the migrants' skills, qualifications and experience leads to their migration and results in a 'brain drain' or loss of skilled personnel. The host nation's similar inability to benefit from the migrants' skills deprives it of the migrants' potential contribution—turning a potential 'brain gain' into a 'brain waste'. The migrants themselves are denied the opportunity to contribute fully to local and regional economies. The organisations which fail to offer suitable employment opportunities to talented migrant workers deprive themselves of these individuals' skills, experience, expertise and global perspective.

A better understanding of contemporary career mobility within the EU is vital if the community's ideals of a more mobile, skilled and adaptable workforce, able to increase the community's competitive ability in the face of growing globalisation, are to be realised (Khapova et al. 2009).

4 Global Talent Challenges for Employers and Migrant Workers

Interest in international career mobility research has centred on the experiences of corporate expatriates (Zikic et al. 2010; Lee 2005). At the same time, there has been an emerging interest in new forms of international working (Mayrhofer et al. 2008) such as 'short-term', 'commuter' and 'frequent flyer', which have begun to replace more traditional expatriation. Indeed, 'self-initiated expatriates'—or individuals who independently seek work in a foreign country—form a much larger proportion of those working overseas than those who are sent overseas by their Multinational Corporation employers (Bonache et al. 2001; Inkson et al. 1997; Lee 2005).

In a Europe-wide analysis of occupational promotion of migrant workers, Barone (2009) identifies clear and widespread overeducation of migrant workers in the EU. Migrant workers with qualifications obtained outside of the destination country had a much higher incidence of overeducation than natives of that country. In other words, an objective measure of the gap between skills held and skills required in the current job revealed that migrant workers were much more likely than native workers to be working in a position below their education level.

5   Methodology

In common with many recent research studies into migrant workers (Trevena 2010; Anderson et al. 2006; Eade et al. 2007), this study adopts a qualitative approach in order to focus on the migrants' own experiences and interpretation of migration. Such an approach allows for personal experiences, aspirations, feelings and responses—which do not lend themselves easily to measurement—to be considered (Anderson et al. 2006). To this end, it differs from research intended to influence labour mobility policy, which generally adopts quantitative methods. Tarique and Schuler (2010) further argue that the use of a variety of qualitative approaches is justified in the study of Global Talent Management., given the relative youth of the field.

In-depth, semi-structured qualitative interviews were appropriate for this study as they generate 'rich' data, allow a greater flow to the discussion, and make it possible for interviewees to broach topics that had not been anticipated when drafting the interview schedule.

A snowball method was used to gain access to participants. As a technique it is most productive when suitable members are readily identifiable and know others who fit the required criteria. It is relatively common in migration studies, particularly in those with a more qualitative approach (Mckenzie and Mistiaen 2009).

5.1   Participants

The interviewees came from a number of different countries, had a range of skills and qualifications (not all of which were necessarily degree qualifications), were residing in several different cities in the UK, and had been in the UK for varying amounts of time. Of the 19 interviewees, 11 were female and 8 male. Nine were Polish, three Brazilian, two Latvian, two Lithuanian, one French, one Iranian and one Portuguese. It is important to note that the Brazilians had dual nationality (two were Italian passport holders and one Portuguese) and had entered the UK accordingly, thus benefitting from the freedom of movement granted to EU nationals. This freedom also applied to the Iranian, who gained Dutch citizenship after being granted political asylum in the Netherlands (Table 1).

5.2   Analysis

The data analysis process saw transcription and analysis as concurrent rather than sequential activities (Silverman 2005). HyperRESEARCH software was used to code the material collected. In order to merge codes effectively, an iterative approach was adopted (Seidel and Kelle 1995) in which previously coded interviews were reviewed to see if new codes from later interviews could replace earlier codes of a similar nature. This approach demanded a great deal of time but resulted in deep familiarity with the interviews, and the recognition of similarities

Table 1 Participants' background

Name	Time in UK	Background	Nationality	Qualifications	Home country job	UK job
Andrzej	21 m	31–35 M Single	Polish	BSc in Veterinary Medicine	Veterinary Surgeon	Factory worker Loughborough
Brigita	1.5 y	51–55 F Married Three children (23,20,15)	Lithuanian	Degree in Medicine	Doctor	Care Worker Stafford
Cecylja	2.5 y	31–35 F Single	Polish	3 years on BA Course in Pedagogy	Pedagogy	Catering Assistant Leicester
Celine	15 y	36–40 F Married (common law)	French	Master's Degree in Geography & Cartography PGCE	Cartographer	Teaching Assistant Derby
Edmund	2 y	25–30 M Married to Marjanna	Polish	CISCO Networking Associate	IT Specialist	Administrator (Police) Northampton
Gabriela	18 m	31–35 F Married children (10, 4 9 m)	Brazilian/ Portuguese	BSc in Veterinary Medicine BA in International Relations	Veterinary Surgeon	Admin Assistant Leicester
Isabella	5 y	25–30 F Single	Portuguese	BA in Pedagogy (ongoing)	Academia	School Caretaker Northampton
Jiri	2 y	55+ M Married Spouse in home country	Polish	BSc Degree in Medicine	Pathologist	Warehouse Operative Leicester
Juliana	1.5 y	25–30 F Married to Ricardo	Brazilian/ Italian	Journalism Diploma	Journalist	Pizza Packer Boston
Kamal	4 y	46–50 M Married, one child (6)	Iranian/ Dutch	BSc in Clinical Psychology BSc in Network Administration	Psychologist/ Network Specialist	Union Organiser West Bromwich
Marjanna	1.5 y	25–30 F Married to Edmund	Polish	BA in Accounting	Accountant	Coffee Shop Assistant Northampton
Ona	4 y	25–30 F Married one child (4)	Lithuanian	Technical Laboratory Diploma	Laboratory Assistant	Union Organiser West Bromwich

(continued)

Table 1 (continued)

Name	Time in UK	Background	Nationality	Qualifications	Home country job	UK job
Pawel	2.5 y	25–30 M In civil partnership	Polish	BA in English Teaching Diploma	Teacher	Self-Employed Decorator Manchester
Ricardo	1.5 y	31–35 M Married to Juliana	Brazilian/ Italian	BSc in IT	Systems analyst	Pizza Packer Boston
Sebastian	3 m	25–30 M Single	Polish	BA in Music	Composer/ Musicologist	Dispatcher Loughborough
Sofija	3 y	25–30 F Single	Latvian	College Diploma	Administrator	Secretary Spalding
Stanislaw	3 y	31–35 M Single	Polish/ German	2 years on BA Course in Economics	Family Business	Factory worker Loughborough
Valeska	1.5 y	51–55 F Married Spouse in home country	Polish	BA in Pedagogy/ Resocialisation	Pedagogy	Warehouse Operative Leicester
Veronika	5.5 y	25–30 F Single	Latvian	BA in Economics and Law	Economics/ Law	Council Officer Spalding

and differences between interviewees' accounts. A visual representation of the relationships between codes—known as concept mapping—was conducted using a mind mapping program to visually depict the interrelationships between related codes.

6   Findings

6.1   Reasons for Coming

In the analysis of the motivations which underlay the migrants' decision to leave their home countries and to come to the UK to work, a number of factors were identified. The most visible of these were financial incentives. Indeed, 14 of the 19 interviewees mentioned money as a motivating factor, for a number of reasons: an urgent need for money due to debts or family pressure; a desire to accumulate funds to sponsor ongoing or future studies or investments; a desire to earn enough to be comfortable, without having to work long hours; and a desire simply to be able to work at all and earn a living.

. . .it is very important for me this financial side, because in Lithuania I was upset about it and I'm not absolutely happy at the moment, but hopefully in future situation will improve, more or less. (Brigita)

. . . working in Latvia I would earn . . . as erm a specialist in law for businesses . . . about two hundred, two hundred and fifty pound a month, so it wasn't really enough . . . I knew that working on a farm here I can earn more money (Veronika)

when I get my first wage, 200 pound, I thought "Oh God, what I'm going to do with such big money?". . . previously I get 80 pound per month (Sofija)

However, there was clear evidence from the interviews that money was not the sole motivating factor behind the decision to come to the UK. For many of the interviewees, financial incentives co-existed with non-economic factors such as a desire to explore a new culture or to learn English. The possibility of improving one's education, or of providing an opportunity for one's children to get a better education was mentioned by six interviewees as a key factor in their decision to come here.

The decision to come may also have been affected by a sense of not wanting to miss out on an 'adventure'. This was true of four of the 19 interviewees. The importance of the freedom of movement which the interviewees enjoyed is also reflected by the decision of 13 of the interviewees to come to the UK without having first arranged a job. The six interviewees who had arranged a job prior to departure were to change jobs soon after arrival, in one case immediately. All of the interviewees arrived with the knowledge that they had the option of going back to their home country should the reality of life here not appeal.

Before leaving Brazil, Juliana and Ricardo had ignored their friends' advice to turn down a job offer from Germany and work in the UK instead. They soon regretted their decision. However, as EU citizens, they were able to leave Germany and come to work in the UK in a very short space of time:

[Our friends in Boston said on the phone] ". . .good money, better than in Germany. If you want to come, you can come, no problem . . . we can help you". The first flight we took it straight (Ricardo)

There was a clear lack of information available to potential migrants as they contemplated seeking work in the UK. The interviewees using a home country agency were content to allow the agencies to advise them as to the nature and location of work available. In particular, they placed little or no importance on the location of the work the agencies could offer them:

I just came here from work agency, straight to Leicester, they got a job here. So that's why. I'm not, not thinking. I just said, 'OK I'm going', I want to go to England, but it doesn't matter where. (Cecylja)

Because, I got an offer from Polish job agency, which recruited, was recruiting, Polish people for a care assistant job in Britain . . . I got two offers, from two different companies and I had problem to choose. But, I got free ticket, plane ticket, so I erm, choose this offer. (Valeska)

You just have to go there and work . . . it doesn't matter where . . . I came through the agency . . . I've been promised work in the onion fields. (Ona)

This lack of attention to their destination region manifested itself later, once the interviewees had come to know the characteristics of the area where they were working. They were, for example, surprised to find that West Bromwich was not a rural oasis, or taken totally aback by the proportion of non-white residents in Leicester. By concentrating on areas with people shortages, the employment agencies that had recruited them were ignoring potentially more suitable employment opportunities for the migrants in other areas of the UK.

The decision to move to the UK was also prompted by the migrants' unhappiness in their home country due to their inability to find work. Five of the interviewees were seeking an escape from redundancy or continued periods of unemployment.

> I've tried to find some job in Latvia but ... because it's, it was a high unemployment in Latvia, so everybody wasn't just interested in qualifications, they were interested in experience. I didn't have experience, so I didn't have chance to get really anything. (Veronika)

> Because my country is not a good country. It's a poor country . . .economy in my country is down. . . (Isabella)

> I've lost my job in August er 2005 ... from the 1st August I was unemployed and I have came to UK the 8th of November. . . I have been working in, in the black way, yes? At about two months, then I was waiting for the going away because we have bought the ticket (Jiri)

6.2   Lack of Recognition of Qualifications

The interviewees encountered scepticism on the part of potential employers and agencies with respect to the value of foreign qualifications, expressing frustration at the dismissive treatment they received in employment agencies:

> Sometimes potential employers look at my diploma "er it's not our diploma, it's not our accent" (Brigita)

> I knew from the start that the agencies, are, it's best to avoid working through an agency, so that's why ... through the other people's experience ... so that's why I avoided it all the way. I never worked for an agency. Never, in England. (Veronika)

> when some ... employer, who see the, some Polish guy finish a Polish school, it's nothing for them, I think, yeah? (Sebastian)

The insistence on UK experience expressed by potential employers and agencies proved highly frustrating for the interviewees. A freshly qualified accountant from Poland, found that her brand new Polish Accounting degree was of little use to her in finding work in her field:

> Do you have any experience in England?" "No", I say "not any but I have experience in Poland, yes?" "No, no, no if you have no any experience in England, you can't start doing something better, yeah. (Marjanna)

Another Pole who had been a teacher in Poland tried to find a job in education. He too was told that he lacked UK experience and found the bureaucracy involved too much to handle:

I wanted to come here and I would be a teacher ... but I literally, I couldn't, it was impossible to have all these documents. There were two or three things, it was impossible for me to have that and it was ... something ... about experience ... of teaching in the UK ... it was like vicious circle, I couldn't, so I couldn't go out of it. (Pawel)

6.3   Taking up Employment

Whether they had been offered posts prior to leaving for the UK or had arrived intending to find a job, the interviewees were faced with the economic need to find work as soon as possible in order to survive. In such cases, sooner or later, the financial pressures of surviving in the UK were such that the interviewees required a job—any job—in order not to have to return home. Faced with the need for money, they took on jobs which they knew to be below their level, often on a short-term contract.

He saw my CV [laughs] and said, I don't know who sent you here, you are too overqualified for this job. I don't know what we can do. But, if this is what you want, it's perfect by me, so why not? I said OK, I took the job. I have to pay the bills anyway. I can't stay with my friends. I took the job. (Kamal)

I had no choice ... because of a simple thing, which is money I needed. I wanted to stay here, I didn't want to come back at that point, I still wanted to stay here. One of my best friends was here and we supported each other, I would say. And she was doing the job she didn't like as well so, I ... I just not have choice because we needed money for rent to live and things like this, ... and we had no savings at this time (Pawel)

... agency found me some one, two week job and I was just taking any assignment I can get: one, two day ... just to get er some money ... because obviously I was starving in this country (Edmund)

Once they had managed to obtain some form of temporary employment and earn enough to survive, however, they set their sights on procuring permanent employment. The desire to find permanent or at least longer term work was mentioned by eight of the interviewees. Their desire to settle for a permanent low skilled job rather than persist in their quest for suitable work aggravated the brain waste in which they found themselves.

I'm really tired when I come back home and Edmund always says "OK, Marjanna, you need to find something different because you drive me crazy with that job. Just try to, to find something better. Just do it for yourself." And it was good excuse for me "But Edmund, you know, it's permanent work, if I find something worse it will be... worse for us, yeah?" (Marjanna)

...my friend just called me and I can doing a job in a canteen, just work for that company. And then she said this is a job from they say permanent job. You've got everything, holiday, everything. And that was for me what was important, have a permanent job. Because, in Poland I've got a mortgage for my flat and I have to pay that and then, ...for that I've got a job, every day and not just you know, waiting for a call from the agency "Oh you cannot go to work today" or "Maybe you can go". That was for me very important and that's why I just agreed to that. (Cecylja)

Their job search strategies, though perhaps not explicitly acknowledged during the interviews, seemed to prioritise certain factors. An awareness of their career capital (especially English language skills) served to give them the courage to seek other jobs. Thus, Ona wasted no time in cashing in on her relatively advanced English language skills in order to escape from the disappointment she felt after taking up the job in the Lincolnshire onion fields which she had procured in Lithuania:

> In the onion fields, for a box, you can get five pounds so ...in a day... let's say four boxes... twenty pounds ...plus they're taking the money from the travelling, from the house and everything like that. So when I went there I said 'No way. I'm not going to do that.' ...I didn't stay in that agency cos I said "Listen I know... English. I'm going to go to the job centre. I'm going to look for a job somewhere else. I'll find it. It doesn't matter where. (Ona)

6.4 Self Image

Those who had, out of financial need, taken on jobs at a lower level than those for which they were qualified, with the expectation that something better would come along, eventually began to notice a change in their self-perception, which required them to reconcile their own self-image. This often resulted in a feeling of frustration when they began to sense that other people did not recognise their educational abilities.

Celine, who had passed her teacher training but failed her qualification year, was working as a teaching assistant and felt frustrated that this led others to undervalue her educational worth:

> Some people here think, think I've got no education. On a par with a peanut, yes. (Celine)

A similar sense of feeling ill at ease with oneself was evident in Marjanna's account, in which a sense of self doubt came through:

> But if somebody...tells you all the ... you know "You are not good enough" you starting to think about that like it's true, maybe I'm not good enough, yeah? Edmund always, always says "Just try believe in yourself. Just try to do something different and"...but [sighs] ...everybody thinks if I work in coffee shop, I'm just ... I'm not smart enough, ...because I can't find something better (Marjanna)

7 Cultural Issues

The migrants were faced with the need to adjust to both work and nonwork situations. Their adjustment was affected by nonwork and family factors, with beneficial effects on significant others, particularly children, offsetting negative aspects of the job to a degree. Their migration had an impact on both their nuclear and extended family both here and in the home country. Their nonwork adjustment

Table 2 Five key GTM challenges, strategies, and future opportunities

Five key points regarding Global Talent Management challenges	Five key points regarding strategies to overcome these challenges	Five key points regarding future opportunities in Global Talent Management
1 More robust mechanisms needed to recognise educational qualifications within EU member countries	Some attempts to set up mutual recognition systems (e.g. MEET/NIACE)	EU skills and qualifications recognition to be coupled with vocational and cultural induction so as to prepare migrants for work in another country
2 Strong willingness to relocate temporarily in search of work not matched by realistic offers of employment commensurate with qualifications	Need to document and share skills and qualifications data more effectively between EU member states	EU labour market information to be made available to migrants *before* they leave their home country
3 Agencies, employers and governments are not systematically addressing the issue of how to avoid brain waste	Need for sustained dialogue to help migrants mould their skills to employers' needs	EU-wide consensus on skills and qualification would produce a more efficient and mobile workforce
4 EU freedom of movement granted to EU citizens leads to large influx of migrants	EU member state governments face legal problems in reducing immigration from EU and have been substantially reducing immigration from outside of the EU	Guidelines for recognising skills and qualifications of non EU migrants to be drawn up, enabling them to be employed where needed throughout the EU
5 Brain waste may lead to lack of self-esteem and mental health issues	Advisors appointed to help migrant workers to cope with their new environment	Possibility of establishing communities of help populated by citizens of those EU countries from which migrants are arriving to the UK

was also affected by marginalisation from UK society but also from other migrants, whom they considered to be of a lower social class than themselves. This was especially the case with the Polish migrants. There was also a widespread resentment of members of ethnic minorities. For many of the interviewees the diversity of the UK population came as both a surprise and a source of friction and they made negative comments about the ethic minorities in their cities which could be described as racist.

Conclusion

The growing demand for global talent has prompted a propensity for people to move temporarily from one nation state to another to secure a job, and then either return to their home country or to another country where new work can be secured. Accordingly, a mind-set of temporary migration is becoming more common.

Within the EU, the right of freedom of movement throughout the community for EU citizens and their families facilitates the decision to visit a member state in order to find work. However, the possibility that this work will be at a level commensurate with the job seeker's skills and qualifications is low as a result of several factors, including lack of recognition of foreign qualifications and a negative attitude by agencies and employers, who have tended to disregard migrants' CVs and offer them menial work.

The increase in worker mobility provides an opportunity for the European community to meet its growth and jobs strategy and become more competitive in the face of the technical and economic challenges of globalisation. However, the study highlights the fact that the human capital of the very group of mobile professionals who would be crucial for the community to achieve these aims is wasted. The most valuable resource in a competitive global market is the talents of people and that talent is best nurtured in gainful employment which is commensurate with the person's experience and qualifications.

The challenges for employers, as previous economic cycles have demonstrated, is that growth follows recessions, so when the next new cycle of growth arrives, businesses will require a skilled and motivated workforce. Accordingly, global organisations also have a significant role to play by investing in employing and retaining a stable workforce (Table 2).

References

Al Ariss, A., Vassilopoulou, J., Ozbilgin, M., & Game, A. (2013). Understanding career experiences of skilled minority ethnic workers in France and Germany. *The International Journal of Human Resource Management, 24*(6), 1236–1256.

Anderson, B., Ruhs, M., Rogaly, B., & Spencer, S. (2006). *Fair Enough?* Central and East European Migrants in Low-Wage Employment in the UK, York: Joseph Rowntree Foundation.

Barone, C., & European Foundation for the Improvement of Living and Working Conditions (Eurofound). (2009). *Occupational promotion of migrant workers.* Dublin, Ireland. Accessed June 25, 2013, from http://www.eurofound.europa.eu/docs/ewco/tn0807038s/tn0807038s.pdf

Bonache, J., Brewster, C., & Suutari, V. (2001). Expatriation: A developing research agenda. *Thunderbird International Business Review, 43*, 3–20.

Eade, J., Drinkwater, S. J., & Garapich, M. (2007). *Class and ethnicity: Polish migrants in London.* Economic and Social Research Council End of Award Report, RES-000-22-1294. Accessed June 19, 2013, from http://www.surrey.ac.uk/cronem/files/POLISH_FINAL_RESEARCH_REPORT_WEB.pdf

Inkson, K., Arthur, M. B., Pringle, J., & Barry, S. (1997). Expatriate assignment versus overseas experience. *Journal of World Business, 32*(4), 351–368.

Khapova, S. N., Vinkenburg, C. J., & Arnold, J. (2009). Careers research in Europe: Identity and contribution. *Journal of Occupational and Organizational Psychology, 82*(4), 709–719.

Lee, C. H. (2005). A study of underemployment among self-initiated expatriates. *Journal of World Business, 40*, 172–187.

Mayrhofer, W., Sparrow, P. R., & Zimmermann, A. (2008). Modern forms of international working. In M. Dickmann, C. Brewster, & P. R. Sparrow (Eds.), *International human resource management: Contemporary issues in Europe* (pp. 219–239). London: Routledge.

McKenzie, D., & Mistiaen, J. (2009). Surveying migrant households: A comparison of census-based, snowball, and intercept surveys. *Journal of the Royal Statistical Society Series A, 172* (2), 339–360.

Mellahi, K., & Collings, W. (2010). The barriers to effective global talent management: The example of corporate elites in MNEs. *Journal of World Business, 45*, 143–149.

Nieto, M. (2013). *An introduction to human resource management: An integrated approach.* London: Palgrave Macmillan.

Penninx, R., Spencer, D., & Hear, N. V. (2008). *Migration and integration in Europe: The state of research.* University of Oxford, Oxford: ESRC Centre on Migration, Policy and Society (COMPAS).

Seidel, J., & Kelle, U. (1995). Different functions of coding in the analysis of data. In U. Kelle (Ed.), *Computer-aided qualitative data analysis: Theory, methods and practice* (pp. 29–40). Thousand Oaks, CA: Sage.

Silverman, D. (2005). *Doing qualitative research: A practical handbook.* Thousand Oaks, CA: Sage.

Tarique, I., & Schuler, R. S. (2010). Global talent management: Literature review, integrative framework, and suggestions for further research. *Journal of World Business, 45*(2), 122–133.

Trevena, P. (2010). *The Polish "Intelligentsia" in London: A case study of young graduates working in the secondary sector* .Unpublished Doctor of Philosophy thesis, Polish Academy of Sciences, Warsaw.

UNFPA. (2005). *Linking population, poverty and development migration: A world on the move.* Accessed March 21, 2011, from http://www.unfpa.org/pds/migration.html

Vandenbrande, T., Coppin, L., Van der Hallen, P., Ester, P., Fouarge, D., Fasang, A., et al. (2006). *Mobility in Europe.* Luxembourg: Office for Official Publications of the European Communities.

Zikic, J., Bonache, J., & Cerdin, J.-L. (2010). Crossing national boundaries: A typology of qualified immigrants' career orientations. *Journal of Organizational Behavior, 31*, 667–686.

Part II

Global Talent Management across Geographical Contexts

Global Talent Management in Brazil: *Jeitinho* as a Managerial Talent

Rosana Silveira Reis and Camilla Quental

1   Introduction

With the opening of borders to trade and foreign investment, globalization has brought opportunities and pressures for firms in emerging markets to innovate and improve their competitive position. A great deal of these pressures and opportunities operate through increased competition from and linkages with mostly developed country multinationals. In this context, BRIC economies—Brazil, Russia, India and China, are facing the challenge of shortage of skilled labour, which can jeopardize their growth. Specifically, in Brazil's booming economy, the B in the BRIC economies, many companies and economists argue that the dearth of highly skilled workers, particularly engineers and tradesmen, can threaten the country's sustained growth, as well as Brazil's economic and political rise. The lack of civil and construction engineers threatens infrastructure projects; areas like banking, aircraft manufacture, petrochemicals and metals are competing for the same top graduates, and are turning to foreign labour, since there are not enough qualified Brazilian workers (Downie 2008).

Consequently, multinational companies are taking additional measures to secure qualified employees. Many of them are launching and increasing internship programs, spending more on training and salaries, and relocating workers from flat and declining markets. They are also relying more heavily on interns to feed the pipeline (Mattioli 2011). In parallel, we observe that cultural integration is pivotal in the context of mergers and acquisitions (M&As), which have become an increasingly popular strategy for achieving corporate growth in emerging countries. The study of Lodorfos and Boateng (2006) finds that culture differences between the

R.S. Reis (✉)
ISG – International Business School, Paris, France
e-mail: rosana.reis@isg.fr

C. Quental
Audencia Nantes, School of Management, Nantes, France
e-mail: cquental@audencia.com

A. Al Ariss (ed.), *Global Talent Management*, Management for Professionals,
DOI 10.1007/978-3-319-05125-3_9, © Springer International Publishing Switzerland 2014

merging firms are a key element affecting effectiveness of the integration process. Booz, Allen and Hamilton, for instance, conducted a survey with more than 200 chief executives of European companies, in which the participants ranked the ability to integrate culturally as a more important aspect than financial or strategic factors in M&As (Pucik et al. 2011).

As organizations increasingly operate in a multicultural context, understanding how global talent management affects outcomes such as satisfaction, creativity, and turnover have been increasing in importance. Although the literature in this area has grown, some points to be clarified remain, notably on how to conceptualize this relatively new construct: Global Talent Management (GTM). Talent management gained popularity in the late 1990s, following the publication of McKinsey & Company's "War for Talent" study (Stahl et al. 2007). According to Lewis and Heckman (2006), three main approaches should be considered: (a) the substitution of the label of human resource management by talent management, focusing in the practices of HR (recruitment and selection, training and development, etc); (b) the emphasis on the development of the talent pool focusing on designing the needs of employees; (c) the focus on managing talented people. Indeed, we use this last perspective in this chapter. A common point emerges from these definitions: the consensus that there is a growing recognition that multinationals need to manage talent on a global basis to remain competitive and that talent can be located in different parts of their global operations (Ready and Conger 2007).

At the same time, with the business environments no longer confined to geographical borders, virtual teams overcome the limitations of time, space, and organizational affiliation as opposed to traditional face-to-face teams (Piccoli et al. 2004). The word "team" can be traced back to the Indo-European word *deuk* (to pull); which indicates that the word has always held an underlying meaning of "pulling together". The modern sense of team, "a group of people acting together," emerged in the sixteenth century (Senge et al. 1994). Today the traditional definition of team has grown to become "a group of people with complementary skills, committed to a common goal, interdependent performance and collectively responsible for results" (Katzenbach and Smith 1993). The new wave of digital technologies has given organizations an enormous opportunity to bring together their distributed workforce and develop the ability to work together despite being apart (Prasad and Akhilesh 2002).

As a result of this changing configuration and management—concerning companies (mergers and acquisitions), global talent management (GTM), and globally distributed teams (GDT)—emerges the identification of an organizational environment where interpersonal relationships are strongly impacted by cultural diversity not yet much explored in the literature. For example, although researchers (e.g., Jackson et al. 2003) have highlighted the positive and negative aspects of the diversity in the teams, they frequently consider teams working together in the same place. In consequence, our main contribution consists in the analysis of these three phenomena simultaneously, taking into account GDT. In line with Baba et al. (2004), a globally distributed team is defined as "an interdependent work group comprised of cultural diverse members based in two or more nations who share a collective responsibility for making or implementing decisions related to a firm's global strategy" (p. 548).

Given that little research has been conducted on innovation and talent management coming from emerging markets, we developed a longitudinal research carried out at Volvo Group. Starting from a global analysis, where the emerging markets impose their culture within globally distributed teams, our practical and empirical contributions in this chapter is to explore the concept of GTM focusing on human capital aspects (Stahl et al. 2007). Our purpose is to show how the Brazilian *jeitinho* can be understood as a cultural characteristic and as a talent management which provides flexibility in dealing with interpersonal relations inside teams, improving their integration and in consequence their performance.

The importance and the original nature of the mediation systems among people are stressed, as well as those between the individual and the organization. In this sense, our research question is: "How does cultural embeddedness of Brazilian GTM contribute to improve the integration within globally distributed teams?"

This chapter is composed of five sections, and is organized as follows. In the Introduction, we present the context analysis, the research question and the structure of the chapter. In the next section, Sect. 2, we present the State of the Art, focusing on Global Talent Management and the Research that led to the empirical data. Our goal in this section is to offer the reader a complete picture of the development of the principle of GTM as "engagement". We also present the research setting where we address the above mentioned research question. Then we present the company in which the data collection was performed—Volvo 3P. Next we explain the method, data collection and data analysis procedures.

In Sect. 3, we focus on *jeitinho*. Our objective is to explain its origins, its positive and negative aspects, and to analyze several facets of this 'Brazilian cultural trait' and its implications for the culture adaptation and integration. In other words, we aim to explain, in a theoretical way, how the *jeitinho* can be useful for the integration of globally distributed teams. We consider how socialization occurs amongst individuals belonging to a geographically dispersed workplace, where interpersonal relationships are mediated by the computer, and where participants have not only multiple addresses but above all different nationalities, and therefore, different cultures, attitudes, thoughts, working patterns and language.

In Sect. 4, we focus on the *jeitinho* as a managerial talent. Our aim in this section is to explore and analyze the elements of this managerial talent that contribute towards the development of the manager flexibility, based on the case study conducted at Volvo 3P. Adopting the premise that "flexible organizations require senior managers who display both personal and strategic flexibility" (Iles et al. 1996), our interest was in investigating how *jeitinho* helps the integration of the GDT. Our empirical evidence shows that the malleability, flexibility and open mindedness to recognize and accept diversity play a role in the integration amongst team members.

Section 5 is the conclusive section, where we outline and synthesize our findings and managerial implications.

2   State of the Art and the Research

Our aim in this section is to explore the concepts about GTM and its historical development. We stress the principle of 'cultural embeddedness' and the importance of employee engagement. In the sequence we present our research and its methodological approach.

2.1   Global Talent Management

There seems to be no consensus concerning the exact meaning and definition of Global Talent Management (GTM). It varies depending on the context it appears in, and has even been used interchangeably with International Human Resource Management (Stahl et al. 2007). Tarique and Schuler (2010) define GTM as follows "global talent management is about systematically utilizing IHRM activities (complementary HRM policies and practices) to attract, develop, and retain individuals with high levels of human capital (e.g. competency, personality, motivation) consistent with the strategic directions of the multinational enterprise in a dynamic, highly competitive, and global environment" (p. 124).

The issue of GTM has become an important area for research for a number of reasons. Indeed, competition between employers has become more generic and has shifted from the country level to the regional and global levels (Ashton and Morton 2005). In various regions of the world, such as Europe and North America, companies are facing significant talent management challenges. However, the challenges are more significant for young professionals and new managers in the emerging markets such as the BRIC economies of Brazil, Russia, India and China (Farndale et al. 2010).

A recent study based on a multiyear collaborative research project on GTM practices and principles looked at 33 multinational corporations, headquartered in 11 countries, and examined 18 companies in-depth. The researchers found that competitive advantage in talent management does not just come from identifying key activities (for example, recruiting and training) and then implementing "best practices". Rather, they found that successful companies adhere to six key principles: (1) alignment with strategy, (2) internal consistency, (3) cultural embeddedness, (4) management involvement, (5) a balance of global and local needs and (6) employer branding through differentiation (Stahl et al. 2012).

Of these six principles, we chose to stress in particular the cultural embeddedness, which appeared especially pertinent in the context of our case study. This principle takes into account that, while companies have traditionally focused on job-related skills and experience to select people, some multinationals have expanded their selection criteria to include cultural fit. Such companies assess applicants' personalities and values to determine whether they will be compatible with the corporate culture. The assumption is that formal qualifications are not always the best predictors of performance and retention, and that skills are easier to develop than personality traits, attitudes and values (Pfeffer and Veiga 1999).

Indeed, as we will see in our case study, the Brazilian trait known as *jeitinho* is a cultural attitude, rather than a skill to be developed.

In addition, the criteria against which HR actions for GTM would be evaluated relate more specifically to the employees and the organization such as employee morale and engagement and organization productivity and innovation (Tarique and Schuler 2010). Articles on retaining talent have focused on two major IHRM policies: reducing repatriate turnover, and increasing employee engagement. Furthermore, studies have looked at universal practices to effectively promote engagement such as the need to be aware of country, regional and cultural differences when designing employee engagement and commitment initiatives (Lockwood 2007). These findings corroborate the importance of analyzing specific cultural aspects, such as the Brazilian *jeitinho*, which we explore in this chapter. In the following sub-section, we present our research and methodological approach.

2.2 The Research

To empirically analyze this phenomenon, we have chosen Volvo Group, as a multinational organisation where GDTs are used for the development of new products. Based upon the concept of cross-functional working groups, the teams allocated for the development of new products for Trucks Volvo (except Powertrain) are based at Business Unit Volvo 3P. Volvo 3P includes Volvo Trucks, Renault Trucks, Mack Trucks and Nissan Diesel Trucks; it is a cross-functional organization responsible for product development, purchasing, product planning and product range management.

In order to grasp Volvo's structure, projects' composition, and the context in which their trucks are developed; we have carried out 29 semi-structured interviews in Brazil at Volvo Powertrain, Volvo Trucks, Volvo 3P and Volvo do Brasil. The objects of this research upon which we base this chapter are the brands Volvo and Renault. Out of all brands of Volvo Group, these two brands have met the criteria set forth for this research. In these sense, we have constricted the participating sites to the units based in Curitiba (BR), Gothenburg (SW), Lyon (FR) and Bangalore (IN).

In our qualitative research, we chose the case study research methodology which aligns with the ideas proposed by Eisenhardt (1989) and Yin (2003). As far as data collection is concerned, some of the respondents have been identified as key informants, or highly knowledgeable informants who were actively involved in the implementation process and who could view the focal phenomena from diverse perspectives; combining retrospective and real-time cases (Eisenhardt 1989).

The instruments chosen for the data collection are the documental analysis, semi-structured interviews and observations, which have enabled data triangulation. We have chosen theory building from case study for the analysis of the data collected as it can be applied, according to Eisenhardt and Graebner (2007), to one or more cases to create theoretical constructs, propositions and/or midrange theory from case-based, empirically. The theory is emergent in the sense that it is situated in and developed by recognizing patterns of relationships among constructs within and across cases and their underlying logical arguments.

3 *Jeitinho*: A Brazilian Cultural Trait Embeddedness in GTM

In this section we explore the origins of the *jeitinho*, as well as its positive and negative aspects in the context of the Brazilian culture.

The *jeitinho* is a cultural trait that is considered unique to the Brazilian society. It is a social mechanism widely used in Brazilian society as a problem-solving strategy (Duarte 2006). This famous concept is widely used in the day-to-day of the Brazilians and in anthropological, sociological, psychological and philosophical analyses. It is rare to find someone in Brazil who does not know how to answer, when asked, what the *jeitinho* is. The Brazilian anthropologist Roberto DaMatta affirms that the *jeitinho* is "like an instrument which helps navigate the turbulent ocean of Brazilian everyday life, an everyday life marked by the hell of inconsistencies between the explicit laws.... and the social practices".[1] The anthropologist also translates it as a "clever dodge" (DaMatta 1991), meaning that the *jeitinho* would entail bending or breaking the rules in order to deal with difficult of forbidding situations that emerge in different social contexts (Duarte 2006). Ramos (1966) considers the *jeitinho* as a strategy that has emerged to deal with the excessive formalism of Brazilian society.

The *jeitinho* has been conceptualized and theorized in a number of ways. It can be seen in a positive or negative way. In the popular context, the *jeitinho* could be understood as a singular form of attaining objectives in a peculiar manner, without going through the pre-established norms, i.e., without respecting the laws, by cheating, tricking, lying with the intention of being able to attain some purpose. Many times, the *jeitinho* is seen in a negative way, as being harmful, as a lack of character. It can be confused with corruption and with favor. Nevertheless, Barbosa (1992) affirms that *jeito* is not the same as favor neither corruption, even though what differentiates them is a very tenuous line. In asking for a favor, there is reciprocity. In general people does others a favor expecting something in return. In contrast, the *jeitinho* does not need to be reciprocated.

Corruption is also distinguished from *jeitinho* through the "material advantage coming from the situation" (Barbosa 1992, pp. 34–35). The distinction between these two terms is confusing since, depending on the situation, *jeitinho* can be confused with corruption and vice-versa. The author affirms that if the amount of the material advantage is significant, the action is considered as corruption. If not, it will be characterized as *jeitinho*.

---

[1] Roberto DaMatta used this sentence in the preface of his doctoral student's book Livia Barbosa (1992), named "O jeitinho brasileiro—a arte de ser mais igual que os outros" (Faller Muniz 2009). Free translation of the authors of this chapter.

In general, when it is used in political and economic questions, *jeitinho* is seen as negative, as "a direct product of institutional distortions". However, when it is employed in social relations, it is seen in a more positive way, as capable of "promoting arrangements in regard of the imponderableness of life and humanizing the rules given the moral equality between men and the social inequalities"[2] (Barbosa 1992, p. 49).

The writer and educator Rega (2000) illustrates the two sides of the *jeitinho* "This is how the Brazilian is: 'arranges' everything (*dá um jeito*). Their versatility encompasses an uncountless number of situations: is the car's mudguard tied instead of fixed; it is the interest comprised in the amount of the fixed installments; it is giving some extra money on the side; it is to kill one's grandmother for the fifth time to justify an absence from an exam, in school. But *jeitinho* is also asking for a friend doctor to care for a lacking person or to make a surgery through the public system; it is the alternation between neighbors to help a sick person; it is to obtain a job for an unemployed father." [3]

Indeed, there is also a positive side of this cultural trait. It is used in response to an extraordinary, unforeseen situation, involving a conscious act of breaking rules; it provides a short-time solution to a problem; it is normally self-serving but can be also altruistic. The *jeitinho* requires certain techniques to foster *simpatia* (e.g. a smile and a gentle, pleading tone of voice). It can be used between strangers, but works more effectively between people who know each other; and it is perceived by Brazilians as an important element of their cultural identity (Duarte 2006).

Some authors conceptualize *jeitinho* as a "para-legal institution" which operates in Latin American societies as an "escape valve" to deal with social tensions (Campos 1966). Other authors analyze the *jeitinho* as a "peculiarly Brazilian way of being", which has emerged from specific historical conditions (Torres 1973).

Rosenn (1971) focuses on two main aspects to understand the omnipresence of *jeitinho* as a problem solving strategy in Brazilian society. He argues that this practice emerges as an answer to the unrestrained formalism and legalism of Brazilian society, inherited from the Portuguese colonizers. The author argues that, back in the seventeenth century, when Brazil was under the absolutist rule of the Portuguese empire, the power was centralized in the hands of the King of Portugal. This system was characterized by an authoritarian, paternalistic, particularistic political regime, which favored a complex, confusing and rigid legal system. In this sense, Brazilian people developed a way to survive in this scenario.

The second main aspect underlined by Rosenn (1971) to explain the omnipresence of *jeitinho* is the fact that this practice is closely related to the personalism of Brazilian society, i.e., the expectation of a "personalized, individualized attention, rather than being treated in a standardized way like everyone else" (Albert 1996). This personalism can be traced back to the relationships between masters and slaves on colonial times, when masters granted their subordinates personal favors and

---

[2] Free translation of the authors of this chapter.
[3] Free translation of the authors of this chapter.

privileges in exchange for their loyalty (Rosenn 1971). According to Barbosa (1992), as personal loyalty is reinforced in work organizations, informal networks flourish and norms of diffuse reciprocity spread among workers through *jeitinhos* routinely granted to each other.

In what concerns the unrestrained formalism, it seems to persist in Brazil of the twenty-first Century. Indeed, time-consuming protocols are still frequently required in bureaucratic settings in order to "get things done". Specific stamps are frequently required to 'authenticate' documents, and Brazilians stand hours in long queues at public bureaucracies, waiting for their turn. To deal with these constraints, as Amado and Brasil (1991: 55) argue, Brazilians "have had to develop a flexible, labile, plastic personality . . . a flexibility of body and spirit", implying that rule are often broken when they prevent people from "getting things done". We can note that, in research conducted about *jeitinho* specifically in the field of Organization Studies, this practice has been analyzed s an informal mechanism to counterbalance excessive bureaucratic rigidity.

Although there are similar social mechanisms in other cultures, such as the *trink-geld* in Germany, the *bustarela* in Italy, and the *speed money* in India (Cavalcanti 1991), we can affirm that the "social weight" attributed to the *jeitinho* in Brazilian society is very strong (Barbosa 1992). More cross-cultural research is needed to find out if the practices in other cultures are equivalent to the Brazilian *jeitinho*. Nevertheless, all Brazilians—from the poorest to the richest—recognize it, value it and use it to define a certain style of solving problems perceived as "essentially" Brazilian (Duarte 2006).

It is also important to note that there is an expectation that the *jeitinho* will always be granted, given the generosity, cordiality, warmth and empathy, highly valued attributes in Brazilian society. As Buarque de Hollanda (1995: 146) commented in his classical analysis of the Brazilian society:

[. . .The Brazilian contribution to the civilization will be cordiality – we will give to the world the 'cordial man'. Sincerity, hospitality and generosity, virtues so exalted by foreigners who visit us, represent in effect a defined trait of the Brazilian character.]

In our point of view, *jeitinho* is a "capacity", a way of facing adverse situations in order to achieve results which, if combined with ethical behavior, can be understood as a managerial talent.

4   *Jeitinho* as a Proven Managerial Talent

In this section we outline and synthesize our findings presenting a comparative analysis between theory and practice. We start with the presentation of a single case study—The VM (Volvo Midlum) project—as an example of the research set. This project illustrates the main competences identified.

First of all, the VM Project was chosen because of the fact that it was the most cited project among the interviewees. The uniqueness of the first Midlum developed by Volvo, following the acquisition of Renault and Mack in 2001, was the driving force in our choice to investigate this project. Although the VM truck was developed to attend primarily the Brazilian market, the core project was formed by team based in Curitiba (BR), Lyon (FR) and Gothenburg (SW). After 20 years producing heavy-duty trucks, Volvo unveiled its new line of medium trucks; the VM 17 and VM 23, available in 4×2 and 6×2 versions along with the new generation of electronic engine available in 210 and 240 hp with TEA technology (Truck Electronic Architecture). The VM was the first semi-heavy model carrying the brand Volvo outside European soil (Internal Report, 2008)***. Two and a half years were needed to complete the development process in Brazil, and the project also relied on support provided by French Renault and Volvo engineering in Sweden.

Some main characteristics such as interaction, adaptability and leading with diversity (recognizing and accepting differences) are presented and reinforce the assumption of *jeitinho* as a managerial talent. Below we present some findings which support our affirmations, putting them into perspective with the existing theory.

4.1   Interaction

Working in distributed teams, which means in a 'virtual environment', is a challenge for the teams in terms of cooperation. Taking the assumption that a team is a collection of individuals who are, on the one hand 'interdependent in their tasks' and, on the other hand, 'who share responsibility for outcomes' (Cohen and Bailey 1997), it is difficult to see how the members of GDT can see themselves and are seen by others as an intact social entity embedded in one or more larger social systems (for example, business units or the corporation). According to Brake (2006), there are reduced social and contextual clues, which mean uncertain or also missing norms and conventions for team members' interactions. As a leader, it is necessary to map out the most likely challenges the team could face. And, in the sequence, to take proactive measures to meet the challenges. This, in turn, increases team confidence.

In our empirical data, we noticed that VM, when compared to other projects, is considered the best example of interaction with the global organization. The Brazilian trait known as *jeitinho*, which includes seeing and dealing with the problems that appeared during the development of this product, was present all the time. The challenge of implementing ready-made solutions was to make them compatible with the Brazilian demands. For example, to be eligible to the Finame[4] credit line, the machinery or equipment to be acquired must have a high level of

---

[4] Finame is the Special Agency for Industrial Financing (Agência Especial de Financiamento Industrial). Its credit line is destined for companies located in any Brazilian region. BNDES (Banco Nacional do Desenvolvimento—Brazilian National Bank of Development) funds are used to finance the acquisition of new machinery and equipment, and working capital associated with the acquisition of equipment alone.

domestic content (at least 60 %). The compliance with this requirement was the first drive of the project. Based on this premise and on the fact that the Brazilian team was globally known for its ability in reducing costs, the VM was considered a "jigsaw" aggregating solutions that had already been developed elsewhere.

Following the acquisition Volvo-Renault Trucks (January 2001), R&D area in Sweden, started a debate on the strategic aspects of the merger, of what would converge and what would not. Meanwhile in Brazil, the team thought, as illustrated by one Brazilian Engineer: "Wait, Renault has a middle truck in France, we have a gap in the Brazilian market, why don't we make the integration between Sweden, Brazil, France and implement it?" As a result, by the end of 2003, the product— Volvo Medium (VM) was available in the Brazilian market. It was the first product from this merger, but not many people acknowledged it. It was also the first synergy effect of the new Volvo Group.

The idea of putting together the 'French know how' with the 'Brazilian market demand', plus the tradition of the 'Swedish brand', exemplifies a facet of the jeitinho of the Brazilian team. This fact is characterized not only by the idea of launching of a new product, but also by its implementation during in a post-merger period, i.e., in an environment of uncertainty, where egos, subtleties and indecisions had to be treated with "kid gloves". With the acquisition, much has been said about cultural aspects, profiles' differences, etc. But they also had processes and working tools. Both companies—Renault (France) and Volvo (Sweden and Brazil)—had different processes to develop new products; they used different terminologies and had different decision-making processes. Volvo had the CAD (Computer Aided Design) system and all electronic documents were generated in this format. However, Renault had a different system altogether. How could they conciliate data and processes on a single database? Volvo had a concept and Renault had a different one. In this line, to agreement all the decisions, it took them 3 to 4 years to understand each other. In the meantime, independent of the constraint environment, against all expectations, through the Brazilian way—jeitinho, by the end of 2003, Volvo do Brasil introduced in the Brazilian market the first medium truck by Volvo.

To exemplify the "interaction aspect", we highlight below two quotes that demonstrated this concern.

> [...] The global vision, plus sensing the opportunity was imperative in the behaviour of our team. (Engineer W, Brazil)

> [...] The cabin was a cabin from a new Renault, chassis and various other electronic and electrical components were already available [...] I see the VM rather as creative process of 'integration', of making use of the opportunities available, of reading the 'other's' language – if it makes sense. (Middle manager, Brazil)

4.2 Adaptability

Another facet of the jeitinho can be identified as the ability to be malleable in the acceptation of different opinions, always trying to reach a consensus considering all the variables. In overall view of the literature dedicated to GDT, the concept of virtual implies permeable interfaces and boundaries; project teams that rapidly form, reorganize, and dissolve when the needs of a dynamic marketplace change; and individuals with differing competencies who are located across time, space, and cultures (Maznevski and Chudoba 2000). Based on this, GDT can be understood as groups of people who interact through interdependent tasks guided by a common purpose, and in consequence need to have great 'adaptability' and 'malleability' in its essence. These aspects are illustrated in the following extract of VM project:

> We wanted this product so we needed to make the language conversion. So we did the conversion in a database, and then integration followed suit, without any bureaucracy of a global movement. Very quickly the Brazilian team was integrated and dominating the local system in Lyon. We got there, we read it and we understood it. We spoke their French and used it in all methods and processes; this shows our agility and flexibility. So those people... they come and say... wow, it is a benchmarking, a reference of adaptability in a global structure, and then they see the opportunities. (Top Manager P, Brazil)

The projects developed by Volvo 3P are very often focused on incremental changes rather than on radical changes, even when referring to Volvo Sweden. One must bear in mind and take into consideration the interpretation of the terminology 'radical'. In the words of Cabin Coordinator in Brazil, the VM was a radical project because it delved into a new segment. Yet it could also be seen as non-radical because the Brazilian market already had medium-size trucks on offer:

> One of our Brands (Renault) already had a medium-size truck... so it really depends on the rigour given to the terminology. (Coordinator, Brazil)

From Volvo's perspective, the project could be seen as radical, as it was Volvo's first product with advanced cabin features and with an engine that wasn't produced by Volvo. For Volvo Powertrain's Manager in Brazil, the VM represented an incremental innovation. Although both market and segment already existed, he believes they managed to spot a gap in the market:

> [...] In terms of Volvo, it was an incremental innovation. The cabin was a cabin from a new Renault, chassis and various other electronic and electrical components were already available, so you can say it was an incremental innovation I see the VM rather as creative process of 'integration', of making use of the opportunities available, of reading the 'other's' language – if it makes sense. Like, I will not sit here and wait till Lyon understands how Volvo Systems works, because it is ours, it is our language, and I'll do my best to understand them, grab what interests me and do whatever I have to do! I think it was phenomenal, absolutely extraordinary! (Powertrain's manager, Brazil)

4.3 Leading with Diversity: Recognizing and Accepting Differences

Globalization is responsible for a paradoxical movement of cultures. On the one hand, emergent global cultures transcend national boundaries and cultures. On the other hand, the synchronizing power of the Internet and wireless digital technologies provide local companies and indigenous cultural values with unprecedented global exposure (Bird and Fang 2009). In today's world, managers increasingly manage diverse groups and the variety of cultures may be complex to handle. A culture gives group members guidance as to how to think and feel, how to act, and how to evaluate the actions of others: it is an orientation system for the behavior in the group. A culture also gives to its members a feeling of belonging and identity. It is the glue that holds the group together (Comfort and Franklin 2008). Globalization is reshaping our modes of thinking and ways of behaving and fostering cultural change in societies. While some scholars (Harrison and Huntington 2000) may argue over a 'clash of cultures', it seems just as relevant to focus on the ways in which cultures may learn from each other, even inspire each other where the beauty of cultural differences and cultural collisions is applauded (Soderberg and Holden 2002).

For GDT whose members hail from different parts of the world, cultural diversity has been singled out as perhaps the greatest obstacle faced by members, a much greater hurdle than communication failures caused by the lack of visual and auditory cues. However, some behavioural aspects have been taken into account to underpin the affirmation that cultural differences could contribute towards the performance: humbleness to recognise and accept that one's working processes may not be the best; predisposition (intrinsic motivation) to work in a cross-cultural environment; awareness of cultural differences to ease the socialisation; and, equalisation of management practices to minimise impacts.

According to its policies, Volvo Group takes diversity as an essential element to create an inclusive work environment where individuals are respected and motivated. Diversity is at the top of Volvo's agenda and its role in the organisation's culture and structure is as crucial as their quest for innovation, market leadership and profitability. Some of the Group's strategies seek to include in its workforce people from all walks of life, regardless of their age, gender, education, ethnicity, race, national origin, sexual orientation, and to welcoming individuals with impairment. We identified some cultural differences between the members of the team, according their countries. Specifically, the *Brazilian team* is known for its whole-view approach, which is crucial for multifunctional teams.

According to the Brazilian and French interviews, traditionally, the Swedish do not have great concerns with costs; they focus on quality to meet European standards. For the Brazilian team, for cultural reasons, the focus is on quality but with costs in mind. The French are recognised for questioning and for debating. It is part of their culture to put their opinion forward; they seem to hardly ever accept things differently. As a Brazilian manager stated:

> If we are told to do something, we do it. No, not with them… they have to question everything, debate everything… it takes ages, and very often we get embroiled in heated

discussions. However, the Swedish, they do not like confrontation whilst for the French confrontation is fundamental. (Manager, Brazil)

We expose below some cultural differences found by the teams:

[...]Sometimes the focus isn't the same, the Swedish have a more holistic view, let's say, really global, they are concerned with what's going on here in Brazil; then you have the French, who aren't that focused on the client, at least in my opinion they aren't. They think the engine is the most important part; everything else is built around it. I don't think so; I need an engine to fit a vehicle and not a vehicle to fit an engine. (Engineer X, Brazil)

[...] The French love a debate, especially a heated one... sometimes they cross the line (chuckles)... they easily do it if they get passionate. [...] they think you win an argument by raising your voice and talking fast. They don't let anyone speak. [...] It's a nuisance for the project. (Team member,Brazil)

To summarise, diversity impacts team outcomes in multiple ways. Taking into account the multiple geographic units that Volvo holds worldwide, regardless of the differences, diversity is perceived as positive to integration and a fruitful source of knowledge from which its workforce can learn with and from. To complete this analysis, we highlight below *jeitinho* as an example of conflict administration:

The Swedish team is recognized, inside of the Volvo Group, for its holistic approach, in depth experience, knowledge, conservatism, and precision in planning. Planning is considered one of the strength of the Swedish team. According to a Swedish Engineer, "In Sweden everything is planed and everything happens according to plans." This same characteristic is interpretate for the French workers in a different perspective:

[...] The Swedish team works on consensus. Everybody should agree to something first...it's more like a collaborative and accountable approach. They want to have more discussions to make sure that we arrive at a conclusion, personally I am quite direct and sometimes I say what I feel quite directly, and it's... I would say it shocks people from Sweden, they are more distant, more shy in the way they bring the solution. (French team member)

[...] The Swedish people are people who don't want to change anything. Remember, we have this PDCA, means "Plan Do Check Act" and the French translate it as "Please Don't Change Anything." (Manager A, France)

The opinions shared on the French team reveal divergences in the way they are perceived by others. Whilst they are seen as dynamic, working with the French team is regarded as a 'challenge', a tiresome process filled with endless debates, a burden caused by cultural differences. Most interviewees have addressed the differences in their organizational practices and business view. Despite this shared impression of the French, they are admired for their eagerness in defending their point of view.

In view of these, we have verified the existence of conflicts arising from cultural differences and organizational divergences. With the merge of Volvo/Renault, although the company's principles have been thoroughly accepted and shared by all, there are evidences that the old French organizational culture is still lingering; this is made noticeable when costs are discussed, or attention is drawn upon the need of a hierarchy chain of command or centralization, which as expected triggers conflict with counterparts of other countries, especially with the Swedish team who is used to dealing with diversity.

> [...] Their top managements are very strong in France, Lyon. The designers can't make their own decisions there. They have to go to their manager as well. So the manager takes a lot of the decisions. And here at Volvo, we are an organization, so we are putting a lot of the decisions to the designers and so on. (Manager Z, Sweden).

> [...] French people, to me they are a little bit more... you don't always know where you are, I should say. You don't really know if you share the same views and then if we have the same actions and so on... (Engineer A, Sweden).

> [...] Sure we have conflict, the French guys are French people. They are quite, their philosophy that is a little bit different. German people I know that if they say something, they say and it will be there in the time. Some boring and also control freaks. But the French people, they take life a little bit more easy. (Manager T, Sweden).

Owing to the flexibility, malleability, in other words, the Brazilian *jeitinho*, all the teams (Swedish, Indian and French) have drawn attention to this 'cultural affinity' with the Brazilian team. For the French participants, working with the Brazilian team is an undemanding process due to the affinity between these two cultures and the similarity in the working characteristics and approach. They perceive Brazilians as straight forward which in their opinion benefits communication between these two teams:

> [...] My feeling is that in Brazil they are very close to European culture. It's not so difficult for me to work with Brazil. I think we have a similar way of working. (Manager A, France).

> [...] I have been in Brazil once, and it's very different the way people are talking to you, they can even touch you just to make sure that you are listening to them; it's much more direct. I would say, that's my feeling, I think that even just speaking on the phone, I think they can be direct and say 'no', and not say 'maybe' not even if you already think that it's a 'no'. (Engineer B, France).

> [...] I think the Brazilian team is really good, easy to communicate with, really clear on what they are saying. So that has been very easy. (Engineer V, Sweden).

> [...] To work with Brazil is similar to how we work in India. Decisions can be quick and implementation is quick, fast, and the approach Brazil and in India I feel like it's mostly similar (Manager Q, India).

For all practical purposes, when considering the impact of cultural differences in GDT we have ascertained that such differences improve the performance of the team. However, far from being an effortless process, it requires team members to identify and work on their differences; interpreting, understanding and assimilating them. In this context, we noticed the importance of *jeitinho* to manage the talents inside of the team. When disassociating working relations from interpersonal relationships, we verified that the working relations are identified with two axiomatic characteristics of individuals working in this type of environment: they have to be open-minded to aggregate knowledge, and they have to be humble to accept and recognize the best options. On the other hand, in terms of relationships, team members need to be aware of and be prone to learn the basic socialization norms of the other nationalities involved in the project; thus avoiding biased judgments and minimizing stereotypes. In sum we can affirm that that *jeitinho* is the glue that permits to integrate the cultural diversity in GDT.

Conclusion and Managerial Implications

In accordance to what has been exposed, we can conclude that the Brazilian cultural trait defined here as *jeitinho* acts as a "catalytic agent" within the teams. It is through the *jeitinho* that the Brazilians translate and mediate the expectations of the different cultures of the team members. This occurs because of the detachment of the Brazilians 'to understand without issuing judgment', and to accept and be accepted in the team without restrictions. The flexibility in response to the adverse situations, and the malleability in dealing with conflicting situations make this 'talent management' a driving force of integration among team members.

Through the empirical analysis of the Volvo case study, we could identify and demonstrate situations where the *jeitinho* presents itself as a talent management which facilitates the integration of different cultures within the team. In this line, we support the affirmation of DaMatta (2001), who argued that "In Brazil, in between the "possible" and the "impossible", we find a way (*jeito*). In its classical form, the *jeitinho* demands precisely this: a way that manages to conciliate all the different interests (. . .) the *jeitinho* is such a way and a style of acting, the art of surviving in the most difficult situations".

In what concerns managerial implications, we believe that this cultural characteristic should be better understood and disseminated in order to develop an open posture in interpersonal relations, in particular regarding the effective acceptation of the other for what "he/she is" and not for what I prefer or I want him/her to be.

Table 1 summarizes five tips on understanding Global Talent Management challenges, five tips regarding strategies to overcome these challenges, and five tips on perceiving future opportunities in Global Talent Management, based on the ideas presented in this chapter.

Table 1 Five key GTM challenges, strategies, and future opportunities

Five key points regarding Global Talent Management challenges	Five key points regarding strategies to overcome these challenges	Five key points regarding future opportunities in Global Talent Management
1 To manage globally distributed teams	Managers have to understand the differences between management teams face-to-face and GDT, and their implications for the project	To develop HR equity practices compatible with the countries integrators of GDT
2 To manage different cultures working in the same project	To recognize and accept the different ways of doing things	To use these differences to improve performance and integration
3 To identify the global types of talents responsible of integrating the teams	To create the managerial tools that make the exchange of these talents possible to the managers	To retain these talents in the company
4 To use *jeitinho* as a connective tissue between workers and a way to resist bureaucratic rules	To create mechanisms which allow *jeitinho* to be used by workers, promoting its positive aspects	To use *jeitinho* as a mechanism of resistance to the power of certain regimes that put in place dehumanizing work practices
5 To use the *jeitinho* as a managerial tool	To embrace the concepts of flexibility and malleability as tools to improve the integration of the teams	To export the concept of *jeitinho* to other cultures, focusing on its positive side

References

Albert, R. (1996). American and Latino/hispanic cultural patterns. In D. Landis & R. Bhagat (Eds.), *Handbook of intercultural training* (pp. 327–348). London: Sage.

Amado, G., & Vinagre Brasil, H. (1991). Organizational behaviors and cultural context: The brazilian "jeitinho". *International Studies of Management and Organization*, 38–61.

Ashton, C., & Morton, L. (2005). Managing talent for competitive advantage. *Strategic HR Review, 4*(5), 28–31.

Baba, M. L., Gluesing, J., Ratner, H., & Wagner, K. H. (2004). The contexts of knowing: Natural history of a globally distributed team. *Journal of Organization Behavior, 25*, 547–587.

Barbosa, L. (1992). *O jeitinho brasileiro – a arte de ser mais igual que nos outros, 2ª edição*. Rio de Janeiro: Editora Campos.

Bird, A., & Fang, T. (2009). Editorial: Cross cultural management in the age of globalization. *International Journal of Cross Cultural Management, 9*(2), 139–143.

Brake, T. (2006). Leading global virtual teams. *Industrial and commercial training, 38*, 116–121.

Campos, R. O. (1966). 'A Sociologia do Jeito', In *A Técnica e o Riso* (pp. 10–22). Rio de Janeiro: Edições Apec.

Cavalcanti, P. (1991). *A Corrupção no Brasil*. São Paulo: Siciliano.

Cohen, S. G., & Bailey, D. E. (1997). What makes teams work: Group effectiveness research from the shop floor to the executive suite. *Journal of Management, 23*(3), 239–290.

Comfort, J., & Franklin, P. (2008). *The mindful international manager – How to work effectively across cultures*. London: Kogan Page Limited.

DaMatta, R. (1991). *Carnivals, rogues and heroes: Towards a sociology of the Brazilian Dilemma.* Notre Dame: University of Notre Dame Press.

DaMatta, R. (2001). *O que faz o brasil, Brasil?* Rio de Janeiro: Rocco.

Buarque de Hollanda, S. (1995 [1936]) *Raízes do Brasil.* São Paulo: Companhia das Letras.

Downie, A. (2008). Wanted: Skilled workers for a growing economy in Brazil. *The New York Times, July, 2,* 2008.

Duarte, F. (2006). Exploring the Interpersonal Transaction of the Brazilian Jeitinho in Bureaucratic contexts. *Organization, 13*(4), 508–527.

Eisenhardt, K. M. (1989). Building theories from case study research. *Academy of Management Review, 14*(4), 532–550.

Eisenhardt, K. M., & Graebner, M. E. (2007). Theory building from cases: Opportunities and challenges. *The Academy of Management Journal, 50*(1), 25–32.

Faller Muniz, L. C. (2009). *A Configuração do Jeitinho Brasileiro em Narrativas Literárias.* Dissertação de mestrado, UNISC

Farndale, E., Scullion, H., & Sparrow, P. (2010). The role of the corporate HR function in global talent management. *Journal of World Business, 45,* 161–168.

Harrison, L. E., & Huntington, S. P. (2000). *Culture matters: How values shape human progress.* New York, USA: Basic Books.

Iles, P., Forster, A., & Tinline, G. (1996). The changing relationship between work commitment, personal flexibility and employability: An evaluation of a field experiment in executive development. *Journal of Managerial Psychology, 11*(8), 19–34.

Jackson, S. E., Joshi, A., & Erhardt, N. L. (2003). Recent research on teams and organizational diversity: SWOT analysis and implications. *Journal of Management, 29*(6), 801–830.

Katzenbach, J. R., & Smith, D. K. (1993). The discipline of teams. *Harvard Business Review, 71,* 111–146.

Lewis, R. E., & Heckman, R. J. (2006). Talent management: A critical review. *Human Resource Management Review, 16,* 139–154.

Lockwood, N. (2007). Leveraging employee engagement for competitive advantage: HR's strategic role. *Society for Human Resource Management.* Retrieved April 23, 2013, from http://www.shrm.org.

Lodorfos, G., & Boateng, A. (2006). The role of culture in the Merger and acquisition process: Evidence from the European chemical industry. *Management Decision Journal, 44*(10), 1405–1421.

Mattioli, D. (2011). Brazil's Boom needs talent. *The Wall Street Journal.* Accessed November 2, 2013, from http://online.wsj.com/news/articles/SB10001424052702304231204576403910374743694

Maznevski, M. L., & Chudoba, K. M. (2000). Bridging space over time: Global virtual team dynamics and effectiveness. *Organization Science, 11*(5), 473–492.

Pfeffer, J., & Veiga, J. F. (1999). Putting people first for organizational success. *Academy of Management Executive, 13,* 37–49.

Piccoli, G., Powell, A., & Ives, B. (2004). Virtual teams: team control structure, work processes, and team effectiveness. *Information Technology and People, 17*(4), 359–379.

Prasad, K., & Akhilesh, K. B. (2002). Global virtual teams: What impacts their design and performance? *Team Performance Management: An International Journal, 8*(5/6), 102–112.

Pucik, V., Björkman, I., Evans, P., & Stahl, G. (2011). Human resource management in cross-border mergers and acquisitions. In A. Harzing & A. Pinnington (Eds.), *International human resource management* (3rd ed.). Thousand Oaks, CA: Sage Publications.

Ramos, G. (1966). *Administração e Estratégia do Desenvolvimento: Elementos de uma Sociologia Especial da Administração.* Rio de Janeiro: Fundação Getúlio Vargas.

Ready, D. A., & Conger, J. A. (2007). Making your company a talent factory. *Harvard Business Review, 85*(6), 68–77.

Rega, L. S. (2000). *Dando um jeito no jeitinho: Como ser ético sem deixar de ser brasileiro.* São Paulo: Mundo Cristão.

Rosenn, K. S. (1971). The Jeito: Brazil's institutional by-pass of the formal legal system and its development implications. *The American Journal of Comparative Law, 19*, 516–49.

Senge, P. M., Kleiner, A., & Roberts, C. (1994). *The fifth discipline fieldbook: Strategies and tools for building a learning organization.* New York, NY: Broadway Business Publisher.

Soderberg, A. M., & Holden, N. (2002). Rethinking cross cultural management in a globalizing business world. *International Journal of Cross Cultural Management, 2*(1), 103–121.

Stahl, G. K., Bjorkman, I., Farndale, E., Morris, S. S., Paauwe, J., Stiles, P., Trevor, J., & Wright, P. M. (2007). Global talent management: How leading multinationals build and sustain their talent pipeline (INSEAD Working Paper Series, 34/OB).

Stahl, G. K., Björkman, I., Farndale, E., Morris, S. S., Paawe, J., Stiles, P., et al. (2012). Six principles of effective global talent management. *MIT Sloan Management Review, 53*(2), 24–33.

Tarique, I., & Schuler, R. S. (2010). Global talent management: Literature review, integrative framework, and suggestions for further research. *Journal of World Business, 45*, 122–133.

Torres, J. C. O. (1973). *Interpretação da Realidade Brasileira.* Rio de Janeiro: José Olimpio Editora.

Yin, R. K. (2003). *Case study research: Design and methods* (3rd ed.). Thousand Oaks, CA: Sage.

Talent Management in China

Tony Fang

1 Introduction

The rise of the Chinese economy has arguably been the most important story in the world economy this past generation. Its rapid rate of growth (about 10 % a year for the last 30 years) brings with it not only a higher standard of living but also challenges around managing employees. The exposure of government-run business operations to world markets and the expansion of private enterprise have led to important changes in operations, especially in how employees are managed, and to the development of what may eventually be a distinctive approach to employee management. At present, the field of human resources in China is both extremely important and at the same time under-developed. The demand for better human resource outcomes is creating considerable interest in human resources among new managers, and the rise of this new generation will likely increase the pace at which practices change.

The chapter begins with the historical evolution of human resource management (HRM) and talent management (TM) since China initiated economic reform and open-door policies in the late 1970s. Although HR remains a support function for most companies (especially the state-owned enterprises or SOEs) in China, the TM landscape is quickly changing. Strategic considerations have been incorporated in the HRM and TM practices, especially among the multinational corporations (MNCs) and even among some of the large SOEs. At the national level, TM has been viewed as a critical component in the transitions from low-cost manufacturing to an innovation-based economy. At the global scale, China has joined the

T. Fang (✉)
Faculty of Business and Economics, Monash University, Caulfield, Melbourne, VIC 3415, Australia

Centre for Industrial Relations and Human Resources, University of Toronto, Toronto, ON, Canada

Sir John Monash Drive, Caulfield, VIC 3145, Australia
e-mail: Tony.Fang@Monash.Edu

A. Al Ariss (ed.), *Global Talent Management*, Management for Professionals, 141
DOI 10.1007/978-3-319-05125-3_10, © Springer International Publishing Switzerland 2014

Table 1 Five Key Global Talent Management (GTM) challenges, strategies, and future opportunities

Five key points regarding GTM challenges	Five key points regarding strategies to overcome these GTM challenges	Five key points regarding future opportunities in GTM
1 Talent management in a transitional economy The old way: Hold a static view about supply and demand for the labour market based on the assumption of an infinite supply of labour in China and rely too much on the external labour market for talent	Be adaptable to the dynamic nature of the Chinese labour market, grow talent internally, and ensure smooth transitions in areas affected by talent shortages	Hold a long-term view of talent management, develop a succession plan for your company, invest some real money in people, and commit to a process or structure of internal management and talent development
2 Global talent mobility and management The old way: Go to a few traditional sources of talents and advertise to job hunters, view recruiting simply as a screening process, specify a compensation level and stick with it	Tap many diverse pools of talent including passive candidates, consider recruiting both as selling and screening, break the compensation rules when necessary to get the talent you want	Anticipate supply and demand of skilled talents in the global labour market, critically assess the make or buy decisions
3 Strategic considerations of talent management The old way: Hire workers as needed with no overall plans. HRM mainly serves the administrative functions such as hiring and pay/benefit administration	Embrace a talent mindset, develop a recruiting strategy for each type of talent, get involved in key people decisions, and be accountable for talent management	Remember that the talent management function is already strategic in many MNCs and even some SOEs, but that in most Chinese companies, HRM remains a support function; change the mindset and instil a talent-focused mindset, and get involved in the important decision-making process
4 The influence of Chinese culture on talent management practices The old way: Hold onto a traditional view of cultures and values, believe Western HRM practices can be applied to the Chinese contexts	Develop a deep understanding of Chinese culture and its implications for the talent management practices in China, provide relevant cross-cultural management training to both HR managers and line managers	Establish a government relation manager, hire a local consultant to deal with some sensitive talent management issues such as household registration system, social security for foreign workers, taxation issues, etc.
5 Talent management as a national development strategy and diaspora option The old way: Face potential free-riding problems, focus on headcounts rather than talent quality, adaptation, and retention, fail to coordinate and critically evaluate both national and regional talent programs	Focus on adjustment and retention of global talents, critically assess and utilize government-initiated and supported talent attraction and management programs	Evaluate short- and long-term effects of talent management and development programs as part of China's national development agenda achieved by assembling national resources

international war for talent and has introduced a number of ambitious talent attraction and development plans to bring home highly skilled and Western-trained talents, while at the same time accepting Chinese diaspora as a viable option for overseas depository and reservoirs for future talents (Zweig 2006). This chapter uses a number of TM and other theoretical frameworks to explain the current state and transitions of TM practices in China, highlights the unique challenges Chinese managers and foreign entrepreneurs are facing, and points out future opportunities in global talent management (GTM) in China and beyond (Table 1).

1.1   The State of HRM and Talent Management in China

According to a renowned Wharton professor of human resource management, Peter Cappelli, talent management is simply a matter of anticipating the need for human capital and then setting out a plan to meet it (Cappelli 2008). Talent management also reflects an organization's commitment to recruit, retain, and develop the most talented employees available in the labour market. It comprises all of the work processes and systems that are related to retaining and developing a superior workforce. The field dramatically gained popularity after McKinsey's research and subsequent book *The War for Talent*, which highlights the looming demographic changes, skill shortages, and extant employment strategies of firms that cannot adapt to the challenges (Michaels et al. 2001). Both Cappelli (2003) and Critchley (2004) acknowledge the changing demographics but criticize the fundamental flaws of McKinsey in firms' inability to adapt to the above-mentioned challenges, and they argue for the need for more creative HR practices to attract and retain talented employees.

A review of strategic HRM literature suggests two theoretical frameworks are significant (Holland et al. 2012). The first is the human capital theory, which links organizations' human assets to increased productivity and sustainable competitive advantages (Smit 1998). The strategic aspect of the theory ascertains that the long-term enhancement of human assets can be achieved through employee skill development, career progression, and employee retention. This is consistent with the second theoretical argument, the resource-based view of the firm (RBV), that the retention and development of human resources will ensure that these human assets that are valuable, rare, and difficult to imitate, and will become the firm's long-term competitive advantages (Barney 1991; Walton 1999; Garavan et al. 2001). Broadly speaking, talent management includes workforce planning, talent-gap analysis, recruitment and selection, training and development, talent review, talent retention, succession planning, and evaluation. Organizations must align these processes and practices with their business strategies in order to drive up performance, cope with rapid change, and create sustainable success.

In sharp contrast with the upcoming skill shortages and war for talent in the advanced economies, the big story behind the growth of the Chinese economy has been the low cost and abundant supply of labour for factory jobs. That abundant supply of labour has created workplace discipline ("do what we say or we will replace you with someone who will") and has kept wages low and performance high. To maintain that supply of labour, the east-coast factories looked west and imported labour from rural western regions, housing them in dormitories. According to Kuruvilla et al. (2011), the average employment arrangement in China is still characterized by highly precarious employment with low job security, relatively low wages, and no benefits. About 40 % of the workforce operates with these arrangements.

Given this simple model, it is not surprising that most of the HR functions in China have been administrative in nature. That is, they mainly processed paper: bringing new hires into the system and administering payroll. Supervision, the design and organization of work, and virtually everything else about the workplace was handled by line managers, who were subject more to government policies than to any company policies. Any HR policies were highly standardized, slow to change, and governed by bureaucratic principles. Especially in the SOEs, which are by far the largest employers in China, HR practices lack sophistication. Workplace problems such as skill shortages, turnover, and workplace conflicts were more likely to be tolerated than addressed systematically, and the ability to tailor solutions to the unique aspects of those problems was limited.

Many of the constraints that continue to cause problems in the Chinese workplace are legacies from earlier communist practices when everyone worked for the government, when operations were not subject to competitive pressures, and when the need for change was limited. In that context, firms did not layoff employees, and it was extremely difficult to fire them. Efficiency was rarely a concern, so improving performance was not a concern, either. Practices effectively treated everyone as equals, and when there was differentiation, as when senior positions had to be filled, the criterion for doing so was political rather than performance-related. These constraints exist now mainly in the SOEs, and they are slowly eroding as fewer individuals remember the old systems.

1.2   HR: Support Function

The overall perception of HR has been as a supporting function: something that is necessary for business success but that does not contribute directly to competitive advantage. There is no well- developed national HR professional association in China, which means a lack of central influence on the HR direction or sharing of best HR practices (Cooke 2009), and there is little evidence that HR leaders have knowledge of overall business operations outside their area.

The most comprehensive study of the current status of Chinese HRM practices and their relationships with firm performance in China was conducted by Akhtar et al. (2008). To investigate strategic HR practices and their impact on firm performance, a large-scale survey was conducted in three major cities: Guangzhou (36.1 % of the sample), Shanghai (26.2 %), and Nanjing (37.6 %). The survey was based on the sampling frame of the China Industrial Enterprises Database, collected by the National Bureau of Statistics of China, to cover both manufacturing and service sectors. Among a sample of 400 Chinese firms, 29.2 % were state-owned, 10.1 % were publicly listed, and 60.6 % were foreign-invested. General managers or their deputies responded to the firm performance questionnaires, and HR directors responded to the strategic HR practices. Data were collected from multiple sources to match the responses so as to reduce the simultaneous bias in survey responses. Responses were obtained on a 4-point scale (1 = not at all accurate to 4 = very accurate) for the dimensions of the strategic HRM practices, and on a 5-point scale (1 = very low to 5 = very high) for the dimensions of firm performance. The responses suggest what practitioners believe is the relationship between specific practices and overall business performance. It is probably best to think of these results as indicating management perceptions rather than actual relationships, but they are nevertheless interesting. The authors asked about the presence of a number of HR practices, then factor-analysed them using principal component factor analysis followed by varimax rotation (Delery and Doty 1996), which resulted in seven instruments (training, participation/voice for employees, employment security, job description, results-oriented performance appraisal, internal career opportunities, and profit sharing).

Given that caveat, job descriptions and results-oriented performance appraisals are seen as most prevalent (mean scores of 2.80 and 2.70, respectively) followed by having better internal career opportunities (2.64), participation/voice for employees (2.59), and training (2.57). Profit sharing and employment security were seen as only weakly related to performance (1.69 and 2.41, respectively) and were not related to other HR practices. In terms of relationships with financial and product/service performance, firms with more of these practices (with the exception of profit sharing) also performed better. Given the limited nature of the cross-sectional data, it is difficult to say whether the HR practices caused these outcomes or were merely associated with them, but the results are intriguing.

1.3   The Changing Reality

The emerging story, and the one breathing new interest into human resources, begins with the exhaustion of the supply of cheap labour. Labour costs have risen from roughly US$ 0.5 per hour in 2000 to US$ 3.5 per hour in 2010, reflecting the tighter labour market for unskilled labour. Accounts from some of those factories suggest that wages for operators have risen 50 % from 2010 to 2012. Turnover has become a real problem in these factories as the tables have turned: Workers now hop from employer to employer, chasing higher wages and "switching bonuses." Shortages in key skills have emerged in the large and coastal cities like Beijing, Shanghai, Guangzhou, and Shenzhen. Anecdotal accounts suggest that wage levels for managers and executives are already at European levels and in some areas are climbing to US levels. The biggest skill gaps relate to managerial skills, especially as companies grow, become more complex, and move into new products and markets.

Further, labour problems and the increase of strikes and other labour disputes raise employee relations challenges that higher wages alone are unlikely to address. The Chinese government has increased minimum wages in several of the key manufacturing provinces by as much as 30 %. Although Chinese unions so far have little bargaining power with employers, they have been effective at lobbying governments to pass new contract and employment standards laws, which reduce working hours and improve working conditions.

2 Strategic Considerations and Talent Management

An immediate result of these developments has been that many employers complain about the rigidity and high costs of the new standards and have made greater use of staffing firms to provide workers and non-standard employment contracts (part-time, contract, temporary, etc.) to avoid the legislative requirements. The consequence is that employment issues have become a much bigger challenge for businesses and a more important factor in shaping their competitiveness.

Many Chinese corporations have become competitive globally, largely benefiting from the "cost innovation" strategy, which centres around leveraging low cost and innovation by offering more technology, performance, and value with less money (Zeng and Williamson 2003, 2007, 2011). They take advantage of the niche areas of the global product market including the low end, the periphery, the eccentric demands, and unique niches. For example, "national champions" are the domestic leaders who build global brands by identifying segments that global market leaders have dismissed because of low volumes or thin profit margins (examples are Haier, Huawei, Chonghong, and Wanxiang).

"Dedicated exporters" set their sights on global markets by leveraging their economies of scale (e.g., BYD, CIMC, Galanz). "Technology upstarts" capitalize on the large government-built infrastructure and on the research and development (R&D) conducted by state-owned laboratories to obtain funding by commercializing the technologies (e.g., Beijing Yuande, Datang Microelectronics, Tsinghua Solar). However, the major weaknesses of the Chinese corporations are weak and intangible initial brands, difficulties early in the product life cycle, and dependence on the Chinese domestic market base; and the major vulnerability is their inability to manage the complex systems of R&D, global supply chains, manufacturing, logistics, marketing, and distribution.

2.1 Managerial Talent: Now an Immediate Priority

At the executive level, the growing complexity of business has made managerial talent an immediate priority. CEOs reviewing their operations understand that every important business development creates the need for new organizational competencies (e.g., how do we do market research, how do we do business in another country?) that in turn create the need for new management skills. Hiring those skills and creating a process where they might eventually be grown from within is now a pressing CEO-level concern, especially in the private sector companies as they are the most innovative.

Along with the emerging labour and skill shortages in the southern and coastal areas of China, hiring and training are increasingly considered to be the strategic functions driving business outcomes. The companies also have increased their R&D investments dramatically to facilitate the transition from labour-intensive manufacturing to knowledge economy focusing on innovation, for which talent is the key. Chinese unions are also found to contribute positively to both innovation inputs and outputs (Fang and Ge 2012).

3   Talent Management as a National Development Strategy

Almost unnoticed, China's shift to a high-tech economy has occurred by cajoling and co-opting Western businesses. China's trade is approaching a tipping point, while China's innovation has not yet reached the tipping point.

The importance of China's new human capital strategy is not limited to the crucial role it plays in evolving to an innovation-driven stage of global competition. Its importance also lies in leading the transformation trends that are in high demand in China, including the transformation from demographic dividend to talent dividend; from "made in China" to "created in China"; from attracting investment to attracting intellectuals; from hardware development to software development; from investment-driven economy to talent-driven economy; from resource-intensive growth to knowledge-intensive growth; from solo economical/technology-focused-innovation development pattern to dual economical/technology-and-social-creativity development pattern; from relying on nationally educated talent to giving attention to both nationally educated and internationally trained talent. To be able to achieve these transformations, high quality human capital is the key.

The international war for talent has intensified in the last decade with both developed and developing countries joining in the game. Five years ago, China announced its desire to make the country an innovation-oriented society—but the Tech War had begun much earlier, so China has much ground to make up.

Market forces have created tremendous economic opportunities which are the single most important factor in attracting talented people back to China. Low salaries and difficulties in maintaining overseas contacts have discouraged returnees to China, but these issues have lessened in recent years. Favourable government policies such as Thousand People Plans and Cheung Kong Scholars may not significantly increase the quantity of returnees, but they may help to increase the quality, as predicted by migration theory (Borjas and Bratsberg 1996).

Surveys also reveal that favourable government policies play an important role (Al Ariss and Crowley 2013). There is consensus that government policy could do more to turn the tide of emigration: develop the economy; improve policies that support intellectuals, including more vigorous protection of intellectual property, as suggested by innovation theory; expand democracy; fully utilize people who have already returned; and invest more in science and technology. Interpersonal relations at work also remain a major concern. This problem is more cultural than institutional, and therefore somewhat beyond the reach of the government to address. For the system to work better within the ever-changing global and national environment, future work needs to critically evaluate the real impact of government policies on talent attraction, development, and retention.

3.1   Human Capital Strategy: The Solution for China's Innovation-Oriented Economic Strategy

As developing countries take steps to progress through middle-income status, modern growth theory predicts that middle-income countries in East Asia will witness three transformations: first, diversification will slow and then reverse as countries become more specialized in production and employment; second, investment will become less important and innovation will accelerate; and third, education systems will shift from equipping workers with skills for adjusting to new technologies to preparing them to shape new products and processes (Kharas and Gill 2007).

3.2   Human Capital: Beyond Research and Development (R&D)

Economists have been working on understanding technology and innovation for quite a few decades. Advanced nations' stories have proven that innovation is the driver of high-value products and services, productivity, competitive advantages, and national prosperity. A presentation by the Organisation for Economic Co-operation and Development (OECD) at a World Intellectual Property Organization (WIPO) innovation seminar clearly argued that "innovation today involves the interaction of a system: R&D is only one element...R&D is critical to innovation and is the main focus of public support, but innovation is more than R&D... It is a bundle that includes services, software and 'network' capital." There are a number of policy implications of moving the focus beyond R&D:

- Innovation can not only be derived from advanced science and technology (S&T), but also from the design of new business models, and organizational change;
- A recognition that a bundle of investments are needed for innovation, both technical and non-technical;
- The importance of broad-based human capital: hard and soft skills, including entrepreneurship;
- Taking a systemic approach: "push"/supply and "pull"/demand policies.

This OECD innovation strategy presentation recommended evaluating and monitoring innovation through improved performance measures (Wyckoff 2010).

When going beyond just R&D in terms of encouraging innovation, factors of human capital— generally seen as a set of knowledge, abilities, and skills of individuals used in activities that stimulate economic growth and development—are considered to be a major stimulus of the innovation process. Human capital carries all the "soft" factors in the innovation process, such as culture, aesthetics, creativity, and intellectual nature. High-quality human capital is the key to the success of R&D investment and innovation.

A Canadian study analysed survey data and concluded that there is a significant correlation between the number of employees with post-secondary education in a firm and whether the firm has produced a new and unique innovation; innovative firms are more likely to have some type of training programs than non-innovative firms (Holbrook and Hughes 2000).

4   Global Talent Mobility and Management: A Diaspora Approach

4.1   Immigrants and Innovation: Diaspora Option and National Complementarity

As developing countries embark on a policy agenda for innovation-based growth, they face an acute shortage of competent individuals who know the country well, but who are not part of the "status quo" and therefore have no vested interests other than the best possible country outcome. Paradoxically, the search for such individuals often leads to the country's talent abroad: its skilled diasporas (Kuznetsov 2010). There is some evidence that returnees have more to offer than people who have not been abroad.

4.2   From "Brain Drain" to "Brain Gain" to "Brian Circulation"

The Chinese education policy that encourages Chinese students to study abroad was heavily criticized in the 1980s because most of the students chose to stay in the host countries after graduation. This is supported by the earlier migration theory of "Brain Drain," first developed by Jagdish Bhagwati, a Columbia scholar in the 1970s (Bhagwati and Hamada 1974). Advanced economies have been able to attract and retain talents from developing countries at low cost, constraining the development capacity of such nations. However, this argument was countered by Chicago scholar Robert Lucas and others in the 1980s (Lucas and Stark 1985) because most overseas talents of the developing nations helped advance the economic development of their home countries by sending back remittances, sharing information and technologies, and boosting bilateral trades between the two countries. This is the so-called "Brain Gain" argument.

At the onset of the twenty-first century, Berkeley scholar Anna Lee Saxenian proposed a new migration framework called "Brain Circulation" (Saxenian 2000). Regardless of their final destination, migrant workers can benefit both host and home countries if their human capital is utilized effectively. When the economies and industrial structures of two countries are complementary, the "win-win" effect of "Brain Circulation" can be found in the interacting relationship: "Brain Circulation," as a bridge between resources that are being exchanged, brings industrial opportunities to countries that lack capital and technology but possess labour and natural resources, while it also benefits industries from advanced countries which possess capital and technology but lack labour and natural resources. Though this exchange process, "Brain Circulation" also offers opportunities for the talented to advance their career. This coincided with the waves of Chinese students returning to their homeland starting at the beginning of the twenty-first century, when China joined the World Trade Organization (WTO) in 2001.

An example of this complementarity can be seen between China and Canada. Canada has abundant natural resources, advanced technologies, and high-quality education, while China's complementary assets include abundant human resources and a huge product market. At a time when the world has not fully recovered from the ongoing economic recession and the United States especially is caught in a debt crisis, China is playing an important role in the economy of Canada, where the recovery is still fragile. In the meantime, Canada is a very strong producer and exporter of resources to China. The economies of the two countries are highly complementary, with a largely untapped potential for further collaborations. Under this context, Chinese immigrants and diasporas are well positioned to cooperate with Canadian firms as well as national, regional, and local governments to promote bilateral trade and investment and to create new science and technology partnerships for both countries.

4.3   Immigrants and Innovation: US and Canadian Evidence

In the United States, immigrants have had a disproportionate role in innovation and technology, founding such companies as Yahoo, eBay and Google. Half of Silicon Valley start-ups were founded by immigrants, up from 25 % a decade ago. A recent study by the Kauffman Foundation found that immigrants are 50 % are likely to start businesses than are native-born Americans. Immigrant-founded technology firms employ 450,000 workers in the United States. And, according to the National Venture Capital Association, immigrants have started one-quarter of all US venture-backed firms. Last year, four out of nine Nobel Prize winners were naturalized US citizens.

In Canada, at least 35 % of Canada Research Chairs (CRCs) are foreign-born, even though immigrants are just one-fifth of the Canadian population (Downie 2010). Immigrants to Canada win proportionally more prestigious literary and performing arts awards (immigrants comprise 23 % of Giller Prize finalists and 29 % of winners, and 23 % of Governor General's Performing Arts Award recipients). Foreign direct investment into Canada is greater from countries that are well represented in Canada through immigration, based on data from the Census and from Canada's Department of Foreign Affairs and International Trade.

4.4 Overseas Chinese Returning Home

A World Bank publication recently studied how countries can draw on their talent abroad. The study shows that in the past decades, expatriates have come to play a critical and highly visible role in accelerating technology exchange and foreign direct investment in China, India, Israel and the United States. Some expatriates became pioneer investors before the widespread decentralization of the supply chain and the internal decentralization of authority assured major capital markets that these economies had rosy futures. This World Bank study suggests that the pool of expatriate expertise can be utilized for the benefit of developing countries through the collaboration of networks of diaspora professionals. These diaspora networks could team up with the governments of developing countries and with external funding agencies to share policy and technological and managerial knowledge in order to improve local conditions and promote a development agenda within developing countries (Kuznetsov 2006).

Using the China Statistical Yearbook to determine the absolute number of overseas Chinese returning home, we find the number has been mostly increasing over the last three decades (National Bureau of Statistics, Various Years). In the 1990s, the annual rate of increase in number of Chinese returnees was at 13 %. The rate jumped to 45 % between 2001 and 2002. In 2006 alone, about 35,000 overseas Chinese returned to China.

The Institute for Competitiveness and Prosperity conducted a comparison between Ireland and China of the relationship between economic sophistication and their return of diasporas. Ireland is a country that successfully navigated the transition to an innovation-competition wave. Ireland completed this transition in the 1990s, and net migration patterns in Ireland can be considered a good gauge of movements from one wave to the next.

However, the dominant view both inside and outside China is that the truly talented stay abroad, even though some very eminent academics have returned. The longer one stays abroad, the more difficult it is to return. Family obligations and professional affiliations can not easily set aside. Therefore, the diaspora option of building a transnational scientific community becomes one more way Western technology can flow into China and strengthen it through "science and education" (Zweig et al. 2008).

Although the positive correlation between Chinese diasporas and economic sophistication needs to be confirmed, it has often been argued that investments by the Chinese diaspora in the provinces along China's south and east coast are one of the key determinants of the continued success of China's economic reforms. Since the mid-1980s, "diaspora Chinese capitalism" is emerging as the most dynamic force throughout the whole region after the introduction of the open-door policy in China, far "out-investing Japan and United States combined by a factor of four." It is also seen that Chinese diasporas simultaneously replaced Japan as the major foreign investor throughout Southeast Asia in the 1990s (Lever-Tracy and Ip 1996).

4.5   Nationally Educated Talent in China

China is not rich in terms of talent as the proportion of the population. Recent research show that in 2005, only 2 % of China's population over the age of 25 held a bachelor's degree or higher, while in the United States it was 27.4 % (Stolarick and Chen 2011). The absolute number of university-educated students paints an overly optimistic picture for China. Articles have stated that in 2004 the United States graduated roughly 70,000 undergraduate engineers, while China graduated 600,000 (Gereffi and Wadhwa 2005). However, when researchers from Duke University adjusted comparability, China's graduates were scaled down to 352,000 and those in the United States rose to 137,000 (270/m in China and 470/m in the United States). A labour market study by the McKinsey Global Institute argues that this estimate is still far too generous. McKinsey concluded that only 10 % of Chinese engineers can compete in the global outsourcing arena (Farrell et al. 2005). If that is the case, then even the absolute number of competitive engineers produced by China is less than that by the United States, even with China's population being four times larger than the United States.

Although China is making great strides in human capital, it is still a long way from competing on the basis of innovation and sophistication. So how can China respond to the threat of a global overhaul? McKinsey attributed the low competency of China's engineers to limited language proficiency, lower educational quality, cultural issues, reduced job accessibility, and the attractiveness of domestic non-outsourced jobs. Individuals with strong interpersonal skills, professional knowledge, and the ability to communicate across borders are virtually always in demand (Farrell et al. 2005).

However, to begin producing more highly skilled individuals, China needs a primary education system that is on par with international standards and practical competencies. It is not only about how high the enrolment rate is within China's colleges and universities, but also about how well the graduates adopt and develop existing ideas, and how well they learn new competencies and adapt to a changing environment—the so-called "soft skills." China's education system is producing huge numbers of technically proficient degree holders, but in order to compete globally, China must add more soft skills to the package.

5   The Transition of Talent Management in China and the Influence of the Chinese Culture

5.1   Chinese Talent Management in Transition

For all these reasons, Chinese talent management is in transition (Cooke 2011; Preece et al. 2011; Zhu 2005; Zhu et al. 2008). Western consulting companies are everywhere in the Chinese business community, offering advice and training programs on topics such as recruiting and skill development. Most of the privately held companies are so new that they represent almost a blank slate for experimenting, and the new ideas are Western HR practices. Not surprisingly, the leaders in this area are foreign-based companies operating in China, which adapt easily to these new challenges by bringing in practices from their home countries. Law et al. (2003) supported this notion by combining the followers' perception of the leader and the role of HRM in a survey of 180 firms. They found that the effect of HRM on performance was stronger in foreign-invested enterprises (FIEs) than in the SOEs. Evidence suggests that the HRM functions have been elevated to a level of strategic importance in FIEs in China (Braun and Warner 2002).

However, this is not to suggest that Chinese practices will converge with Western HRM. Many factors affect the willingness to adopt Western practices, such as firm size, age, ownership, and competitive strategy (Ding and Akhtar 2001; Warner 2003). Ahlstrom et al. (2005) noted that WTO membership has increased the motivation for Chinese firms to implement strategic HRM, while Wang and Zang (2005) suggest that, because innovation is a top national priority for China now, HRM practices that contribute to it will more likely increase.

5.2   The Continuing Influence of Chinese Culture

Cultural and political factors present the greatest barrier to a convergence of HRM practices with those in the West and are most likely to contribute to the development of HRM practices with "Chinese characteristics."

More than 5,000 years of a continuous civilization creates a national culture that has far-reaching effects on management practices in general and HR practices in particular (Ding and Akhtar 2001; Chen and Wilson 2003; Zhu and Warner 2004a, b). Most observers suggest that any successful practices will need to adapt to the Chinese culture and that forms of management hybrids are already developing (Taylor et al. 2001; Chen and Wilson 2003).

To illustrate, consider the topic of loyalty. In China, employees typically build attachment with the leaders of the organization rather than to the organization per se. It is fairly common that, when a leader leaves a company, many of the employees will follow him/her (Wang 2011). This is perhaps not surprising in the business world, given that the idea of a corporation is still relatively new, and there is no history of iconic corporations that transcend generations the way there is in the West. Whether we can expect organizational commitment in Chinese companies is an interesting question. Perhaps commitment to the leaders is enough, but what needs to be done to develop that commitment to leaders is likely to be different.

5.3   Shaping Organizational Culture

Chinese business leaders do seem very aware of the issue of organizational culture and their role in shaping it. This is arguably the "glue" that ties individuals to the leaders of these companies, and it is likely to become a more explicit focus of attention in the future.

Chinese culture values hard work. Many employees work extra hours on the weekend and weekdays until late at night, even without overtime pay. Tung (1981) was one of the first to extol the virtue of the Chinese worker and to emphasize the need for foreign investors to understand the moral basis for the Chinese motivation. Perhaps the Western focus on motivating employees is less of a concern in China. The bigger concern might be to avoid those factors that might distract and demotivate them.

One of those factors might be harmony. Chinese culture values harmony as crucial to its view of a welcoming work environment. Chinese managers rely on Confucian principles to achieve that harmony or benevolence (Chew and Lim 1995). Market pressures create changes that disturb harmony, however, and Western HRM practices that focus on individuals rather than the workforce as a whole and that differentiate individuals in terms of rewards may further disturb harmony.

Relationship-building is often seen as the most distinctive aspect of business in China. The concept of "guanxi" refers to informal social networks that influence not only social interactions but also business interactions such as employment and financial transactions (Luo 2000; Parnell 2005). Guanxi is often considered a major barrier for foreign nationals attempting to establish Western HRM practices such as purely merit-based recruitment and selection (Chen et al. 2004; Zhu 2005). For HRM, guanxi reflects the notion of trust that comes from experience. It is reflected in the fact that business leaders like to work with a team of employees that they know. Executive "churn" does not happen as commonly as in US firms, and there is a fair amount of loyalty from leaders to their followers in return. In that sense, these practices at the top level may resemble older corporate models in the United States where lifetime employment was assumed. How CEOs will deal with the need to bring in new skills, though, or whether talent can be rotated across roles to develop it—breaking at least in the short term those working relationships—remains to be seen.

A final Chinese value, which exists in many Asian countries, is the value placed on "face," or avoiding personal embarrassment (Wang 2011). Western HRM practices rely on promotions, dismissals, and other individualized outcomes that create winners but also losers. Whether those practices can be adapted to the Chinese context remains an open question. If not, how Chinese businesses will deal with the challenge of moving the right people into positions whose requirements change is not obvious.

HR professionals also need to "manage" and "educate" senior leaders on important HR issues, showing them the value of HR activities and practices. For example, the succession planning process in China is not transparent; HR professionals need to get involved in the decision-making process rather than to take orders (Wang 2011). HRM also needs to develop world-class leaders to meet the demands of local and multinational corporations.

6   The Future of Talent Management in China

This chapter illustrates the evolving HRM and TM practices in China since the late 1970s and explains why the TM practices deviate from the Western model. This deviation is largely driven by the large population of China and the almost infinite supply of labour that was available for a considerable period of time. There was little incentive for the Chinese managers to adopt sophisticated TM practices. Although HR remains a support function for most companies (especially the SOEs) in China, the TM landscape is quickly changing. Strategic considerations have been incorporated into the HRM and TM practices, especially among the MNCs and even in some large SOEs. At the national level, TM has been viewed as a critical component and major driving force for the crucial transitions from low-cost manufacturing to innovation-based economy. At the global scale, shortly after its entry into the WTO in 2001, China joined the international war for talent and introduced a number of ambitious talent attraction and development plans to bring home highly skilled and Western-trained talent, while at the same time accepting Chinese diaspora as a viable option for overseas depository and reservoirs for future talent. This chapter used a number of strategic HRM and TM theoretical frameworks to explain the current state and transitions for TM practices in China; highlighted the unique challenges that Chinese managers and foreign entrepreneurs are facing—in particular, the far-reaching effects of Chinese culture on the TM practices; and pointed out future opportunities in GTM in China and beyond.

In his influential article, Peter Cappelli offered the following prescriptions for talent management in the twenty-first century (Cappelli 2008). First, in order to strike the make or buy decision, we need to understand the relative costs of under- and over-estimation. The cost of over-estimation appears to be considerably high. China is a notable exception, given that many firms now need to be prepared for pockets of labour and skill shortages and high turnover in the workforce. Second, we need to adapt to uncertainty in talent demand. This is especially true now in China since the demand is volatile, and supply is also difficult to predict. Therefore, most of the suggestions made by Cappelli could apply to China, such as breaking up long training programs into discrete pieces, splitting smaller training groups into more intervals, and centralizing training across divisional groups. Third, we must improve return on investment (ROI) of employee training and skill development. This can be done by requiring employees to share the training costs and to sign a binding contract to reduce attrition, and by bringing "leavers" back into the firm. Although the rationale works well in theory, Chinese employees often consider training and development as an entitlement and are reluctant to share the costs. Fourth, we need to give employees more choices in their career path. This fits well with the aspirations of the new generation of Chinese workforce, as the young Chinese workers are less committed to the organization and place more emphasis on their own career development.

China now is the second largest economy in the world, and the World Bank (2012) forecasts that it will be the largest economy by 2030. The business model that brought it to this point—factories that relied on surplus labour to keep wages down and maintain workplace discipline—is already on the way out. Chinese businesses will have to find ways to deal with competitive labour markets, to train workers to meet skill needs, and to engage workers in ways that substitute for labour market discipline. Much of those TM practices can be borrowed from the West.

Chinese businesses will also need to deal with the problems of change in the workplace: changing skill requirements and changing demands of workers. The pressures from markets for responsiveness will lead to intense pressures for adaptation at the managerial level. Western solutions to those problems conflict not only with existing Chinese practices but also with Chinese culture. It is therefore unlikely that Chinese businesses will use these exact solutions. The path they will end up following is bound to be both unique and interesting.

References

Ahlstrom, D., Foley, S., Young, M. N., & Chan, E. S. (2005). Human resource strategies in post-WTO China. *Thunderbird International Business Review, 47*, 263–285.

Akhtar, S., Ding, D. Z., & Ge, G. L. (2008). Strategic HRM practices and their impact on company performance in Chinese enterprises. *Human Resource Management, 47*(1), 133–156.

Al Ariss, A., & Crowley, H. M. (2013). Self-initiated expatriation and migration in the management literature: Present theorizations and future research directions. *Career Development International, 18*(1), 78–96.

Barney, J. (1991). Firm resources and sustained competitive advantage. *Journal of Management, 17*, 99–120.

Bhagwati, J., & Hamada, K. (1974). The brain drain, international integration of markets for professionals and unemployment: A theoretical analysis. *Journal of Development Economics, 1*(1), 19–42.

Borjas, G. J., & Bratsberg, B. (1996). Who leaves? The outmigration of the foreign-born. *The Review of Economics and Statistics, 78*(1), 165–176.

Braun, W. H., & Warner, M. (2002). Strategic human resource management in western multinationals in China: The differentiation of practices across different ownership forms. *Personnel Review, 31*(5), 553–579.

Cappelli, P. (2003). Will there really be a labor shortage. *Organizational Dynamics, 3*, 15–24.

Cappelli, P. (2008). Talent management for the twenty-first century. *Harvard Business Review, 2008*(3), 76–81.

Chen, C. C., Chen, Y., & Xin, K. (2004). Guanxi practices and trust in management: A procedural justice perspective. *Organization Science, 15*, 200–209.

Chen, S., & Wilson, M. (2003). Standardization and localization of human resource management in Sino-foreign joint ventures. *Asia Pacific Journal of Management, 20*, 397–408.

Chew, I. K. H., & Lim, C. (1995). A Confucian perspective on conflict resolution. *International Journal of Human Resource Management, 6*, 143–157.

Cooke, F. L. (2009). A decade of transformation of HRM in China: A review of literature and suggestions for future studies. *Asia Pacific Journal of Human Resources, 47*, 6–40.

Cooke, F. L. (2011). Talent management in China. In H. Scullion & D. Collings (Eds.), *Global Talent Management, a volume in the Global Human Resource Management series edited by Randall Schuler, Susan Jackson, Paul Sparrow and Michael Poole* (pp. 132–154). London: Routledge.

Critchley, R. (2004). *Doing nothing is not an option: Facing the imminent labor crisis.* Australia: Thomson/South-Western.

Delery, J. E., & Doty, D. H. (1996). Modes of theorizing in strategic human resource management: Tests of universalistic, contingency, and configurational performance predictions. *Academy of Management Journal, 39*(4), 802–835.

Ding, D. Z., & Akhtar, S. (2001). The organizational choice of human resource management practices: A study of Chinese enterprises in three cities in the PRC. *International Journal of Human Resource Management, 12*, 946–964.

Downie, M. (2010) *Immigrants as innovators boosting Canada's global competitiveness* (60 p). Canada: The Conference Board of Canada.

Fang, T., & Ge, Y. (2012). Unions and firm innovation in China: Synergy or strife? *China Economic Review, 23*(1), 170–180.

Farrell, D., Laboissière, M., Rosenfeld, J., Stürze, S., & Umezawa, F. (2005). *The emerging global labor market: Part II – The supply of offshore talent in services* (p. 24). McKinsey Global Institute.

Garavan, T., Moreley, M., Gunnigle, P., & Collins, E. (2001). Human capital accumulation: The role of human resource management. *Journal of European Industrial Training, 25*, 48–68.

Gereffi, G., & Wadhwa, V. (2005). *Framing the engineering outsourcing debate: Placing the United States on a level playing field with China and India.* Durham, NC: Duke University.

Holbrook, J. A. D., & Hughes, L. P. (2000). *Innovation and the management of human resources* (CPROST Report # 00-03). Centre for Policy Research on Science and Technology, Simon Fraser University at Harbour Centre. http://www.sfu.ca/cprost/docs/0003.pdf

Holland, P., Sheehan, C., Donohue, R., Pyman, A., & Allen, B. (2012). *Contemporary issues and challenges in HRM* (2nd ed.). Australia: Tilde University Press.

Kharas, H., & Gill, I. (2007). *An East Asian renaissance: Ideas for growth.* East Asia & Pacific: World Bank. http://siteresources.worldbank.org/INTEASTASIAPACIFIC/Resources/226262-1158536715202/EA_Renaissance_full.pdf

Kuruvilla, S., Lee, C. K., & Gallagher, M. E. (2011). *From iron rice bowl to informalization: Markets, workers, and the state in a changing China.* Cornell University Press

Kuznetsov, Y. (2006). *Diaspora networks and the international migration of skills: How countries can draw on their talent abroad.* World Bank Publications. http://web.worldbank.org/WBSITE/EXTERNAL/WBI/WBIPROGRAMS/KFDLP/0,,contentMDK:20946758~menuPK:1727232~pagePK:64156158~piPK:64152884~theSitePK:461198,00.html

Kuznetsov, Y. (2010). Talent abroad promoting growth and institutional development at home: Skilled diaspora as part of the country. *World Bank - Economic Premise, 44*, 1–7.

Law, K. S., Tse, D. K., & Zhou, N. (2003). Does human resource management matter in a transitional economy? China as an example. *Journal of International Business Studies, 34*, 255–265.

Lever-Tracy, C., & Ip, D. (1996). Diaspora capitalism and the homeland: Australian Chinese networks into China. *Diaspora: A Journal of Transnational Studies, 5*(2), 239–273.

Lucas, R. E. B., & Stark, O. (1985). Motivations to remit: Evidence from Botswana. *Journal of Political Economy, 93*(5), 901–918.

Luo, Y. D. (2000). *Guanxi and business.* Singapore: World Scientific.

Michaels, E., Handfield-Jones, H., & Axelrod, E. (2001). *The war for talent.* Boston: Harvard Business School Press.

National Bureau of Statistics. China statistical yearbook. Various issues.

Parnell, M. F. (2005). Chinese business guanxi: An organization or non-organization? *Journal of Organizational Transformation and Social Change, 2*, 29–47.

Preece, D., Iles, P., & Chuai, X. (2011). Talent management and management fashion in Chinese enterprises: Exploring case studies in Beijing. *International Journal of Human Resource Management, 22*(16), 3413–3428.

Saxenian, A. (2000). The Bangalore boom: From brain drain to brain circulation? In K. Kenniston & D. Kumar (Eds.), *Bridging the digital divide: Lessons from India.* Bangalore: National Institute of Advanced Study.

Smit, A. (1998). *Training and development in Australia* (2nd ed.). Sydney: Butterworth.

Stolarick, K., & Chen, X. (2011). *Understanding the creative economy in China*. Martin Prosperity Institute. http://martinprosperity.org/media/CreativeChina_EnglishVersion.pdf

Taylor, R., Chu, Y., & Hyun, J. (2001). Korean companies in China: Strategies in the localization of management. *Asia Pacific Business Review, 7*, 161–181.

Tung, R. L. (1981). Patterns of motivation in Chinese industrial enterprises. *Academy of Management Review, 6*, 481–489.

Walton, J. (1999). *Strategic human resource development*. Great Britain: Pearson Education Limited.

Wang, B. (2011). Chinese HRM in action: An interview with Wayne Chen of Hay Group China. *Journal of Chinese Human Resource Management, 2*(1), 61–68.

Wang, Z., & Zang, Z. (2005). Strategic human resources, innovation and entrepreneurship fit: A cross-regional comparative model. *International Journal of Manpower, 26*, 544–559.

Warner, M. (Ed.). (2003). *The future of Chinese management*. London: Frank Cass.

World Bank. (2012). *China 2030: Building a modern, harmonious, and creative high-income society*. http://wwwwds.worldbank.org/external/default/WDSContentServer/WDSP/IB/2012/02/28/000356161_20120228001303/Rendered/PDF/671790WP0P127500China020300complete.pdf

Wyckoff, A. (2010). OECD's innovation strategy: Getting a head start on tomorrow. *Executive Summary*. OECD. http://www.oecd.org/dataoecd/3/14/45302349.pdf

Zeng, M., & Williamson, P. J. (2003). The hidden dragons. *Harvard Business Review, 81*(10): 92–99, 137

Zeng, M., & Williamson, P. J. (2007). *Dragons at your door: How Chinese cost innovation is disrupting global competition*. Boston: Harvard Business School Press.

Zeng, M., & Williamson, P. J. (2011). How China reset its global acquisition agenda. *Harvard Business Review*

Zhu, C. J. (2005). *Human resource management in China: Past, current and future HR practices in the industrial sector*. New York and London: Routledge Curzon.

Zhu, J. C., Thomson, S. B., & De Cieri, H. L. (2008). A retrospective and prospective analysis of HRM research in Chinese firms: Implications and directions for future study. *Human Resource Management, 47*(1), 133–156.

Zhu, Y., & Warner, M. (2004a). Changing patterns of human resource management in contemporary China: WTO accession and enterprise responses. *Industrial Relations Journal, 35*, 311–328.

Zhu, Y., & Warner, M. (2004b). The implications of China's WTO accession for employment relations. *European Business Journal, 16*, 47–58.

Zweig, D. (2006). Learning to compete: China's efforts to encourage a reverse brain drain. *International Labour Review, 145*(1/2), 65–90.

Zweig, D., Fung, C. S., & Han, D. (2008). Redefining the brain drain: China's 'diaspora option. *Science, Technology and Society, 13*(1), 1–33. doi:10.1177/097172180701300101.

Zweig, D., Fung, C. S., & Vanhonacker, W. (2006). Rewards of technology: Explaining China's reverse migration. *Journal of International Migration and Integration, 7*(4), 449–471.

Global Talent Management in Japanese Multinational Companies: The Case of Nissan Motor Company

Masayuki Furusawa

1 Introduction

A number of studies of international human resource management have pointed to the slow progress made in localizing top management positions at overseas subsidiaries of Japanese multinational companies (Furusawa 2008; Harzing 2004; Kopp 1994). However, to complete in the global arena, which requires the balancing of local responsiveness and global integration, localization of top management positions is not enough (Bartlett and Ghoshal 1995; Doz et al. 2001). It is also important to achieve the optimum utilization of human resources on a global scale. Nevertheless, so far only limited research has been conducted on the global integration aspect of international human resource management in Japanese multinationals.

This chapter reports on the Global Talent Management of Nissan Motor Company based on a series of in-depth interviews with the company's managers. Global Talent Management in this research is defined as the process of international human resource management required to identify, develop, evaluate, utilize and retain high-potential employees for global competitive advantage (Schuler et al. 2011; Tarique and Schuler 2010). The purpose of this research is to explore the Global Talent Management of Nissan in order to present implications on international human resource management of multinational companies, especially of Japanese multinationals which have been suffering from difficulties in attracting and retaining capable local human resources owing to their ethnocentric HRM practices (Kopp 1994). Through the case study of Nissan, two theoretical and practical contributions are expected. They also account for why we chose Nissan. First, we

This article is a part of the research achievements from the 2012 Overseas Research Program of Osaka University of Commerce.

M. Furusawa (✉)
Osaka University of Commerce, Higashi-Osaka, Japan
e-mail: furusawa@daishodai.ac.jp

A. Al Ariss (ed.), *Global Talent Management*, Management for Professionals,
DOI 10.1007/978-3-319-05125-3_11, © Springer International Publishing Switzerland 2014

hope to shed some light on the latest international HRM practices of the leading Japanese multinational company. The overseas sales and production ratios of Nissan exceed those of Toyota Motor Corporation. As to the workforce, about 60 % of their total employees are non-Japanese. Second, we will be able to present the best practice for overcoming the HRM challenges Japanese multinationals have faced for decades from the 'peculiarity' of Nissan: although Nissan is headquartered in Japan, they have a strategic alliance with Renault as well as a French Lebanese Brazilian CEO, Mr. Carlos Ghosn. Our research hopes to break down some of the stereotypes about international HRM in Japanese multinationals.

This chapter takes the following form. We begin by discussing the relevant aspects of the literature on international human resource management and outline the theoretical framework for this case study. Next, we explain our methodology and present the case of Global Talent Management in Nissan. Finally, we draw implications for our understanding of international human resource management and its practitioners.

2   Theoretical Framework

Studies of international human resource management have centred on issues concerning the expatriation of parent country nationals (PCNs) or the development and utilization of host country nationals (HCNs). As for Japanese multinational companies, it has been argued that the slow progress localizing top management positions at their overseas subsidiaries can be seen as their "Achilles heel" (Bartlett and Yoshihara 1988). From an external viewpoint, localization is expected to help eliminate the ethnocentric image of human resource management and gain access to locally-embedded knowledge. Internally, it is expected to contribute to the acquisition and retention of capable local human resources as well as reducing personnel expenses (Evans et al. 2002).

However, while localization is a necessary condition, without more, it is not sufficient to compete in the global arena, where balancing of local responsiveness and global integration is required. As suggested by Bartlett and Ghoshal (1995) and Doz et al. (2001), the overseas subsidiaries of the "transnational company" and the "metanational company" have to take on the dual responsibilities of contributing to their global network as well as providing local expertise in each domestic market. Localization strategies without global integration might make their overseas subsidiaries 'uncontrollable kites' that end up as a medley of stand-alone companies.

For companies to manage the dual pressures of local responsiveness and global integration, two kinds of integration are needed in international human resource management (Furusawa 2008). One is what we call "normative integration". Multinational companies have to present a global corporate philosophy that can be accepted by their employees with diverse cultural backgrounds and make a commitment to spread this philosophy out as global glue to local managers of their overseas subsidiaries. Within network-type organizations such as the transnational company and the metanational company, the flow of knowledge and information between the headquarters and their overseas subsidiaries can be complex. In particular, tacit knowledge embedded in the local environment is often intangible, and thus might be extremely difficult to transfer through information technology or hierarchy (Doz et al. 2001). The senders and receivers of this knowledge must trust each other (Szulanski 1996). Normative integration includes using measures to promote the process of global socialization such as training programmes on corporate philosophy or values, international assignments, corporate ceremonies and rituals, employee opinion surveys, and so on (Deal and Kennedy 1982; Edström and Galbraith 1977; Furusawa 2008).

The other necessary type of integration is "systems integration". The fundamental advantage of multinational companies over domestic ones lies in the global-wide availability of capable human resources (Vernon 1971). The models of the transnational company and the metanational company assume situations wherein excellent ideas are exchanged and human resources are utilized across borders to create and diffuse innovation on a global basis. In order to develop these organizational capabilities, global headquarters must come up with a system to make the best use of their competent employees scattered around the globe from the perspectives of global optimization. The practices for systems integration encompass globally-standardized systems of job grades, personnel appraisals, and compensation, as well as global HR databases, and so forth (Furusawa 2008). The headquarters also should be keen to identify and develop high-potential individuals on a global scale for sustainable competitive advantage (McDonnell and Collings 2011).

With these issues in mind, Furusawa (2008) conceptualized a framework of "Global Human Resource Management" for global competitiveness which reaches beyond the localization theory (Fig. 1). This model emphasizes the importance of both normative integration and systems integration in international human resource management, which will lead to "HRM performance" and eventually to "global innovation performance".

HRM performance consists of two aspects. The first is the aspect of global corporate culture and mutual trust. Through the measures for global socialization (normative integration), it is assumed that mutual trust and human networks among the key persons of the headquarters and their overseas subsidiaries will be cultivated. The sharing of corporate philosophy will also nurture a global mindset (Evans et al. 2002; Gupta and Govindarajan 2002; Sparrow et al. 2004) in their local managers and will sublimate into the global corporate culture where greater importance is attached to worldwide learning capabilities (Bartlett and Ghoshal 1995). The second aspect is on global utilization of human resources. International transfers will be facilitated by globally-integrated personnel systems (systems integration) and capable people will be promoted irrespective of their nationalities. This means that global career opportunities can be presented to local employees who were originally hired by their overseas subsidiaries. To sum up, companies can realize the globally-optimized utilization of human resources and build up their "employer brand" to attract and retain capable future leaders.

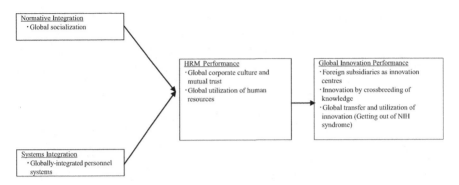

Fig. 1 The framework of "Global Human Resource Management" (Furusawa 2008)

Global innovation performance is the fruit of global collaborations promoted by HRM performance. Global innovation performance has three major characteristics. The first is that foreign subsidiaries become innovation centres. The transnational company and the metanational company that value environmental diversity, will enable their subsidiaries to act as innovation centres in their global network. Moreover, involvement with local employees and foreign subsidiaries through both normative and systems integration will give them the energy and motivation that lead to innovation. The second characteristic is its multi-dimensional innovation process. In the conventional theory of international management, the source of each innovation was thought to exist within the boundaries of a country (Bartlett and Ghoshal 1995; Fayerweather 1969). On the other hand, the transnational company and the metanational company are grounded in a mentality that utilizes local knowledge for global interests. Similarly, in our Global Human Resource Management model, the crossbreeding of knowledge that yields innovation is expected through the global interaction of human resources. Finally, the third characteristic is the global transfer and utilization of innovation. "NIH"— the Not Invented Here syndrome—has been a serious obstacle to the global competitiveness of multinational companies (Katz and Allen 1982). Conversely, we believe that such a parochial mindset can be overcome by nurturing mutual trust among key persons and the multi-directional transfers of employees.

Furusawa (2008) conducted a questionnaire survey of 128 Western and Japanese multinationals based on the framework of Global Human Resource Management and showed that the Japanese multinationals lag behind their Western counterparts in all the aspects of the model. More importantly, Furusawa demonstrated the validity of the model by examining the relationship among the three major components of it. The results revealed that the practices for normative and systems integration were associated with increasing levels of HRM performance, and that HRM performance statistically correlates with global innovation performance.

3   Methodology

This research adopted a qualitative method. The author conducted in-depth interview surveys of Nissan six times (1 August, 2003; 13 June, 2008; 12 September; 2008; 19 June 2009; 10 January 2013; 17 May 2013). Each survey lasted 1.5–2.0 h and took the form of a semi-structured interview. The author met with eight informants. They were all general managers or managers in charge of the Global Talent Management of Nissan at the global headquarters located in Japan and the European headquarters in France. The key questions in the interviews were concerned with the background, the practices, the results, and the challenges of their Global Talent Management. The answers to them were given orally with some relevant materials. The qualitative data was categorized and processed following the framework of Global Human Resource Management by using the KJ (Kawakita Jiro)-method.

4   Global Talent Management of Nissan Motor Company

4.1   Background of Global Talent Management

Nissan used to be a typical Japanese multinational company in terms of international human resource management. Their HRM systems were different from country to country and each functional department of the company had latent power concerning personnel reshuffles. The HRM department at their headquarters did not pay much attention to the management of local employees at their overseas subsidiaries. The international HRM of Nissan was almost synonymous with the management of Japanese expatriates. One of the informants looked back over the past and said, "we had very few global-wide HRM practices." Under these HRM systems, the local employees faced three "glass ceilings": (1) a glass ceiling for top management positions at the subsidiaries; (2) a glass ceiling for global career opportunities; and (3) a glass ceiling for trans-functional career opportunities. Due to these glass ceilings, Nissan found it difficult to attract and retain capable local employees at their overseas subsidiaries. The optimum utilization of human resources on a global basis had hardly been realized and, in addition, the company suffered from a huge deficit. In fiscal year 1999, their consolidated net loss reached 684.4 billion Yen (USD 6.46 billion, EUR 6.71 billion) and Nissan was burdened with 1.35 trillion Yen in net debt.

Facing these challenges, Nissan launched their Global Talent Management under the leadership of President Carlos Ghosn in 2000. In the previous year Nissan announced the strategic alliance with Renault and Mr. Ghosn was appointed as COO of Nissan. The basic philosophy of the programme is that the global headquarters takes the initiative in managing capable human resources from a global perspective in order to utilize them as company-wide assets, with the authority of the HRM department in each region or country restricted significantly for total optimization.

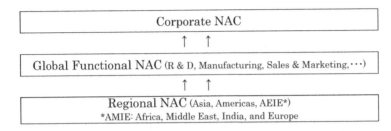

Fig. 2 The nomination process of high-potential persons at Nissan

4.2 Practices of Global Talent Management

4.2.1 Setting up the "NAC" (Nomination Advisory Council)

As one of the first measures of Global Talent Management, Nissan set up a personnel committee named the "NAC" (Nomination Advisory Council) in 1999 in order to build a global talent pipeline. Candidates for recognition as high-potential persons (HPPs) are nominated to the Corporate NAC (the global-level NAC) by the Global Functional NAC and Regional NAC (Fig. 2). The Global Functional NAC corresponds with their ten major functions such as R & D, manufacturing, sales & marketing, and so on, and the Regional NAC is made up of three councils (Asia; Americas; Africa, Middle East, India, and Europe). The Corporate NAC is held monthly and chaired by the CEO (Mr. Ghosn), with the COO, Executive Vice Presidents, and HR Director as its members. It is responsible for approving and developing high-potentials and succession planning for their "Global Key Posts", which are of great importance to Nissan's global strategy. Individual HPPs are reviewed for replacement at least once a year by the Corporate NAC.

The Corporate NAC also appoints five "career coaches", who are general managers with the mission of identifying candidates as HPPs and proposing a development plan for each HPP as well as making a list of successor candidates for the Global Key Posts. Career coaches are allowed to attend all meetings held in Nissan across the world, including the Corporate, Global Functional, and Regional NAC, so as to execute their mission.

4.2.2 Development Measures for HPPs

High-potentials are to be developed through training programmes as well as a variety of assignments, which means through both off-the-job training (Off-JT) and on-the-job training (OJT). For the Off-JT, Nissan started a programme called "GET" (Global Executive Training) in 2002. GET comprises two courses ("Advanced" and "Intermediate"). Each course lasts for 1 year and is held at Nissan's corporate university, the Nissan Learning Center Management Institute, in Japan. About 20–25 managers of Nissan from all over the world participate in the Advanced course, while 40–50 join the Intermediate course every year. Approximately, 40 % of the participants are non-Japanese. The training content encompasses leadership assessment, intensive MBA-level lectures (furnished in collaboration with INSEAD) and action learning. Action learning is a group project to work out proposals for management innovation at Nissan. All GET programmes are in English. As for the OJT, diverse tasks are prepared following individual career development plans approved by the Corporate NAC that nurture broad management perspectives and a global mindset. These tasks include international or trans-functional assignments or both, appointments as a pilot (leader) of their cross-functional teams, or problem-solving activities. Some HPPs are given work opportunities in Renault to learn their best practices.

4.2.3 Establishment of the "Nissan Way"

The third measure is the establishment of Nissan's global corporate values, known as the "Nissan Way". Needless to say, Nissan had a corporate philosophy before the Nissan Way, but it had not been actively promoted to local employees of their overseas subsidiaries, nor was it connected with Nissan human resource management systems. In contrast, with the Nissan Way Mr. Ghosn emphasized its significance as global glue in order to integrate Nissan's diverse workforce and manage cultural synergy. In 2006 the Nissan Way was identified through discussion by the top executives as the 'DNA' of Nissan for business success, which should be passed down to succeeding generations. It consists of five mindsets and five actions, with the core message of 'The power comes from inside' (Fig. 3). Nissan is keen on sharing the Nissan Way among its employees across the world through various HRM practices. For example, they intend to diffuse the Nissan Way by sponsoring workshops (the "Nissan Way Workshop") or teach-ins (the "Nissan Way Town Hall Meeting") with top executives or general managers. "Our basic policy is that leader coaches leader," one HRM manager explained. Nissan also provide its employees with tools or media such as portable cards, in-company newsletters, and intranet pages to inculcate the philosophy of the Nissan Way. Additionally, Nissan has introduced many recognition programmes to help ensure normative integration. The "Global Nissan President Prize" is awarded every year to individuals and teams which have made global-wide contributions based on the mindsets and actions articulated in the Nissan Way. At each workplace level, all managers of Nissan are encouraged to give "Thanks Cards" to employees to whom they wish to express their appreciation for excellent behavior and performance connected with the Nissan Way. Furthermore, Nissan regularly conducts a full-scale employee survey (the "Nissan Global Employee Survey") to determine the depth to which the Nissan Way has permeated its workforce worldwide.

4.2.4 Globally-Standardized Personnel Evaluation System

In 2007 Nissan standardized a personnel evaluation system for managers across the globe as an infrastructure for effective Global Talent Management. This system is composed of two appraisals, namely an "objectives appraisal" and a "contribution appraisal". The objectives appraisal is a kind of MBO (management by objectives) system. Managers are required to set their individual goals and group goals at the beginning of the fiscal year. Each objective should contain both "commitment"

【The power comes from inside.】 The focus is the customer, the driving force is value creation and the measurement of success is profit.	
Mindsets	Actions
1.Cross-functional, Cross-cultural Be open and show empathy toward different views; welcome diversity.	1.Motivate How are you energizing yourself and others?
2.Transparent Be clear, be simple, no vagueness and no hiding.	2.Commit & Target Are you accountable and are you stretching enough toward your potential?
3.Learner Be passionate. Learn from every opportunity; create a learning company.	3.Perform Are you fully focused on delivering results?
4.Frugal Achieve maximum results with minimum resources.	4.Measure How do you assess performance?
5.Competitive No complacency, focus on competition, and continuous benchmarking.	5.Challenge How are you driving continuous and competitive progress across the company?

Fig. 3 The "Nissan Way"

(indispensable goals) and "target" (stretch goals). The objectives appraisal measures the achievement rate of individual and group goals. The results of the objectives appraisals affect the variable compensation of managers. When all the targets are attained, the amount of variable compensation will reach 20–30 % of their annual basic salary. Meanwhile, the contribution appraisal is operationalized by the extent to which each manager embodies the Nissan Way. The four-grade rating system is applied to each mindset and action stipulated in the Nissan Way. This appraisal affects annual basic salaries. Outstanding performance in both appraisals is a pre-requisite for nomination as high-potentials.

4.3   The Result of Global Talent Management

In respect to the results of normative integration in international human resource management, the permeation of the Nissan Way has contributed to establishing mutual trust and global human networks among the leaders in key positions regardless of their nationalities or locations of assignment. At the same time, a global mindset for local managers by which they are able to balance respect for diversity with the pursuit of global optimization has been nurtured. These have been confirmed by the results of the Nissan Global Employee Survey. Furthermore, the hierarchical or dyadic relationships between the headquarters and their overseas subsidiaries are disappearing and a new organizational climate is being developed to generate the best global practices through mutual learning among diverse members. One informant emphasized, "we work as a team without distinction of nationalities or assignment locations by sharing global KPIs (key performance indicators)." On the other hand, through systems integration in international HRM, multi-directional and trans-functional personnel transfers have been realized for the optimum utilization of human resources as well as for the attraction and retention of capable employees. As a result, global career opportunities for local employees are increasing. About 48 % of Nissan's global top 100 positions are now held by non-Japanese. The nationalities of executive positions at the headquarters are also diversifying: the ratio of non-Japanese members on their board of directors and in corporate officer positions has jumped from 0 % in 1999 to 29 % in 2013. A general manager in charge of their Global Talent Management proudly remarked, "the three 'glass ceilings' have been successfully broken through."

Concerning global innovation performance, which is assumed to be led by the HRM performance mentioned above, a new innovation process has emerged as in the case of the new model of car: the DUALIS. It was originally developed by Nissan Europe as the QASHQAI and was reverse-imported into Japan, where it became a big hit. Later, with some modification to the design, it was introduced in the North American market as the ROGUE. We should also take note of the crossbreeding of knowledge across borders. Concretely, it has become ordinary for design centres in various regions to compete and cooperate for the design of global models such as the CUBE and the GT-R. The global innovation process in Nissan is no longer based on a "one-way model from Japan" (Yoshihara 1989) and free from NIH syndrome. Consequently, the company has made a remarkable turnaround. Nissan has already cleared off the net debt and posted a net income of 342.4 billion Yen (USD 4.13 billion, EUR 3.21 billion) in fiscal year 2012. They also have increased global market share from 4.9 % in 1999 to 6.4 % in 2011.

However, Nissan still has a long way to go in their Global Talent Management. One of the most pressing challenges is the promotion of female employees. The ratio of female corporate officers in Nissan is still very limited. As Nissan enjoys a high reputation for its efforts to create an attractive and supportive work environment for women, synergistic effects between Global Talent Management and diversity management should be sought more vigorously. In Table 1 we summarize the key GTM challenges, strategies, and future opportunities from the case study.

Implications and Conclusions

There are five main implications from this case study. The first is that coupling normative integration and systems integration in international human resource management can bind diverse workforce of multinational companies together, promoting greater global collaboration. Systems integration without normative integration could lead to a hotbed of opportunism and hurt team spirit for the global collaborations beyond national borders. On the other hand, normative integration without systems integration is liable to be regarded as ethnocentrism and lead to loss of capable employees (Furusawa 2008). Nissan focused on global socialization by disseminating the Nissan Way throughout the company and by positioning the Nissan Way as an essential factor in its personnel evaluation system for managers in the Global Talent Management process. In short, the two types of integration function like the two wheels of a cart with the Nissan Way as the axle. Through such a coupling of normative integration and systems integration, companies will be able to intensify the 'adhesiveness' of their corporate philosophy or values to use as global glue and promote global collaborations among members with various cultural backgrounds.

The second implication is that there should be a balanced approach to local responsiveness and global integration in the context of international HRM. Concerning their non-management positions, Nissan adapts human resource management to local circumstances in order to be competitive in each labour market. On the contrary, they are keen to integrate the HRM of managers into globally-standardized systems for global competitiveness. This approach could be an effective solution to manage the dual pressures of local responsiveness and global integration that multinational companies are destined to face.

The third implication is that one-size-fits-all methods of Global Talent Management will not work in multinational companies, because of their cultural and geographical diversity. Apart from the standardized systems such as the nomination process of high-potentials, the Off-JT for high potential persons or the personnel appraisals for managers, we can find that Nissan employs hands-on approaches in the individual career development plan for each HPP and the roles of career coaches.

The fourth implication concerns the initiative of the global headquarters in the process of Global Talent Management. One of the troublesome challenges in Global Talent Management is "silo thinking", the tendency of managers to stick to the interests of their own units rather than the whole organization (Stahl et al. 2007). They might resist the personnel transfers of capable subordinates in pursuit of their partial optimization. In Nissan, total optimization has been achieved by centralizing the HRM of HPPs to the Corporate NAC while restricting the authority of the HRM department in each region or country.

The fifth implication is that international strategic alliances can enlarge the reference group for HRM and greatly expand the exchange of knowledge among the different companies in the alliance. Nissan has made the best use of their 'peculiarity' for organizational learning, which we touched upon at the beginning of this chapter. In other words, the existence of Renault as an alliance partner has enlarged the reference group for the international human resource management of Nissan and accelerated the process of Global Talent Management. For instance, the nomination systems of high potential persons found in the NAC were originally developed by Renault and transferred to Nissan. But, recently, Renault has brought in some HRM practices from Nissan. Now, Nissan and Renault have regular meetings to exchange information on their Global Talent Management systems, which means that double-loop learning is occurring between the two companies.

This case study of Nissan's Global Talent Management extends our understanding of international human resource management in Japanese multinational companies and presents the best practice to overcome the persistent challenges they have been suffering from for decades.

Table 1 Five key Global Talent Management challenges, strategies, and future opportunities

Five key points regarding Global Talent Management challenges	Five key points regarding strategies to overcome these challenges	Five key points regarding future opportunities in Global Talent Management
1 Differences of national cultures	Integration through global socialization ("normative integration")	Synergy with diversity management
2 Glass ceiling for global career opportunities among host country nationals	Globally-integrated personnel systems ("systems integration")	Balanced approach to both internal and external labour markets
3 Silo thinking of managers	Initiative of the global headquarters	Double-loop learning of Global Talent Management through strategic alliance
4 Sapping of motivation among employees who are not nominated as high-potentials	Regular reshuffle of talent pools	Utilization of new HR pools such as self-initiated expatriates, migrants, or returnees
5 Risk of opportunism or ethnocentrism	Coupling of "normative integration" and "systems integration"	HRM function as a business partner

References

Bartlett, C. A., & Ghoshal, S. (1995). *Transnational management: Text, cases, and readings in cross-border management.* New York: Times Mirror Higher Education Group.

Bartlett, C. A., & Yoshihara, H. (1988). New challenges for Japanese multinationals: Is organization adaptation their achilles heel? *Human Resource Management, 27*(1), 19–43.

Deal, T. E., & Kennedy, A. A. (1982). *Corporate cultures.* New York: Addison-Wesley Longman.

Doz, Y. L., Santos, J., & Williamson, P. (2001). *From global to metanational: How companies win in the knowledge economy.* Boston: Harvard Business School Press.

Edström, A., & Galbraith, J. R. (1977). Transfer of managers as a coordination and control strategy in multinational organizations. *Administrative Science Quarterly, 22*(2), 248–263.

Evans, P., Pucik, V., & Barsoux, J. L. (2002). *The global challenge: International human resource management.* New York: McGraw-Hill/Irwin.

Fayerweather, J. (1969). *International business management: A conceptual framework.* New York: McGraw-Hill.

Furusawa, M. (2008). *Global jintekishigen kanriron (The theory of global human resource management).* Tokyo: Hakutou Shobou.

Gupta, A. K., & Govindarajan, V. (2002). Cultivating a global mindset. *Academy of Management Executive, 16*(1), 116–126.

Harzing, A. W. (2004). Composing an international staff. In A. W. Harzing & J. V. Ruysseveldt (Eds.), *International human resource management* (2nd ed.). London: Sage.

Katz, R., & Allen, T. J. (1982). Investigating the not invented here (NIH) syndrome: A look at the performance, tenure, and communication patterns of 50 R & D project groups. *R & D Management, 12*(1), 7–20.

Kopp, R. (1994). International human resource policies and practices in Japanese, European, and United States multinationals. *Human Resource Management, 33*(4), 581–599.

McDonnell, A., & Collings, D. G. (2011). The identification and evaluation of talent in MNEs. In H. Scullion & D. G. Collings (Eds.), *Global talent management.* New York: Routledge.

Schuler, R. S., Jackson, S. E., & Tarique, I. (2011). Global talent management and global talent challenges: Strategic opportunities for IHRM. *Journal of World Business, 46*(4), 506–516.

Sparrow, P., Brewster, C., & Harris, H. (2004). *Globalizing human resource management.* London: Routledge.

Stahl, G. K., Björkman, I., Farndale, E., Morris, S., Paauwi, W., Stiles, P., Trevor, J., & Wright, P.M. (2007). Global talent management: How leading multinationals build and sustain talent pipeline. *Faculty and Research Working Paper*, INSEAD.

Szulanski, G. (1996) Exploring internal stickiness: Impediments to the transfer of best practice within the firm [Winter special issue]. *Strategic Management Journal, 17*, 27–43.

Tarique, I., & Schuler, R. S. (2010). Global talent management: Literature review, integrative framework, and suggestions for further research. *Journal of World Business, 45*(2), 122–133.

Vernon, R. (1971). *Sovereignty at bay: The multinational spread of U.S. Enterprises.* New York: Basic Books.

Yoshihara, H. (1989). *Genchijinshachou to uchinaru kokusaika (HCN presidents and internal internationalization).* Tokyo: Toyokeizaishinposha.

Talent Management in ASEAN: A Study of Thailand

Opas Piansoongnern

1   Introduction

The financial industry particularly the securities business is one of the Thailand's fastest growing industries. Multinational corporations (MNCs) are using Thailand as one of their financial hubs for penetrating the Southeast Asian region. ASEAN Economic Community (AEC) is the important factor that encourages a number of MNCs to spend plenty of their investment in Thailand. One critical issue of MNC's operation is people management. A number of high performance financial consultants are urgently needed by both Thai and global corporations in the industry. According to the study of Piansoongnern and Anurit (2007), it is obviously seen that the relationship with marketing staff is the most influential factor to investor's loyalty to the companies in Thailand because the marketing staff always directly contact with the investors. In this regard, Piansoongnern and Anurit point out that the best way to sustain profitability in long-term operation the securities companies need to manage their high performance marketers or talented employees appropriately.

However, in the current situation, the emerging battle for talent in Asia can be intensified because severe skilled labor shortages in the manufacturing and service sectors. The labor shortages across Asian countries such as China, Japan, Korea, Malaysia, Singapore and Taiwan have been repeatedly reported in the media. As a part of strategies to win the emerging talent battle, many global and local companies often use attractive salary packages to motivate talented people such as managers and professionals from overseas or poach them from competitors. Achieving talent management with strategy requires global and local companies to change their mindset especially reorientation of their organizations, operations, and processes to reflect the new order to talent management. As indicated by Cappelli

O. Piansoongnern (✉)
Faculty of Business Administration, Nation University, 1854 Bangna-Trad Road, Bangna, Bangkok 10260, Thailand
e-mail: opasplk@gmail.com

A. Al Ariss (ed.), *Global Talent Management*, Management for Professionals, DOI 10.1007/978-3-319-05125-3_12, © Springer International Publishing Switzerland 2014

171

(2008), talent management is easier said than done and it is time for a fundamentally new approach to talent management that takes into account the great uncertainty business face today. In this regard, this study should prove to be valuable and beneficial scholars in terms of talent management theory expansion and also assist human resource practitioners how to manage talents effectively in order to gain competitiveness in fierce global competition. The key objectives of the study are: (1) to discover talent management practices of Thai executives; and (2) to investigate the reasons that influence engagement and performance of talented employees in the Thai securities industry.

2 Talent Management in Thailand

In the Thai business context, talent management is deemed as a new and challenging issue amongst HR practitioners as revealed by a study of Piansoongnern and Anurit (2010). The study discloses that talent management is still a new and challenging HR issue in which the succession planning is recognized and utilized as the foundation of talent management in both public and private organizations. The majority of in-depth interview participants suggested that they wish to manage individual talent as such encouraging and unleashing employees' potential, but they do not know how and where to begin the process. These problems significantly discourage HR practitioners from proposing any creative ideas about managing talent to their top executives. Thus, the participants mutually agree that to provide some promising scientific information is an urgent HR agenda. In addition, there are currently few empirical investigations in the field of talent management in the Thai business context as an important country in the global competition.

The link between human resource practices and organizational performance is found in the study of Wattanasupachoke (2009). The research focuses on how human resource strategies of Thai enterprises can influence business performances. All Thai firms listed in the stock market are investigated in order to represent the overall picture of Thai business. Regarding the relationship between human resource strategies and the firms' performances, the analysis results indicate that the extra pay and profit sharing scheme significantly influences the non-financial performances. The extra pay and profit sharing scheme lead to lead to sense of belonging and greater commitment of staff because their wealth will be directly linked to firms' financial performances. For the non-financial performances, the only influential group of variables is positive inner characters, consisting positive attitudes and politeness. The employees with these characters tend to be dedicated, faithful and committed to firms and customers. This results in better image, reputation, and satisfaction of customers.

The researches that are mainly focused on talent management have mostly found in comparative studies among Asian nations. In this regard, the link between human resource practices and talent management has focused and examined. Zheng et al. (2008) examine the issues relating to recruiting highly skilled managerial and professional staff experienced by multinational companies (MNCs) manufacturing in six Asian countries, namely Indonesia, Malaysia, Philippines, Singapore, Taiwan and Thailand. Data collected from 529 MNCs are used to examine critical human resource planning and recruitment concerns of companies operating in high growth "Dragon" and newly developed "Tiger" economies. The study examines the differences in recruitment practices between manufacturing and service companies and the issues relating to how manufacturers maintain an adequate skills basis. There appears a considerable extent of battle for talent between Dragon and Tiger economies with the latter required being more aggressive as they attempt to sustain growth. Manufacturing companies are experiencing a higher demand for more job-related managerial and technical capabilities whilst competing with service companies that are also in need for more talent. To succeed, manufacturing MNCs will need to adopt a strategic approach for recruitment and retention, and internal capability training to maintain their skilled employees in order to sustain competitive advantage. Zheng (2009) further surveyed 281 service MNCs in six Asian countries as discussed earlier in order to test the link between HR practices, employee retention, and service firm performance. The results confirm that there are statistically significant linkages between HR practices, talent retention and firm performance. In particular, various skill training and development programs are seen to be significantly associated with capacity to deliver quality service and on firm growth as perceived by managers surveyed. Informal recruitment methods that are used more by Asian-bred firms have contributed to better retention rates. Not all formalized HR practices lead to talent retention; and the degree to which HR is perceived to have impacted on firm performance varies.

In the micro perspective on talent management, Japanese companies in Thailand are interested by scholars particularly the implementation and transferability of Japanese managerial styles are mainly concentrated. Onishi (2006) examines the transferability of Japanese human resource management to Thailand. Attitudes toward lifetime employment, seniority system, consensual decision-making, quality circles, and house unions are considered. The sample included 560 managers and staff of Japanese companies in Thailand. The results indicate that all five practices except seniority are transferable. The Thai employees have more positive attitudes toward consensual decision-making, quality circles and house unions than the Japanese managers in the Japanese manufacturers in Thailand. Some Japanese managers think that consensual decision-making and quality circles are not appropriate or accepted in Thailand. This belief may limit the implementation of these practices. Regarding seniority, both the Japanese mangers and the Thai employees agreed that performance should be evaluated by achievement, but years of service should be part of any evaluation criteria. Petison and Johri (2007) point out that trust and respect are significant factors that influence the development of local talent in Japanese subsidiaries. Petison and Johri (2007) analyze the implementation of Thainization philosophy at Toyota Motor Thailand (TMT) by using in-depth interviews with Thai and Japanese employees, and Imai Hiroshi, one of the architects of Thainization philosophy. The findings demonstrate that the challenges and solutions in developing local employees for managing subsidiaries—implementation of Thainization philosophy in TMT, the management has to demonstrate

Table 1 Five key GTM challenges, strategies, and future opportunities

Five key points regarding Global Talent Management challenges	Five key points regarding strategies to overcome these challenges	Five key points regarding future opportunities in Global Talent Management
Emerging talent mobility in Association of Southeast Asian Nations (ASEAN)	Categorization of different kinds of talent	Develop a framework for managing talent in the ASEAN business context
Launching corporate policy supporting talent management	Leveraging executive's supports on talent management	Increase executive's awareness about talent management
Demanding talent management specialist in ASEAN	Develop specialist's competencies for some specific regions such as ASEAN	Develop global talent management specialists and their competencies
Women in management	Create management frameworks for managing female talent	Develop career path for female talent
Skill portability of talent	Planning and managing portable skills of talent in a new environment	Develop organizational supports and environment facilitating portable skills of talent

respect for local employees and build trust between Thai and Japanese employees. Once the employees related to each other on the basis of mutual respect and trust, it was relatively easy to collaborate and find solutions. A study of Petison, and Johri is supported by a recent study of Piansoongnern et al. (2011) that investigate talent management strategies and employee engagement implemented in three leading cement companies in Thailand ranged from the largest to smallest ones. In-depth interviews are conducted with multi-level employees involved in managing talent including executives, potential employees, and human resources (HR) staff, while 350 questionnaires are also distributed for an investigation of factors influencing employee engagement. The findings revealed that robust talent management planning, well supports of top management, fair salary, good safety and health insurance, training opportunity, career advancement, organizational unity, a balance of work and daily life, and other environmental factors are crucial factors that keep talent rooted to organizations (Table 1).

In summary, the research in the topic "talent management" in Thailand is mainly focused on the link between human resource practices and organizational performance, and the factors affecting talent management. These empirical studies demonstrated high value of human resource practices in managing talent through macro and micro perspectives. Data from different Asian countries are analyzed, while Japanese companies are mainly employed as the significant data source. Apparently interesting issues, such as, What do Thai firms mean by talent and talent management? What human resource practices do they use in managing talent? And the comparison of Thai and MNCs in different nationalities and industries regarding talent management, are left unaddressed.

3   Research Methodology

The qualitative research is deemed as the most appropriate for this study since the research questions are targeted to investigate on "how" and "why" questions which are (1) How do Thai executives describe and manage talented employees?; and (2) Why do Thai talented employees engage and perform their jobs in the organization? The overall purposes of qualitative research were to achieve an understanding of how people make sense out of their lives, delineate the process of meaning-making rather than the outcome or product, and describe how people interpret what they experience. This matches researcher's objectives for conducting this study. However, the qualitative case study research is selected because it is focused on a contemporary phenomenon and do not require the control of behavioral events (Yin 2008). The researcher wishes to understand talent management processes, developments, and implementations that are going on in the natural setting or real business situations. The researcher do not need to control some behavioral events, but would like to explore and understand how people interpret their experiences, how they construct their words, and what meaning they attribute to their experiences about talent management naturally.

For the case selection, one financial and investment brokerage company is selected as a case study because two main reasons:
1. It is one of the large financial and investment brokerage companies in Thailand. Also, it is a subsidiary of one of Asia's leading financial and investment brokers.
2. It is identified as the high performance financial and investment brokerage organization in Thailand. This is proven by its champion position with the highest market share for 8 consecutive years. In this regard, without any high performance employees, the firm will never occupy this position definitely. However, the data were collected from 2 Chief Executive Officers (CEOs), 1 Managing Director (MD), 25 Branch Managers, and 75 high performance employees

In order to protect the privacy of the selected company, it is named as "Company X" in the study. However, a single case is focused for two reasons. First, the case is relatively unusual in context and provides the opportunity to build theory through analysis of a number of unit cases within the firm. That is divergent individual views from key people at different levels from the senior management (i.e. Chief Executives and senior managers), and at the middle-management and operational levels (i.e. middle managers and employees) could be identified and used to point a collective portrait of the talent management phenomenon under the study. Different groups of people may have disparate interpretations of the same issue. Second, because of the nature of the research, the researcher opts for depth and rich data, which necessarily requires a thorough immersion in the organization.

As for data analysis, content analysis is used in order to find the themes, stories and patterns in the data. The process unpacks the evidence from interviews, documents, and archival records to determine how stakeholders' perceptions and understanding of talent management in their organization. The unit of measurement is centered on the communication of meaning, especially the frequency and variety of messages, the number of times a certain phrase or speech pattern is used during the interviews. Essentially, content analysis looked for insights in which situation, settings, styles, images, meanings and nuances are key topics. The important concerns for content analysis are: (1) selecting the right data to answer the research question; and (2) susceptibility of the analysis to bias. The data are not usually immediately accessible for analysis but required some processing. Raw field notes needed to be corrected, edited, noted, typed up and re-corrected. After that, the data are aggregated and analyzed to ensure the consistent themes of the study. Then, the obtained dada is analyzed using content analysis techniques to measure the semantic content of the communication to diagnose findings with anonymity protection for academic purposes. The researcher checks the data once it is interpreted and cooperated with highly experienced researchers and professionals to ensure validity and reliability before finalizing the finally completed report.

Thus, the researcher uses various methods for increasing validity and reliability. First, validity is enhanced by triangulation; respondent validation; and adequate engagement in data collection.

1. Triangulation: The use of multiple data sources is employed for the study;
2. Respondent validation: The researcher solicited feedback on emerging results from some of the participants that the researcher interviewed;
3. Adequate engagement in data collection: The researcher collected data until the researcher sees or hears the same things over and over again, and no new information surfaces as the researcher collected more data;

Second, thick description is employed for enhancing reliability and generalizability of the study. This is the most common method involving the generalizability of qualitative research. It refers to a description of the setting and participants of the study as well as a detailed description of the findings with adequate evidence presented in the form of quotes from participant interviews. Reader or user generalizability involves leaving the extent to which a study's findings apply to other situations up to the people in those situations. The person who reads the study decides whether the findings can apply to his or her particular situation. In this regard, the results of the study are reviewed by the HR practitioners for their application.

4   Results and Discussion

Based on the findings, two research questions which were: (1) How do Thai executives describe and manage the talented employees?; and (2) Why do Thai talented employees engage and perform their jobs in the organization?, were answered.

For the research question one, talent is defined by the top executives as a group of high performance employees called "Manus Thongkhum (in Thai: มนุษย์ทองคำ)". More than 80 % of corporate revenue is generated by this group of employees. The result is similar and supported to the survey of Thai HR practitioners' perspectives on talent management conducted by Piansoongnern and Anurit (2010) which reveals that talent is very important factor leading to corporate success and sustainable profitability of the firms, but this result is divergent with the recent study about talent management in the Thai cement industry of Piansoongnern et al. (2011) which states that the competition of talented employees is not fierce. The study discloses that the competition of talented employees in the Thai securities industry is very aggressive as the talented employees are the key revenue generator. This is the reason that why they are directly and closely supervised by the top executives. The HR department plays just a supportive role. Every employee is equally treated, although, he or she is not identified as a talented one because the top executives believed that all employees should have an equal opportunity to be identified as one in a group of talented employees. Since they believe that everyone had hidden potential. The company has a responsibility of unleashing individual potential from every employee.

However, the key characteristics of talented employees desired by the securities firm are honesty, optimism, enthusiasm, and tolerance because they have to work under pressure from both the nature of the job and the external effects such as economic crunch. No matter what they graduate from leading business schools and had extensive experiences, these characteristics still plays more important. The study reveals that a group of people who graduated from leading business schools and hold a honor degree is not difficult to employ but the persons who have both excellent qualification and desired characteristics are very hard to find and retain as revealed by the top executives. For this reason, growing the talents from within is mainly employed as the unofficial policy of the company because it is the most effective method for acquiring and retaining talents for sustainable profitability. The talented employees grown from within are likely to stay with the company longer than the ones recruited from the competitors. The top executives also use personal relationship as the important tool for managing talents. It is the respect between the top executives and talented employees ranged from the branch managers to operational staff. In the Thai business context, respect is very important particularly in the securities industry where job performance is chiefly depended on individual knowledge, skills, and capability. The talented employees will not effectively work under the superiors who they are not respected. Once the talents feel like that, they are likely to move from the current firm to the new one.

These findings are in line with the data obtained from the interview with the talented employees that is employed to answer the research question two. In the talented employee's perspectives, talent management is not widely recognized because there is not any talent management activity officially organized in the organization in the study. The HR department is just recognized as a payroll unit that involves mainly in salary payment and related paper works. Therefore, to be identified as a talent is not important for them because it has no effect on individual performance and career advancement. Equal employment and career advancement opportunity are identified as the important factors for retention of the talented employees. In the individual performance oriented firm, educational background should not be used as the crucial determinant of employment and career advancement. Every employee expects to be promoted and rewarded on the basis of his or her performance. If this practice can be implemented, the talented ones are likely to sustainably stay with the company for long time.

By the way, an informal mentoring is revealed as a powerful practice used to unleash incredible potential of all talented employees because it is based on the voluntary basis and the matching of mentor and mentee's personal characteristics and interests. Most of the talented employees are successful in their careers because they impress their mentors and look them as the role model. In this regard, the top executives are deemed as the most important factor. They must act as the first mentor in the entire process of talent management. The top executives must firstly train the branch manager because they are the direct superiors of the talented ones. If they have positive attitude toward mentoring conducted by the top executives, they are likely to deliver all the knowledge and tactics to their subordinates. Therefore, leader's characteristics are very important. In a Thailand's leading securities firm, characteristics of leaders desired by the talented employees are openness, approachability, and trustworthiness. The financial benefits issue was not only a focus of the talents in the Thai securities industry. They wished the leaders to be more than just their bosses. For this reason, the brother-sister relationship is strengthened and used by the executives as the powerful instrument for managing talents (Petison and Johri 2007). This is not strange or seen as a new relationship pattern in the Thai business context. The brother-sister relationship is respectfulness between the top executives and their subordinates. The higher level of the brother-sister relationship leads to the higher level of engagement of the talented employees according to the findings of the study.

Therefore, the study shows that to be successful in talent management the equal employment opportunity practices must firstly be implemented. According to the findings of the study, the equal opportunities for talent identification, development, rewarding, and retention are highly desired by the talented employees at all levels. The HR department is just a supportive unit that acts as a unit to provide information and material supports for the executives in managing talents. In the study, the equal employment opportunity is not officially announced as the corporate policy but it was widely recognized by the employees that everyone has an equal chance to be identified as one in a group of talented employees. In this regard, leaders are very important to encourage the equal opportunity practices. Leader's characteristics desired by the talented employees are openness, approachability, and trustworthiness. The leaders who possess these characteristics are expected to encourage the success of talent management because they are likely to create the brother-sister relation between them and their talented employees. This is an exchange relationship but is differentiated by fulfilling the respect into it. In the Thai business context, respect is very important. The talented employees do not contribute to the company where they feel that they are not respected and included by the executives particularly the top ones. Once the brother-sister relationship is actively implemented, the firm will possess the talented ones who are honesty, optimism, enthusiasm, and tolerance. At the same time, the informal mentoring will be used as the instrument to transform the respect to the power that pushes employees to work hard for the company. Sense of belonging is created and emerged by this practice. Afterward, the engagement will be emerged. As obviously shown in the study, the Company X can sustain its champion position for 8 consecutive years because of its leaders implement these practices. The talent management model emerged from this study is also confirmed by the study of Petison and Johri (2007) which states that trust and respect are important factors that influence talent management in the Thai business context.

5   Recommendations for Future Research

First, quantitative research is recommended to examine and confirm the findings found from this qualitative study. Some factors that influence the effective talent management should be quantitatively investigated such as leader's characteristics. As the nature of quantitative research, a number of samples could use to effectively confirm the findings and expand some perspectives of talent management in Thailand.

Second, a comparison of Thai and foreign executives' practices in managing Thai talents is recommended to investigate. The different practices of Thai and foreign leaders are a very important factor in developing an effective talent management framework for the organizations in the Thai business context. Both Thai and foreign executives should have different practices, experiences, and solutions in managing talents. This means that Thai and foreign executives working in a same company may have different methods for managing talents. Their diverse practices will expand the perspectives of the HR practitioners in the Thai business context because the researcher believes that in a specific context likes Thailand; a unique talent management practice is needed to enhance the success level of talent management implementation.

Third, a comparison of talent management in different industries is recommended. Talented employees in one industry may be managed or needed the different management practices compared with the others. However, the researcher believes that all the industries should have a mutual point or factor that uses to manage talents effectively.

Fourth, a comparative study of the firms from different nationalities is recommended to conduct for comparing the practices done by various foreign corporations. A comparison of the Japanese and Chinese firms in Thailand, for example, is an interesting talent management issue since the Japanese is the biggest investors in Thailand, while the Chinese is increasing their power in the Thai economy. Many Chinese corporations are hunting the local talents. The Chinese practices of hunting and the Japanese practices of retaining are very interesting.

Fifth, the career path of the talented employees should also be investigated. The success factors and barriers of career progression will be revealed. To recognize these factors will be useful for structuring and developing an effective talent management framework. The talent retention program, for example, could be effectively implemented by using the factors that really affect on talents.

Sixth, the exchange relationship between the top executives and the talented employees is recommended to investigate. As shown in the study, the brother-sister relationship has an important impact on the success of talent management. Therefore, a comparative study between two companies, industries or countries is interesting.

Last, a comparative investigation of female and male talented employees should be conducted in order to investigate the factors that influence the success level of talented employees from different genders. Because in the same business context, female and male employees may have different career path, even though, they are classified as the high performance ones. In the Thai business context, an interesting issue is what factors have high impact on their career.

6   Recommendations for Managerial Implication

Apart from the financial packages the company offers to the talented employees, the global managers must create trust in order to encourage commitment of talented employees in Thailand. It is very easy for the managers to position themselves as the elder brother or sister. This approach leads to higher level of trustworthiness and respectfulness of the superior and his subordinate, respectively. The relationship between them in Thailand is not reciprocal. The subordinates are reluctant to leave and also do not to hesitate to contribute their resources and capabilities, if they accept that their superiors are their elder brothers and sisters.

References

Cappelli, P. (2008, March). Talent management for the twenty-first century. *Harvard Business Review*, 74–81.

Onishi, J. (2006). The transferability of Japanese HRM practices to Thailand. *Asia Pacific Journal of Human Resources, 44*(3), 260.

Petison, P., & Johri, L. M. (2007). Developing local talent in international subsidiaries: The importance of trust and respect in Toyota. *Development and Learning in Organizations, 21* (3), 10–13.

Piansoongnern, O., & Anurit, P. (2007). A global competitiveness study of Thai securities industry: A case study of factors influencing investors' loyalty to securities companies in Bangkok. *Global Journal of Flexible Systems Management, 8*(1&2), 1–16.

Piansoongnern, O., & Anurit, P. (2010). Talent management: Quantitative and qualitative studies of HR practitioners in Thailand. *International Journal of Organizational Innovation, 3*(1), 280–302.

Piansoongnern, O., Anurit, P., & Kuiyawattananonta, S. (2011). Talent management in Thai cement companies: A study of strategies and factors influencing employee engagement. *African Journal of Business Management, 5*(5), 1578–1583.

Wattanasupachoke, T. (2009). Strategic human resource management and organizational performance: A study of Thai enterprises. *Journal of Global Business Issues, 3*(2), 139–148.

Yin, R. K. (2008). *Case study research: Design and methods* (4th ed.). Thousand Oaks, CA: Sage.

Zheng, C. (2009). Keeping talents for advancing service firms in Asia. *Journal of Service Management, 20*(5), 482–502.

Zheng, C., Soosay, C., & Hyland, P. (2008). Manufacturing to Asia: Who will win the emerging battle for talent between dragons and tigers? *Journal of Manufacturing Technology Management, 19*(1), 52.

Global Talent Management in Knowledge Intensive Firms in Europe and India

Vijay Pereira and Rita Fontinha

1   Introduction

This chapter concerns global talent management in knowledge intensive firms in and between Western Europe and India. It also discusses the extent of talent flow between the two regions (specifically from Western Europe to India), and the challenges faced by these expatriates in India. In doing so it aims to identify and suggest future research directions.

The need for organisations to be as competitive as possible in the global marketplace has increased dramatically over the last 20 years. This phenomenon has led practitioners and researchers to rethink the traditional strategies used to manage human resources, now adding an international perspective. International human resource management follows the premise that organisations' global competitive advantage depends on the effective management of their workforces (Bryan 2010). Within the field of international human resource management, global talent management has been developing as a crucial topic for both researchers and managers. The relevance of this topic is due to the fact that, since the late 1990s, organisations around the world have been confronted with a major threat to doing business: a demand for talented employees that far surpassed the supply, thus creating a global talent shortage (Michaels et al. 2001). As a consequence, talent acquisition, retention and management have become a matter of great importance in the global business arena (Guthridge et al. 2008).

There is no unanimity in the definition of global talent management. However, from the large set of definitions in the literature, a key and common notion emerges: i.e. that there should be a focus on the talent of employees, so that organisations can attract, select, develop and retain this talent in order to enhance organisational performance in a global setting (Schroevers and Hendriks 2012; Farndale et al. 2010).

V. Pereira (✉) • R. Fontinha
Portsmouth Business School, University of Portsmouth, Portsmouth, UK
e-mail: vijay.pereira@port.ac.uk; rita.fontinha@port.ac.uk

A. Al Ariss (ed.), *Global Talent Management*, Management for Professionals,
DOI 10.1007/978-3-319-05125-3_13, © Springer International Publishing Switzerland 2014

Most of the research on international human resource management, and more specifically on global talent management has been developed in North America. In fact, there has been mention of the existence of a 'Gulf Stream' of ideas in this field, drifting from the USA and hitting the UK first, then crossing the Benelux countries … and Germany and France, and proceeding finally to southern Europe (Scullion and Collings 2011). Research outside North America and Europe is even sparser. Nevertheless, even with the global economic slowdown of 2008, there are continuing challenges in attracting, managing, and retaining talent, especially in the developing regions of the world where economic activity has outpaced the availability of skilled employees (Tymon et al. 2010), as these regions are witnessing greater growth rates.

In this chapter we decided to focus on talent management in Western Europe and India for the following two interrelated reasons. First, we wanted to focus on two representatives of Western and Eastern talent management strategies. The emphasis and focus of research is now moving from developed countries such as the US, EU and Japan to developing countries such as the BRICS (Brazil, Russia, India, China and now South Africa). However, the majority of research on Western vs. Eastern comparisons focused on contrasting Western Countries and Eastern Asian countries, mostly China. We decided to focus on a less researched topic and compare Western Europe and India in order to explore the specificities of the two regions and the challenges for talent management, and in the process help identify future research directions. Our second motive relates to the growing links between the two regions and talent management flows, especially from Western Europe to India. According to the Expat Explorer Survey (HSBC 2012), India is the 11th out of 30 countries of destination in terms of economic incentives for Western expats. These economic advantages are likely to be extremely relevant in a context of the current European economic crisis. Additionally knowledge sharing between the two regions is envisaged to be mutually beneficial.

Also, in this chapter, we will focus specifically on the context of knowledge intensive firms. For knowledge-intensive firms (Alvesson 2004) the strategic capacity to compete derives from knowledge: this knowledge is mainly derived from people (Kessels 2004). Because the emphasis is on knowledgeable people in knowledge-intensive firms, organisations constantly need to find ways to make better use of this knowledge (Schroevers and Hendriks 2012). Considering the relevance of the workers for organisations' competitive advantage, the strategy has been to manage knowledge via human resource management (HRM). However, simply thinking of knowledge management as incomplete without human resource management would be too vague considering the amplitude of the HRM field. The specific area of 'talent management' may be able to provide the missing link between the people side to management and knowledge-related challenges and problems within organisations (Schroevers and Hendriks 2012). Accordingly, we focus on the specific challenges for talent management and possible strategies to overcome them in the particularly fertile context of knowledge intensive firms.

Further, considering the multinational dimension of numerous organisations, and the arguments made above, there has been a growing concern with the management of talent at a global level. There is a vast gap in research in this area. Accordingly, in this chapter, we focus on important theoretical and empirical research related to talent management in knowledge intensive firms, focusing specifically on Western Europe and India, with an aim to provide future research directions. We provide a thorough description of talent management strategies implemented in Western Europe and then move on to discuss, much more in detail, the emerging talent management strategies in India, especially the business process offshoring industry, aiming to emphasise some specificities between the two regions. We additionally describe and analyse the talent flow patterns from Western Europe to India, and challenges for expatriates in India. Our overall aim is to understand the specific challenges of these flows from the perspective of talent management, aiming to provide some suggestions to both researchers and practitioners.

2   Talent Management in Western European Knowledge Industries

Alongside North America and Japan, Europe has long been a privileged location for the development of knowledge intensive firms. Knowledge-intensive business services in particular grew significantly since the early 1990s. During this time, the perception of the services area shifted from a role of 'adapters of innovation stemming from the manufacturing sector' to the role of 'important players in the innovation process' (Muller and Doloreux 2007: 19). However, as expected, there are several inequalities in terms of the distribution of knowledge intensive firms throughout Europe, with Scandinavia, the Benelux countries and the UK leading the charts, and with the Mediterranean and the new EU members at the bottom. Despite these expected regional differences, the most remarkable contrasts are between some urban poles and the remaining territories. In particular, the highest concentration of workers in knowledge intensive firms is in Î}\^{I}{le de France, Lombardie, Comunidad de Madrid, Outer London, Cataluña, Rhône-Alpes, Düsseldorf, Andalucia, Inner London, Lazio and Upper Bavaria (descending order; European Commission 2012). These areas are all located in Western European countries, which is why we chose to focus on Western Europe in the current chapter (leaving out the new EU countries).

The high number of highly-skilled global workers in European capitals has soon led to a managerial and academic interest in the management of this talent (e.g., Pettigrew 2002; Scullion and Collings 2011). Nevertheless, Europe is a very heterogeneous continent, which leads to the existence of different forms of managing talent across different regions. The most common regional division is: Anglo Europe, Germanic Europe and Latin Europe (Carter and Galinsky 2008). Each of the three regional profiles poses challenges to talent management. We advance some possible solutions to overcome them.

Research has shown that in Anglo-Europe, organisations and their employees have common 'value-based' behaviour that predicates rewards on merit, are highly individualistic and male dominated, despite the efforts to reduce gender inequality and implement a better work-life balance (Carter and Galinsky 2008). The main challenges for talent management, especially in the context of knowledge intensive firms relate to team-work and knowledge sharing, which are crucial for the success of this type of firms. One possible strategy to overcome these challenges might reside in a better team leadership, where group achievements would have a direct impact in the extremely valued individual careers. For this individualistic culture, it would also be relevant to consider the emerging perspectives of leadership as a collective process: collective leadership within a team, particularly the development and mentoring dimensions are predictors of supervisor-rated team performance (Hiller et al. 2006).

Workers from the Germanic Europe cluster are likely to value traits such as assertiveness and being results-oriented, reporting a greater concern for standardisation, being focused on the future, avoiding uncertainty and appreciating collectivism (Carter and Galinsky 2008). The particular talent management challenges for Germanic Europe relate to being able to break standardised processes and readapt when situations suddenly change (difficulty dealing with uncertainty). This spontaneity might be extremely relevant in the constantly changing business of knowledge intensive firms. One possible strategy to overcome these challenges might relate to extra training aiming to develop skills such as creativity and fast resolution of unknown problems.

In the Latin Europe cluster, workers have been found to be less likely to engage in collective action, and leaders are less likely to exhibit and promote altruistic ideals or reward members for performance improvement and excellence. This culture is more characterised by affective autonomy, in which individuals are independent and pursue positive experiences for themselves (Carter and Galinsky 2008). The main talent management challenges for Latin Europeans relate to the idea that collective performance might not necessarily lead to individual rewards. The suitable talent management strategies for this context would be similar to the ones appropriate for the Anglo European context: the implementation of better leadership strategies that would develop a stronger altruistic feeling, where the investment of the whole group would be directly linked to rewards to all individuals. This would be relevant for knowledge intense firms where team-work is crucial.

Despite the relevance of the aforementioned challenges related to specific regional business characteristics, the major challenge for the talent management of all Europeans, since 2008, has been the economic recession. The 'war for talent', which characterised the years up to the economic crisis, has been quelled as companies have fewer funds. According to the Eurostat (2013), the overall unemployment rate in Europe was 12 % in August 2013. Among the Member States, the lowest unemployment rates were recorded in Austria (4.9 %), Germany (5.2 %) and Luxembourg (5.8 %), and the highest rates in Greece (27.9 % in February) and Spain (26.2 %). Figures are even more concerning when we focus on youth unemployment, since they are a crucial source of talent, especially for knowledge-intensive firms. From the beginning of 2009, the gap between the youth and the total unemployment rates has increased, so that at the end of 2012 the youth unemployment rate was 2.6 times the total rate. The economic recession has impacted knowledge intensive areas and we have been witnessing, not only a brain drain from Southern to Northern Europe, but also a brain drain from Europe to the US or to emerging economies (OECD 2013).

Whether companies are in the midst of restructuring, recruiting and developing talent on shoestring budgets, or struggling to maintain and motivate top talent, changes of this magnitude must be actively managed with workforce capabilities as a key consideration (Davidson et al. 2008). The major strategy in this situation may reside in the identification of crucial sources of talent in knowledge intensive firms, both at the managerial and at the technical levels. Attempts for retention at this level may involve strategies that promote job security and work-family balance. Furthermore, we believe that there is a relevant strategy that would, not only help manage talent in the context of economic recession, but also contribute to overcoming the recession: the reinforcement of the bridge between science and practice (McDonnell 2011). Bridging this gap is crucial for talent search and retention in knowledge intensive firms, since it will promote the faster application of innovative ideas and thus increase the market value of these firms. In particular, there should be a stronger reliance in partnerships between profit-oriented organisations and Universities/Research & Development Centres. Excellence at the scientific and technological levels may be one of the most relevant factors to differentiate Europe from its worldwide competitors and boost the recovery from the European recession. Initiatives such as 'Horizon 2020'[1] might become important instruments to bridge this gap between science and practice in Europe.

Having described some of the key features that influence the way talent is (and should be) managed in Europe, we now discuss the talent management strategies in the newly evolving knowledge intensive industries in India, such as the business process offshoring industry. We start with discussing the specific knowledge intensive industries, its extent and growth and then the talent management strategies, practices and challenges and the ways in which they are managed.

3   Talent Management in Indian Knowledge Industries

Globalisation has transformed the way business and work is conducted, both in the global north and south. The increased use of offshore outsourcing or 'offshoring' of knowledge intensive work has meant stakeholders are affected by work being carried out in geographically different global destinations. This trend has changed global employment patterns and talent management strategies and has as a result led to management implications and consequences. India is a major destination for such knowledge intensive work, such as for e.g. work in 'information technology

---

[1] 'Horizon 2020' is the financial instrument implementing the Innovation Union, a Europe 2020 flagship initiative aimed at securing Europe's global competitiveness.

enabled services' (ITeS), 'business process offshoring' (BPO) and 'pharmaceutical' industries. Activity has grown rapidly for India in recent years, with success in attracting both relatively low skilled transactional work, and high skilled 'professional' work. There is increased interest in this phenomenon from academics, researchers and practitioners worldwide to understand these new trends and their implications. Relatively little research on talent management strategies in knowledge intensive firms investigates the phenomenon's consequences and implications for human resource management strategies and practices of those firms in destination countries supplying such services to external clients. What is the balance between 'indigenous' and 'novel' talent management practices, for example, and 'best-practice' policies that may be adopted in these knowledge intensive industries? Also, what is the extent and challenges of talent management flows between Western Europe and India? These and others below are important questions that future research needs to address.

3.1 Why India?

India is seen as the second largest growing economy of the world after China (Budhwar and Varma 2010, 2011). The growth of the Indian economy, growth in Indian firms and their resources are salient issues in the current environment (Cappelli et al. 2010; Kumar et al. 2009). The Information and Communication Technology (ICT) sector is still the fastest growing segment of the economy, both in terms of production and exports. With complete de-licensing of the electronics industry with the exception of aerospace and defence electronics, and along with the liberalisation in foreign investment and export-import policies of the entire economy, this sector is not only attracting significant attention as an enormous market but also as a potential production base by international companies. These are knowledge intensive industries and hence need talented knowledge workers to service these sectors. The Indian IT sector has shown remarkable resilience during the current global financial downturn. Arguably the greatest area of growth in this respect is with regards to the knowledge intensive BPO industry which was worth $69.4 billion in 2009, and growing; in 2012, estimated at almost 7.5 % of India's GDP and employs close to 2.2 million people (NASSCOM 2012). However, for established firms the outsourcing of business processes potentially carries a number of risks (Earl 1996; Aron and Singh 2005; Aubert et al. 1998; Hoecht and Trott 2006). These risks include unsuccessful outsourcing experiences in which suppliers have failed to meet expected service levels and deliver the expected cost savings. Therefore, for Indian firms the development of sustainability, through a strategic talent management process, is a key issue in order to compete with more established firms, particularly those originating or associated with countries that have a more established reputation with regards to the knowledge intensive sector, to extend their success to an international level. Several Indian organisations are now well known globally and hence it becomes imperative for them to sustain this and remain competitive, through a sustainable talent management strategy. In this context, how can successful 'best-practice' talent management strategies and practices from Western Europe be adopted and adapted in these Indian business process offshoring organisations?

The next section discusses the growth of the Indian knowledge intensive industries and the global linkages.

3.2 Growth of Indian Knowledge Intensive Firms: Global Linkages

A feature of the Indian knowledge intensive industries is its incredible rate of expansion. However, it is less clear to what extent, and how, talent management practices of such firms have fluctuated over time, and more recently as a result of the turbulent international business environment. In particular, what have been the consequences and implications for talent management practices in such firms of the recession where impact on Western countries may have led increased incidence of offshore work? As a prime destination for knowledge intensive outsourced work, India is a critical case for research into talent management. For e.g. Lahiri et al. (2012) state several reasons for investigating into the Indian BPO industry. First, India remains the top choice among various offshoring destinations for western client firms (Luo et al. 2010; Zaheer et al. 2009). Second, Indian BPO industry has evolved from low-value added services (e.g., call centers) to high-value added knowledge-based services. Finally, as one of the world's largest and most dynamic economies, India-based studies add value to the overall understanding of the global business environment. In terms of HR research, some studies of Indian call centres and BPO organisations have highlighted the formal, structured and rationalised human resource management (HRM) systems (Budhwar et al. 2006a, b), with some evidence of innovative practices in 'high end' services (Raman et al. 2007). The rapid growth of the outsourcing industry has resulted in both high turnover and skill shortages, as employers compete for a restricted talented segment of the labour force and have been forced to consider new types of response (Kuruvilla and Ranganathan 2010).

Over time, the Indian IT/BPO industry's performance was marked by sustained revenue growth, steady expansion into newer services, increased geographic penetration, and an unprecedented rise in investments by MNCs, in spite growing concerns about gaps in talent and infrastructure impacting cost competitiveness. NASSCOM (2012) further reported that as a proportion of national GDP, the sector revenues have grown from 1.2 % in the financial year 1998 to an estimated 7.5 % in 2012. Thus, the Indian IT/BPO sector has portrayed itself to be building a strong reputation in terms of its high standards of service quality and information security. The industry also continues to portray its drive to set global benchmarks in quality and information security through a combination of provider and industry-level initiatives and at strengthening the overall frameworks, creating greater awareness and facilitating wider adoption of standards and best practices. Within the broad-based industry structure, IT is led by large Indian firms, BPO by a mix of Indian and

MNC third-party providers and captives, and this reflects the talent supply-base. Whilst the larger players continue to lead growth, gradually increasing their share in the industry aggregate; several high-performing small and medium enterprises (SMEs) also stand out. In terms of the extent of talent, today, India leads the world in terms of the number of quality certifications achieved by centres in any single country (NASSCOM 2012). The US and the UK remain the key markets for Indian IT/BPO exports (excluding hardware), accounting for nearly 80 % of the total exports, followed by the remaining countries in Western Europe. Though these two markets account for the largest share of worldwide technology spends, the EU has a fair share of the market. In terms of global standing and competition, Indian business process outsourcing (BPO) providers have proved to be stiff competition to western BPO providers, accounting for 5 % of market revenue generated among the top 150 providers in 2008, according to Gartner Inc. (2008). In 2002 there were few, if any, India based BPO vendors in the top 150 worldwide providers, but by the end of 2008, the top 20 India based BPO providers accounted for $4 billion in revenue, representing 5 % of the $80 billion revenue of the top 150 BPO vendors globally. Gartner expects this trend to accelerate because of economic pressures that are contributing to demand for low-cost BPO. This again could not have been achieved without the sustained talent management practices and strategies of the Indian firms.

3.3 Talent Management and HRM Challenges in Indian Knowledge Intensive Industry

Above all sectors in India, the experience of talent management specifically in IT/BPO organisations is often flagged as standing apart from those in more traditional parts of the economy (Khandekar and Sharma 2005, 2006; Saini and Budhwar 2008) with more emphasis on formal, structured and rationalised HRM systems that reflect the importation of practices in the call-centre industry in other countries (Budhwar et al. 2006a, b). The workforce's identity is constructed as 'professional' rather than proletarian by the graduates themselves and the BPO firms that hire them, although this may belie the actual nature of much of the work (Noronha and D'Cruz 2009). Part of the reason for the formalisation of HRM can be found in the double-edged nature of the IT/BPO industry's expansion. The rapid growth of the outsourcing industry has resulted in both high turnover and skill and talent shortages, particularly evident in large cities, as multiple employers fish within the same relatively small pool for a restricted segment of the graduate labour force (Chatterjee 2009: 276–277; Kuruvilla and Ranganathan 2010). Numerous sources, including the BPO industry body NASSCOM (2010), suggest that relatively few fresh graduates are employable without further training. For example, Bayadi (2008: 24) claims that, despite the two and a half million graduates that India produces annually, 'human resource managers at multinationals consider only 10–25 % as employable'. With the Indian IT/BPO industry faced with recruitment, attrition and poaching problems, one recent survey finds the sector of the opinion that use of better HR practices is the main key to future success (Rajeev and Vani 2009: 59). Companies have been forced to consider new types of response (Kuruvilla and Ranganathan 2010). Some evidence exists of more innovative HR practices in 'high end' knowledge processing services, intended to recruit, retain and manage the performance of the relatively scarce group of graduates deemed to possess the right skills (Raman et al. 2007). Longitudinal data suggests a degree of movement in the governance and organisational features of IT/BPO firms from an initial transactional orientation to one more focused on achieving resource complementarity through the development of trust and a longer-term orientation to the provision and delivery of the offshore services (Vivek et al. 2009; Pereira and Anderson 2012).

Despite a hiatus in the fortunes of India's inherently globalised IT/BPO sector as a result of the international financial crisis, with recruitment freezes and even lay-offs in some firms particularly dependent on Western contracts (Ghosh and Chandrasekhar 2009: 728–729), there appears little reason to think that the hiring and retention problems outlined above are not recurrent. The challenge to recruit and retain talented people in the knowledge intensive industries in India is thus complex, evolving and on-going. Whilst Indian companies look towards the global north or Western countries for talent management models and strategies, they are also looking inwards towards indigenous way of managing its talented workforce in knowledge intensive sectors. In this context, what is the extent of the talent flow between Western Europe and India and what are the challenges faced? These questions are addressed below, with suggestions for future research in this area.

4   Knowledge Based Talent Flow from Western Europe to India

In the last two decades, there has been a growth in the two-way flow of trade between India and member states of the European Union, mostly Western Europe. This flow has led to the creation of organisations such as the EU Chambers of Commerce in India and the European Business Group in India. The major talent flows from Europe to India and from India to Europe have been occurring in the context of knowledge intensive firms, particularly the ones aiming at innovation and research and development activities (EBGI 2012). These talent flows are likely to persist in the future, especially due to initiatives such as the "Horizon 2020" strategy in Europe and the recently launched "Innovation Union" as it is in India with the "Decade of Innovation". We will now describe the way talent has been flowing from Western Europe to India, giving particular emphasis to the context of knowledge intensive firms.

The largest talent flow from Western Europe to India has started in the early 1990s, with the implementation of multinational organisations in this country. Today it is estimated that over 750 research and development subsidiaries of multinational organisations employing 200,000 engineers exist in India (EBGI 2012). There are several reasons why multinational organisations would decide to enter India. These reasons are initially more related to pure market considerations, sighting cost advantage, qualified workforce and attractive market conditions as prominent reasons. However, a medium term strategy is also leveraging India as a design base and research and development centre. The other reasons identified for entering India include: providing service support for high-end equipment imported from Europe, offering environmental services to the parent organisation and local customers, funding India specific projects, providing securing services, marketing and sales operations, mineral, and oil and gas exploration, delivering IT consulting services to global and Indian customers, and geographical expansion.

The majority of the talent flow from Europe to India occurs at a top managerial level. The implementation of subsidiaries of multinational organisations in India has led to a flow of European expatriates with high skills, performing managerial jobs and with high responsibility levels. Although these expats may belong to knowledge intensive organisations, they are unlikely to perform technical jobs. They might have strong technical skills in their field, but their roles as expatriates are more likely to involve the supervision of this type of jobs.

Talent management of European expatriates in India is intrinsically related to the management of the expatriation process. This involves specific organisational management strategies before, during, and after the expatriation period. Gesteland and Gesteland (2010) wrote a comprehensive book about the expatriation of 'Westerners' in India ('Westerners' would involve Northwest Europeans, Americans, Australians and New Zealanders). They describe the specificities of the business culture in India, which may present some difficulties for the western expats. The specific differences between the business cultures in Europe and in India are related to a monochronic vs. polycrhonic interpretation of time, respectively. Gesteland and Gesteland (2010, p. 22) exemplify: "German and German-Swiss expatriate managers in particular often experience great stress" due to their strongly monochronic interpretation of time. Other crucial aspects to account for considering western expatriates' adaptation to the Indian business culture involve the climate, the relationship-focus vs. deal-focus, hierarchical and egalitarian business behaviour, communication challenges and intercultural leadership challenges. Organisations need to be extremely careful in managing the talent of these expatriates. One strategy is to provide them training, which will allow them to be ready for some of the differences in the way of doing business. Furthermore, organisations' talent management strategies should also involve not only financial support, but also guidance related to the settlement of the expatriates' families.

In summary, though there is an increased flow of talented expatriates between Western Europe and India, research on talent management of these expatriates in India is largely missing. Future research thus needs to keep pace with this topical and evolving area. We hope the discussions above (and the subsequent Table 1) has pointed to several areas for future research.

Table 1 Talent management challenges of knowledgeable workers in Western European and Indian knowledge intensive industries

Five key points regarding Global Talent Management challenges	Five key points regarding strategies to overcome these challenges	Five key points regarding future opportunities in Global Talent Management
1 Recruitment and Retention of Talent by Knowledge Intensive firms (applicable to both Western Europe and India, see special emphasis on Indian firm under point 3 below)	Reinforcement of the investment in partnerships between the Academia and Private Organisations	Talent Management Strategies should pay special attention to career transitions between Academia and Private Organisations and vice versa
2 Impact of the Recession in Europe and Brain Drain	Widespread implementation of R&D initiatives such as 'Horizon 2020'	As Europe is affected by the recession, it is crucial to identify the most talented individuals, providing them several inducements (related to increased job security in particular) in order to promote their retention
3 Attraction and retention of key talent personnel in newly evolving knowledge intensive firms (e.g. IT-BPO)	The utilisation of Western (e.g. European and US) best-practices and local indigenous talent management practices and models	Identifying the hybridisation of talent management practices through research
4 The need for talent management to keep pace with the fast growing knowledge intensive work coming into India through offshore outsourcing and dealing with the complexities of such work	Using practices that are best-fit to overcome the challenges rather than mere global or local best practices	Greater research needed to unbundle the complexity facing talent management and thus keep pace with the growth
5 Talent Flow from Western Europe to India: Management of the Expatriation Process	Preparation for the Indian Business Culture and close monitoring of the expatriation process	Future research should focus on the identification of strategies for talent management post-expatriation process

Conclusion

In the current chapter, our aim was to address some of the specificities of talent management in knowledge intensive firms. We focused on the particular cases of Western Europe and India, describing thoroughly these two contexts and the talent management challenges and strategies implemented to overcome them.

In the case of Western Europe, these challenges may differ according to the main geographical differences (Anglo Europe, Germanic Europe and Latin Europe). However, the biggest challenge for talent management in knowledge-intensive firms in Western Europe relates to the current context of economic recession, which has led to high unemployment rates, talent flows within Europe and brain drain from Europe to the U.S. or to some of the emerging economies, such as India. We advanced some possible talent management strategies involving the appropriate identification and retention of key talented workers thought increased job security and work-family balance. We also suggest that talent management in knowledge intensive firms should involve the reinforcement of strategies to bridge the gap between science and practice. In India, the current economic situation is in a much better shape, largely led by the phenomenal growth of the Indian business process offshoring industry, meaning that there has been a large proliferation of such knowledge intensive firms in this country. The particular challenges that arise relate to the attraction of quality talent and skilled personnel and then the retention of such talented people. Furthermore, we focused on the Western Europe-India talent flow. Concerning the flow from Western Europe to India, we described the main talent management challenges that arise from the expatriation process and the possible strategies to overcome them. However, we also argue that there is a glaring gap in research in this area and that future research on talent management should concentrate on addressing this gap.

In summary, we chart the following five key points regarding challenges within talent management of knowledgeable workers in Western European and Indian knowledge intensive industries (Table 1), with relevant strategies to overcome these challenges and future opportunities in global talent management.

References

Alvesson, M. (2004). *Knowledge work and knowledge-intensive firms*. Oxford: Oxford University Press.

Aron, R., & Singh, J. (2005). Getting offshoring right. *Harvard Business Review, 83*, 135–143.

Aubert, B., Patry, M., & Rivard, S. (1998). Assessing the risk of IT outsourcing. In *Proceedings of the Thirty-First Hawaii International Conference on System Sciences*, Hawaii, 1998.

Bayadi, J. (2008, May 22–25). Will BPO remain as India's pride? *Siliconindia.*

Bryan, L. (2010, June 7–15). Globalization's critical imbalances. *The McKinsey Quarterly.*

Budhwar, P., Luthar, H., & Bhatnagar, J. (2006a). The dynamics of HRM systems in Indian BPO firms. *Journal of Labor Research, 27*(3), 339–360.

Budhwar, P., & Varma, A. (2010). *Doing business in India*. London: Routledge.

Budhwar, P. S., & Varma, A. (2011). Emerging HR management trends in India and the way forward. *Organizational Dynamics, 40*(4), 317–325.

Budhwar, P., Varma, A., Singh, V., & Dhar, R. (2006b). HRM systems of Indian call centres: An exploratory study. *International Journal of Human Resource Management, 17*(5), 881–897.

Cappelli, P., Singh, H., Singh, J., & Useem, M. (2010). *The Indian way: How India's top business leaders are revolutionizing management*. Boston: Harvard Business Press.

Carter, N. M., & Galinsky, E. (2008). *Leaders in a global economy: Talent management in European cultures*. Accessed October 12, 2013, from http://familiesandwork.org/site/research/reports/globaltalentmgmt2.pdf

Chatterjee, S. (2009). From Sreni Dharma to global cross-vergence: Journey of human resource practices in India. *International Journal of Indian Culture and Business Management, 2*(3), 268–280.

Davidson, V., Harshak, A., Rabb, S., & Blain, L. (2008). *Managing talent at a time of crisis: A cross-industry look at challenges and opportunities.* London: Booz & Co.

Earl, M. (1996). The risks of IT outsourcing. *Sloan Management Review, 37*(3), 26–32.

EBGI—European Business Group India. (2012). *Innovation and research & development activities of European Companies in India: Study report.* Accessed October 12, 2013, from http://ebgindia.com/contents/EBGI_r&d_innovation_surveyreport2012.pdf

European Commission. (2012). *Knowledge-intensive (business) services in Europe.* Brussels: European Commission. Retrieved from http://ec.europa.eu/research/innovation-union/pdf/knowledge_intensive_business_services_in_europe_2011.pdf. Accessed October 12, 2013.

Eurostat. (2013). *Unemployment rates, seasonally adjusted, August 2013.* Retrieved from http://ics_explained/index.php?title=File:Unemployment_rates,_seasonally_adjusted,_August_2013.png&filetimestamp=20131001065748. Accessed October 12, 2013.

Farndale, E., Scullion, H., & Sparrow, P. (2010). The role of the corporate HR function in global talent management. *Journal of World Business, 45*(2), 161–168.

Gartner Inc Report. (2008). Accessed October 12, 2013, from http://enea.ro/download/pdf/Gartner%20Why%20Romania%202008

Gesteland, R. R., & Gesteland, M. (2010). *India cross-cultural business behaviour: For business people, expatriates and scholars.* Copenhagen: Copenhagen Business School Press.

Ghosh, J., & Chandrasekhar, C. P. (2009). The costs of 'coupling': The global crisis and the Indian economy. *Cambridge Journal of Economics, 33*(4), 725–739.

Guthridge, M., Komm, A. B., & Lawson, E. (2008, January). Making talent management a strategic priority. *The McKinsey Quarterly,* 49–59.

Hiller, N. J., Day, D. V., & Vance, R. J. (2006). Collective enactment of leadership roles and team effectiveness: A field study. *Leadership Quarterly, 17*(4), 387–397.

Hoecht, A., & Trott, P. (2006). Innovation risks of strategic outsourcing. *Technovation, 26*(5–6), 672–681.

HSBC. (2012). *Expat explorer survey.* Retrieved from http://www.expatexplorer.hsbc.com/files/pdfs/overall-reports/2012/report.pdf

Kessels, J. W. M. (2004). The knowledge revolution and the knowledge economy: The challenge for HRD. In J. Woodall, M. Lee, & J. Stewart (Eds.), *New frontiers in HRD* (pp. 165–179). London: Routledge.

Khandekar, A., & Sharma, A. (2005). Managing human resource capabilities for sustainable competitive advantage: An empirical analysis from Indian global organization. *Education and Training, 47,* 628–639.

Khandekar, A., & Sharma, A. (2006). Organizational learning and performance: Understanding Indian scenario in present global context. *Education and Training, 48,* 682–692.

Kumar, N., Mohapatra, P. K., & Chandrasekhar, S. (2009). *India's global powerhouses: How they are taking on the world.* Boston: Harvard Business School Press.

Kuruvilla, S., & Ranganathan, A. (2010). Globalisation and outsourcing: Confronting new human resource challenges in India's business process outsourcing industry. *Industrial Relations Journal, 41,* 136–153.

Lahiri, S., Kedia, B., & Mukherjee, D. (2012). The impact of management capability on the resource-performance linkage: Examining Indian outsourcing providers. *Journal of World Business, 47*(1), 145–155.

Luo, Y., Zheng, Q., & Jayaraman, V. (2010). Managing business process outsourcing. *Organizational Dynamics, 39*(3), 205–217.

McDonnell, A. (2011). Still fighting the 'War for Talent'? Bridging the science versus practice gap. *Journal of Business and Psychology, 26,* 169–173. doi:10.1007/s10869-011-9220-y.

Michaels, E., Handfield-Jones, H., & Axelrod, B. (2001). *The war for talent.* Boston: Harvard Business School Press.

Muller, E., & Doloreux, D. (2007). *The key dimensions of knowledge-intensive business services (KIBS) analysis: A decade of evolution* (Working Papers Firms and Region No. 1/2007).

NASSCOM. (2010). *Nasscom strategic review.* Retrieved from http://www.nasscom.in/upload/SR10/ExecutiveSummary.pdf

NASSCOM. (2012). *IT-BPO sector in India: Strategic review 2010.* New Delhi: NASSCOM.

Noronha, E., & D'Cruz, P. (2009). Engaging the professional: Organising call centre agents in India. *Industrial Relations Journal, 40*, 215–234.

OECD. (2013). *International migration.* Accessed June 29, 2013, from http://www.oecd.org/migration/

Pereira, V., & Anderson, V. (2012). A longitudinal examination of HRM in a human resources offshoring (HRO) organisation operating from India. *Journal of World Business, 47*(2), 223–231.

Pettigrew, A. M. (2002). Management research after modernism. *British Journal of Management, 12*, 61–70. doi:10.1111/1467-8551.12.s1.8.

Rajeev, M., & Vani, B. P. (2009). India's export of BPO services: Understanding strengths, weaknesses and competitors. *Journal of Services Research, 9*, 51–67.

Raman, R., Bhudhwar, P., & Balasuramanian, G. (2007). People management issues in Indian KPOs. *Employee Relations, 29*(6), 696–710.

Saini, D. S., & Budhwar, P. S. (2008). Managing the human resource in Indian SMEs: The role of indigenous realities. *Journal of World Business, 43*, 417–434.

Schroevers, M., & Hendriks, P. (2012). Talent management in knowledge intensive organisations. In H. T. Hou (Ed.), *New research on knowledge management models and methods.* Rijeka: InTech. ISBN 978-953-51-0190-1.

Scullion, H., & Collings, D. G. (2011). *Global talent management.* New York: Routledge.

Tymon, W. G., Stumpf, S. A., & Doh, J. P. (2010). Exploring talent management in India: The neglected role of intrinsic rewards. *Journal of World Business, 45*, 109–121. doi:10.1016/j.jwb.2009.09.016.

Vivek, S. D., Richey, R. G., & Dalela, V. (2009). A longitudinal examination of partnership governance in offshoring: A moving target. *Journal of World Business, 44*, 16–30.

Zaheer, S., Lamin, A., & Subramani, M. (2009). Cluster capabilities or ethnic ties? Location choice by foreign entrants in the services offshoring industry in India. *Journal of International Business Studies, 40*(6), 944–968.

Talent Management in the MENA and GCC Regions: Challenges and Opportunities

Mhamed Biygautane and Khalid Othman Al Yahya

1   Introduction

The recent global economic and institutional performance problems have triggered a serious debate about the capacity of both government entities and private sector firms to develop, incorporate, and manage human capital and knowledge resources in a more strategic and sustainable manner. The MENA countries in general, and GCC ones in particular, have historically faced critical challenges related to the formation and management of their talent: the shortage of national skills and knowledge resources, the continued need for investments in these resources, and the reliance on large numbers of foreign workers and firms to fill the national skill-knowledge gap and shoulder the implementation of ambitious economic development goals (Farndale et al. 2010; Michaels and Handfield-Jones 2001). In part, the region was able to afford this reliance due to abundant financial resources, improved working and living conditions, and greater integration into the global economy (Pfeffer 1998).

However, recently, conditions have changed in terms of shrinking budgetary allocations for major expansion projects and human resource development, departure of talent from many sectors, and the quest for workforce nationalization and employment opportunities for locals (Blass et al. 2006). This highlights the limitations of previous approaches to organization and management development activities adopted by both public and private sectors in the GCC region. These new conditions raise many questions about the importance of how talent and knowledge—with their different forms and sources—are captured, organized, stored, and used to achieve strategic developmental goals. As illustrated in the 2009 *Arab Knowledge Report*, talent and knowledge constitute a pivotal lever in the service of growth and development. Hence, effective talent management is a necessary vehicle for realizing and

M. Biygautane (✉)
Dubai School of Government, Zayed University, Dubai, UAE
e-mail: mhamed.biygautane@dsg.ac.ae

K.O. Al Yahya
Managing Director, Accenture, Dubai, UAE

A. Al Ariss (ed.), *Global Talent Management*, Management for Professionals,
DOI 10.1007/978-3-319-05125-3_14, © Springer International Publishing Switzerland 2014

maximizing the potential of knowledge for sustainable performance in work organizations, as well as in society at large (UNDP and MBRF 2009).

Effective talent management is of vital importance to MENA and GCC countries. Governments have invested generously in developing or attracting human capital and knowledge resources through education, research, and training (Kumari and Bahuguna 2012). In spite of this expansion in human capital resources, recent studies suggest low returns in terms of achieving positive results concerning the empowerment and management of local (national) talent, as well as in improving performance (Lawler 2008; Wood 1999; Guthridge and Komm 2008). One factor is the prevalent high level of underutilization of knowledge and skills, especially in the public sector. The advent of the global financial crisis reinforced the gravity of some organizational and managerial problems that public organizations have been facing in the Arab world and the Gulf countries in particular. The region has historically faced three significant challenges: the "organizational management system challenge," the "knowledge management challenge," and the "talent management challenge." These three intertwined constitute a solid stumbling block for the success of organizational reforms' initiatives in the region (Biygautane and Al Yahya 2010).

The chapter is organized as follows: Sect. 2 starts with defining and providing a brief overview of global talent management, its opportunities and challenges from a general perspective. Section 3 sheds light on the various structural, economic, educational, and technical challenges that hinder the efforts of governments in the MENA region to benefit from the pools of young talent it hosts. To effectively evaluate these challenges, the chapter looks at the socioeconomic context in the MENA region, which includes unemployment, deficiencies in educational systems, literacy rates, and other indicators that explain the challenges associated with proper investment of talent. Section 4 looks at the opportunities that exist in the region's market place and how the purposeful formation, utilization, and management of talent can serve as a vehicle for their empowerment. It provides a holistic image of the efforts governments of the MENA, particularly in the GCC, have made to transform their economies to ones based on knowledge, diversify their economies, and protect the local labor force through policies like 'nationalization' implemented by governments of GCC. The case of the United Arab Emirates (UAE) in nationalizing its workforce will be discussed in more detail given its success in implementing effective nationalization policies over the past decade. Section 5 addresses specific recommendations to policymakers in the region on how to better utilize and manage their pools of talent and identify gaps in their current policies and practices. The recommendations will be based on the analysis of the challenges and opportunities identified in this chapter, and allow policymakers to learn from the opportunities embedded in global talent management best practices.

1.1   Research Methodology

This chapter conducts an extensive literature review on global talent management and identifies the global trends, drivers, opportunities, and challenges associated with talent management from a global perspective. To contribute to the paucity of research on talent management in the MENA region, the chapter relies on data collected from websites of governmental and non-governmental international organizations, analysis of the findings the few studies conducted on the MENA region, and the personal experience of the author, who has researched and taught in the region and understands the challenges that are associated with its talent management practices.

2   Definition and Brief Overview of Global Talent Management

In the past two centuries, the abundance of natural resources and adequate labor were instrumental for higher productivity and fiercer competition in domestic and international markets. However, the transition to a knowledge economy in the twenty-first century has drastically transformed the means of production. It has resulted in the scarcity of and competition over another viable source of productivity and sustainable growth: talent (Schuler and Jackson 2009).

The first difficulty that faces researchers when dealing with the topic of talent and global talent management is the "disturbing lack of clarity" regarding its definition, scope, and goals (Lewis and Heckman 2006). Ashton and Morton (2005) put it directly when they stated that "there is not a single consistent or concise definition" of the concept. To demonstrate this, Creelman (2004) defines talent management as ". . .not a set of topics, but as a perspective or a mindset. A talent management perspective presumes talented individuals play a central role in the success of the firm" (p. 3). Schweyer (2004) defines it as "what occurs at the nexus of the hiring, development and workforce management processes and can be described alternatively as talent optimization" (p. 38).

Lewis and Heckman (2006) addressed effectively the inconsistency in defining talent management and identified the three major trends in how the subject is tackled by academics and practitioners. They argue that there are three main streams in the literature: (1) the first one looks at the issue from the ordinary HR viewpoint regarding the processes involved in hiring, retaining, and development, (2) the second looks from a talent pool perspective in terms of identifying the precisely needed talents to fill specific positions within the organizations, and (3) the third one, which is, according to the authors, more complex and tricky, categorizes the workforce by performance levels. However, a fourth dimension can be added to these three, which is the identification not of talent, but of critical positions within the organization that can serve its long term strategic objectives (Huselid et al. 2005; Boudreau and Ramstad 2005).

Due to the waves of globalization and easy mobility of people across continents, the notion of talent management is no longer considered a domestic issue, but an international and global one (Singh et al. 2012). Concepts like "global workforce" and "global talent management" have received substantial attention from academics and corporate heads in the past two decades (Mellahi and Collings

2010; Mercuri Urval 2010). Global talent management looks at the various processes and organizational, human, and economic factors that impact talent on a global scale (Sparrow et al. 2004). Employers all over the world compete fiercely to attract and retain talent to achieve competitive advantages for their companies (Collings and Mellahi 2009; Blass et al. 2006).

Global talent management has emerged as one of the most challenging and key strategic issues for organizations and HR managers in the twenty-first century (Cappelli 2008a, b; Ready et al. 2008; Mellahi and Collings 2010; Ashton 2005). Public and private organizations are increasingly faced with the difficulty of attracting, recruiting, and retaining appropriate talent (Coy and Ewing 2007). This competition and challenge concerning talent was first predicted by a McKinsey study entitled "The War for Talent" (1998). The study surveyed 77 large corporations in the US and found that "successful organizations tend to have a dominant talent segment, while their weaker peers have a bit of everything" (p. 4). The study served two purposes: first, it provided an astute analysis of the complexity of the new global economic climate and the role of talent in producing value and comparative advantage, and second, it triggered an unprecedented interest in the topic of talent and why it had to be a "burning" priority for organizations if they wanted to survive in the increasingly globalizing markets (Aguirre et al. 2009; Becker and Huselid 2006).

Since the publication of "The War for Talent," a growing body of literature proves that competition over talent is a phenomenon that organizations need to effectively deal with in order to grow and flourish. Athey (2008) notes that "despite millions of unemployed workers, there is an acute shortage of talent: science educators to teach the next generation of chemists, health care professionals of all stripes, design engineers with deep technical and interpersonal skills..." (p. 1). Cappelli (2008a, b) considers the essence of talent management to be the proper identification of the talent needs and setting a coherent strategy to meet them. His study provides a systematic analysis of the history of talent in the US, starting from its excess supply during the recession of 1988 to its scarcity again during the 1990s US economic boom. Cappelli (2008, b) looks at the concept of talent management in a holistic manner and does not consider it an end in itself, but rather as an instrument that supports the overall objectives of organizations of maximizing their profits (Boudreau et al. 2007).

Research findings by major international corporations prove that organizations that implement effective global talent management programs witness significant improvement in their performance (Schuler et al. 2011; Farley 2005). It is no longer hiring and developing talent that is the main ingredient for organizational effectiveness and competition in the growingly complex global economic system, but proper management of this talent (Government of Newfoundland and Labrador 2008). This is largely dependent upon having the right people in the right place at the right time with the necessary skills to produce competitively (Lane and Pollner 2008).

Global talent challenges emerge as a result of numerous intertwined factors and drivers. First, globalization is the key element that has been pointed out by many studies (Schuler et al. 2011; Scullion et al. 2007; Beechler and Woodward 2009;

Tung 2008). The spread of multinational corporations all over the world and the mobility of labor have facilitated the immigration of talent or the brain drain phenomenon (Hewitt's Human Capital Consulting 2008). The ease of moving from one country to another to pursue education or look for better job opportunities has affected many developing countries and caused them to lose significant pools of talent (Chartered Institute of Personnel and Development 2006). The second challenge is associated with demographic transitions and trends within developed and developing countries (Faust 2008). While the population growth in developed economies like those in the US, UK, Australia, and so forth remains relatively stable with great potential for decline in the years to come, developing and emerging countries are witnessing significant baby booms (Tarique and Schuler 2010). The ease of emigrating from one country to another makes these young and talented generations a threat to the workforce in developed economies (Adecco Institute 2008). A third major factor is the shift toward a knowledge economy which entails the dire need for training and equipping "knowledge workers" with the necessary skills to operate within a dynamic and fast changing global environment (Oracle 2012; Iles et al. 2010; Stroh and Caligiuri 2008). A knowledge economy is inherently driven by innovation and creativity, which are embedded in human minds.

3   Challenges of Talent Management in the MENA Region

To provide a coherent and inclusive picture of talent management challenges and opportunities in the MENA region, one is unable to escape pointing out the intertwined structural, socioeconomic, and educational factors that constitute the core hindrance to the best utilization and investment in talent. The MENA region enjoys abundant energy reserves, strategic geographic location, and a generation of those younger than 30 years old that comprises 60 % of its population. Nevertheless, the UNDP and MBRF's Report (2009) indicated, "For nearly two and half decades after 1980, the region witnessed hardly any economic growth." High rates of unemployment, educational systems that do not deliver quality programs, and a public sector that is the main recruiter in the market constitute mounting and long-term challenges that the region needs to take the necessary measures to address.

The World Bank (2008) classifies the countries of the MENA region into three categories: (1) resource-poor, labor-abundant countries like Egypt, Jordan, Morocco, Tunisia, and so forth. These countries have no natural resources, but massive pools of labor that mostly seek jobs in Europe or the Gulf states. (2) Resource-rich, labor-abundant countries Algeria, Iraq, and Iran. (3) Resource-rich, labor-importing countries, which are generally the GCC countries in which the expatriates constitute up to 80 % of the population, as is the case in the United Arab Emirates. Understanding the comparative advantages of each country within these categories will explain the challenges related to both talent and resources.

The recent political turmoil that swept through the region in the past 3 years was the ultimate result of the dire economic and social circumstances in which many, the youth particularly, have lived for decades. Hence, addressing talent management in the MENA region goes beyond the boundaries of HR departments and practices in public or private organizations to include government policies and strategies for youth education, training, formation, and integration into the market. As Ali (2011) puts it, "talent management (TM) is strategically suited to play a vital role in the region's economic progress. For years it was neglected by both corporations and governments. In recent years, however, it has taken on an added value as economic development programs have generally failed to produce tangible improvement in the wellbeing of people in the region" (p. 34).

Talent management in the MENA region is a major structural and governmental issue, rather than a purely organizational and institutional one. Unlike Organization for Economic Co-operation and Development (OECD) and high-income countries where the challenge involves how to get the most from the "war for talent," MENA countries still struggle with mounting socioeconomic and educational obstacles that prevent them from forming and training adequate talent pools that can be absorbed easily by the job market.

3.1 Unemployment: Talent in Waiting

The MENA region has undeniably the highest unemployment rates worldwide. Despite the relentless, yet ineffective, attempts of governments to curtail the rising rates of unemployment, they only managed to reduce it by 1 % in the decade from 2000 to 2010. Yet, the rates are almost double the world average of 6 %, as Fig. 1 demonstrates. GCC countries witness the lowest unemployment rates at around 5 %, given the generous revenues from the oil sector that subsidizes other sectors and creates job opportunities. Countries like Iraq, Tunisia, and Jordan top the list of unemployment rates, which range around 15.3 %, 14 %, and 13.4 %, respectively. Qatar is on the other extreme of the spectrum with an unemployment rate of 0.5 %, as shown in Table 1.

Long-term structural unemployment among the youth in the MENA region is alarmingly high compared to other parts of the world. It stands at 25.1 % in the Middle East and 23.6 % in North Africa, while the global average is only 12.6 % (ILO 2010). As Table 1 further illustrates, it is around 50 % in Yemen, 45.6 % in Algeria, 43.5 % in Iraq, and 29.4 % in Tunisia. The lowest rate is found in the UAE, where it reaches 6.3 %. Arab World Competitiveness Report (2012) argue that unemployment is high especially among the most educated. For example, 43 % of students with tertiary education are unemployed in Saudi Arabia, 22 % in Morocco and the UAE, and 14 % in Tunisia. What exacerbates these figures is the negative economic growth in some countries like Sudan and Yemen, where GDP growth is −10 %, and sluggish ones like Lebanon at 1.4 %, Algeria at 2.5 %, and Morocco at 2.71 %.

The cost of unemployment and inefficient use of talent in MENA reaches around 40–50 billion dollars annually based on a report by McKinsey, which surveyed 1,500 employers and conducted 200 interviews. These losses result from the governments' investment in education and preparation of talent that becomes unemployed after graduation or emigrates to other countries that offer better opportunities. The brain drain phenomenon is experienced mostly in countries

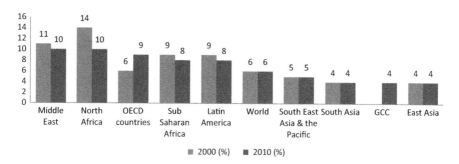

Fig. 1 Unemployment rates in different parts of the world: *Source.* Economist Intelligence Unit (2006)

Table 1 Socioeconomic indicators in the MENA region

Countries	Literacy rate % (2011)	Knowledge index	Brain drain index (1–7)	Total unemployment	Youth unemployment	GDP growth % 2011
UAE	90	7.09	5.6	2.4	6.3	4.4
Kuwait	94	5.15	5.4	2.2	23.3	6.1
Bahrain	92	6.98	4.7	15	20.7	2.5
Qatar	96	5.5	5.7	0.5	17	1.6
Oman	87	5.87	3.9	15	19.6	
Saudi Arabia	87	6.05	4.6	10.8	25.9	2.13
Lebanon	90	4.65	–	13	22.1	1.4
Syria	83	3.01	2.3	8.3	18.3	−2.3
Jordan	93	4.71	2.8	13.4	28.1	2.8
Iraq	78	–	–	15.3	43.5	8.43
Egypt	72	3.54	2.3	9.7	24.8	2.21
Libya	89	–	–	–	–	–
Morocco	56	3.25	3.1	9.8	17.6	2.71
Algeria	73	4.28	2.4	9.9	45.6	2.5
Tunisia	78	4.8	3.9	14	29.4	3.6
Mauritania	58	1.52	2.4	–	–	7.57
Sudan	–	1.82	–	–	–	−10.1
Yemen	64	1.58	–	–	–	−10.5

Source. World Bank Data Bank (2013), UNDP and MBRF (2009), United Nations (2008), (IMF)

with no resources and abundant talent like Egypt, which scored 2.3 % in brain drain index, Algeria at 2.4 %, Jordan at 2.8 %, and Mauritania at 2.4 % (Table 1). Arab World Competitiveness Report (2012) found that the countries facing a harder time retaining their talents were Lebanon and Egypt, and the same result was confirmed by the Bayt.com Middle East Salary Survey (2012) survey, which stated that 31 % showed their readiness to relocate to other countries where they could get higher salaries and promising opportunities.

3.2   Education: Mismatch Between the Market Requirements and Students' Education and Skills

The acutely high rates of unemployment are strongly correlated with the quality of education in the MENA region (UNDB (2002); Arab World Competitiveness Report (2011); Ali 2011). While MENA countries have significantly improved their literacy rates over the past two decades, the quality of education, its contents, and its applicability to the market needs are still questionable (Qari 2013). More importantly, tertiary school enrollments stand at a very low rate of 26.3 % in the region compared to 90.3 % in OECD countries (Arab World Competitiveness Report 2012). Businesses in the region constantly complain about the inherent mismatch between the skills that are required in the market place, and the materials primarily taught at public schools and universities. A comprehensive survey run by the International Finance Corporation (2011) found that 38.8 % of firms blame inadequate talent as a constraint for recruitment, compared to a mere 14.4 % in OECD countries.

The prevalent educational systems do not train and prepare students with the necessary technical, personal, entrepreneurial, and analytical skills that are essential in today's competitive world, but rather demand traditional rote memorization to pass the tests (UNDP (2002); World Bank 2008). Numerous reports by international organizations stress the lack of practical skills taught in educational systems in the region. The PWC (2007), which is based on 585 surveys from eighteen Arab countries and interviews with more than forty prominent senior Arab executives, reveals interesting findings about employment and talent management in the region. It found that 54 % of respondents state that the educational systems do not provide the adequate skills in sufficient quantities. Moreover, 97 % of respondents in Jordan, 92 % in Morocco, and 86 % in Algeria all agreed that the curricula are essentially based on theoretical rather than practical foundations. Moreover, the World Bank Enterprise Surveys found that firms find talents' lack of skills a key stumbling block for recruitment in Lebanon (38 %), Syria (36 %), Jordan (33 %), and Egypt (31 %).

The low quality of educational programs affects the academic achievements of students in the MENA region compared to other parts of the world. Salehi-Isfahani and Dhillon (2008) state the results of a World Bank study that found that MENA students who participated in the Third International Mathematics and Sciences Studies (TIMSS) and the OECD Program for International Student Assessment (PISA) standard exams scored close to the bottom of the list of participating countries. Moreover, the UNDP and MBRF (2009) made a comparison of test results between US and Arab students taking Business Administration tests.

As Table 2 shows, 63 % of the American students scored good or above compared to 31 % of the Arab students. Boudarbat and Ajbilou (2007) argue that despite the strenuous efforts made by the government of Morocco to improve the quality of its public sector education, the country remained the only one that did not meet the minimum acceptable participation rate in TIMSS examinations among

Table 2 Comparison of results of tests in business administration

Grade categories	Rating	Percentage of students in Arab countries (%)	Percentage of students in the United States (%)
120–130	Nil	15	0
131–140	Poor	26	15
141–150	Fair	28	22
151–160	Good	19	39
161–170	Very good	9	10
171–200	Excellent	3	14
Total		100	100

UNDP and MBRF (2009)

eighth graders in 2007. Moreover, it also failed to meet the minimum requirements in 2003, especially in exams of math and science. This weakness in the classes of science and math is what principally forces students to major in the humanities thus missing the opportunity to pursue fields of education that promise careers in the private sector.

All of these studies and indicators demonstrate the complexity of talent management in the MENA region. Unlike the OECD and developed countries, where the main challenge involves how to attract talent to organizations and retain and develop them, in the Arab world the main challenge that faces the private sector is how to find properly educated and trained employees, the skills that are compulsory for entry to the job market. Therefore, over 70 % of students with higher education degrees graduate in the humanities and social sciences, which does not make them attractive to the private sector. Their only remaining alternative is to embrace life jobs with the public sector, which guarantees higher paying jobs (Assaad and Barsoum 2007; Salehi-Isfahani and Dhillon 2008).

One critical element that inhibits the proper preparation and training of talent, and is not discussed or researched adequately, involves the skills and teaching methodologies of teachers. Salehi-Isfahani and Dhillon (2008) refer to the socio-economic circumstances of teachers in the region, which include being paid low salaries, receiving insufficient and sometimes improper training, the use of violence against students, and so forth. Teachers constitute the backbone of educational experience, and if they are not psychologically prepared to deliver, their impact on students will most likely be negative.

Another challenge that faces talent in the MENA region is the weak governance structures and prevalence of nepotism especially while trying to access the job market. Despite the fact that Islamic believes stress on values like moderation, keeping promises, accountability and discipline (Eabrasu and Al Ariss 2012), these values seem to be absent from the practical life style of managers within organizations in the MENA region. Al Ariss (2010) indicates in a study that was based on field work and extensive interviews that merit is not necessarily the criteria that guarantees a job in the Lebanese market. The cases Al Ariss interviewed and examined demonstrated that religious affiliations and confessional diversity schemes play a significant role in securing a job. This obliges many talents to travel abroad in search of equal access to job opportunities that prioritize merit and qualifications rather than religious believes or connections.

3.3   Public Sector as a Dominant Recruiter

As discussed in the previous section, around 75 % of graduates in the MENA region find the public sector a promising venue to secure a career given their limited qualifications for the private sector. To meet its social contract obligations, the public sector absorbs as much talent as it can afford; thus raising the MENA region's percentage of government wages relative to GDP around 9.8 % compared to a global average of 5.4 % and making it the highest in the world (IMF 2012, 2013).

The private sector in the MENA region is also responsible for the lack of trust and interest among talent in the region. It does not provide sufficient incentives to recruit the best performing talent, and thus risks losing it to other countries. Bayt. com runs the Middle East Salary Survey, which found that 38 % of surveyed employees were not satisfied with their salaries and compensation packages, while 58 % only expressed medium satisfaction. More importantly, 63 % of the respondents said that they got paid much less than their peers in the same industry. In terms of training opportunities, only 26.7 % of the respondents of the survey mentioned receiving any form of training compared to 41.1 % in OECD countries (IFC 2009).

However, there are various factors that encourage talent in the Arab world to opt for the public sector as the first employer of choice. Some of these factors are: a better pay scale, longer vacations, shorter working hours, lifelong job security, and regulations that make it hard for the employer to fire public servants (O'Sullivan et al. 2011; Al-Masah Capital 2012). Looking carefully at these factors indicates that the public sector, in fact, stimulates an environment of stagnation and lack of motivation, development, or competition.

The public sector in GCC countries recruits nationals more than the private sector for the benefits and rewards it provides to them, such as fewer working hours, less expected productivity, and less focus on qualifications and merit. In Kuwait, for example, the public sector recruits more than 91.3 %, and in Saudi Arabia more than 79 % is recruited. The Middle East Policy Council states that 72.3 % of public sector jobs in the Gulf are held by nationals, with ratios as high as 91.3 % in Saudi Arabia, 90.8 % in Bahrain, 80.5 % in Oman, and 74.6 % in Kuwait (as cited in Al-Masah Capital 2012).

3.4   National Versus Expatriate Workforce in the GCC

The discovery of petroleum and the resultant accumulation of abundant revenues have dramatically changed the shape of GCC countries, demanding urgent employment of foreign expatriate employees to run the newly established institutions and organizations. As a result, since the late 1980s, the Gulf countries in general have embarked on an unprecedented wave of modern state construction. However, since GCC countries have lacked sufficient local human capital with the necessary qualifications and skills to run these institutions, they have heavily relied on the expertise and knowledge of foreign consultants, experts, and advisors to fill in this gap (Robinson 1990). At the same time, the GCC governments have generously invested in their citizens' education to improve the human capital resources to support their rapid economic growth.

In the meantime, GCC talents find it difficult to compete with the imported expatriate workforce, who often possess higher levels of education and the professional experiences that are desired by a range of employers supporting the GCC's development, both public and private. Previous studies have confirmed that the private sector in the Middle East responds more positively to expatriate applicants than to nationals, since they cost less, they work longer hours, and companies will not face the same legal challenges as if they recruit nationals (Attiyah 1996; Cateora and Graham 2007). The Arab Labor Organization (2007) indicates that in the UAE the rate of foreign labor force as a percentage of total labor force was 91.6 %, in Kuwait 82.2 % and in other GCC countries around 70 %. Therefore, to provide job protection to GCC citizens, the governments have introduced nationalization policies that aim to facilitate citizens' access to local job markets.

4   Opportunities for Talent Management in the Arab World

4.1   Economic Growth and Investment in Talent Creation

The MENA region enjoys an unmatched abundance of human and natural resources that can be invested effectively to propel development and growth (Ali 2011). The region is a home to more than 490 million people, and 60 % of them are under the age of 30. This vibrant, energetic, and young population can serve as the engine of economic prosperity in the region if their talent and potential are tapped. In order to curb the rising unemployment that is occurring in parallel with the increasing fertility rate in the region, the World Bank estimates that the region needs to create 100 million jobs by 2020 (World Bank 2008). Moreover, around 60 % of all global energy reserves are located within the boundaries of the Arab world, and investing them in sustainable development projects can yield progressive results that will improve the overall performance of the region and employ the unemployed and "waiting generations" (Dhillon and Yousef 2009).

Despite the current economic and political obstacles that inhibit the region from properly utilizing its talent, the future socioeconomic trends are very promising.

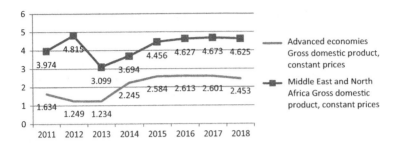

Fig. 2 GDP growth % at constant prices in MENA countries and advanced economies. *Source.*
IMF (2013)

Figure 2 shows that GDP growth will pick up again from 2014 onwards. The
International Monetary Fund (IMF) predicts that GDP in the MENA region will
reach 4.67 % by 2017 despite the economic downturn that has affected OECD
countries (IMF 2013). Furthermore, the political turmoil that swept through the
region recently promises the reconstruction of political institutions and implementation of transparent, responsive, and accountable governments. The creation of
democratic political institutions will significantly impact the business environment
in the region and attract more foreign direct investment opportunities.

More importantly, the recent Arab Youth Survey (2013) found that the majority
of Arab youth strongly believe that "the best days are ahead of us" (p. 7). The
youth's belief in a better future is of crucial significance to allow for their empowerment, energizing and incentivizing them to give the best they can for their
countries (ASDA'A Burson-Marsteller Arab Youth Survey 2013).

Job creation has also become the main priority for governments in the MENA,
especially after the Arab Spring events. The newly elected governments of
Morocco, Tunisia and Libya realize that if they do not deliver what they promise
to their people, they will eventually be voted out of power. Thus, they are
strategizing job creation by empowering the creation of small and medium
Enterprises (SMEs), providing the necessary technical training for unemployed
talents to facilitate their integration into the workforce, and providing them with
micro-finance loans to establish small businesses. In this way they will nurture their
skills and capitalize on their young age to prepare them to become the future
entrepreneurs of the region. In the light of the political turmoil, Saudi Arabia
dedicated $36 billion for job creation, benefits, and allowances for the jobless in
the country.

Gulf countries realize that investments in research and education are the key
pillars for successful transition to the knowledge economy. Thus, they are competing to build the necessary infrastructure to attract high talent globally and train and
form the local nationals as well. Qatar Foundation was established by the government to "support Qatar on its journey from a carbon economy to a knowledge
economy by unlocking human potential" (Qatar Foundation website). The foundation invests massively in science, education, and research. It attracted top niche

universities like Georgetown University, Carnegie Mellon, University College London in Qatar, and others to create a vibrant, competitive, and innovative culture of serious scholarship in Qatar. Hundreds of millions of dollars are given every year in grants to conduct scientific research in the region. In Dubai, the Sheikh Mohammed Bin Rashid Al-Maktoum Foundation was established for the purpose of creating leaders that are equipped with the talent, knowledge, and training to make a difference in the region. The mission of the foundation is to "Provide Arabs with opportunities to guide the region towards a knowledge economy through promoting entrepreneurship, research and innovation, enhancing access to quality education and professional development; and supporting the production, acquisition and dissemination of Arab knowledge sources." (MBRF website). This is carried out by offering generous full scholarships for Arab students to attend the most prestigious universities worldwide, training teachers on how to deliver quality teaching, and supporting research and translation of prominent books. Saudi Arabia is also pursuing the same path by establishing the biggest "economic city" in the world with a cost of $86 billion dollars. The city will be a hub of research, commerce, and environmentally friendly industry, and provide more than one million jobs (SAGIA 2013).

Gulf countries are also diversifying their economies to rely less on natural resources, and nurture the talent and skills of its people by exposing them to new market opportunities. There is a growing shift away from the traditional channels of job creation in the region, and provision of incentives to the private sector to create and provide jobs. Governments are increasingly trying to reform investment policies, facilitate the process of starting businesses for young entrepreneurs, and enhance the ease of doing business to attract foreign direct investment.

4.2   Nationalization as a Policy to Manage and Empower Nationals' Talent: The UAE as a Successful Case

'Nationalization' processes are typically initiated as a result of a nation's confrontation of the challenges posed by waves of globalization and the increasingly easy movement of goods and human capital from one place to another. Abdelkarim (2001) provides a succinct definition of what nationalization means: "A multilevel process through which dependency on the expatriate labor force is reduced and nationals are prepared to take up jobs performed by expatriates. Such preparation entails enabling nationals to perform their jobs equally as good, if not better, than expatriates in the shortest possible period" (p. 38). Such experiences thus typically threaten the exploitation of national resources by indigenous people and their access to job markets, and risk compromising their national identity (Al Dosary 2004; Mellahi and Wood 2003).

Emiratization is an example of "the interventionist approach often taken by governments of the region", and one of the most successful experiences of workforce nationalization in the Gulf region (Harry 2007), with the main purpose of the *Emiratization* policy being to reduce the UAE's dependence on expatriate workers and enhance national participation in the workforce (Wilkins 2001). As a result, along with abounding globalization, the integration of economies and information technologies, as well as the trend of spreading globalized cultures, there has been a direct influence on sustaining the UAE's national identity. Therefore, the *Emiratization* policy has come into place with the main function of forcing the recruitment of Emiratis. In addition, Emiratization plays a role in protecting and sustaining the national identity of Emiratis in the workplace. As it is stated in the National Human Resource Development and Employment Authority's (*Tanmia*) website, the emphasis on nationalization in the UAE (Emiratization) is a result of "serious thinking and careful policy-making that sets targets with a long-term vision" (p. 3). *Tanmia* has been established mainly to address issues related to the nationalization of the UAE's workforce and recommend relevant policy options to the government, as well as to assist Emiratis in matching skills to job placements.

The government of the UAE announced 2013 as a year of Emiratization to further strengthen the foundations of this policy. This demonstrates the willingness of the government to gradually decrease its dependence on expatriates and start building national homegrown expertise. It is the vision of the UAE to, in a decade or two, achieve milestones in enabling local talents, training them, and qualifying them to hold challenging and leading roles in the public as well as private sectors.

However, to fully benefit from the experiences of a foreign labor force, it is in the best interest of the UAE's government to intensify the implementation of knowledge management programs and tools. Such will allow a smooth transfer of knowledge to the national workforce and enable them to learn from the expertise of expatriates more effectively. Among the repercussions of the financial crisis was the loss of vibrant, diversified, and talented employees. These employees left their posts and took along with them the experiences and knowledge that they had gained over the years. Hence, their organizations lost twice: they lost experienced staff and also the knowledge they took with them (Biygautane and Al-Yahya 2011). The UAE strongly needs to capture, document, and disseminate the knowledge and expertise of its work force.

5   Recommendations and the Way Forward

5.1   Curbing Unemployment Rates by Reinvigorating the Role of the Private Sector in the Economy

Unemployment is a universal phenomenon requiring scrupulous policymaking that identifies the role of education, society, and the private sector's impact on the labor force. Given that the region has the highest unemployment rates in the world, along with the challenges associated with creating 100 million jobs by 2020, carefully designed, well-informed, and implemented policies to trigger economic growth are a must for MENA governments especially in light of the political unrest in the region.

Job creation has to be the burning priority for the MENA region in the short and medium run to mitigate the losses incurred by governments due to the departure of talent or its underutilization. However, traditional channels of recruitment through public sector agencies and entities should be avoided to curtail the burden of heavy public spending that consumes substantial portions of GDP in the region.

Diversifying the economy, establishing a business-friendly environment, attracting FDIs and providing micro-finance possibilities for youth should be taken into serious consideration by governments in the Arab world.

Furthermore, supporting a culture of entrepreneurship and SME creation is another path to unlock the talent of youth and allow them to be potential recruiters rather than job seekers in the market. Since the political uprisings in the region, various governmental and non-governmental organizations have been providing significant support to young people in the region by facilitating micro-finance loans and offering training sessions on entrepreneurship.

GCC countries should focus on the proper training and education of their national workforce before they can expect to see the fruits of nationalization policies. The expatriate workforce is still essential for the economic growth of the region, and implementing knowledge management tools and mechanisms is critical to guarantee effective knowledge transfer and knowhow from expatriates to nationals.

5.2   Reforming Educational Programs and Policies

Educational systems and policies have to be revisited and redesigned to align them with the job market needs. New educational systems that rely on critical thinking, quantitative methods, communication skills, problem solving, team work, and entrepreneurial skills need to be introduced to the schooling system in the region.

Moreover, students need to be acclimatized to the working environment before they graduate through internships programs that have to be a mandatory component of their learning experience. Selecting a specific educational stream should emanate from the interest of the students, who should be supported by proper advising and guidance well before they reach high school to know what career path they want to take and what is the best academic program that can lead them there.

Educational policies, on the other hand, need to stress introduction of international best practices while developing the curricula, implementing them, and training teachers to properly deliver them. Also, government policies need to indicate the importance of updating textbooks, teaching materials, and methodologies to cope with the dynamic and changing job market requirements. Continuous training and support for teachers should be emphasized through clear government policies that articulate the number of hours that they need to train and what aspects they should focus on.

Table 3 Five key GTM challenges, strategies and future opportunities

Five key points regarding Global Talent management Challenges	Five key points regarding strategies to overcome these challenges	Five key points regarding future opportunities in Global Talent Management
1 Shortages of talent in some countries	Build a pool of local talent by effectively investing in education and training	Growing interest in global talent management practices and programs by private and public sector organizations
2 Difficulty of attracting and retaining talent	Providing the necessary incentives and career growth opportunities for talent to work and remain in the organization	Mobility of talent and "knowledge workers" facilitates the implementation of best practices and lessen the knowledge gaps
3 Demographic transitions and trends within developed and developing countries	Establishing a competitive and rewarding working environment will attract talent	Better understanding of challenges facing global talent management offers innovative ways for organizations to tackle them
4 Low quality of educational systems that do not prepare qualified talent	Develop educational systems that are pertinent to the global market needs	The recovery from the economic downturn will provide new opportunities of growth for global talent and organizations
5 Brain drain in some countries affects their human capital and growth	Implement talent management programs to effectively benefit from the available pools of talent	Growing appreciation of the positive results from investing in development of global talent

5.3   Implement Talent Management Programs

Research has found that public and private organizations that have effectively running talent management departments outperform those that do not. Hence, government policies should emphasize the need of managing talent properly and effectively through making talent management departments part of organizational charts (Table 3).

Conclusion and the Way Forward

This chapter reviews the challenges and opportunities associated with global talent management in the MENA region. It has come to the conclusion that while OECD and high-income countries struggle to identify mechanisms to attract, retain, and develop the pools of talent in a fierce war over talent, the MENA region is still hampered with chronic socioeconomic challenges This is essentially due to the failure of policymakers to foresee the quality of educational systems and their applicability to the job market needs. However, if the governments of the region make the proper movements to correct the mistakes of the past, the future of talent in the region might seem brighter.

References

Abdelkarim, A. (2001). UAE labor market and problems of employment of nationals, an overview and policy agents. Tanmia.

Adecco Institute (2008). Talent, talent, talent. Finding it, developing it, and keeping it. The new role of HR in the future. Adecco Institute. [Report].

Aguirre, D., Hewlett, S., & Post, L. (2009). *Global talent innovation: Strategies for breakthrough performance [report]* (pp. 1–25). San Francisco: Booz and Company.

Ali, A. (2011). Talent management in the middle east. In H. Scullion & D. Collings (Eds.), *Global talent management*. New York: Routledge.

Al Ariss, A. (2010). Religious diversity in Lebanon: Lessons from a small country to the global world. In M. Ozbilgin & J. Seyed (Eds.), *Managing cultural diversity in Asia: A research companion* (pp. 56–72). New York: Edward Elgar Publishing.

Al Dosary, A. S. (2004). HRD or manpower policy? Options for government intervention. *Human Development International, 7*(1), 123–135.

Al-Masah Capital. (2012). MENA education report. Accessible from: www.Almasahcapital.com

An Oracle White Paper. (2012). *The future of talent management: Underlying drivers of change* [report]. Oracle Taleo Cloud Service, pp. 1–20.

Arab Labor Organization's Statistics. (2007). Accessible from: www.alolabor.org

Arab World Competitiveness Report. (2011, 2012). World economic forum. Accessible from: www.oecol.org

ASDA'A Burson-Marsteller Arab Youth Survey. (2013). Accessed September, 2013, from http://arabyouthsurvey.com/wp-content/uploads/2013/04/AYS-2013-Brochure-White-Paper-Design-ARTWORK-REV.pdf

Ashton, C. (2005). Managing talent for competitive advantage. CRF publishing and Lynne Morton, *Performance Improvement Solutions, 4*, 28–31.

Ashton, C., & Morton, L. (2005). Managing talent for competitive advantage. *Strategic HR Review, 4*(5), 28–31.

Assaad, R., & Barsoum, G (2007). Youth exclusion in Egypt: In Search of "Second Chances". Youth Initiative Working Papers. Dubai School of Government.

Athey, R (2008). It's 2008: Do you know where your talent is? Why acquisition and retention strategies do not work. Deloitte Development LLC.

Attiyah, H. S. (1996). Expatriate acculturation in the Arab Gulf countries. *Journal of Management Development, 15*(2), 37–47.

Becker, B., & Huselid, M. (2006). Strategic talent management: Where do we go from here? *Journal of Management, 32*, 898–925.

Beechler, S., & Woodward, I. (2009). The global "war for talent". *Journal of International Management, 15*, 273–285.

Biygautane, M., & Al Yahya, K. (2010). *Knowledge management in Dubai's public sector: Opportunities and challenges* (Policy Brief no. 27). Published by the Dubai School of Government.

Biygautane, M., & Alyahya, K. (2011). Knowledge management in Dubais public sector: The case of Dubai Working Papers. Dubai School of Government.

Blass, E., Knights, A., & Orbea, A. (2006). *Developing future leader: The contribution of talent management* (pp. 1–21). UK: Ashridge Business School.

Boudarbat, B., & Ajbilou, A. (2007). Youth exclusion in Morocco: Context, consequences and policies. Youth Initiative Working Papers' Series. Dubai School of Government.

Boudreau, J., & Ramstad, P. (2005). Talentship, talent segmentation and sustainability: A new HR decision science paradigm for a new strategy definition. *Human Resource Management, 44*, 129–136.

Boudreau, J., & Ramstad, P. (2007). *Beyond HR: The new science of human capital*. Boston: Harvard Business School Press.

Cappelli, P. (2008a). *Talent on demand*. Boston: Harvard Business School Press.

Cappelli, P. (2008b). Talent management for the twenty-first century. *Harvard Business Review, 86*, 74–81.

Cateora, P. R., & Graham, J. L. (2007). *International marketing*. New York: McGraw–Hill, Irwin.

Chambers, E., Foulon, M., Handfield-Jones, H., Hankin, S., & Michaels, E. (1998). The war for talent. *The McKinsey Quarterly, 3*, 1–8.

Chartered Institute of Personnel and Development. (2006). *Talent management: Understanding the dimensions*. Change agenda [report]. CIPD, pp. 1–24.

Collings, D., & Mellahi, K. (2009). Strategic talent management: A review and research agenda. *Human Resource Management Review, 19*, 304–313.

Coy, P., & Ewing, E. (2007). Where are all the workers? Business week, April 9, pp 28–31.

Creelman, D. (2004). *Return on investment in talent management: Measures you can put to wont right now*. Washington: Human Capital Institute.

Dhillon, N., & Yousef, T. (2009). *Generation in waiting: The unfulfilled promise of young people in the middle east*. Washington, DC: Brookings Institution Press.

Eabrasu, M., & Al Ariss, A. (2012). Socially responsible employee management case studies from Saudi Arabia and Lebanon. In D. Jamali & Y. Sidani (Eds.), *CSR in the middle east* (pp. 93–113). Hampshire: Palgrave and Macmillan.

Economist Intelligence Unit. (2006). *The CEO's role in talent management: How top executives from ten countries are nurturing the leaders of tomorrow [report]*. London: The Economist.

Farley, C. (2005). HR's role in talent management and driving business results. *Employment Relations Today, 32*, 55–61.

Farndale, E., Scullion, H., & Sparrow, P. (2010). The role of corporate HR function in global talent management. *Journal of World Business, 45*, 161–168.

Faust, C. (2008). *State of the global talent nation report 2008: Organizations' struggle to prepare workforces to meet growth demands*. Accessible at http://www.softscape.com

Government of Newfoundland and Labrador. (2008). *Developing an integrated talent management program* [report]. Newfoundland Labrador, pp. 1–15.

Guthridge, M., & Komm, A. (2008). Why multinationals struggle to manage talent. *The McKinsey Quarterly*, 1–5.

Harry, W. (2007). Employment creation and localization. The arrival human resource issue for the GCC. *International Journal of Human Resource Management, 18*(1), 132–146.

Hewitt's Human Capital Consulting. (2008). *The state of talent management: Today's challenges, tomorrow's opportunities* [report]. Human Capital Institute, pp. 1–34.

Huselid, M., Beatty, R., & Becker, B. (2005, December). 'A players' or 'A positions'? The strategic logic of workforce management. *Harvard Business Review*, 110–117.

Iles, P., Chuai, X., & Preece, D. (2010). Talent management and HRM in multinational companies in Beijing: Definition, differences and drivers. *Journal of World Business, 45*(2), 179–189.

ILO (2010). International Labor Organization's Statistics. Accessible from: www.ILO.org

IMF. Accessible at: http://www.imf.org

International Finance Corporation. (2009). Annual report. World Bank Institute. Accessible from: www.IFC.org

International Finance Corporation Report. (2011). World Bank Institute. Accessible from www.WorldBank.org

International Monetary Fund's Statistics. (2012, 2013). Accessible from: www.IMF.org

Kumari, P., & Bahuguna, P. (2012). Measuring the impact of talent management on employee behaviour: An empirical study of oil and gas industry in India. *Journal of Human Resource Management, 2*(2), 65–85.

Lane, K., & Pollner, F. (2008). How to address China's growing talent shortage. *McKinsey Quarterly, 3*, 33–40.

Lawler, E. (2008). Strategic talent management: Lessons from the corporate world. *Strategic Management of Human Capital*, 1–34.

Lewis, R., & Heckman, R. (2006). Talent Management: A critical review. *Human Resource Management, 16*, 139–154.

MBRF. Accessed September 14, 2013, from http://www.mbrfoundation.ae

Mellahi, K., & Collings, D. (2010). The barriers to effective global talent management: The example of corporate elites in MNEs. *Journal of World Business, 45*, 143–149.

Mellahi, K., & Wood, G. T. (2003). From kinship to trust: Changing recruitment practices in unstable political contexts. *International Journal of Cross Cultural Management, 3(3)*, 369–381.

Mercuri Urval. (2010). *Talent Management: A summary of quantifiable surveys and relevant reports* [report]. pp. 2–26.

Michaels, E., & Handfield-Jones, H. (2001). *The war for talent*. Boston: Harvard Business School Press.

Middle East Salary Survey. (2012). Accessible from www.bayt.com

Pfeffer, J. (1998). *The human equation: Building profits first*. Boston: Harvard Business School Press.

PWC. (2007). Arab human capital challenge the voice of CEOs. Accessible from: www.PWC.com/publications.pdf

Qari, R. (2013). How to capitalize on human capital. *Endeavor Insight*, 5–19.

Ready, D. A., Hill, L. A., & Conger, J. A. (2008). Winning the race for talent in emerging markets. *Harvard Business Review, 86*, 62–70.

Robinson, A. (1990). Corporation on exploitation? The argument against cooperative learning for talent students. *Journal for Educational of the Gifted, 14*(1), 9.

SAGIA. Accessed September 15, 2013, from http://www.sagia.sa

Salehi-Isfahani, & Dhillon, N. (2008). Stalled youth transitions in the middle east. Broking & Institute Working Papers' Series.

Schuler, R., & Jackson, S. (2009). *The global talent management challenge: Drivers and HR actions for attaining and sustaining global competitive advantage* (pp. 1–35). Zurich: Rutgers University.

Schuler, R., Jackson, S., & Tarique, I. (2011). Global talent management and global talent challenges: Strategic opportunities for IHRM. *Journal of World Business, 46*, 506–516.

Schweyer, A. (2004). *Talent management systems: Best practices in technology solutions for recruitment retention*. Toronto: Wiley.

Scullion, H., Collings, D., & Gunnigle, P. (2007). International HMR in the 21st century: Emerging themes and contemporary debates. *Human Resource Management, 17*, 309–319.

Singh, A., Jones, D., & Hall, N. (2012). Talent management: A research based case study in the GCC region. *International Journal of Business and Management, 7*(24), 94–107.

Sparrow, P., Brewster, C., & Harris, H. (2004). *Globalizing human resource management*. London: Routledge.

Stroh, L., & Caligiuri, P. (2008). Increasing global competitiveness through effective people management. *Journal of World Business, 33*(1), 1–16.

Tarique, I., & Schuler, R. (2010). Global talent management: Literature review, integrative framework, and suggestion for further research. *Journal of World Business, 45*, 122–133.

Tung, R. L. (2008). Human capital or talent flows: Implications for future directions in research on Asia Pacific. *Asia Pacific Business Review, 14*(4), 469–472.

United Nations. (2008). *Fertility rates* [online].

UNDP and MBRF. (2009). Knowledge development report.

UNDP (2002). Arab Human Development Report. Accessible from: www.arab-hdr.org

Wilkins, S. (2001). Human resource development through vocational education in the UAE. *Journal of Vocational Education and Training, 54*(1), 5–26.

Wood, S. (1999). Human resource management and performance. *International Journal of Management Reviews, 1*, 367–413.

World Bank. (2013). Accessible at http://www.worldbank.org

World Bank Annual Report. (2008). Year in review. World Bank Publications.

Talent Management in Poland: Challenges, Strategies and Opportunities

Sylwia Przytula

> *"I just splits the parts of the stone, which is unnecessary and the release of the angel who has always been in the closed"*
> Michelangelo

1   Introduction

Interest in global talent management (GTM) has increased considerably in the past decade (Farndale et al. 2010), but most research in this area, is based on North American and Anglo-Saxon countries. Although recently there has been an increase in research on TM in such emerging economies as BRIC (Brazil, Russia, India, China), there is still a dearth of such research in some of the other evolving markets in Central and Eastern Europe (Vaiman and Holden 2011). While economic transition process might be considerably advanced in CEE countries (Alam et al. 2008), the cultural processes influencing managerial practices are still in a period of change and believed to be far from converging with Western models (Vaiman and Holden 2011). The lack of research on management in post-communist countries may be even more critical to foreign firms, because foreign managers find it difficult to understand the mental models in these economies. This may lead to misunderstandings between local subsidiaries and foreign headquarters (see: Dobosz-Bourne and Jankowicz 2006). And the richness and variety of institutional and managerial realities, as well as research traditions in Eastern Europe, may allow good opportunities to further develop knowledge of TM (Collings et al. 2011).

Identifying, developing and keeping talented employees in the company, has become a key task in the area of HR departments in the knowledge-based economy. Talent management processes are growing in importance every year. 85 % of

S. Przytula (✉)
Wroclaw University of Economics, Wroclaw, Poland
e-mail: s_przytula@wp.pl

A. Al Ariss (ed.), *Global Talent Management*, Management for Professionals,   217
DOI 10.1007/978-3-319-05125-3_15, © Springer International Publishing Switzerland 2014

companies said that acquiring and retaining the right talent is crucial (for: Stedt 2010). In addition, talent management was on the list of the top five priorities for the HR policy in the study The European HR Best Practice Report in 2011.

In the literature, there are in fact different terms, such as "high potential employee" (Burke 1996), "core employees" (Lepak et al. 2007), "best performers" (Kwon et al. 2010), which tend to be used interchangeably. Some authors regard the term "talent" as a synonym for the entire workforce of the organization (for: Hansen 2007), while A Global Talent Mobility Study (2012) shows that no more than 15 % of all employees belong to the talent pool. State of the theory is very important, since it implies the selection criteria of subject and object of empirical research.

The specific contribution of the current chapter is in developing a concise definition of "talent" and "talent management". A theoretical model of talent management was developed in relation to traditional structure of TM (recruitment & selection, motivation, development, performance and leave). In so doing, insights from a number of existing Polish and international literature bases were drawn. This chapter should contribute to future research in the field of talent management through (1) providing a theoretical framework that could help researchers in framing their comparative research devoted to talent management in developing countries (2) helping researchers to clarify the conceptual boundaries of talent management. In business practice it may help managers in identifying "talents" to their organisations and developing talent management programs.

2 Importance of Talent Management in Economic Practice

Talent management has a strategic dimension (Davis et al. 2010). Firstly, staffing and retention of talents is important for an organisation in the context of achieving strategic goals. Secondly, in order to adapt talent management processes, organisations must allocate substantial material and non-material resources for that purpose and the decisions made in such respect are difficult to reverse. Review of the literature on talent management strategies shows two parallel trends. The first trend promotes activities related to *staffing of talented* employees and the issue of retaining such employees is considered less important. In the second trend, priority is given to *retention of talented employees*, whereas activities aimed at acquiring such employees are secondary to the company's strategy (Pocztowski 2008).

Studies conducted in the last decade also prove that TM has been gaining strategic meaning in numerous organisations (Collings and Mellahi 2009). Research conducted in 17 countries shows that talent management has become the most important part of HRM in an organisation (BCG 2008). According to report by Talent Mobility 2020 (2010), employment of talents is expected to rise from 26 to 48 % in Europe, from 34 to 43 % in the USA and from 41 to 56 % in Asia-Pacific countries.

It is worth mentioning that TM appeared as a result of evolution of the concept of human capital management and the basic difference between such concepts is the fact that talent management can concern a more or less limited number of employees (Pocztowski 2008). According to T. Listwan (2009), "although the components of this process are similar to the procedures for the personnel function in relation to other skilled workers, in this case, there is often more complex interaction of psychological and ethical factors. Mostly because we have to deal with the subject more complex, difficult and sensitive". TM is also a part of knowledge-based economy (Morawski 2009).

One definition of global talent management (GTM) that is broadly used is that of Mellahi and Collings (2010): "GTM involves the systematic identification of key positions which differentially contribute to the organisation's sustainable competitive advantage on a global scale, the development of a talent pool of high potential and high performing incumbents to fill these roles which reflects the global scope of the MNE [multinational enterprise], and the development of a differentiated human resource architecture to facilitate filling these positions with the best available incumbent and to ensure their continued commitment to the organisation". The development of the issue of GTM results from the following social and economic trends being challenges for global organisations at the same time:

2.1   Dynamic Development of Knowledge-Based Economy

Specialization in all fields of science related to the explosion of knowledge results in demand for knowledge workers with special skills and qualifications that need to be improved on an ongoing basis. P. Drucker, who coined the term *"knowledge worker"* in 1970s, pointed to the need of using knowledge in production processes (for: Grycuk 2002). According to Cannon and McGee (2012) "in the future, talent management will be less about development of tools, implementation of systems or trying to squeeze people in the competence patterns and more about the way of thinking, attitude, inborn sense and approach to science".

In relation to Poland, the speed of economic development did not allow the process of management development to keep pace with market demands. Development of HR practices in many companies is rather slow which can be linked to the country's status as a low-cost 'production centre' acquired in the first decade of transition (for: Skuza et al. 2013).

2.2   Shortage of Talented Workers on a Both Local and Global Scale

A study conducted in the UK showed that 82 % of the companies have had difficulties in finding right employees (for: Cannon and McGee 2012). A shortage of highly-qualified managers able to manage on an international level is also apparent on a global scale. Workforce borders will continue to fall as global talent mobility creates new pathways to deal with skill shortages affecting both established and emerging markets. Poland takes place in the pool of top ten most popular countries for supplying global talents (Fig. 1).

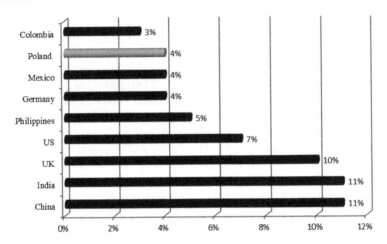

Fig. 1 The most popular countries for supplying global talents (10 min on global talent mobility 2012)

2.3 Demographic Changes

Workforce demographics are evolving. Today, 60 % of workers over the age of 60 are electing to postpone their retirement due to the financial crisis. Many hold top positions, squelching the opportunity for lower-level talent to advance and leaving younger workers feeling stuck (and potentially looking for opportunities with other organisations). At all levels, each deferred exit from the workforce is one less new hire in an already depressed job market (Wellins et al. 2009).

2.4 Human Capital Mobility and Changes in the Psychological Contract

Although 97 % of people in the world do not belong to the group of migrants (Castles 2011), it is worth to paying attention to 3 % of the population of migrant workers because of new tendencies in international mobility. The scale of international migration was as follows: in 1990, 80 million people changed their country of residence; in 2005, there were 191 million migrants and in 2010—almost 214 million (for: Murdoch 2011).

Migration has had an immense impact on Poland. Since 2004, more than one million Poles have migrated to other EU countries (Vaiman and Holden 2011) with over 60 % under 35 years old.

Employee expectations are also changing. Employees today are: increasingly interested in having challenging and meaningful work, more loyal to their profession than to the organisation, less accommodating of traditional structures and authority, more concerned about work-life balance, prepared to take ownership of their careers and development. Responding to these myriad challenges makes it difficult to capture both the "hearts" and "minds" of today's workforce. Yet, it is critical to do so, as research from IBM and the Human Capital Institute highlights. Their study showed, that 56 % of financial performers understand and address employee engagement. This is just one piece of a large body of evidence that illustrates how the cultures built within our organisations are crucial to attracting and retaining key talent (Wellins et al. 2009).

3   Definition of "Talent" and "Talent Management"

In formulating the definition of "talent" or "talent management", an interdisciplinary approach can be seen. The authors allure to different definitions of talent because of the achievements of concept in other disciplines of the social sciences, such as psychology (behavioural, cognitive), philosophy and management (HRM, strategic HRM).

Numerous authors have attempted to define talent for years. The word "talent" originates from Latin *talentum* (scales and money) and from Greek *talanton* (balance). Further, it means exceptional aptitude for creative or reproductive work, as well as a person gifted with such aptitude. However, being talented does not guarantee success itself. Talents must be fostered and developed. Talented persons must be encouraged to work on themselves, to seek new development paths and to think outside the box (Maliszewska 2005).

The definition of talent most commonly found in literature relates to a person with a great potential. In T. Ingram studies (2011), 22 definitions of talent together with their key words were analysed in order to make the definition of talent more precise (NVIVO 7 software was used for that qualitative analysis). The results showed that almost every key word contained in the analysed definitions can be assigned to one of the three basic categories:

– Characteristics of talent as a person. The most commonly appearing characteristic feature of talent as a person was potential in the broad sense, as well as aptitudes, motivation, knowledge and skills.

   The results of the studies conducted by HRM Partners suggest such understanding of talent among business practitioners (Fig. 2).

– Talent-specific activities. The scope of activities taken up by talents included: creation and erection of something new, inspiration.

– Talent's area of influence. The talent's area of influence includes organisation in the first place, then achievements, results, development combined with passion and work itself.

Psychologists have made significant contributions to the conceptualization. According to A.J. Tannenbaum (for: Chełpa 2005), talent is composed of general skills (exceptional intellectual potential), specific skills (skills relating to specific areas of activity), factor connected with thinking-achievement motivation, emotional maturity and psychological resilience. The definition offered by J.S. Renzulli (1986) also refers to psychological categories and "talent" is composed of: exceptional skills (increased intellectual potential), specific skills, creativity (originality,

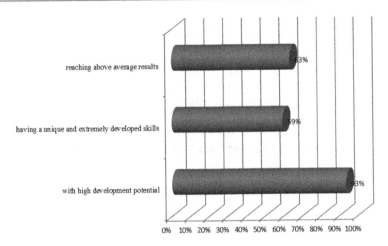

Fig. 2 Talent is a person... (Praktyki zarządzania talentami w Polsce 2010)

novelty, fluidity, flexible thinking), work commitment (self-discipline, persever-
ance, diligence, resistance, fascination with work).

Talent is a quality that does not belong to a specific role in an organization, but
results from exceptional achievements of a given person. Therefore, talent does not
belong to an organization, but to its employees (Listwan 2005). According to
J. Grodzicki (2011), "human talent depends on genetic predispositions, social
environment, self-motivation and coincidence". Talent cannot be created, but it
can be developed, improved and also destroyed" (Kwiecień 2005). Talents are
carriers of *tacit knowledge*, as we know more than we can express (Pocztowski
2008).

As far as the global pool of talents is concerned, we can mention expatriates,
with regard to whom qualification requirements are above standard and relate to
soft skills and psychological features to a large extent. The available literature
mentions such predispositions as open-mindedness, emotional stability, extraversion, intercultural competence, cultural intelligence, adaptive skills and high stress
resistance (Scullion and Collings 2006; Jokinen 2005; Caligiuri 2000) that may be
necessary for their success in work abroad.

"Talent management"(TM) means a host of activities relating to exceptionally
gifted persons, taken up with a view to development of their skills and achievement
of corporate goals (Listwan 2005). The term can simply relate to management
succession planning and actions aimed at its development, as this notion adds
nothing to the already known processes but a new, suggestive name. It is better to
treat TM as a more complex and integrated set of activities aimed at securing the
flow of talents within an organisation, remembering that talent is one of the main
resources of a company (Armstrong 2011). Similarly to E. Blass (2007) who
defined TM as "the additional management processes and opportunities that are
made available to people in the organization who are considered to be 'talent".
Talent management is thus about the additional elements that are afforded to high

potentials, not about the general processes that are available to every member of the organisation.

To sum up this discussion on definitions, it can be assumed that:

– "Talent" means a creative person with a high intellectual potential, exceptional skills and psychological qualities (e.g. abstract thinking, achievement motivation, psychological resilience, emotional maturity). Talent is not connected with position held or role played in the organisational ladder, it is an inborn quality of an individual, therefore it cannot be created, but can be shaped and improved.

– "Talent management" is a process of strategic importance for an organisation. It is a host of activities (relating to talented individuals) aimed at achieving and maintaining advantage over competitors. The most important activities under such process include: identification, acquisition, development and retention of talents in an organisation.

4   The Practice of Talent Management in Poland

Interest in the topic of talent management in Poland is growing, both in terms of the conceptual and research area, and to the significant researchers who bridge the gap in this area and offer their own models belongs S. Borkowska (2005) and A. - Pocztowski et al. (2008). It is also worth recalling the position of M. Morawski (2009), who claims that talent management is always behind knowledge-based economy issues and the book "Managing talent in an enterprise" by J. Kopeć (2012).

In order to present the TM practice in Polish companies, the results of studies conducted by various research institutions operating on the Polish market in recent years will be presented.

The Company HRM Partners S.A. conducted a study in 2010 "Talent Management Practices in Poland". It included 53 companies operating on the Polish market, representing a variety of industries. The popular solutions for talent management were the key issue among participants.

The Polish version of The Conference Board (Glowacka-Stewart 2006). Challenges, trends, examples of solutions was also taken into consideration. Data were collected using both quantitative and qualitative methods. In quantitative approach data consisting of the results of questionnaires were sent out to the registered HR directors of 300 largest companies in the country. Qualitative data were based on 36 interviews.

A report entitled "Talent management in the organization", edited by A. Pocztowski presents research conducted in 36 firms in Poland.

The results of HRM Partners (Praktyki zarządzania talentami w Polsce 2010) show that talent management processes will still be developed in Polish companies—over 50 % of the respondents have implemented development schemes for talents and 35 % plan to implement such schemes. Many organisations in Poland is currently in the "maturing stage" with regard to implementation of TM processes.

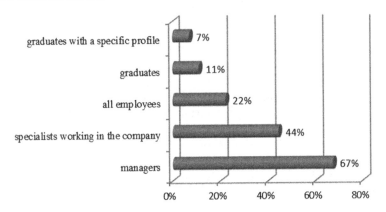

Fig. 3 Programs for talents are offered to:... (Praktyki zarządzania talentami w Polsce 2010)

In The Conference Board study (Glowacka-Stewart 2006), 94 % of HR managers expect that TM process will become more important in the years to come and 73 % of the companies participating in the study have a program dedicated to TM. Similarly, 85 % of the respondents in the study by ACCA (2006) believe that the importance of talent management will be growing. In the studies by A. Pocztowski (2008), the issue of TM has a strategic dimension in over 50 % of the analyzed companies in Poland (it is a part of a companies' strategy).

The respondents in the study by HRM Partners dedicated talent schemes mainly for managers and specialists (Fig. 3):

The Conference Board report shows that only in 15 % of the analysed companies, talent schemes are offered to all the employees, in the majority of companies such a scheme is offered to selected employees (39 %), usually to the managing staff (30 %) (Glowacka-Stewart 2006).

It can be noticed that the Polish companies focus mainly on identification and development of already employed employees. Still, the main beneficiaries of talent schemes are managers. Development schemes for young talents, aimed at graduates of higher education institutions, are less frequent.

Diagnosis of TM practice in Polish companies will be presented in the following structure: acquisition of talents through recruitment and selection, motivation, training & development, talent assessment and leaving the organisation.

4.1 Recruitment and Selection of Talented Employees

Talent management is all about putting the right people in the right jobs. The organisations place the higher priority on staffing rather than development because not everything can be developed. Many elements of qualification profiles are impossible, or at least very difficult, to develop. Lack of creativity or a poor fit between employees' values and those of the organization leads to poor performance, and no learning activity will change this fundamental mismatch. Hiring for

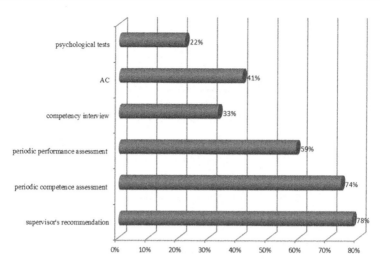

Fig. 4 Forms of identifying talented employees (Praktyki zarządzania talentami w Polsce 2010)

the right skills is more efficient than developing those skills. Moreover assessing the most demanded qualifications is likely to cost less than developing them later.

Usually, the tools used in the talent recruitment process mentioned by the Polish companies that have implemented schemes for talents are as follows: superior's recommendation, periodic competence assessment and periodic performance assessment (Fig. 4).

Very similar results were obtained by The Conference Board (Glowacka-Stewart 2006), respectively: superior's recommendation 73 %, result of periodic assessment 55 % and goal achievement level 33 %.

In the study by A. Pocztowski, both external and internal forms of talent acquisition were analysed. External forms, used in 75 % of the companies, included internships and direct search and internal forms consisted of interviews with managers (64 % of the respondents), goal achievement assessment in the last year (44 %) and work performance assessment (42 %).

As far as the global managing talents (expats) are concerned, the major sources of recruitment are internal personnel resources of a corporation (Przytula 2013b). Studies conducted in 3165 European companies all over the world show that internal candidates prevail on all the management levels (Schroeder 2010).

The most frequently used staffing techniques in the study by HRM Partners were as follows: Assessment Centre, competence interview and competence tests. Moreover, many companies also take into consideration management's recommendations or propose potential talented candidates to be later discussed by the management staff.

In the study by A. Pocztowski, most of the analysed companies (53 %) use at least three selection techniques—interview, analysis of applications and work samples (Fig. 5).

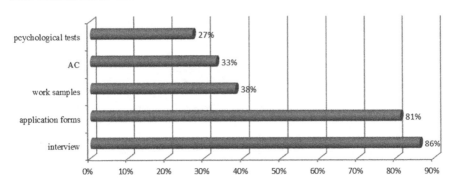

Fig. 5 Techniques of talents' selection (Pocztowski 2008)

It is worth mentioning, that psychological tests, AC-techniques considered as highly predictive (Witkowski 2000), are not very popular despite the fact that according to most of the definitions of talent, it is the exceptional and unique psychological qualities that constitute "talent". Therefore, it would seem that psychological tests (personality, competence and aptitude tests) would be very helpful in identifying a candidate as a "talent". Yet, such tools are underrepresented.

In global talent management practices, identifying talents for future managerial positions should be based on assessment of personal skills such as ability to learn, communication skills, flexibility, adaptability to change and entrepreneurship.

According to A. Skuza et al. (2012) the competencies and skills that are typical regarded as a key in identifying high potentials in western organizations appear not to be currently used in organizations in Poland, particularly in domestically owned firms. Polish managers are very cautious in identifying talented employees for fear that they may take their own positions.

4.2   Training and Development of Talents

After putting a candidate in a talent pool, the next stage is "polishing rough diamonds" which takes the form of various development schemes and trainings. Schemes for talents are held periodically and last usually 1–2 years (Fig. 6).

According to The Conference Board, in 39 % cases such schemes last from 1 to 3 years. HRM Partner's report states that the most commonly offered development activities include participation in corporate projects and trainings planned together for the whole group of talents (81 %), mentor's supervision (56 %), coaching sessions with an external coach (44 %). Participation in international projects is available at 33 % of the companies, but internships abroad make up only 11 % (Fig. 7).

The results of A. Skuza et al. (2012) highlighted the similar approach to developing talents in Polish companies. Almost two-thirds of participants from Polish companies pointed on low value of training because many managers do not

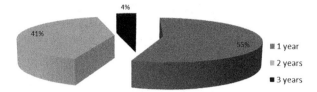

Fig. 6 Duration of TM programs (Praktyki zarządzania talentami w Polsce 2010)

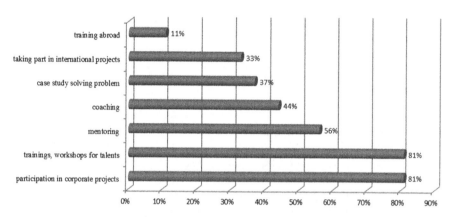

Fig. 7 Forms of developing talents (Praktyki zarządzania talentami w Polsce 2010)

believe in any form of training except from 'on-the-job' training. It is worth mentioning that a low emphasis put on gaining international experience by talents results in a deficit of local and global talents able to face global challenges. In large multinational organisations, 'international experience' and 'changing jobs every 2 years', are key to talent development. Moreover, in some organisations an individual cannot progress beyond a certain level without international experience (Blass 2007).

The Conference Board lists the following development initiatives: group training and development schemes (76 %), opportunity to work in foreign subsidiaries (52 %) and opportunity to work in various corporate departments (45 %). In smaller companies, development paths are very individualized and "tailor-made".

In the studies by A. Pocztowski et al. (2008), almost 67 % of the companies offer a talent development scheme individually for each talent. It includes open trainings (63 %), internal trainings (50 %), self-education (52 %) and job rotation (18 %). In large companies, where a group of talents consists of several dozens of persons, there are universities or knowledge centers operating on all corporate levels.

The practice of development global talents has been confirmed by the statistics, according to which only 11 % of American, 10 % of Japanese and 25 % of Finnish experts were promoted after the end of a foreign contract lasting at least 2 years. 77 % of American, 43 % of Japanese and 54 % of Finnish managers were offered lower positions in the mother company than those they had held before leaving their home country (Stroh et al. 2005). The results of GMAC research show that 72 % of the companies do not have a formal career management schemes for such expats and 85 % of the analysed corporations do not have a repatriation strategy resulting from an expat's career plan.

4.3   Motivating Talented Employees

The report by HRM Partners shows, that financial and non-financial incentives are very weak and they are not differentiated in any way with regard to "talents" and other company employees. 41 % of the analyzed companies do not use any additional incentives for talents, the same percentage of companies considers "talent recognition within the company" as an incentive. For 18 % of the companies, awards and remuneration are considered incentives (Fig. 8).

4.4   Performance Appraisal of Talents

In the area of appraising talents, the results of their achievements are translated into the following activities: in 70 % of the Polish companies, an employee is placed in the pool of potential successors and in the opinion of 30 % of the respondents completing a talent scheme does not result in any changes for the employee (Fig. 9).

The study of A. Skuza et al. (2012) proved also that evaluation processes in Polish companies not only lack standards and advanced tools, but it is also historically dominated by short-term goals and operational priorities.

The most commonly used tools for appraising talents were HR documents and results of 360° appraisal, AC and psychological tests. Almost 70 % of the analyzed companies appraised talents, resulting in the following actions: employee promotion, planning career paths for talents, transfer to another department and changes in remuneration (Pocztowski 2008).

4.5   Leaving the Organization

Leaving a company is a natural process and some small number of employees leaving their companies is desired, however, excessive employee turnover with regard to talented workers should be discussed. The three main areas of talent management responsible for retention of talents include staffing, development and motivating. These processes, carried out properly, are indispensable for retaining talents. According to the studies (Pocztowski 2008), ca. 80 % of employee turnover results from employing the workers in wrong positions—it is therefore a result of improper selection.

In the studies conducted by The Conference Board (Glowacka-Stewart 2006), trainings, professional development opportunities, interesting tasks and friendly atmosphere at work play the major role in retaining talents. However, as it has been

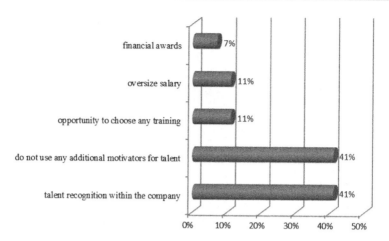

Fig. 8 Motivators for talented employees ((Praktyki zarządzania talentami w Polsce 2010)

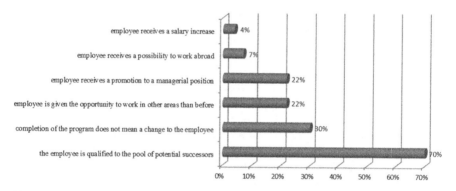

Fig. 9 The results of evaluation of talent (Praktyki zarządzania talentami w Polsce 2010)

shown earlier, the financial aspect does not have a huge impact on retaining employees, especially talents. The main reason for leaving companies by talents is lack of movement within organisations and lack of promotion opportunities. Some reasons also include interpersonal relations and cooperation with superiors, according to the rule that "people come to a company, but they leave their boss".

It is worth to mention the practice of management of global talents, to which expatriates belong. Preparation and transfer of an expat to a foreign trip constitutes an important item of personnel costs for corporations, being sometimes three times the cost of maintaining a manager in a similar position in the mother country of a given corporation (Przytula 2013a). It turns out, that sending employees and their families on international assignments does not in itself contribute to global talent management. Quite the opposite often is the case. When a high-potential expat returns after a 3-year international assignment and is given a series of lesser domestic jobs, the result can be global talent deterioration. Other expatriates will

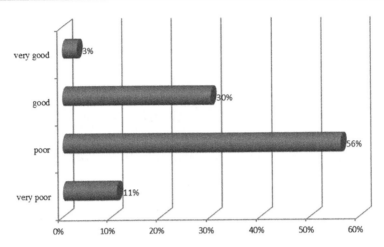

Fig. 10 Using the knowledge and experience of repatriates (Global Benchmarking Survey 2010)

observe keenly that an international assignment is a career killer. The "talent" will seek employment elsewhere. The organisation will fail to take advantage of the special knowledge and business acumen the foreign assignment produced in the individual.

The research by Global Benchmarking Survey (2010) show that organisations can utilise expats' knowledge and experience gained during a foreign contract to a small extent only (Fig. 10).

Therefore, the companies take up actions related to measurement of effectiveness of talented employees and development schemes. Indicators used to measure effectiveness or ROI of TM process include: business effects achieved by a team participating in the scheme (42 %), ability to fill job vacancies in key positions (36 %), results of assessment processes and level of employee commitment (27 %). Almost 30 % of the respondents do not measure the effectiveness of their schemes (Glowacka-Stewart 2006).

5 Summary and Conclusions

The analysis of the current state of theory and practice in the area of TM shows, that Polish companies have established good practices concerning identification and development of talents. However, many organisations still have some difficulties or commit errors, making their initiatives a failure. Among them, special attention should be paid to the following issues:

Talent management should be an integral part of strategic HR management and connected with it harmoniously.

Talent development schemes in Polish companies are limited to managerial staff provided for only 2–3 % of company employees. The idea of elitism seems to dominate in Polish companies, which has been reflected in the above mentioned reports. Only 15 % of companies declared that all employees have a chance to take part in the program; whereas mainly it was reserved only for managers.

The need to involve key subjects of such management, i.e. top management, line managers and acquisition of essential support of personnel services is apparent. Mentors and coaches could play a special role in this area.

Limited managers' skills in development of talented employees are also an important problem in this area. Polish managers are still not prepared for an individual approach to talents and making appropriate decisions in such respect. It also means the use of various development paths and tools, such as regular meetings, feedback or progress monitoring.

Ineffective strategy for employees who have completed a talent scheme can result in loss of valuable employees to competitors. According to the ineffective and outdated HR policies observed in Polish companies increased the risk of losing talented employees to foreign corporations.

In many cases, TM scheme is only a popular, good-looking expression improving company's image and all the activities regarding talent development do not differ significantly from standard forms of development of other employees.

It can be said that TM in Poland, although increasingly popular, seems to be still rather only a separate process than the deep philosophy and strategy of the organisation. However, the value a talented employee brings into the organisation, is the greater the more open and natural is the process of talent management, as well as the more engaged, prepared and convinced managers are to this process.

Polish companies still face many challenges with regard to TM—however, it is important that talent schemes are being developed and improved on an ongoing basis. It is worth to add that the achievements in theoretical and empirical areas concerning TM in Poland become a part of the global academic achievements, supplementing the issue of global talent management by Polish experiences and practice.

In Table 1 there are several guidelines concerning GTM challenges, as well as some strategies to overcome these challenges and future opportunities in this respect.

5.1 GTM Challenges and Strategies to Overcome These Challenges

Development of knowledge-based economy. This challenge requires a reconstruction of personal function consisting in distinguishing the talent management scheme from the area of development and improvement. In many Polish cases, TM is nothing but a nice expression, meaning actually training schemes for employees. In fact, talent management is about development of strengths of talented employees through proper selection of trainings. It also entails the need for creation of new jobs and roles for talent management professionals across the globe, who would build motivation and identification of talents with a company,

Table 1 Key GMT challenges, strategies and future opportunities

Five key points regarding GTM challenges	Five key points regarding strategies to overcome these challenges	Five key points regarding future opportunities in GTM
1 Development of *knowledge based economy*	Reconstruction of the HR function, the creation of new roles for GTM professionals	Global sources of attracting talents (from emerging markets)
2 Talent shortage in the local and global scale	The emphasis not on the development of talented employees but on their retention, linking GTM with global strategy	Technology development helps to gain information about the talents and facilitates the selection process
3 Global demographic changes	New sources and pools of talented employees	Built a base of global talents
4 Global mobility of employees	Employees are more loyal to their profession than to organization, individualized programs for talents, talent management as a concept to build employee loyalty	Socio-cultural changes (lifestyle, the role of women, work life balance issues, generation Millennials on job market, flexpatriate contracts)
5 Creating an organizational culture conducive to talent management	Transparency of the criteria to attract talents, open and clear communication within the organization	Cross-border projects and cooperation among organizations

support talent development, as well as represent the scheme outside of the organization.

A shortage of talented workers on both global and local scale. The global management practice shows that expensive schemes for high-potentials do not ensure retention of such employees within an organization. Therefore, more emphasis should be put not on development, but on retention of talents in a company. The most satisfied employees are those who believe their talent and skills are being well utilized by their employers. In order to retain talented employees, companies must provide them with continuous development, which is a long-term process. It means that talent management should have a strategic dimension and become a part of the general vision of HRM.

Demographic changes. Demographic and generation issues figure prominently in the changing talent mobility picture. Companies will need to move beyond their traditional recruiting patterns and talent sources. While the populations of many developed economies are aging and shrinking in size, the populations of developing and emerging economies are expanding and getting younger. These changes prompted international companies to explore new destinations for their foreign affiliates which take into account the availability of skilled workers in the host countries.

Global mobility of employees. Todays' generation of employees is more loyal to their profession than to organisation, more concerned about work-life balance. Employee expectations are changing-they are increasingly interested in having challenging and meaningful job. Customisation of schemes for talents (preceded by a diagnosis of exceptional skills and personality traits using proper selection tools), would bring together individual talent's goals and corporate goals. Ability to change one's place of work with ease is a challenge for TM today. An employee's intellectual property is their knowledge, experience, specific skills not limited by the company's walls or national borders. It seems that talent management could be an *antidote* to the above problems and become a basis for building loyalty and limiting the number of key employees leaving their organisations.

Creating an organizational culture supporting talent management. A proper work environment favours creativity, expression of oneself and initiative. Clarity of talent acquisition criteria for development schemes, clear communication within an organisation—such conditions are necessary to develop and retain talents. A positive organisational atmosphere also contributes to the sense of responsibility for one's own development.

5.2   Opportunities

Global talent acquisition sources know no national or ethnical boundaries. Global talents can be derived from various sources. Those include not only traditional PCNs (parent country nationals), TCNs (third country nationals), HCNs (host country nationals), but also specific countries or geographical regions abundant with talents (emerging markets). On the other hand, there are countries that lack talents and seek them abroad.

Development of technology. More employers have already been using social media to track skilled employees who are willing to relocate abroad, broadening their potential candidate pools at the same time. E-technology used by organisations to send messages about themselves is also a part of building a company's image.

Building a global database of talents, able to work in different cultural environments, having international experience and intercultural background. As companies become international, the demand for the services of such specialist (identified as high-potential) among corporations will be growing.

Lifestyle change. The generation of "Millennials" on today's market, role of women in global management, social issues, such as *work life balance*, favour the creation of persons who will belong to the global pool of talents in the future. Many people are comfortable with lifestyle based on moving from one place of residence or country to another and meeting new friends. Business trips show a trend or even a fashion for international business. Social changes entail alternative approach to contracts for work in an international corporations and traditional expatriate contracts are being replaced by various forms of flexpatriate assignments.

The cross border projects and cooperation seems to be another increasingly important method for developing global talents. Such projects involve working through local-global. The opportunity to work with people who have very different experience, perspectives and national provenience is the added value of the project, not only in economic terms (made for business purposes), but also in the social terms (building base of global skills, experiences, best practices).

References

ACCA Global Survey Report. (2006). Talent management in the finance profession, 49. Accessed September 15, 2012, from http://www.accaglobal.com

A Global Talent Mobility Study. Regional Differences in Policy and Practice. (2012). http://www. towerswatson.com. Accessed 16 May 2013.

Alam, A., Anos Casero, P., Khan, F., & Udomsaph, C. (2008). *Unleashing prosperity: Productivity growth in Eastern Europe and the former Soviet Union*. Washington, D.C: World Bank.

Armstrong, M. (2011). *Zarządzanie zasobami ludzkimi* (p. 503). Warszawa: ABC Wolters Kluwer Business.

Blass, E. (2007). *Talent management: Maximizing talent for future performance* (p. 33). London: Routledge.

Borkowska, S. (Ed.). (2005). *Zarządzanie talentami*. Warszawa: IPiSS.

Burke, L. A. (1996). Developing high- potential employees in the new business reality. *Business Horizons, 40*, 18–24.

Cannon, J., & McGee, R. (2012). *Zarządzanie talentami i planowanie ścieżek karier. Zestaw narzędzi* (pp. 16–64). Warszawa: ABC a Wolters Kluwer business.

Caligiuri, P. M. (2000). The Big Five personality characteristics as predictors of expatriates desire to terminate the assignment and supervisor-rated performance. *Personnel Psychology, 53*(1), 67–88.

Castles, S. (2011). *Migracje we współczesnym świecie*. Warszawa: PWN.

Chełpa, S. (2005). Samorealizacja talentów-możliwości i ograniczenia intrapersonalne. In S. Borkowska (Ed.), *Zarządzanie talentami*. Warszawa: IPiSS.

Collings, D., & Mellahi, K. (2009). Strategic talent management: A review and research agenda. *The Human Resource Management Review, 19*(4), 304–313.

Collings, D., Scullion, H., & Vaiman, V. (2011). European perspectives on talent management. *European Journal of International Management, 5*(5).

Davis, T., Cutt, M., Flynn, N., Mowl, P., & Orme, S. (2010). *Ewaluacja talentu. Nowa strategia zarzadzania talentami w organizacji* (p. 15). Warszawa: Oficyna a Wolters Kluwer business.

Dobosz-Bourne, D., & Jankowicz, A. D. (2006). Reframing resistance to change: Experience from General Motors Poland. *International Journal of Human Resource Management, 17*(12), 2021–34.

Farndale, E., Scullion, H., & Sparrow, P. (2010). The role of the corporate HR function in global talent management. *Journal of World Business, 46*(2), 161.

Global Benchmarking Survey. (2010). Accessed February 12, 2013, from http://www. worldwideerc.org

Glowacka-Stewart, K. (2006). Zarządzanie talentami-wyzwania, trendy, przykłady rozwiązań. The Conference Board. Accessed February 10, 2013, from http://www.conference-board.org

Grodzicki, J. (2011). *Talent w przedsiębiorstwie opartym na wiedzy*. Gdansk: Wydawnictwo Uniwersytetu Gdanskiego.

Grycuk, A. (2002). Peter Drucker. The essential Drucker. *Organizacja i Kierowanie*, nr 2.

Hansen, F. (2007). What is 'talent'? *Workforce Management, 86*(1), 12–13.

Ingram, T. (2011). *Zarządzanie talentami. Teoria dla praktyki zarzadzania zasobami ludzkimi* (pp. 17–64). Warszawa: PWE.

Kopeć, J. (2012). *Zarządzanie talentami w przedsiębiorstwie*. Kraków: Wydawnictwo Uniwersytetu Ekonomicznego w Krakowie.

Kwiecień, K. (2005). Zarządzanie talentami w międzynarodowych korporacjach. In S. Borkowska (Ed.), *Zarządzanie talentami*. Warszawa: IPiSS.

Kwon, K., Bae, J., & Lawler, J. (2010). High commitment HR practices and top performers. Impacts on organizational commitment. *Management International Review, 50*, 57–80.

Jokinen, T. (2005). Global leadership competencies: A review and discussion. *Journal of European Industrial Training, 29*(3), 199–216.

Lepak, D. P., Taylor, M. S., Tekleab, A. G., Marrone, J. A., & Cohen, D. J. (2007). An examination of the use of high-investment human resource systems for core and support employees. *Human Resource Management, 46*(2), 223–246.

Listwan, T. (2005). Zarządzanie talentami-wyzwanie współczesnych organizacji. In S. Borkowska (Ed.), *Zarządzanie talentami* (pp. 20–21). Warszawa: IPiSS.

Listwan, T. (2009). Kierunki zmian funkcji personalnej w przedsiębiorstwach. In A. Potocki (Ed.), *Globalizacja a społeczne aspekty przeobrażeń i zmian organizacyjnych*. Difin: Warszawa.

Maliszewska, E. (2005). Zarządzanie talentami—rozważania praktyka. In S. Borkowska (Ed.), *Zarządzanie talentami*. Warszawa: IPiSS.

Mellahi, K., & Collings, D. G. (2010). The barriers to effective global talent management: The example of corporate elites in MNEs. *Journal of World Business, 45*(2), 143–149.

Morawski, M. (2009). *Zarządzanie profesjonalistami* (p. 107). Warszawa: PWE.

Murdoch, A. (2011). Zespoły międzykulturowe -konflikt źródłem kreatywności. In *Proceedings of the conference on creativity as a source of innovation*, Nowy Sącz, 4 March 2011.

Pocztowski, A. (Ed.). (2008). *Zarządzanie talentami w organizacji* (pp. 63–137). Kraków: Oficyna a Wolters Kluwer Business.

Praktyki zarządzania talentami w Polsce (2010). Accessed April 25, 2013, from http://www.hrmpartners.pl/publikacje

Przytula, S. (2013a). Compensating expatriates in Polish subsidiaries-pilot research findings. *Argumenta Oeconomica, 1*(30).

Przytula, S. (2013b, May 9–10). *HRM in relation to expatriates working in Poland-research findings*. Paper presented at the global conference of International Human Resource Management, Pennsylvania State University, USA.

Renzulli, J. S. (1986). The three-ring conception of giftedness: A developmental model for creative productivity. In R. Sternberg & J. E. Davidson (Eds.), *Conceptions of giftedness*. New York: Cambridge University Press.

Schroeder, J. (2010). *Międzynarodowe zarządzanie zasobami ludzkimi* (p. 63). Poznań: Wydawnictwo UE w Poznaniu.

Scullion, H., & Collings, D. (2006). International recruitment and selection. In H. Scullion & D. Collings (Eds.), *Global staffing* (p. 69). London: Routledge.

Skuza, A., Scullion, H., & McDonnell, A. (2013). An analysis of the talent management challenges in a post-communist country: The case of Poland. *The International Journal of Human Resource Management, 24*(3), 453–470.

Stedt, J. (2010). *Harmonizacja talentów. Jak rekrutować pracowników aby firma odnosiła sukcesy*. Warszawa: Oficyna a Wolters Kluwer Business.

Stroh, L., Black, J. S., Mendenhall, M., & Gregersen, H. (Eds.). (2005). *International assignments. An integration of strategy, research and practice* (p. 65). Mahwah, NJ: Lawrence Erlbaum Associates, Publishers.

Talent Mobility 2020. (2010). The next generation of international assignments. http://www.pwc.com/managingpeople2020. Accessed 29 March 2013.

The BCG World Federation of Personnel Management Associations. (2008). *Creating people advantage*. Boston: BCG.

Vaiman, V., & Holden, N. (2011). Talent management perplexing landscape in Central and Eastern Europe. In H. Scullion & D. Collings (Eds.), *Global talent management* (pp. 178–193). London: Routledge.

Wellins, R., Smith, A., & Erker, S. (2009). White paper-nine best practices for effective talent management. *Development dimensions international*. http://www.ddiworld.com/locations. Accessed 10 Jan 2013.

Witkowski, T. (Ed.). (2000). *Nowoczesne metody doboru i oceny personelu*. Kraków: Wydawnictwo Profesjonalnej Szkoły Biznesu.

How to Attract and Retain Global Careerists: Evidence from Finland

Vesa Suutari, Olivier Wurtz, and Christelle Tornikoski

1   Introduction

Organisations have probably never looked for global managers as zealously as they are now, given the increasing globalisation of corporate activities and a growing scarcity of talent, which is particularly evident in European countries. The "war for talent" identified by McKinsey in 1998 is more prevalent than ever. These global talents range from an ability to apply skills or transfer knowledge quickly and efficiently, to an ability to lead foreign groups of activities abroad. Organisations need global employees, particularly at managerial level, with international experience, who are ready to assume responsibilities in global or regional headquarters, or to manage international organisations. These global managers are required in order to meet organisational demands, such as the need to control their subsidiaries' activities, making sure that they operate in accordance with headquarters' policies and guidelines, and to ensure the transfer of knowledge between different foreign units and from these units back to headquarters. One archetype of such a global employee is that of the "global careerist" (e.g., Suutari 2003). These managers have been described as employees whose careers encompass a succession or collection of multiple international assignments. They have thus experienced several relocations, and are accustomed to working in different countries. Companies value such employees as they are likely to have developed the ability to adjust to new situations and cultures, to be willing to move abroad again, to be flexible, and to

More in-depth reports on the experiences of Finnish global careerists can be found in "Further Reading"

V. Suutari (✉) • O. Wurtz
University of Vaasa, P.O. Box 700, 65101 Vaasa, Finland
e-mail: vsu@uva.fi; olivier.wurtz@uva.fi

C. Tornikoski
Grenoble Ecole de Management, B.P. 127 - 12, rue Pierre-Sémard, 38003 Grenoble, Cedex 01, France
e-mail: Christelle.TORNIKOSKI@grenoble-em.com

A. Al Ariss (ed.), *Global Talent Management*, Management for Professionals,
DOI 10.1007/978-3-319-05125-3_16, © Springer International Publishing Switzerland 2014

possess the skills and experiences that enable them to facilitate the working of others in international environments.

However, global careerists have also been described as "boundaryless careerists" (e.g., Stahl et al. 2002) meaning that they are individuals who move between jobs, firms, and countries (Sullivan and Arthur 2006) "independent [ly] from, rather than dependent[ly] on, traditional career arrangements" (Arthur and Rousseau 1996). Companies, such as Schlumberger, that have been successful in developing global careerists for decades, have experienced difficulties in retaining such individuals (Evans et al. 2011). Thus, it is vital for today's organisations to identify the means of attracting, developing and retaining global managers.

The aim of this paper is to address this issue by examining current approaches to the talent management of global careerists. First, global talent management is introduced, with a particular focus on global careerists. Secondly, reflections on four different aspects of talent management of global careerists are developed (identification, attraction, retention and support), based on studies conducted among Finnish business professionals. This book chapter ends with conclusions, recommendations and future directions for research.

2 Global Talent Management: Focus on Global Careerists

"Talent management is the process through which organisations anticipate and meet their needs for human capital" (Evans et al. 2011: 257). More precisely, it refers to the HRM activities which aim to "attract, develop and retain individuals with high levels of social capital" (Schuler and Tarique 2012). In other words, talent management is the aspect of HR practice that is dedicated to the acquisition, development and retention of key employees. It involves "putting the right person into the right place at the right time" (Evans et al. 2011: 257). Various definitions have been used to describe "talent", ranging from all the employees of a company (they all have talent), to only a few high potential individuals (e.g., Evans et al. 2011). In this discussion, we define "talent" as "individuals with high levels of human or social capital". By "global talent", we refer to individuals that not only fit this description but who can also succeed in international environments, such as within multinational corporations, working abroad in any kind of international setting. "Global careerists" are employees who have accumulated experience from several international positions and can be considered global talent, given their experiences, competences and profiles. This point is developed in the next sections.

Global talent management encompasses different activities. The first consists of identifying the employees who need to be included in global talent management programmes, i.e. individuals possessing the talents and potential needed by the company. These can be found both inside and outside the company. Companies have been advocated to "Make *and* Buy" talent (Cappelli 2008: 77), that is to say, to identify and develop talent from within the company, but also to recruit talent from outside in case of shortfall, since a perfect forecast of required talents is impossible (Cappelli 2008).

The second activity, and related set of HR practices, of global talent management consists of attracting and recruiting key employees. This involves finding such individuals and rendering the company attractive for them (e.g. Tarique and Schuler 2010). This implies building a positive corporate image, or at least succeeding in communicating a positive image to the target audience.

The third key action of global talent management consists of retaining the existing international talent. Hiring talent is often not enough; being highly valuable, such individuals are also likely to be attractive to other companies, often competitors. They are therefore likely to be head hunted, to receive indirect job offers through their professional and social networks, and to leave the company at some point. Such departures represent heavy losses for the organisation, not only in terms of talent, skills and knowledge, but also in terms of the previous investment in the departing individual (including the cost of recruitment, training, compensation etc) and the cost of finding someone else. Additional potential costs may be incurred for the period of time that the position is vacant, between the departure of the previous job holder and the recruitment of the new one, along with the cost of any potential leakage of key professional knowledge to competitors. Retention issues seem to have increased in recent years due to the current tendency of individuals to change jobs more and more frequently (Schuler and Tarique 2012).

A fourth and related area of activity of global talent management consists of providing appropriate organisational support to talented employees. Organisational support may take many forms, from supervisory support, for instance, to various measures to facilitate work-life balance (e.g., Evans et al. 2011). Organisational support has been found to increase employee retention and performance (e.g., Kraimer and Wayne 2004).

Talent management of global careerists differs from talent management of first-time expatriates from several perspectives. Global careerists are more experienced, more attractive to companies due to their broad international experience, more able to adapt easily to different contexts, and more aware of what they can ask for in terms of company support. We will investigate the four areas of activity involved in the talent management of global careerists, based on the results of empirical studies, in the following sections. First, in terms of talent identification, global careerists are likely to be strong assets for companies, and should therefore, when relevant, be identified as "talent". Their unique and rich experience provides them with specific skills and competencies. We reflect on what, precisely, global careerists have learned from their previous experiences and what they consequently bring to a company. Second, in order to recruit global careerists, it is necessary to understand what they value specifically, and what attracts them. Their careers, and their lives, differ widely from domestic employees, and so their preferences may also be dissimilar. Third, the retention of global careerists can present a challenge to organisations, given that these individuals are accustomed to changing locations, countries, and subsidiaries regularly. Thus an examination of what motivates global careerists to change employers and to relocate is crucial in order to understand what can be done to gain their commitment. Finally, global managers as expatriates usually receive more support than many other employees due to the demanding nature of their careers. The company has a key role to play in supporting global careerists, helping them to settle-in well and ensuring that their working and living circumstances meet their expectations and requirements.

3   Reflections on Talent Management from Studies Among Finnish Global Careerists

This chapter utilises interview materials and related observations from six different studies, built upon three data collection rounds, all of which were conducted during the last 10 years. A total of 62 experienced international professionals from a variety of industries were interviewed to gain their perspectives on various aspects of their careers, including career tracks, career anchors, career capital, social capital, career decision making, total rewards and work-family interface. On average, the respondents had spent more than 15 years abroad and their assignment locations covered 13 countries and four continents.

3.1   Why Are Global Careerists an Interesting Group for MNCs to Consider? What Have They Learned and What Can They Do?

The findings on the developmental nature of work experiences of global careerists indicate that, over the course of their careers, these professionals assume various challenging roles in a number of different international environments, which develops their competencies considerably (Suutari and Mäkelä 2007). One framework to describe their development is that of "the career capital framework". Individual career capital includes three different types of knowing: knowing-why, knowing-how, and knowing-whom (Inkson and Arthur 2001). "Knowing-why" career capital refers to motivation and personal meaning, which provides the individual with energy, a sense of purpose and identification with work. "Knowing-how" career capital consists of work-related knowledge, skills, and expertise. Finally, "knowing-whom" career capital refers to the networks, both within and outside the organisation, that are relevant and helpful for an individual's career.

Global careerists reported that their career experiences had strongly increased their knowing-why career capital. These global professionals believed that their experiences had developed their self-awareness, including an understanding of their personal strengths and weaknesses, their work-related values, and career-related motives, and had improved their self-confidence. As a result of such development, global careerists felt that they were well-prepared to take on other challenging tasks in the future and were capable of handling such future demands. Similar development had taken place in the area of knowing-how career capital, where global careerists had developed both general management (e.g., social skills, change management and leadership skills) and international managerial competencies (e.g., managing cross-cultural teams or international projects, cross-cultural communication skills and adjustment skills). Global careerists realised that they had acquired new managerial expertise from handling diverse and demanding tasks abroad while, at the same time, developing the global leadership skills necessary in an international business environment. As a result of their mobility and experience of working in many different organisational units and national business environments, global careerists had also developed extensive social networks (knowing-whom career capital) which they utilised extensively when working in challenging environments.

The main reasons for the extensive professional development of the global careerists interviewed were the considerable breadth of their responsibilities, the demanding nature of their tasks and the high level of autonomy involved in their international jobs. Furthermore, each of their international relocations offered new learning opportunities, as did the challenging nature of their international and/or cross-cultural working and living. They considered their experiences to have forced them to test and push their limits in terms of handling challenging tasks in new contexts where there was typically little corporate support.

Global careerists had also developed a global career identity throughout their international experiences. This identity typically manifested as an awareness of their own high level of career capital and a related high degree of faith in their employability. They considered their job-markets to be global and were highly committed to continuing their work careers in an international environment. They were driven by their internal career motivation, were interested in facing new challenges in their future career and, overall, had a clear career identity involving high levels of self-understanding and significant self-confidence. They were also clear about their values and career interests, and knew their market value.

As these findings indicate, global careerists had developed a wide range of general managerial skills. Besides being the most experienced professionals in managing international teams and projects, they also understood the nature of the international business environment and had the undeniable ability to adapt to various and very different work environments. It is of no surprise that their talent is thus highly sought-after by MNCs facing increasing globalisation.

3.2   How to Attract Global Careerists: What Do They Value?

Companies aiming to recruit global careerists need to identify what they should offer in order to attract, recruit and integrate them properly. The results from the studies of Finnish global careerists indicated that international professionals valued the nature and characteristics of their job over the financial compensation (salary, benefits and allowances) involved (Suutari et al. 2012). This confirmed that a "total rewards" perspective would be a useful compensation approach for MNCs (see also Tornikoski 2011) This does not mean that financial compensation is unimportant when global careerists are making decisions on whether to change job or employer.

Financial rewards "simply" appear as necessary prerequisites in any possible negotiations, while the key motivational factors lie elsewhere. Indeed, our research has shown that it was only after a job offer was perceived as potentially interesting and challenging enough, from a motivational perspective, that the monetary and financial issues were considered and raised in the discussions. Furthermore, if the job offer was considered interesting, global careerists appeared to be more concerned about their standard of living in the host country than their financial package in itself, i.e. they wanted to make sure that the level of salary offered by the organisation allowed them to cover all of their living costs abroad.

Since global careers include a succession of international assignments, which may be long- or short-term, organisationally imposed or self-initiated, the issue of compensation becomes extremely complex for corporations to handle, particularly in relation to issues such as pensions. Typically, MNCs have defined policies on expatriate compensation. However, the recruitment of global careerists from the external job market does not fit the expatriate assignment scenario. Also, as experienced global professionals, global careerists with self-initiated assignments often manage to negotiate benefits and allowances which are usually reserved for assigned expatriates, in addition to a locally-based compensation package.

Since the financial issue is not the primary motivational factor for global careerists, the main question, naturally, is then: What should companies offer to attract the interest of such professionals? The perspective of the Finnish global careerists interviewed was clear: The nature of the job and the job design were the key elements of interest. These professionals were looking for meaningful, strategic jobs in which they could fully exploit their experiences and developed skills, and develop these still further. To gain the attention of global careerists, organisations should focus on the job itself, the competencies required and the developmental challenges involved. Global careerists enjoyed working in challenging job environments that they considered interesting though complex, and so were attracted to challenging new roles. The other aspect that attracted global careerists was the developmental potential of the role. Given that their international jobs often involved a high level of managerial autonomy, it is also likely that global careerists find narrow and restrictive job descriptions less interesting.

Global careerists typically valued the international dimension of their jobs and wanted to work in international job environments—an element that many MNCs can offer, as a result of their organisational structure, and/or by assigning more specific international responsibilities to the role in question. Global careerists were accustomed to leading multinational teams and projects and to travelling internationally. If a role involved such elements, its attractiveness to global careerists increased. This finding was shown clearly when the career anchors of global careerists were analysed (Suutari and Taka 2004). Almost 80 % of those interviewed saw the international dimension of the job as of such central importance to their careers that it was identified as one of their main career anchors. Whenever tasks in the home country did not involve an international element, a high proportion of assignees expressed interest in looking for a new international job either in the home country or abroad.

The repatriation stage of international assignments typically presents particular challenges. It is common that companies, after repatriating their managers, place these individuals in roles that are not as interesting or as challenging as those that the global careerists enjoyed abroad. Repatriation may also present difficulties for organisations, both in terms of recognising the skills that their expatriates have developed in international jobs, and in terms of acknowledging that global careerists often lack social connections within domestic career markets (both internally to the organisation and externally) due to their long or successive absences (including the so-called "out of sight—out of mind" phenomenon).

An analysis of the social capital developed by global careerists during their careers showed that, due to their mobility and related experiences in many different organisations and contexts, global careerists had a wide range of social connections (Mäkelä and Suutari 2009). They considered their social capital to be a very important aspect of their ability to handle their challenging roles, in terms of using their connections to get help or information at any time it was required. This was closely related to their recruitment, in the sense that they often found new jobs through their networks, i.e. external colleagues or customers offered them jobs in other organisations. In fact, in many cases the respondents changed employers without ever formally applying for the external position. Therefore, active head hunting is required if companies wish to identify and recruit such international professionals, given that these individuals are not often active themselves in seeking external career options.

3.3   How to Retain Global Careerists: What Motivates Them to Stay in an Organisation?

Having recruited a global careerist, it is important for organisations to understand what motivates the individual to commit to the organisation. The discussion on what they value (above) has already shown what companies ought to be offering, in terms of packages based on total rewards and interesting job roles, in order to attract and motivate these individuals. Additional insights can be gained by analysing the reasons behind previous changes in employers and jobs during their careers.

The Finnish global careerists interviewed cited external pressures unrelated to individual motivation as a frequent reason for career changes (Suutari et al. 2012). This reflected the turbulence of the international business environment and the global career path, which was often related to business logistics such as organisational restructuring, a merger or acquisition. Such changes often led to the disappearance of the respondents' job, or to their resignation in cases where the organisational changes implied a modification of the initial agreement of their employment relationship and of the nature of the job role. The second reason usually given for career changes was connected to the periodic nature of international jobs such as international assignments or international projects. The high degree of uncertainty in terms of the global careerist's next career opportunity resulted in a tendency to frequently analyse what they could be doing next. This analysis often involved the question of whether and when they should repatriate back to the home country, or if they should continue working abroad in the same country or in new countries. At this stage, global careerists typically thought through their external as well as their internal employment options.

Besides these external factors pushing global careerists to change jobs or employers, there were also other personal interests involved in career decision-making. Supporting the findings discussed in the previous section, the global careerists reported that they had looked for new career options in order to gain exposure to new challenges, new learning opportunities, and more meaningful jobs in which they could fully capitalise on their earlier career experiences. Global careerists were often interested in new posts in bigger, global organisations which were perceived to offer career opportunities that better enabled these individuals to fully employ their global expertise. As well as job-related factors, career decisions were also affected by location (i.e. the attractiveness of the host country) and family-related concerns. Financial benefits and related life-style possibilities were also considered, but typically played a secondary role in the career decision, i.e. the main motivation for career moves came from the internal and job-related factors discussed above.

Given that financial compensation has been found to rank fairly low among the key factors motivating global careerists, companies need to pay great attention to the "human" side of the employment relationship—career/professional opportunities, development possibilities, and the personal/relational context of the job—since these are perceived as essential. When global careerists have developed their career capital to a high level, it also means that they are sensitive to what is offered to them: The job needs to "mean" something to them and to have a real purpose in terms of their career perspective. The job also needs to allow them to develop their competencies further, should involve some international aspects, and allow the job-holder a level of autonomy and discretion comparable to the levels that they had typically enjoyed in their previous international jobs. Global careerists will naturally compare any new jobs offered to them with their existing roles, taking account of how the new role measures up to their current international job in terms of these important dimensions.

3.4 How to Support Global Careerists: What Specific Support Do They Need?

Our findings among Finnish global careerists clearly indicate that a global career has extensive implications in terms of the overall life of both the careerists and their families (Suutari 2003; Mäkelä and Suutari 2011; Mäkelä et al. 2012). One of the main challenges concerns the work-family interface: Global careers involve frequent international moves, necessitating constant adjustment at the family level, and typically involving extremely demanding jobs for the global careerists themselves.

Although global careerists and their families are already experienced in relocating, they still value (or even require) corporate support with practical arrangements (e.g., settling-in programmes), family training (e.g., cultural training with the focus on the new host country and language training), and career support for the spouse as well. Furthermore, our findings showed that global careerists had learned that, due to the complexity of their situations, they often needed assistance with practical matters provided by legal counsellors, pension specialists, insurance advisors, and investment and tax consultants. They had also learned that thorough personal preparation was essential to ensure that the entire family got off to a good start (e.g., careful selection of living environments, schools and child-care, and before-arrival visits to the host country in order to make arrangements). It was clear from the interviews that a global career is not a choice made by global careerists alone, but needs to be a family decision, and that a supportive corporate policy boosts the chances of success. Thus, organisations should be mindful of family concerns at all stages, from the selection of the expatriate through to the planning and provision of necessary relocation support and training. In dual-career situations, the career possibilities for the spouse often presented a challenge. Dual-career support practices, such as job-search support for the spouse, career counselling and covering the costs incurred in the job-search, were valued.

Due to the international nature of their jobs, global careerists typically worked long hours, travelled a great deal and were expected to have 24/7 availability. As compensation, they expected flexibility from their employers in arranging their schedules and also in arranging time when they could stay at home (e.g., through distant working). If there was much international travelling involved, travelling time was expected to be taken into account in discussions about working time. Global careerists also found staying in touch with their extended families and friends challenging when living in different countries. Thus, MNCs usually paid for the expatriate to travel back to their home country during vacations; self-initiated expatriates may be able to negotiate similar benefits (for more on self-initiated expatriates, see Al Ariss and Crowley-Henry 2013).

It should be stressed here that because international job contracts are often fixed-term, they typically involve uncertainty with regard to the next career stage. Global careerists need corporate career support in order to be able to negotiate the next assignment well in advance of the end of the contract. Otherwise, the motivation for looking at external options increases. In cases where companies had taken good care of the wider career issue, the loyalty of global careerists towards their employer increased, and they were not as interested in looking at external options. Whenever the respondents repatriated back to their home country (e.g., to work at HQ), they highly valued organisational support, such as repatriation training and help with practical arrangements. Still, the organisational support concerning job-related arrangements for both partners was top of their priority list.

Conclusions and Recommendations

The first conclusion of this work is that global careerists should, when relevant, be identified as "talent", as key assets for the company. Over the course of their working lives, global careerists experience international careers that offer extensive learning opportunities (Cappellen and Janssens 2005). Supporting this assertion, the Finnish global professionals interviewed over the past 10 years have reported extensive development experiences, thanks to challenging job situations in different institutional contexts. Bearing in mind that a single international assignment is already considered to be an extremely efficient management development method (Carpenter et al. 2000), it is far from surprising that individuals who have lived and worked in several, often different, environments acquire extensive career capital and international expertise.

The Finnish global careerists also developed a high level of social capital, which they frequently utilised in their challenging international jobs. The development of global social capital has important consequences for MNCs. Borgatti and Cross (2003) found that MNC managers often sought and shared their knowledge through interpersonal interaction, rather than using written materials or corporate intranets. In this way, knowledge existing within their social networks forms their most important knowledge base, which these managers draw upon in order to succeed in their jobs and careers. Consequently, extensive international experience increases the career capital necessary to take on more demanding roles at higher organisational levels within MNCs. In the study, the global career identity of the respondents was found to include an awareness of their own career capital and employability. Other elements comprising this identity included a global job market orientation, interest in seeking new challenges, and well-defined career aspirations. They also reported that their social capital had influenced their career opportunities and advancement. However, the respondents recognised that international roles carry a risk in terms of losing home country connections and that is was thus important to make an effort to remain active in important home country networks as well.

The career findings of this study support the protean career approach: Global careerists were clearly in charge of their own careers and were motivated more by internal than by external career issues (Hall and Moss 1998). Global careerists also seem to share many features with "boundaryless careerists", moving across national, organisational and job boundaries (Suutari et al. 2013). However, the global careerists were found to act less individualistically than the boundaryless theory suggests: i.e. some of them were very loyal to their companies over a long period of time. Thus, if a company takes good care of the career interests of global careerists and supports them and their families well, these professionals are more likely to remain committed to that company. An appropriate talent management approach to global careerists is therefore likely to retain them.

When we analysed the career orientations and total rewards preferences of global careerists, it was clear that they valued non-financial over financial rewards. This supports the importance of using a total rewards approach, i.e. providing a package that includes all of the elements of reward that the employee values the most, when aiming to attract and motivate global professionals (Tornikoski 2011). The experiences of global careerists also emphasised the importance of family-related concerns in a global career context. Taking family-related aspects into careful consideration in contract negotiations provides a means by which companies can signal their empathy with the international professional and convey their interest in helping to address the unique challenges faced by them and their families.

From a retention perspective, it is necessary to identify the elements of reward that are perceived as critical and decisive by the employee, and which consequently influence their decision to stay with a company (Stahl and Cerdin 2004). The findings among global careerists indicate that their reasons for changing employers are typically related to the characteristics of the role, in combination with a personal orientation that leads them to look for new challenges and learning possibilities within an international work context. In line with this, a recent study by Tornikoski (2011) shows that expatriates' perceptions regarding their traditional, financial, expatriate compensation package (i.e. base salary, incentives, insurances and benefits, and allowances) were unrelated to their affective commitment to the employer organisation; while perceptions of the non-financial elements of their reward package did influence their commitment. In addition to job-related factors, the location of the assignment and family-related preferences were usually explicitly considered when deciding upon the next career move.

Domestic studies have shown that perceived organisational support has an impact on employee retention (e.g., Rhoades et al. 2001). Global careerists were committed to their employer whenever the organisation had managed the assignments well, provided them with interesting new tasks over the course of their careers and given them a good level of overall support. Thus, organisational support and good management of these professionals increased their reluctance to face the uncertainty and risk typically involved in any employer change. This overall organisational support consisted of practices provided at different career stages or in various situations, for example, in career planning situations, relocation situations, dual-career situations, at the repatriation stage or when attempting to find a satisfactory work-life balance. In order to succeed well in supporting global careerists, companies should closely monitor the unique challenges faced by their key global talent and understand the support practices required in order to help these professionals cope in this special career environment. In a turbulent international business environment, where job contracts are typically fixed-term, the career planning of global talent is both an important and extremely difficult task.

In Table 1 we summarise some of the main recommendations from the studies of Finnish global careerists.

Table 1 Key global talent management challenges, strategies, and future opportunities regarding global careerists

Four key points regarding Global Talent Management challenges	Four key points regarding strategies to overcome these challenges	Four key points regarding future opportunities in Global Talent Management
1 Should global careerists be identified as talent?	Experienced global careerists form an attractive labour pool for MNCs due to their extensive global experiences and related high level of global career capital	There is a growing global careerist population—employees valuable for many companies. Active headhunting is often necessary to identify and recruit global careerists
2 Focus on financial issues alone is not enough to attract and retain global careerists	A "total rewards" approach with a focus on non-financial rewards is necessary to attract global careerists	Companies need to better identify global talent internally. For example, self-initiated expatriates are not always tracked by HR
3 Family issues are an important aspect of career management among global careerists	Focus should be on the family unit as a whole when recruiting, supporting and managing global careerists	Once global talents have been identified, appropriate global talent management policies need to be identified and implemented
4 Appropriately supporting global careerists can be a challenge	Active career planning and support is required to retain global careerists who live in uncertain career situation within a dynamic international business environment	Multinationals can attract global careerists by developing targeted communication and support programmes

Further Reading

Mäkelä, L., Saarenpää, K., Suutari, V., & Wurtz, O. (2012). How to cope with work-family conflicts in an international career context? In B. Molinelli & V. Grimaldo (Eds.), *Handbook of the psychology of coping: New research* (pp. 151–168). Hauppauge, NY: Nova Publishers.

Mäkelä, K., & Suutari, V. (2009). Global careers: A social capital paradox. *International Journal of Human Resource Management, 20*(5), 992–1008.

Mäkelä, L., & Suutari, V. (2011). Coping with work-family conflicts in the global career context. *Thunderbird International Business Review, 53*(3), 365–375.

Suutari, V. (2003). Global managers: Career orientation, career tracks, life-style implications, and career commitment. *Journal of Managerial Psychology, 18*(3), 185–207.

Suutari, V., & Mäkelä, K. (2007). The career capital of managers with global careers. *Journal of Managerial Psychology, 22*, 628–648.

Suutari, V., & Taka, M. (2004). Career anchors of managers with global careers. *Journal of Management Development, 23*(9), 833–847.

Suutari, V., Tornikoski, C., & Mäkelä, L. (2012). Career decision making of global careerists. *International Journal of Human Resource Management, 23*(16), 3455–3478.

Other References

Al Ariss, A., & Crowley-Henry, M. (2013). Self-initiated expatriation and migration in the management literature: Present theorizations and future research directions. *Career Development International, 18*(1), 78–96.

Arthur, M., & Rousseau, D. M. (1996). *The boundaryless career.* New York: Oxford University Press.

Borgatti, S. P., & Cross, R. (2003). A relational view of information seeking and learning in social networks. *Management Science, 49,* 432–445.

Cappellen, T., & Janssens, T. (2005). Career paths of global managers: Towards future research. *Journal of World Business, 40,* 348–360.

Cappelli, P. (2008, March) Talent management for the twenty-first century. *Harvard Business Review,* 74–81.

Carpenter, M. A., Sanders, W. G., & Gregersen, H. B. (2000). International assignment experience at the top can make a bottom-line difference. *Human Resource Management, 39*(2&3), 277–285.

Evans, P., Pucik, V., & Björkman, I. (2011). *The global challenge: International human resource management* (2nd ed.). Boston: McGraw-Hill.

Hall, D. T., & Moss, J. E. (1998). The new protean career contract: Helping organizations and employees adapt. *Organizational Dynamics, 26*(3), 22–37.

Inkson, K., & Arthur, M. (2001). How to be a successful career capitalist. *Organisational Dynamics, 30*(1), 48–61.

Kraimer, M., & Wayne, S. (2004). An examination of perceived organizational support as a multidimensional construct in the context of an expatriate assignment. *Journal of Management, 30*(2), 209–237.

Rhoades, L., Eisenberger, R., & Armeli, S. (2001). Affective commitment to the organization: The contribution of perceived organizational support. *Journal of Applied Psychology, 86,* 825–836.

Schuler, R., & Tarique, I. (2012). Global talent management: Theoretical perspectives, systems, and challenges. In I. Björkman & G. Stahl (Eds.), *Handbook of research in IHRM.* London: Edward Elgar Publishing.

Stahl, G. K., & Cerdin, J. L. (2004). Global careers in French and German multinational corporations. *Journal of Management Development, 23*(9), 885–902.

Stahl, G. K., Miller, E. L., & Tung, R. L. (2002). Toward the boundaryless career: A closer look at the expatriate career concept and the perceived implications of an international assignment. *Journal of World Business, 37*(3), 216–227.

Sullivan, S. E., & Arthur, M. B. (2006). The evolution of the boundaryless career concept: Examining physical and psychological mobility. *Journal of Vocational Behavior, 69,* 19–29.

Suutari, V., Brewster, C., & Tornikoski, C. (2013). The careers of self-initiated expatriates. In V. Vaiman & A. Haslberger (Eds.), *Managing talent of self-initiated expatriates: A neglected source of the global talent flow.* Hampshire: Palgrave Macmillan.

Tornikoski, C. (2011). Expatriates' affective commitment: A total reward perspective. Cross cultural management—An International Journal (CCM) [Special issue]. *Expatriate Management: New Issues and New Insights, 18*(2).

Global Talent Management in French Multinationals

Vincent Sponton and Akram Al Ariss

1 Introduction

In order to grow within a crisis market and be closer to resources and/or customers, companies need to grow internationally. This internationalization of companies is achieved through the international mobility of human resources (HR) and talents, and companies use international assignment (IA) as a lever to develop these global talents (GTs). Given the huge investment that companies make in IAs, it is crucial to ensure that they are managed effectively (Franck and Ramirez 2003; Bournois et al. 2007). This means looking at how IAs can be successful in achieving the objectives of the companies and of the individual talents; in short, how to develop successful international mobility of talents. This chapter will consider companies' global mobility (GM) and identify possible practical improvements for the management of talents on IAs. Our focus is on corporate expatriations lasting between 1 and 5 years.

We begin with a review of the literature on GM and talent management (TM), which enables us to identify key elements in the process of IA and specific links with global talent management (GTM). Key reports from consulting agencies have also been analyzed to identify the best practices ongoing in both GM management and TM (e.g. World Economic Forum/Mercer 2012). We then introduce to our discussion voices drawn from in-depth interviews conducted in three French multinationals and a French association of international human resource management (IHRM) professionals. Finally, we present the practical as well as the research implications of our work.

V. Sponton
Freelance consultant, France
e-mail: vincentspontonrh@gmail.com

A. Al Ariss (✉)
Université de Toulouse, Toulouse Business School, France
e-mail: info@akramalariss.com

A. Al Ariss (ed.), *Global Talent Management*, Management for Professionals,
DOI 10.1007/978-3-319-05125-3_17, © Springer International Publishing Switzerland 2014

2   What Are the Dynamics of a Successful International Assignment?

The topic of IAs has grown in importance within international management literature (Collings et al. 2007; Al Ariss 2014), and as multinational enterprises (MNEs) struggle to attract, retain, and develop managerial talents for their global operations, the efficient management of GTs has been specifically identified as an area in need of further research (Sidani and Al Ariss 2013; Tarique and Schuler 2010). Though not yet focused upon in the literature, management of talent assignment is critical for business success in MNEs (Waxin and Barmeyer 2008; Dickmann and Baruch 2010; Cerdin 1999).

One reason for which companies use international transfers is to develop their GTs. In some firms, GM is even mandatory in attaining management positions (Waxin and Barmeyer 2008; Dickmann and Baruch 2010). Global assignments are created to develop the international mindset of assignees. Typical motives behind accepting an IA depend upon the nature of the job offered, the opportunity for new experiences, and the chance to develop new skills (Dickmann et al. 2008).

Unlike self-initiated expatriation/international migration, where individuals are mainly in charge of their own international mobility (Al Ariss and Crowley-Henry 2013), the success of corporate expatriation, during and after, can be classified as both the individual's and the organization's success (Cerdin and Le Pargneux 2009). Thus, we can define a successful international assignment c as mobility enabling both the organization and its employee to attain their objectives (Al Ariss et al. 2013), with organizational success denoting the accomplishment of key organizational objectives, knowledge transfers, network construction, and retention of the expatriate; and individual success comprising success in the job and individual development during and after assignments.

The financial cost of one IA can reach up to three to five times the amount of an assignee's home salary per annum. As a result, organizations have a great interest in finding ways to make IA worthwhile: efficient and successful. Preparation for IA has, for example, been identified as fundamental. Figure 1 presents a model which synthesizes the main stages of managing the IA of talents. Building on the work of Waxin and Barmeyer (2008) we use this model as a theoretical guideline for our discussion in this chapter as we consider the possible means of achieving successful international assignment. The principle components of this model are (1) the organization of a GM policy—a pillar of IA management (IAM); (2) strategic planning of assignments; (3) recruitment and selection of candidates; (4) choice of compensation and benefit (C&B) profile; (5) preparation for the assignment; (6) organizational support during and after expatriation; (7) performance evaluation and management of expatriates; and (8) repatriation and retention of those talents (Waxin and Barmeyer 2008).

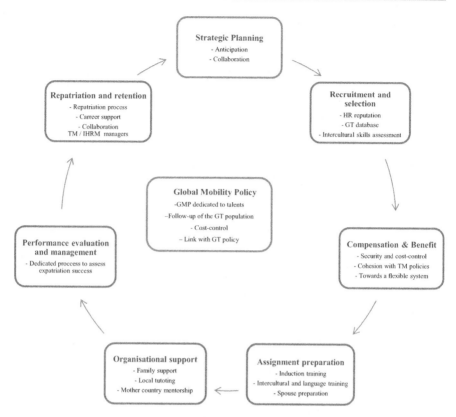

Fig. 1 Model for the management of global talents' international assignments [also see Waxin and Barmeyer (2008)]

2.1 Global Mobility Policies

A global mobility policy (GMP) enables an overview of all the policy benefits as well as the terms and conditions the company would like to offer assignees. This document contains the regulations and specifications regarding pre-assignment preparation; shipment of goods and travel expenses; home and host accommodation; family, dual careers, and training provisions; compensation, benefits, and assignment allowances; tax treatment, social security, pensions, and insurance; and repatriation and information concerning assignment termination (Dickmann and Baruch 2010). This document has to be conceived as a "living document" and updated following the evolution of the strategic objectives of GM and the assignee population. Most of the companies have one global policy while others develop policies dedicated to different employee populations. In these cases, it is worthwhile developing GMPs dedicated to talents which address their needs and problems while remaining coherent with the company TM policy.

2.2   Strategic Planning of Assignments and Recruitment and Selection Process

Any strategic planning of IAs requires that HR professionals have a global view of the needs of IAs in advance (Dickmann and Doherty 2010). A comprehensive analysis and early preparation of the assignment enables a smooth process of recruitment and selection. This will inevitably minimize problems in the whole IA process if all elements have been well accounted for. With the increase in dual career couples and the increasing demand for GTs, many MNEs have difficulty in finding appropriately qualified workers willing to accept IAs (Schuler et al. 2011). MNEs need to work on developing their HR reputation to attract individuals with interest in international work. Most importantly, they should develop a talent pool strategy by which to recruit young talents for future IAs (Tarique and Schuler 2010). Recruitment methods for international transfers currently include the use of both external websites and internal databases to identify candidates for expatriation. This international mobility database could be linked to a company's TM database so as to keep track of internationally mobile talents.

A key part of the IA selection process is minimizing the risk of failure by ensuring that the candidate has the necessary skills or the potential to develop them (Graf and Harland 2005). Considering that the selection process may involve some bias in the methods and criteria of selection used by recruiters, it might be useful to obtain objective tools for testing and training the intercultural competencies of international recruiters and stakeholders in recruitments. In this regard, technical competence, personal traits, family situation, and the ability to adapt to another environment are pertinent factors for IA selection (Tung 1989; Dickmann and Baruch 2010). Assessments of intercultural skills can be used to select the appropriate candidates and equally to identify the required training. Suutari and Brewster (2001) suggest that the most commonly used criteria are centered upon work-related skills, while language skills and a willingness to work abroad belong to a second group of criteria. From our review of the literature and consultancy reports, we note that there seems to be a gap between researchers' recommendations as per IA recruitment and selection and companies' application of such advice. Notably, companies do not seem to use psychometric tools to select international assignees (Harvey and Novicevic 2001). Once the right person is selected, mobility managers should then define the appropriate compensation and benefit proposition according to the GMP.

2.3   Compensation and Benefits

Compensation and benefits (C&B) constitutes an important aspect of the expatriation and key determinant of the expatriate's decision to accept an assignment (Franck and Ramirez 2003). However, the very topic of expatriation costs and benefits seems to remain neglected by most organizations (Collings et al. 2007; Saint-Onge et al. 2002).

Internally, such compensations could be expected to be part of a company-wide system of compensation and TM policies. Externally, the expatriate compensation should be competitive, motivating, and must ensure the security of GTs (Dickmann and Baruch 2010). Compensating internationally mobile employees requires four components: base salary, bonus, indemnities, and fringe benefits. Nowadays, companies are evolving towards a 'cafeteria' approach that allows the employee to choose different kinds of allowances and support for mobility within a defined amount. This approach, offering flexible international assignee compensation, can reduce costs and enable companies to better respond to assignees' needs in the most appropriate way (Burns 2003). Practical issues such as taxation, total salary level, and car/transportation allowance have a clear influence on the level of satisfaction. For GTs, the calculation of these bonuses and allowances is important and offer an attractive package that promotes GM of talents (Dickmann and Baruch 2010). Apart from that, a good preparation of the assignee will enable a better adaptation of the expatriate.

2.4   Preparation for the International Assignments

Since smooth adaptation to the new environment is integral for the success of any expatriation, solid support in cultural adaptation for the GTs, their partners, and families is crucial (Cerdin 2001; Fish and Wood 1997; Katz and Seifer 1996). Preparation for adaption might include a preliminary visit, language lessons, and intercultural training. A comprehensive cross-cultural management training program enables expatriates and their families to enhance their cross-cultural aptitude and awareness, gain substantive knowledge, and develop appropriate skills for working with and within other cultures (Kline Harrison 1994; Godiwalla 2012). On top of this preparation before expatriation, expatriated talents will need support during and after the assignment.

2.5   Organizational Support for Adaptation

Perceived organizational support refers to employees' general belief as to the extent to which their organization values their contribution and cares about their wellbeing. This perceived organizational support is positively related to commitment to the organization (Kraimer et al. 2001). Thus, headquarters and local support will impact the performance and retention of international assignees (Lazarova and Caligiuri 2001). Pre-departure assistance, support at arrival, and support during expatriation can help the assignees to maintain the link with their headquarters and allow them to focus on their job.

As the global adaptation of the partner and family has a strong impact on the global adaptation of the expatriate (Cerdin 1999), MNEs might provide support for the partner, schooling support, informal networking opportunities, and financial support to pursue studies (Merignac and Roger 2012). In addition to this, the social support of a local coach or tutor who can help in times of difficulties (Andreason 2008) could also be provided. Some companies propose having sponsors or mentors for talents in the mother country, which helps the assignee remain visible to the organization and to prepare for his/her return (Shawn et al. 2008; Carraher et al. 2008).

In addition to providing logistical, financial, or tax support during assignment, global companies could also consider other services for talents, such as on-going career counseling, psychological counseling for expatriates, and a dedicated evaluation of performance.

2.6 Evaluation and Management of Performance

To evaluate and manage the performance of an international assignee, some companies develop expatriate performance appraisals (Martin and Bartolk 2003; Tahvanainen 2000). Recent studies point out the importance of expatriate assignments that target the success of expatriates. To manage the performance of an expatriate, it is important to adapt the appraisal system, taking into account a number of key factors, such as the host context, the articulation of performance objective, and the designation of the evaluator (Collings et al. 2007).

2.7 Repatriation and Retention

High turnover among expatriates is an old phenomenon (Harzing 1995; Tung 1998). For companies, this represents a bad return on substantial investments, the possibility of losing to competitors, and a damaging impact on the willingness of other employees to embark upon IAs in the future. Three organizational variables are known to play a key role in assignees' turnover intentions (Stahl et al. 2009; Tung 1988): perception of repatriation concerns, perceived career advancement opportunities (Barmeyer and Davoine 2012), and satisfaction with the support provided by the company. A deficient combination of these elements can induce a feeling that the international experience is not fully appreciated at headquarters.

To overcome this difficulty, better career support coordinated with the TM services is required. This can improve the perceived organizational support for the repatriate, develop a greater satisfaction and belonging within himself/herself, and can lower feelings of uncertainty and anxiety (Jassawalla et al. 2004; Tarique and Schuler 2010). Therefore, a career-orientation, the utilization of expatriate experience, and post-assignment tracking would all greatly improve retention (Sanchez Vidal et al. 2008). Nevertheless, it seems that most firms lack appropriate repatriation management policies (Smida 2006). Instead, most of the support consists in housing, schooling, medical, and tax-return support. There is a lack of preparation in identifying the job upon the return of the repatriates, with many companies neglecting to manage the transition from an IA to a new position effectively.

Models for effective repatriation propose to work on repatriation at each step of the IA (Jassawalla et al. 2004) and to handle the process of expatriation and repatriation in the career management (Baruch 2002): prior to departure, during assignment, and on the return of the assignee. For companies, this support enables improved retention of international assignees and improved return on investment (ROI) in human capital (Van Der Haijden et al. 2009; Scelba 1995). In order to illustrate some of the issues mentioned above, we focus on the cases of three French multinationals.

3   Methods

For this exploratory and practice-oriented chapter, semi-structured interviews were conducted with HR directors of three French multinationals as well as with a key French association of IHRM professionals in France. At the time of the interviews, the number of employees in each of the three multinationals was 6,000, 10,000, and 130,000, respectively. Their respective business sectors were in energy, chemicals, and aeronautics. The interview method was chosen in order to obtain qualitative results on the challenges and successes of IAs of GTs and to collect examples of good practice. A specific invitation letter and interview guide were prepared. The questions in this interview guide were developed from the literature (Waxin and Barmeyer 2008; Cerdin 2001; Dickmann and Baruch 2010). The questionnaire contains four groups of questions: (1) the organization of international assignments; (2) the process of international mobility; (3) the link between international mobility and human resource management; and, (4) organizational challenges and successes of international assignments.

The average duration of each interview was approximately 1 h. The interviews were carried out in 2012 and have been recorded, transcribed, and analyzed. To protect the privacy of the participants, all collected data has been kept anonymous. Participants received the transcription of their interview. Of course, these results are not generalizable; rather, they offer a snapshot of how the IA of talents is managed in three important French multinational companies.

4   Results and Analysis

The interviewees understood successful mobility as the realization of three separate goals: (1) achievement of the company's mission objectives; (2) good adaptation and development of the expatriate during expatriation; and, (3) the opportunity for the company to use expatriates' human capital upon their return. For the interviewees, successful mobility can be realized through careful planning, ensuring that employees are fully prepared to go abroad, and fluent and coherent communication throughout the expatriation process. Participants underlined the fact that they would need more HR management (HRM) support to measure and achieve full efficiency in the management of assignments.

4.1 Global Mobility Policies

The interviewees identified integral elements for the development of a document of GMP that encourages successful mobility. Firstly, the GMPs must be linked to business and companies' HR activities; secondly, they should address the cost and security problems; thirdly, they must be competitive and offer optimum support for expatriation; and fourthly, they should enable the transfer of the acquired competency and culture, linking this to the recruitment and management of talents, allowing the development of horizontal mobility.

The interviews show that the GMP has to be strongly connected to the business strategy and to strategic HRM vision of the company. For this, it is important to adapt the mobility policies to the population of talents. It follows that if one is to adapt the GMP as a "living document" it is integral to know the demographic of the employees. Follow-up indicators (such as age, sex, country of origin, business unit) can help to gage the population and adapt the mobility policies to its needs.

4.2 Strategic Planning of Assignments

Interviews confirm that international mobility professionals are not always informed of assignments in advance, having to work in a state of emergency. This emerged as being detrimental to both the company and employees. The need for the strategic planning of assignments was therefore acknowledged in all of the three multinationals. More specifically for talent assignments, the international mobility professionals would prefer to anticipate and prepare the recruitment with TM services rather than manage an emergency. The Talent Deployment team at Abbott Laboratories, for example, developed and structured a mobility program aligned with strategic goals.

For the strategic planning of one assignment, this anticipation has to be followed by frequent meetings between business and operational managers and HR professionals to prepare for the assignment. These regular meetings between international human resource (IHR) and talent managers can help identify the next IA for talents and prepare the way for recruitment.

4.3 Recruitment and Selection Process

The companies consulted mentioned the difficulty of finding appropriately qualified talents for some IAs. Various recruitment techniques are used, including job postings and virtual networks to recruit internationally mobile candidates, and the synthesis of previous recruitments or appraisals to identify potential candidates for international mobility. Two of the three companies developed a talent pool of internationally mobile talents: "recruitment for GM is part of TM". For them, the development of GM explicitly requires the recruitment of talents.

Interviews highlighted that recruiters and mobility managers can build upon the recruitment synthesis and/or annual appraisals, and develop databases of the internal and external candidates for a mobility assignment. With an instant view of the candidates' specificities, this mobility candidate database can enable rapid detection of potential candidates for an IA. When this database is constructed with talent managers it can also help to identify GTs for IAs. The recent emergence of internal "talent marketplaces", used in Procter & Gamble for example, proposes a system connecting open job postings, corporate performance management, and salary systems (Stahl et al. 2007).

Two of the three companies focus their selection of internal candidates on their drive and motivation, the ability of a partner and family to adapt, and the personal environment of the candidate. Some companies are beginning to develop language and/or personality tests dedicated to international mobility, which can help to identify the needed adaption support for talents. After the selection, the companies work on the definition of the C&B package for the international assignee.

4.4   Compensation and Benefit

For the three companies, IHR handle the security of the assignees. They also propose an attractive compensation, but are vigilant on the cost and the risk that their employees opt for international mobility simply for money. Regarding the cost of a talent's IA, there is great importance attached to tracking each part of the compensation with indicators. In this way, for example, the 'cafeteria' approach developed by Xerox enabled flexibility while managing the overall cost of the mobility program.

4.5   Preparation for the International Assignment

Before expatriation, each of the companies interviewed offer language and intercultural training where needed, inviting spouses to the intercultural training and mobility meetings. For talents, preparation for the IA includes full induction in management and communication, which might be prepared with recommendations from the TM team. Only one of the companies we consulted stated that there is no need for language and intercultural training. This goes against a general tendency followed by companies such as Novartis, which proposes a checklist to help the assignee verify that each preparation step is well managed (Waxin and Barmeyer 2008). Such tools help the assignees to take maximum advantage of the organizational support of the company.

4.6   Organization Support for Adaptation

We found that during assignments, the support and allowances offered depend on the company's culture. For example, one company accords particular importance to spousal support. It is important to evaluate the global outgoings of this support in order to optimize the services and costs. The remuneration services can create a compilation of these support expenses by type (i.e. housing, immigration, relocation etc.) to obtain a global perspective on the expenditure required for such support. This also permits the obtaining of an internal benchmark for those different costs and negotiation of future contracts with suppliers.

In the same way, it is important to obtain feedback from the expatriates on service providers for evaluation and to determine the quality of support. The host country HR services are present to support the international assignee during their integration; however, no specific system of tutorship is established in two of the three companies. Continuous coaching on culture, country, and business is only provided informally by managers or colleagues of the expatriates. In the case of specific talents, one of the companies proposes an identified internal tutor or an external coach, but globally this is rare.

During the interviews, it was noted that the expatriate may be forgotten and that his/her repatriation job may be found only opportunistically and might not be the most appropriate. Thus, for TM, it can be beneficial to propose a mentor as is done by L'Oreal or Accor.

4.7   Evaluation and Management of Performance

We found that expatriates conducted their annual appraisals with their local country or home-country manager, and they are tracked by a local HR manager in coordination with competency management services from headquarters. Two companies manage the careers of their employees abroad by way of informal contact between HR, the expatriates, and business managers abroad or at headquarters. A dedicated career manager and/or an IHR manager ensure/s their career progress. None of the case companies developed a specific system to evaluate the success of their IA. It was noted during the interviews, however, that these international assignees, specifically the talents, were closely followed by the IHR managers, mobility managers, or talent managers in this respect. They are there to detect the specific needs of the expatriate, to accompany them, and to prepare for repatriation.

4.8   Repatriation and Retention

During the interviews, two points of improvement on repatriation were identified as means to increase the retention of GTs. Firstly, it was noted that the service and financial support are less important on repatriation than at departure, and this is sometimes considered as a problem by repatriates. In some cases, participants mentioned that their companies propose a new position to most of their expatriates. The aim is to enable them to use their developed skill set in their new job. However this was not always the case, as it was mentioned that most repatriates find their jobs upon their return by chance. The collaboration between TM and IHR managers could therefore be enhanced to ensure better career support and follow-up for talents. For example, bi-annual meetings between TM, IHRM, and business managers to consider future repatriates and an overview written by headquarters and made available to the expatriates/future repatriates of the next available job can help to anticipate job opportunities and prepare for repatriation. A formal policy of repatriation, such as the one developed by PricewaterhouseCoopers, can allow the facilitation of repatriation, and there are a number of studies that show the positive impact of a career planning and development process to follow and accompany the GT throughout the entire assignment process (Scelba 1995).

Secondly, knowledge sharing after repatriation was identified as a key gap in IHRM practices. None of the interrogated companies have developed knowledge sharing systems to distribute newly acquired skills on transversal projects such as training or induction programs. One way to capitalize on the new abilities of expatriated talents would be to ask them to be mentors for new GTs. However, a difficulty with this, identified during the interviews, is that most of the international assignees struggle to share their new abilities. An IA competency assessment, with the support of a coach, may help the repatriate to identify his/her new competencies, share his/her experience, and develop himself/herself.

Discussion and Conclusions

Based on a literature review and illustrative cases, this article presents practical elements and proposes solutions for the GM of talents. Even though our discussion is rich, this remains a limited explorative study on the topic of GTM and expatriation and is rather oriented for practitioners. Furthermore, the persons interviewed were IHR managers in multinational French companies, therefore some of their experiences, positions, contexts, and difficulties may be set explicitly within a French context. For future research, more interviews are required in order to better elucidate this topic. It would also have been interesting to meet people other than IHR managers, such as talent managers, local HR managers, expatriated talents, business managers, or general managers, to develop a more comprehensive view of expatriation of GTs.

In Table 1, we note five challenges for GTM, five recommendations to overcome them and five future opportunities for the assignment management of GTs. One challenge identified in this article is that the expatriation process is not always connected to TM. Regular meetings and common tools, such as a shared internationally mobile GTs database, can provide a partial solution to this problem. In the future, the model in Fig. 1 can be utilized by companies to coordinate activities between IHR services and TM services. This model can also represent a support for further research.

Another challenge is that IHRM directors mentioned facing difficulties in their attempts to be fully efficient with their actual resources. Considering the

Table 1 Five key GTM challenges, strategies, and future opportunities

Five key points regarding global talent management challenges	Five key points regarding strategies to overcome these challenges	Five key points regarding future opportunities in global talent management
Connection between expatriation process and TM	Common tools for TM and IHR teams	Coordination between IHR and TM services following the proposed model of GT' IA
Efficiencies, difficulties for IHRM directors	Evolution of the coordination between TM team and other HR services	Creation of a GT mobility manager job
Dissatisfaction of expatriated talents with IA process and support	Formal feedback by the international assignees on the IAM and support	Evolution towards a continuous improvement of the management of IA
Dissatisfaction and difficulties with the repatriation	Evaluation of the repatriation process	Development of repatriation processes
No measure of efficiency of IAs	Clear definition of IA objectives and set-up of a ROI of GTs' IA	Measure of IAs' ROI

global reduction of support function positions in MNEs, this tendency would only proliferate in the future. An update of the mobility team, a different coordination with TM team, and other HR services would begin to address this problem. In the future, the creation of a GT mobility manager could provide dedicated support for talents before, during, and after their IA.

Another important challenge is the dissatisfaction of expatriated talents with the IA process and support. This dissatisfaction is still present and impacts the retention of GTs. Formal feedback by the expatriate talents on the IAM and organizational support can help identify the most important levers of improvements and ameliorate this process. For the future, the use and study of feedback can provide a continuous means of improvement to the management of IAs for talents.

Repatriation is clearly the least developed part of the expatriation process. The evaluation of the repatriation process has already been studied (Scelba 1995) but should nonetheless represent a future line of research given the importance and persistence of this challenge.

None of the companies in this study measure the efficiency of their IAs. The clear definition of IA objectives and the setup of a ROI of GTs' IA might support MNEs in improving their IAM and in measuring the efficiency of their TM. McNulty and De Cieri (2011) developed models for a ROI of IAs and studied their implementation in various companies (McNulty 2008). The study of the ROI for GTs' IAs could be an opportunity to measure the efficiency of this process.

References

Al Ariss, A. (2014). Voicing experiences and perceptions of local managers: Expatriation in the Arab Gulf. *The International Journal of Human Resource Management.* doi:10.1080/09585192.2013.870288.

Al Ariss, A., Cascio, W., Paauwe, J. (2013). Talent management: Current theories and future research directions. *Journal of World Business.* http://dx.doi.org/10.1016/j.jwb.2013.11.001

Al Ariss, A., & Crowley-Henry, M. (2013). Self-initiated expatriation and migration in the management literature: Present theorizations and future research directions. *Career Development International, 18*(1), 78–96.

Andreason, A. W. (2008). Expatriate adjustment of spouses and expatriate managers: An integrative research review. *International Journal of Management, 25,* 382–393.

Barmeyer, C., & Davoine, E. (2012). Comment gérer le retour d'expatriation et utiliser les compétences acquises par les expatriés? *Gestion, 37,* 43–53.

Baruch, Y. (2002). Management of expatriation and repatriation for a novice global player. *International Journal of Manpower, 23,* 659–671.

Bournois, F., Point, S., Rojot, J., & Scaringella, J. L. (2007). *RH : Les meilleures pratiques du CAC 40/SBF 120.* Paris: Editions d'Organisation.

Burns, S. M. (2003). Flexible assignee compensation plans. *Compensation and Benefit Review, 35,* 35–44.

Carraher, S. M., Sullivan, S. E., & Crocitto, M. M. (2008). Mentoring across global boundaries: An empirical examination of home- and host-country mentors on expatriate career outcomes. *Journal of International Business Studies, 39,* 1310–1326.

Cerdin, J. L. (1999). *La mobilité internationale: Réussir l'expatriation.* Paris: Editions d'Organisation.

Cerdin, J. L. (2001). *L'Expatriation.* Paris: Editions d'Organisation.

Cerdin, J. L., & Le Pargneux, M. (2009). Career and international assignment fit: Toward an integrative model of success. *Human Resource Management, 48*(1), 5–25.

Collings, D., Scullion, H., & Morley, M. (2007). Changing patterns of global staffing in the multinational enterprise: Challenges to the conventional expatriate assignment and emerging alternatives. *Journal of World Business, 42,* 198–213.

Dickmann, M., & Baruch, Y. (2010). *Global careers.* London: Routledge.

Dickmann, M., & Doherty, N. (2010). Exploring organizational and individual career goals, interactions and outcomes of developmental international assignments. *International Business Review, 52,* 313–324.

Dickmann, M., Doherty, N., Mills, T., & Brewster, C. (2008). Why do they go? Individual and corporate perspectives on the factors influencing the decision to accept international assignment. *The International Journal of Human Resources Management, 19,* 731–751.

Fish, A., & Wood, J. (1997). Managing spouse/partner preparation and adjustment: Developing a meaningful portable life. *Personnel Review, 26,* 445–466.

Franck, G., & Ramirez, R. (2003). *Meilleures pratiques des multinationales.* Paris: Editions d'Organisation.

Godiwalla, Y. H. (2012). Training and development of the international US executive. *Journal of Modern Accounting and Auditing, 8,* 32–39.

Graf, A., & Harland, L. K. (2005). Expatriate selection: Evaluating the discriminant, convergent, and predictive validity of five measures of interpersonal and intercultural competence. *Journal of Leadership and Organization Studies, 11,* 46–62.

Harvey, M., & Novicevic, M. (2001). Selecting expatriates for increasingly complex global assignments. *Career Development International, 6,* 69–86.

Harzing, A. W. (1995). The persistent myth of high expatriate failure rates. *Human Resource Management, 6,* 447–476.

Jassawalla, A., Connolly, T., & Slojkowski, L. (2004). Issues of effective repatriation: A model and managerial implications. *SAM Advanced Management Journal, 69,* 38–46.

Katz, J. P., & Seifer, D. M. (1996). It's a different world out there: Planning for expatriate success through selection, pre-departure training and on-site socialization. *Human Resource Planning, 19*, 32–47.

Kline Harrison, J. (1994). Developing successful expatriate managers: A framework for the structural design and strategic alignment of cross-cultural training programs. *Human Resource Planning, 17*, 17–35.

Kraimer, M. L., Wayne, S. J., & Jaworski, R. A. (2001). Sources of support and expatriate performance: The mediating role of expatriate adjustment. *Personnel Psychology, 54*, 71–99.

Lazarova, M., & Caligiuri, P. (2001). Retaining repatriates: The role of organizational support practices. *Journal of World Business, 36*, 389–401.

Martin, D. C., & Bartolk, K. M. (2003). Factors influencing expatriate performance appraisal system success: An organization perspective. *Journal of International Management, 9*, 115–132.

McNulty, Y. (2008). How a major multinational is working to overcome the barriers to improved expatriate ROI. *Global Business and Organizational Excellence, 27*, 38–47.

McNulty, Y., & De Cieri, C. (2011). Global mobility in the 21st century—Conceptualizing expatriate return on investment in global firms. *Management International Review, 51*, 897–919.

Merignac, O., & Roger, A. (2012). Comprendre les préoccupations du conjoint qui doit suivre un expatrié à l'étranger. *Gestion, 37*, 23–33.

Saint-Onge, S., Magnam, M., Prost, C., & Biouele, S. P. (2002). Gérer la rémunération dans un contexte de mobilité internationale: L'art de jongler avec les différentes perspectives. *Gestion, 27*, 41–55.

Sanchez Vidal, E., Sanz Valle, R., & Barba Aragon, I. (2008). International workers' satisfaction with the repatriation process. *The International Journal of Human Resources Management, 19*, 1683–1702.

Scelba, M. A. (1995). Developing an effective repatriation process at Chubb & Son Inc. *Employment Relations Today, 22*, 55–61.

Schuler, R. A., Jackson, S. E., & Tarique, I. (2011). Global talent management and global talent challenges: Strategic opportunities for IHRM. *Journal of World Business, 46*, 506–516.

Shawn, M., Sherry, E. S., & Crocitto, M. M. (2008). Mentoring across global boundaries: An empirical examination of home- and host-country mentors on expatriate career outcomes. *Journal of International Business Studies, 39*, 1310–1326.

Sidani, Y., Al Ariss, A. (2013). Institutional and corporate drivers of global talent management: Evidence from the Arab Gulf Region. *Journal of World Business.* http://dx.doi.org/10.1016/j.jwb.2013.11.005

Smida, N. (2006). Optimiser la gestion du retour des cadres expatriés français. *Gestion, 31*, 59–68.

Stahl, G. K., Björkman, I., Farndale, E., Morris, S. S., Paauwe, J., Stiles, P., Trevor, J., Wright, P. M. (2007). *Global talent management: how leading multinationals build and sustain their talent pipelines* (Faculty and Research Working Paper). INSEAD.

Stahl, G. K., Hwee Chua, C., Caligiuri, P., Cerdin, J. L., & Taniguchi, M. (2009). Predictors of turnover intentions in learning-driven and demand driven international assignments: The role of repatriation concerns satisfaction with company support and perceived career advancement opportunities. *Human Resources Management, 48*, 89–109.

Suutari, V., & Brewster, C. (2001). Expatriate management practices and perceived relevance: Evidence from Finnish expatriates. *Personnel Review, 30*, 554–577.

Tahvanainen, M. (2000). Expatriate performance management: The case of Nokia Telecommunications. *Human Resources Management, 39*, 267–275.

Tarique, I., & Schuler, R. (2010). Global talent management: Literature review, integrative framework, and suggestions for further research. *Journal of World Business, 45*, 122–133.

Tung, R. L. (1988). Career issues in international assignments. *Academy of Management Executive, 2*, 241–244.

Tung, R. L. (1989). Career issues in international assignments. *Academy of Management Executives, 2,* 241–244.

Tung, R. L. (1998). American expatriates abroad: From neophytes to cosmopolitans. *Journal of World Business, 33,* 125–144.

Van der Haijden, A. V., Van Engen, M. L., & Paauwe, J. (2009). Expatriate career support: Predicting expatriate turnover and performance. *The International Journal of Human Resources Management, 20,* 831–845.

Waxin, M. F., & Barmeyer, C. (2008). *Gestion des ressources humaines internationales.* Paris: Editions Liaisons.

World Economic Forum/Mercer. (2012). *Talent mobility good practices—Collaboration at the core of driving economic growth.* http://www.weforum.org/reports/talent-mobility-good-practices-collaboration-core-driving-economic-growth

Global Talent Management and the American Female Executive

Laura Sankovich

1   Introduction: What Is GTM Anyway?

Companies may use different definitions of Global Talent Management (GTM) as what works for one may not work for another. In general, GTM is an approach that builds integration of business units by selecting and promoting individuals who most closely model the guiding principles of the organization as a whole. GTM creates opportunity for balance in gender equity, power, and diversity throughout business units, creating a uniform culture even in the largest organizations. The purpose of a qualitative study I conducted in 2012 was to understand executive women's experiences of power and gender; two critical elements in GTM.

Much of the data cited throughout this chapter comes from women's real-life experiences in the expatriate and domestic workplace, and focused specifically on *how* they perceived and interpreted those experiences. Using narrative inquiry, this method allowed participants to share their first-hand accounts of experiences in U.S.-based headquarters and overseas locations.

Executive women in this study are defined as women who hold or have held Director or Vice President-level positions or above within transnational corporations (TNCs) in the Fortune 500, for at least 1 year within the past 3 years. Participants are American-born, range in age from their early 40s to mid-50s, had work experience at the Director or VP-level both in North America at US-based companies and abroad, 5–7 years experience in "line" or "staff" positions, and at least a Bachelor's degree at the time of the interviews.

This chapter explores challenges and opportunities in the following:

- Underrepresentation of women
- The importance of mentoring

L. Sankovich (✉)

The Human Resource, Capella University, Minneapolis, MN, USA

e-mail: laura@the-human-resource.com

A. Al Ariss (ed.), *Global Talent Management*, Management for Professionals,
DOI 10.1007/978-3-319-05125-3_18, © Springer International Publishing Switzerland 2014

- Gender diversity
- Gender challenges in decentralized organizations
- Gender culture inside and outside the organization

1.1 The Challenge of Underrepresentation of Women

Most publically traded companies are evaluated by their profitability and size, as evidenced by their rank in the Fortune 500. Women's presence in management is highly correlated to financial success and organizations need leadership teams that mirror the diverse populations they serve. Organizations with a higher representation of women at the executive level have a higher return on equity and higher total return to shareholders as compared to organizations with fewer women executives (Cormier 2007).

1.1.1 Overcoming the Underrepresentation of Women

Opportunities for GTM have expanded and having women on the executive team is a sound financial decision, as women's presence improves the bottom line of these organizations. Nevertheless, women remain underrepresented in the executive ranks of American global companies, and their representation is on the decline. Women's representation in executive ranks in American-based organizations accounts for only 13.5 % of corporate officers even though women make up 46.7 % of the workforce (Catalyst, Inc. 2010). These numbers are highly disproportionate; however, for individuals looking to advance in global businesses, "international experience is increasingly considered as a requisite for promotion to the top of the organizational hierarchy" (Caligiuri and Tung 1999, p. 764). A 1998 study reported 58 % of companies acknowledged that international assignments are important to career advancement (McClenahen 1997) and "internationally competent managers represent a key component of global business success" (McDonnell et al. 2010, p. 150), a key outcome in GTM. Despite the importance of gender balance, a dangerous phenomenon in employee selection known as *homophily* exists in both in domestic and GTM.

1.1.2 Opportunities in Overcoming the Underrepresentation of Women

Northouse (2004) described that "homophily refers to the tendency to prefer to work or interact with people who are similar demographically and attitudinally" (p. 277). A participant in my study shared that when she was hired, she was the only female in field sales in the organization. While she was hired because she was female (and told so by her manager), she persevered and excelled in her role from the start but it was clear she was hired to break the cycle of homophily.

In 1977, Kanter reported that corporate leaders implicitly favored promoting individuals from the same or similar socioeconomic, racial, and gender groups because doing so reduced anxiety. Male leaders may specifically select males to fill other leadership roles in the organization to bring familiarity to their teams, thereby minimizing anxiety. "The role of the expatriate involves even more uncertainties than that of the domestic manager and as uncertainty increases, the need for trust is perceived as having further implications for limiting women expatriate managers" (Linehan and Scullion 2004, p. 439). This conscious or unconscious behavior of homophily limits gender equity in corporate leadership as men have historically dominated the upper ranks of organizations.

Given that the executive ranks are typically male dominated, males may be receiving greater consideration over their female counterparts, regardless of qualifications for the job. For the incumbent male executive, it may seem easier to promote other males into executive positions based on the similarity of gender alone. GTM practitioners should consider the severity of homophily in their workplaces striving for an equitable work environment in all ranks of the organization.

1.2 The Mentoring Myth

Finding and retaining truly great employees can be challenging. When we consider the cost of recruiting, staffing, hiring, and developing employees, retention of the best in the organization becomes more critical. Mentor/mentee relations can help promote retention by creating greater intrinsic workplace value for both parties.

I found female executives reported the importance of a mentor as a significant factor in their success, both in their youth and as adults. One participant, Janice described building her own "board of directors" in support of her career path and decision making. She built a network of three mentors and a couple of others to give herself a "good 360 view." She described herself as a business: "I look at myself as Janice, Inc. and there's no reason I shouldn't manage my brand and myself that way and so I have a board of directors." She said that when she considers making a career change, she consults the individuals on her board of directors. These participants consistently spoke of the positive impact mentors had on their careers and personal development. As each of these women advanced in their careers, their experiences as mentees led them to mentoring roles themselves. Bringing others along and creating a more inclusive process in the organization helps employee retention and productivity.

Traditionally, mentoring programs have sought to match mentors and mentees of the same gender. Since men are the gender majority in executive roles throughout large organizations, there are few executive women to mentor other women in the organization. In addition, a commitment to matching male mentors with other males and female mentors with other females may promote homophily, a dynamic discussed earlier in the chapter.

1.2.1 Developing Great Mentorships for GTM

Matching genders in mentoring relationships may lead to unintended consequences by solidifying more male to male relationships in the workplace. Mentoring initiatives seem well intended but may hinder women from cultivating a strong network with their male counterparts in the workplace. Women already have less availability of same-sex networks than men (Ibarra 1993) so the opportunity to cultivate relationships with their male counterparts is important for building networks in the organization. Research shows the dominant demographic group (white males) typically selects mentees or new subordinates who already share their characteristics of color and gender. Nevertheless, the advancement of the women in my study suggests otherwise. The women in my study reported their success as mentees through relationships with solely male mentors throughout their career development (Sankovich 2012). If homophily was a pervasive phenomena in the organization, the male-dominated leadership would have chosen other men for the leadership roles in these companies. Instead, the male leadership in the organizations selected great mentees who happened to be women, rather than making selections based on sameness of gender. Male leaders in the TNCs from this study made a positive impact in supporting women's advancement in executive leadership roles.

1.2.2   Dispelling the Mentoring Myth

Given that the executive ranks of global organizations are typically male dominated, males may often receive greater consideration for mentee and promotion opportunities over their female counterparts, regardless of the qualifications. Mentoring relationships built at the individual level have a great impact on workplace equality and inclusion when both genders see beyond the natural preference of working with similar individuals. Rather than assuming the success of a mentor-mentee relationship is based on a female mentor working with a female mentee, HR practitioners, mentors, and mentees should work together to define the desired developmental outcomes these relationships. Defining outcomes for GTM also educates mentors and mentees through a richer experience through exposure to diverse backgrounds over what an individual may normally seek in a mentor or mentee on his or her own.

1.3   Promoting Gender Diversity

Many international HR texts on GTM discuss the ideal mix of host country nationals and corporate country nationals. Integrating local talent as a piece of global talent expansion is often a consideration as companies look at being inclusive of the local culture. Traditionally, HR texts focus on basic assessment practices for evaluating local talent, a discussion about hiring an appropriate mix of locals when possible, and how to create solid relationships between the expatriates who are typically in management roles. All of these factors can lead to an imbalance in gender. While return on investment and general effectiveness of expatriate assignments is currently debated, companies committed to expatriate assignments as an approach to their GTM should take a close look at the selection process.

The field of HR is typically touted as gender-blind. While this trait may be seen positively from an equality perspective, "gender-neutrality is itself a form of gendering, in the sense of obvious gender divisions not being talked about" (Hearn et al. 2012, p. 515). Women are typically considered in two categories: as expatriate candidates; as the trailing spouse or partner to a male expatriate. From a GTM staffing perspective, there can be "many ways of promoting and conceptualizing diversity management that are less or more challenging to existing power structures, including gender power" which may lead to "downplaying gender power and diverting attention away from gender" (Hearn et al. 2012). As practitioners try to identify the best balance at offshore locations, looking closely at the benefits brought to the role by the individuals under consideration, and building important skill sets for the future is an equally important consideration.

1.3.1 Opportunities for Gender Diversity

While international mobility is becoming increasingly problematic for both male and female employees due to "unwillingness to disrupt children's education," "the problems associated with dual-income and dual-career couples," and challenges in caring for elderly parents (Hearn et al. 2012, p. 515), specific and pointed dialogue is important in assessing an individual's willingness and ability to relocate overseas. Decision-makers should engage in dialogue with employees, regardless of gender, to explore with the employee whether the personal situation is a barrier to relocation.

Women's representation in executive ranks in American-based organizations accounts for only 13.5 % of corporate officers (Catalyst, Inc. 2010) and the number of women as expatriates is unreported but likely much lower. "This might be surprising given the characteristics identified for effective international managers, such as interpersonal, intuitive, and cooperative management styles, as often associated with women" (Hearn et al. 2012, p. 515). Key skills such as nurturance, Hofstede (1984) reported, are traditionally associated with women. Their leadership style consists of an open, consensus-building, collegial approach; a huge asset to working in the international arena. Still, diversity management may be perceived as a threat to existing power. Nevertheless, diversity initiatives give GTM an opportunity to thrive, choosing the best talent that builds and integrates a company's business units with those who best reflect the values of the organization and the customers it serves.

In November 2012, the European Commission, the executive body of the European Union, pushed for gender balance in both non-executive and executive board-member positions in publicly listed companies (Andreeva and Bertaud 2012). This initiative is a great example of proactive GTM, requiring companies to make appointments to those positions on the basis of a comparative analysis of the qualifications of each candidate, by applying clear, gender-neutral and unambiguous criteria.

1.3.2 Embracing Gender Diversity

On the whole, Western countries have embraced equality in the lower and middle ranks of their organizations through equality initiatives. A glass ceiling preventing gender equality in the senior ranks of organization still exists. While gender-neutrality is itself a form of gendering, the future looks more balanced between the genders, even in the upper ranks of organizations. That said, the discussion of gender equality, mentioned above, from the European Commission began in the late 1950s and did not take legislative form in the United States until 1964 with the Civil Rights Act. Both efforts required ongoing dialogue and supplementation over the decades, prompting this latest push for gender balance from the European Commission. Debate continues on whether governments should meddle in the affairs of business but GTM initiatives such as these do raise awareness, stressing the importance of gender balance and equality.

1.4   Gender Challenges in Decentralized Organizations

Advancing in the ranks of TNCs often depends on gaining global experience; how the female executive is able to be successful in each environment is important, particularly if the organization is committed to creating a more inclusive and diverse workforce. Companies that select leaders from a broader, more inclusive talent pool and value skills and results regardless of gender position themselves for better financial performance (Joy 2008). Fisher and Eiben (1992) declared, "The best reason for believing that more women will be in charge before long is that in a ferociously competitive global economy, no company can afford to waste valuable brainpower simply because it's wearing a skirt" (p. 56). A participant in my study shared this story:

> In Japan when I was there, [I was] the only woman in the room. At multiple times I was asked to take notes, get coffee, things like that...and you pick your hill, right? But sometimes I go, "You know what? I'm going to get the frikin' coffee because it's not worth it!" But I would demonstrate [my expertise] in the meeting as questions came up and as I'm facilitating the meeting and what's going on.

A key challenge of balanced GTM is having sufficient female representation, preventing situations like the one described above. Businesses do not have the luxury to continue to select only men in the most senior ranks. The organizational benefits that come from having a diverse workforce make a strong case for the need to not only increase the number of women in leadership positions, but to better understand how both internal and external culture influence the individual. The overall success of women in global executive roles coupled with the benefits of diverse leadership creates a strong case for the continuation of women's advancement in these roles. The well-documented success of women as expatriate managers in all geographies throughout the globe is an endorsement of women's effectiveness and a sign to employers to continue sending women abroad, even in male-dominated cultures (Adler 1987; Moran et al. 1988).

1.4.1   Opportunities to Balance Decentralized Organizations

The business benefits of diversity include better decision-making which results in stronger financial performance through diversity of thought, increases employee retention through respect and inclusion, more favorable opinions from the company's customer-base and business partners in representing the global world in which we live, and allows for a larger pool of great talent. Diversity efforts should not be focused solely on the recruitment and promotion of women, but rather part of an overall strategy to diversify an organization. Efforts should include diversity of age, race, gender, sexual orientation, and physical ability, particularly since research shows that race, class and gender are built into transnational organizations' construction, often leading to disadvantages for women (Berry and Bell 2012, p. 10). The occasional misunderstanding that this is a quota-driven agenda should be mitigated by developing a strategy to recruit and promote a diverse workforce, whereby all parties have access to promotion opportunities. GTM should invite thoughtful dialogue and engagement of each qualified individual, leaving assumptions behind.

A diverse GTM strategy cannot be successful without the support of senior management. In organizations where diversity and balance does not hold priority, HR practitioners must facilitate discussions with senior management about both the intrinsic and extrinsic benefits diversity brings to the organization. In addition, leaders must look to skills in addition to the traditional pedigree of business acumen. Intercultural leaders require a more robust set of skills to navigate different cultural, national, religious and ethnic background to meet global business demands. In a 2005 interview, Jack Welch said "We have to send our best and brightest overseas and make sure that they have the training that will allow them to be the intercultural leaders who will make GE flourish in the future." The complexity of the global business environment demands individuals in the GTM pipeline with the cultural intelligence, awareness, and understanding to interact with the diversity of the global environment.

1.4.2 Hierarchy and Equality in Decentralized Organizations

As TNCs develop and expand their global presence, they create a network of partners throughout the globe. These partnerships force organizations to be more dynamic and flexible in executing their business goals increasing the importance of GTM. Adler and Bartholomew suggested that TNCs are less hierarchically structured than firms operating solely in domestic markets (Adler and Bartholomew 1992, p. 56) or even those operating as a multidomestic organization.

As organizational complexities increase, organizations direct greater emphasis on the dependence of subsidiaries on HQ and interdependence among peer subunits and between subunits HQ. The physical distance between business units in TNCs forces them to decentralize, which results in a system of business networks and operations that flattens the organization as a whole. This flattening is beneficial because hierarchy lessens as the organization flattens and becomes more nimble. TNCs are embedded in ongoing networks of diverse relationships that are economic, social, cultural, and political. The TNC becomes a constellation of diverse relationships that provides the central dynamic to the TNC activities (Yeung 1998, p. 5) and a more decentralized set of subunits.

Even in a decentralized organization with diverse relationships, it is possible that there are strong hierarchies within the subunits, but those subunits are most likely flatter than the organization as a whole. Further, these flatter organizations may instill greater power to the individual by granting more authority at lower levels, more control over organizational goals and strategies, and a greater sense of mastery in a given profession.

Kanter (1977), whose research occurred prior to the evolution of today's TNCs, interviewed executives who felt that flattening managerial hierarchies is a good idea. One of the more obvious outcomes of Kanter's research demonstrated how the on organizational structure impacted the individual. "In a flat organization, people underneath become better managers. They are more autonomous, and they feel more powerful" (p. 276). Kanter discovered that decentralization can empower as well as enhance opportunity, provided that the result is more autonomous work units. This perception of power, enhanced opportunity, and accessible authority may have a connection to women's advancement into leadership positions. Helgesen (1990) suggested:

> Women . . . are countering the values of the hierarchy with those of the web . . . when describing their roles in their organizations, women usually refer . . . to themselves as being in the middle of things. Not at the top, but in the center; not reaching down, but reaching out . . . inseparable from their sense of themselves as being in the middle was the women's notion of being connected to those around them. (pp. 45–46)

A participant from my study echoed this assertion. "Depending on what country you're working in abroad is probably going to be more relationship-based, certainly not saying that results aren't important but it may vary." Supporting this more contemporary perspective, Schein (2004) also acknowledged that decentralized organizations push authority down as low as possible because they believe that the strength of their organization is in their people (p. 264). The benefits of decentralization coupled with a mindful GTM approach toward gender can balance the organization from top to bottom.

1.5   Country and Organization: Gender Culture's Impact on Advancement

The success of women as expatriate managers in all geographies throughout the globe is an endorsement of women's effectiveness and a sign to employers to continue sending women abroad, even in male-dominated cultures (Adler 1987; Moran et al. 1988). Further, Adler found that 97 % of the female expatriates in her study self-reported that their assignment had been successful. Additional indicators (e.g., being offered another global assignment after completion of the current one) suggested that these women were successful (Caligiuri and Tung 1999, p. 765).

The relationship between organizational culture and country culture may hold the key to understanding the collective impact on the female executive. Given the small population of female executives in U.S.-based TNCs, it is important to understand what dynamics work well in engaging female employees. Advancing in the ranks of TNCs often depends on gaining global experience; how the female executive is able to be successful in each environment is important, particularly if the organization is committed to creating a more inclusive and diverse workforce. Although companies may have a fairly uniform culture in their U.S.-based locations, a single culture is often lacking in the TNC due to its size and geographical networks (Schein 2004). According to the Javidan and House (2001), "Beliefs are people's perceptions of how things are done in their countries. They are the reported *practices* in a particular culture" (p. 293). These intangibles contribute to a perceived standard definition for culture in countries and organizations alike.

The GLOBE Study's cultural dimension of gender egalitarianism measures "the degree to which a collective minimizes (and should minimize) gender inequality" (Javidan et al. 2006, p. 70). Countries that minimize gender inequality may promote a more equitable environment, not only to those native to the country but even to the expatriate working in that country. U.S. executive women may more easily adjust to their work environment where gender egalitarianism (or gender equity) is high.

In my research, I used the Javidan and House (2001) and Hofstede's (1984) research on power distance to gauge the degree of inequity of women's experiences in the U.S. corporate location and abroad. The dimension developed by the GLOBE Study focuses on the society, whereas Hofstede's index helps us drill down to the individual level. Hofstede defined that "power distance is the degree of inequality in power between a less powerful individual and a more powerful other" (p. 71). Executive women may thrive because of less rigidity and demand for conformance to organizational rules and instead, greater acceptance of the individual, resulting in a strong organizational fit (Sankovich 2012). Like any good business leader, some decisions come with great risk. One of my participants shared she had full authority to make decisions in her region, but felt she needed to take her team to Japan to ensure that their counterparts had everything they needed to deliver product into their local marketplace. Taking this trip was a huge risk as it took much of her operating budget to execute. If the trip did not achieve the business objectives or she needed additional resources for the remainder of the year, she would be stuck with only the residual monies. The trip was successful so the risk was worth the reward. Another participant shared how her risks helped build her reputation and fit in the organization:

> And so I learned how to take my international experience, my tolerance for "it's okay to be different," to take risks, so not opting out and then how to function on a team that's very different. How do I take all of those elements, use that to our advantage so that I can capitalize on a strategy...and I did it. And that became my niche.

The findings from my study include:

1. When executive women were successful, they reported feeling that they fit into the organization because of feedback from their leaders, peers, and even subordinates.

2. Themes about values and beliefs indicated that fit came from management's willingness to trust participants to do their jobs independently. As a result of this trust, these women made decisions based on their own expertise, helping them develop into and secure their positions as leaders in the organization.

3. Executive women created fit through a conscious process of building relationships throughout the organization.

1.5.1 Host Country Culture's Impact

While Hofstede (1984) suggested that country culture would influence the work environment within the TNC, country culture generally does not have a significant influence on executive women's abilities to be successful in the workplace. I found that in day-to-day operations, participants felt that off-site locations are organically more diverse, reflecting the diversity of their country. These locations have a more accepting culture around gender, ethnic diversity, and diversity of ideas. GTM practices are organically part of the host country environment in many offsite locations for transnational corporations.

1.5.2 Gender Egalitarianism and Power Distance

Not surprisingly, findings from my study suggested the executive women studied thrived in work environments with greater gender equity and balanced power distance. Power distance demonstrates the level of inequality between the power holders and the less powerful within a society or organization. The degree to which individuals submit to authority in these environments can be evaluated by this dimension. The ease with which an executive woman leads and feels empowered to be a decision-maker in her job may be directly related to the level of power concentrated in the roles above her and the gender equity around her.

1.5.3 Benefits of a Balanced GTM Approach

In an environment where GTM excels in balancing equity and power, women who are either host nationals or expatriates enjoy equality with their male counterparts in society and in the workplace. While participants from my study shared that they were successful both at the corporate headquarters and overseas, they felt a higher acceptance of their ideas overseas, easier execution of their jobs, and a lessened hierarchy between themselves and their supervisors. Participants attributed the benefits of working overseas directly to a more diverse setting where individual differences had greater acceptance. These benefits reflect solid GTM practice that embraces individual differences while promoting a uniform culture for the organization (Table 1).

2   Summary

This chapter demonstrates that advancing in the ranks of TNCs often depends on gaining global experience. How the female executive is able to be successful in each environment is important, particularly if the organization is committed to creating a more inclusive and diverse workforce. Companies that select leaders from a broader, more inclusive talent pool and value skills and results regardless of gender, position themselves for better financial performance (Joy 2008). Companies must expand their pool to choose the best talent available, regardless

Table 1 Five key GTM challenges, strategies, and future opportunities

Five key points regarding Global Talent Management challenges	Five key points regarding strategies to overcome these challenges	Five key points regarding future opportunities in Global Talent Management
1 Organizations desire greater diversity in the executive-level of their organizations	Women must have the same opportunities for international experience	Practitioners should consider the organizational dynamics that promote and hinder women's advancement
2 Retaining top talent can be challenging for all organizations, especially on the global stage	Stronger retention and promotion of existing talent is helped by mentorship throughout the organization	A solid mentor of either gender is more important than matching the gender of the mentee
3 Assumptions are often made about women's ability to adjust to different work cultures, due to masculine or feminine work values	Inclusivity of both genders offers better decision-making throughout the organization and even better financial performance, regardless of work values	The corporation can support gender diversity through equality of GTM practices
4 Many international HR texts on global talent management discuss the ideal mix of host country nationals and corporate country nationals	Understanding both organizational gender issues and the country culture can lead to other ways of thinking about the prescribed diversity mix in a host country	As our world continues to shrink, the ideal mix of host country nationals and corporate country nationals must come from GTM thinking without a one-size-fits all approach
5 Understanding gender culture within transnational corporations and the countries in which they operate may be critical to understanding the influences impacting women's advancement	Deep understanding of an individual's connection to the organization may help identify barriers to women's advancement in the unique global environment	Understanding and dissolving barriers to advancement at the top of the organization may help expand global opportunities for employees in all ranks of the organization

of gender and rank in the organization. A key challenge of GTM is having sufficient female representation. The organizational benefits that come from having a diverse workforce make a strong case for the need to not only increase the number of women in leadership positions, but to better understand how both internal and external culture influence the individual.

References

Adler, N. J. (1987). Pacific basin managers: A gaijin, not a woman. *Human Resource Management, 26*(2), 169–191.

Adler, N. J., & Bartholomew, S. (1992). Managing globally competent people. *Academy of Management Executive, 6*(3), 52–65.

Andreeva, M., & Bertaud, N. (2012, November 14). *Women on boards: Commission proposes 40% objective*. Retrieved from http://europa.eu/rapid/press-release_IP-12-1205_en.htm

Berry, B. P., & Bell, M. P. (2012). 'Expatriates': Gender, race and class distinctions in international management. *Gender, Work and Organization, 19*(1), 10–28.

Caligiuri, P. M., & Tung, R. L. (1999). Comparing the success of male and female expatriates from a U.S.-based multinational company. *International Journal of Human Resource Management, 10*(5), 763–782.

Catalyst, Inc. (2010). *Women are not half of the U.S. labor force and other data clarifications.* Retrieved February 6, 2010, from http://www.scribd.com/doc/26314402/Women-Are-Not-Half-the-U.S.-Labor-Force-2-3-10

Cormier, D. (2007). Retaining top women business leaders: Strategies for ending the exodus. *Business Strategy Series, 8*(4), 262–269.

Fisher, A. B., & Eiben, T. (1992). When will women get to the top? *Fortune, 126*(6), 44–56.

Hearn, J., Metcalfe, B., & Piekkari, R. (2012). Gender, intersectionality and international human resource management. In G. Ståhl, I. Björkman, & S. Morris (Eds.), *Handbook of research in international human resource management.* Cheltenham: Edward Elgar.

Helgesen, S. (1990). *The female advantage: Women's ways of leadership.* New York: Doubleday Currency.

Hofstede, G. (1984). *Culture's consequences: International differences in work-related values.* Beverly Hills: Sage.

Ibarra, H. (1993). Personal networks of women and minorities in management: A conceptual framework. *Academy of Management Review, 18*(1), 56–87.

Javidan, M., Dorfman, P. W., De Luque, M. S., & House, R. J. (2006). In the eye of the beholder: Cross cultural lessons in leadership from project GLOBE. *Academy of Management Perspectives, 20*(1), 67–90.

Javidan, M., & House, R. J. (2001). Cultural acumen for the global manager: Lessons from project GLOBE. *Organizational Dynamics, 29*(4), 289–305.

Joy, L. (2008). *Advancing women leaders: The connection between women board directors and women corporate officers.* Retrieved from Catalyst Publication database.

Kanter, R. M. (1977). *Men and women of the corporation.* New York: Basic Books.

Linehan, M., & Scullion, H. (2004). Towards an understanding of the female expatriate experience in Europe. *Human Resource Management Review, 14*(4), 433–448.

McClenahen, J. (1997). To go-or not to go? *Industry Week, 246*(2), 33.

McDonnell, A., Lamare, R., Gunnigle, P., & Lavelle, J. (2010). Developing tomorrow's leaders: Evidence of global talent management in multinational enterprises. *Journal of World Business, 45*, 150–160.

Moran, Stahl, & Boyer, Inc. (1988). *Status of American female expatriate employees: Survey results.* Boulder, CO: International Division.

Northouse, P. (2004). *Leadership theory and practice* (3rd ed.). Thousand Oaks, CA: Sage.

Sankovich, L. (2012). Executive women in transnational corporations: Case studies of power in the United States and abroad (Doctoral dissertation). *Retrieved from ProQuest Dissertations and Theses.* (UMI No. 3510686).

Schein, E. H. (2004). *Organizational culture and leadership* (3rd ed.). San Francisco: Jossey-Bass.

Yeung, H. W. (1998). *Transnational corporations and business networks: Hong Kong firms in the ASEAN region.* New York: Routledge.

Author Biographies

Professor Akram Al Ariss, PhD is Professor of Human Resource Management (HRM) at Toulouse Business School (France). He works on international HRM and his research is focused on the topic of international mobility. He has a Habilitation à Diriger des Recherches from Université Paris-Dauphine, the highest academic qualification an academic can achieve in France. He serves as Associate Editor for *Career Development International* and is a member of the editorial boards of *Journal of World Business*, *British Journal of Management*, *Thunderbird International Business Review*, and *Personnel Review*, among others. He has published on IHRM in journals such as *Journal of World Business*, *Thunderbird International Business Review*, *British Journal of Management*, and *International Journal of Human Resource Management*. He has edited or coauthored books including *Human Resource Management* (with Dessler, Pearson, Arab World Edition) and *Self-Initiated Expatriation* (Routledge). He has worked internationally in universities like the London School of Economics and Penn State University. With Lebanese and French citizenship and cultural background, he has experience in management consultancy in organizations across Europe and the Arab Middle East. Akram can be contacted at info@akramalariss.com

Dr. Khalid Al Yahya has nearly 20 years of global experience in development of public management and policy; transformational governance and innovation; employment and human capital strategy; and strategic thinking and leadership development with special focus on the GCC and Middle East context. His previous work experience includes being the managing director of Accenture Management Consulting, Middle East; professor and director of the Governance and Public Management Program at the Dubai School of Government; fellow at Harvard University Kennedy School (2008–2012); professor of Policy and Management at Arizona State University (USA) and the University of Denmark; and official at the Saudi Ministry of Finance and UN. He also served as a senior advisor to several international organizations and firms, government agencies, and local businesses in the GCC region.

Prof. Silvia Bagdadli, Ph.D. in Management, is Associate Professor of Organization and Human Resource Management at Bocconi University (Milan, Italy) and Senior Professor of HRM at SDA Bocconi, the Business School of Bocconi University. Since 2008, she has been the director of EMSHRM (Executive Master

A. Al Ariss (ed.), *Global Talent Management*, Management for Professionals,
DOI 10.1007/978-3-319-05125-3, © Springer International Publishing Switzerland 2014

in Strategic Human Resource Management), an international program for HR executives. She is a member of the AOM (HR and Career Division), Egos network (Career SWG—Co-Convenor in 2006) and Euram (Co-Convenor in 2013). Her research and teaching are in the areas of HRM and career and talent management (TM) where she is interested in the intersection of the individual and the organizational perspective.

Prof. Mhamed Biygautane is a researcher in the Public Management program at the Dubai School of Government, specializing in governance, public management and administration, and sustainable economic growth for the UAE and wider MENA region. He also serves as a Middle East and North Africa expert in the European Geopolitical Forum where he provides strategic advice on the economic development of the MENA region. Mhamed has also been featured in international and regional media such as BBC, the *New York Times* and other prestigious outlets, for his expert opinion. He has published more than 70 studies on political economy of development, knowledge management in the public sector, modernization and reforming of the public sector and improving its performance, governance challenges in the Arab world and contributed as well to case studies that the DSG has copublished with the World Bank. He has also worked on consultancy projects with the OECD, UNDP, World Bank, Saudi Ministry of Labor, and the UAE's Prime Minister's office.

Dr. Joost Bücker (1955) is Senior Lecturer of Strategic Human Resource Management in the Department of Business Administration at the Nijmegen School of Management, Radboud University Nijmegen (Netherlands). He studied sociology (M.A.) at the University of Tilburg (Netherlands). He is an expert in training and consultancy on global leadership and cross-cultural management. His research interests are in the area of cross-cultural management and international HRM, more specifically in the topic of "global leadership competencies". He finished his Ph.D. in March 2013 on the topic of "cultural intelligence measurement and development". Joost Bücker can be contacted at J.Bucker@fm.ru.nl

Prof. Jean-Luc Cerdin is Professor of Human Resource Management at ESSEC Business School in France. He gained a doctorate from Toulouse University and a M.Sc. from the London School of Economics (UK). He worked as a practitioner in HRM before becoming an academic. He has served as a visiting professor at Rutgers University (US) and University of Missouri St-Louis (US) and a visiting scholar at Wharton (US). He researches, publishes, and consults in three primary areas: IHRM, expatriation management, and career management. He has contributed numerous articles to academic and professional journals. He has also published books on expatriation and career management.

Dr. Richard D. Cotton is an assistant professor at the Walker College of Business at Appalachian State University in Boone, North Carolina, USA. His research interests include developmental networks and mentoring, extraordinary career achievement, IHRM, career development, TM, cross-cultural management, and relational dynamics. Prior to completing his Ph.D. in Organization Studies at

Boston College, he worked in industry for nearly 15 years as a consultant and manager with Accenture, Senior Vice President of HR at Putnam Investments, and as an independent consultant. He has published several peer-reviewed articles and can be contacted at: cottonrd@appstate.edu

Dr. Nicky Dries (1982) is a research professor at the KU Leuven, Faculty of Business and Economics (Belgium). She conducted her doctoral research on TM and (subjective) career success at the Vrije Universiteit, Brussels, during which time she was also a visiting scholar at the Vrije Universiteit, Amsterdam. Since then, she has been a visiting scholar at the University of Tilburg (Netherlands), at Wirtschaftsuniversität Vienna (Austria), at Reykjavik University (Iceland) and a Fulbright scholar at Boston University (US). Nicky is on the editorial board of the *Journal of Vocational Behavior* (JVB) and the *European Journal of Work and Organizational Psychology* (EJWOP). Currently, she is the supervisor of four Ph.D. projects on TM, as well as a co-supervisor of the Policy Research Centre on Work and Social Economy. In addition, she is actively involved in two large-scale cross-cultural projects on contemporary careers, i.e. 5C (Consortium for the Cross-Cultural Study of Contemporary Careers) and the Career Adaptability/Life Design project.

Dr. Tony Fang is Director of the Master of International Business Program and at Monash University in Melbourne, Australia and an associate professor at the University of Toronto in Canada. He is also a visiting scholar at Harvard University and NBER and holds the J. Robert Beyster Faculty Fellowship at Rutgers University (US). He was a visiting professor at the Wharton School of the University of Pennsylvania, University of Toronto, and City University of Hong Kong. He served as President of the Chinese Economists Society (2012–2013). Professor Fang published widely in HRM, industrial relations, and labor economics.

Dr. Rita Fontinha, Ph.D., is a research fellow in the Organisation Studies and Human Resource Management group at the Portsmouth Business School, University of Portsmouth, UK. She started her career in HR in 2006, having moved to academia in 2008. She has a Joint Ph.D. from KU Leuven (Belgium) and the University of Lisbon (Portugal). She has published in journals such as *Personnel Review*, *Journal of Work and Organizational Psychology* and *Journal of Career Development*. She can be contacted at University of Portsmouth, Richmond Building, Portland Street, Portsmouth, Hampshire, PO1 3DE, United Kingdom. E-mail: rita.fontinha@port.ac.uk

Prof. Masayuki Furusawa, Ph.D., is Professor of International Human Resource Management at Osaka University of Commerce in Japan and a former visiting research fellow at Henley Business School of the University of Reading in the UK. He is a member of the board of directors at the Academy of Multinational Enterprises in Japan. He has conducted extensive research in the field of IHRM and engaged in numerous training and consultancy projects for HR specialists from all over the world. He has published more than 40 books and articles and was awarded three academic prizes for his publications on IHRM.

Prof. Michael L. Nieto Cert Ed; B.Ed. (Hons.); M.A. (HRM); Adv Dip Consultancy (Henley), F.C.M.I., Academic F.C.I.P.D., F.H.E.A.

Michael is Head of the Department of Management and Human Resources and Principal Lecturer with Regent's University London. He has also held senior academic posts as MBA Director, Dean, and International Officer with other leading British higher education providers and presented visiting professor lecture series to Marymount University USA, the ACI Paris, and Valencia University (Spain). Michael is currently the external examiner for postgraduate programs with Kingston University and also Buckingham University, overseeing post-graduate programs at the European School of Economics.

Dr. Vijay Pereira, Ph.D., is Senior Lecturer (Associate Professor) of International and Strategic Human Resource Management and Leader in Knowledge Services (Human Capital Development) in the Organisation Studies and HRM group at the Portsmouth Business School, University of Portsmouth, UK. He holds six academic qualifications and has published in journals such as the *Journal of World Business, International Studies of Management & Organization, Culture & Organisation, International Journal of Indian Culture & Business Administration*, etc. He has also contributed to several book chapters. His previous experiences have been in consulting and industry. He can be contacted at the Centre for Organisation Research and Development (CORD), Dept. of Organisation Studies and Human Resource Management, University of Portsmouth, Richmond Building, Portland Street, Portsmouth, Hants, UK- PO1 3DE. Telephone: (+44) (0)23 92 844815. E-mail: vijay.pereira@port.ac.uk

Dr. Opas Piansoongnern is a lecturer at the Faculty of Business Administration, Nation University, Bangkok, Thailand. He is also Visiting Assistant Professor at Carlos III University of Madrid, Spain and the University of Applied Sciences, Ravensburg-Weingarten, Germany. He holds a Ph.D. in Management Science from Shinawatra University (Thailand) where he was granted the Royal Golden Jubilee Ph.D. Scholarship of the Royal Thai Government. Opas Piansoongnern is interested in interdisciplinary approaches to teaching and researching HRM especially TM in the ASEAN business context. He always welcomes teaching and research opportunities from researchers and business practitioners all over the world. He can be contacted at opasplk@gmail.com.

Dr. Sylwia Przytula holds a Ph.D. in Management. She works in the HRM department at Wroclaw University of Economics in Poland. Her scientific interests are expatriates, cultural differences in global business, and psychology of manage-ment. She is a member of SIETAR Poland (Society for Intercultural Education, Training, and Research). She also participated in many foreign studying visits for academic staff: (among others) RSM Erasmus University (The Netherlands), Aalborg University (Denmark), University of Cagliari (Sardegna), DCU Dublin (Ireland), and ESCIP School of International Business (France).

Dr. Camilla Quental is Assistant Professor in Management and Human Resources at Audencia Nantes School of Management, France. Her research focuses on gender and diversity in organizations, women's careers, and professional identity. She received a master's degree from Sciences Po Paris and a Ph.D. in Management from HEC Paris, having completed her Ph.D. thesis on the topic of women's careers in professional services firms and the "glass ceiling" phenomenon in these firms. She published her research in academic journals such as *Revue de Gestion des Ressources Humaines* and *Revue Internationale de Gestion*. She was a visiting scholar at Darden School of Business, USA.

Dr. Jenny K. Rodriguez is Lecturer in Human Resource Management at Newcastle University Business School, UK. Her research interests traverse gender and organization and IHRM. Her current work looks at intersectional inequality in work and organizations, more recently exploring the relationship between intersectionality, transnationalism, and globalization. She is also working on projects exploring the interplay between identity, work, and regulation in the context of transnational migration, focusing on different analytical levels of regulation of work and employment (i.e., macro-country, meso-organizational and micro-individual) and how these interplay with transnational identities and experiences of skilled migrants.

Mrs. Raija Salomaa, Doctoral Candidate at the University of Vaasa, Department of Management, is completing her Ph.D. on "Coaching of international managers: individual and organizational perspectives". Raija did her M.A. degree at the University of Turku (Finland), School of Languages and Translation, and has completed Change Management studies at the Technical University of Helsinki. She holds an Evidence-Based-Coaching Certificate from the Fielding Graduate University, USA and is a professional certified coach by International Coach Federation. Prior to her career as an executive coach Raija held several executive positions in Sales & Marketing in the travel trade and the international hotel industry.

Dr. Laura Sankovich is Professor of Human Resources Management at Capella University. Her research interests include gender equity in the workplace, social justice, and employment compliance. Laura is also the owner of The Human Resource, founded in 2004. The Human Resource focuses on HR compliance and preventing employment issues for small and medium-sized businesses. Laura is from Chicago and enjoys international travel with her family, with a home base in Coeur d'Alene, Idaho.

Dr. Bradley Saunders, B.A.(Hons.), P.G.C.E., M.Sc., M.A., Ph.D., M.C.M.I., A.A. C.I.P.D.
Bradley oversees online programs in Business and Management at the University of Derby. After some 20 years teaching English in South East Asia and the Arabian Gulf, Bradley took an M.A. in Human Resource Management by distance learning, before taking up a Loughborough University scholarship to conduct doctoral research into the motivations and aspirations of highly educated migrant workers in the UK employed in low status jobs. Bradley has taught at Regent's University London and the University of Northampton. His research interests are in IHRM and e-learning.

Dr. Tracy Scurry is a lecturer at Newcastle University Business School. Her main research interests are in the area of careers from the perspectives of the individual and the organization Her research focuses on careers from the perspectives of the individual and the organization. There are three main strands to her research (1) graduate careers, (2) global careers, and (3) extended working lives. She has also worked on numerous projects exploring organizational change in the workplace. She has successfully secured funding from the British Academy and is a coinvestigator on an ESRC-funded seminar series which explores the "Regulation of Work and Employment". She recently coauthored a report for the Department for Business Innovation and Skills exploring the relationship between SMEs and graduates. Her work has been published in the *International Journal of Human Resource Management, Personnel Review and Career Development International.* She is Book Reviews Editor for *Personnel Review.*

Mr. Kushal Sharma is a Ph.D. candidate at ESSEC Business School, France. His area of focus is HRM. Before starting his Ph.D. studies, he worked as an HR manager for several organizations in Kathmandu, Nepal. His research interest is in TM, employee retention, IHRM, and cross-cultural HRM. He focuses on TM practices of multinational organizations and seeks to understand how TM strategies are implemented in large-scale organizations.

Dr. Rosana Silveira Reis is Associate Professor at ISG—International Business School in Paris (France) and a regular visiting professor at Fundação Dom Cabral, Belo Horizonte (Brazil). She has 28 years of experience in HR, 15 of them as a manager in large organizations. Since 2000 she has been teaching HRM and Cross-Cultural Management in graduate and M.B.A. courses. She received her scientific master in Business Administration from the Federal University of Santa Catarina (Brazil) and her Ph.D. in Management from the University of Bologna (Italy). Her research interest focuses on Creativity and Innovation, Human Resource Management, Culture, and Globally Distributed Teams.

Mr. Vincent Sponton, after developing his skills in sales, management, and training within Procter & Gamble, evolved towards HR as Human Resources Officer for Pierre Fabre Dermo-Cosmetic. For his professional thesis for Toulouse Business School, Vincent worked on Global Mobility Management. He proposed various solutions and developed specific operational tools to improve global mobility.

Prof. Vesa Suutari is Professor at the Department of Management and Dean of the Faculty of Business Studies, at the University of Vaasa, Finland. He has published various international journal articles (e.g. in *Human Resource Management, International Business Review, International Journal of HRM* and *Journal of World Business*) and book chapters on issues such as cross-cultural leadership, expatriation, self-initiated expatriation, global leadership, and global careers. His expertise and experience covers a number of different positions including Board Member of the European Academy of Management, Vice Chairman of the Association of Business Schools Finland, Board Member of Finnish Association for HR Professionals, and member of editorial boards in several journals.

Prof. Christelle Tornikoski is an academic professor in HRM at Grenoble École de Management (christelle.tornikoski@grenoble-em.com). She investigates what motivates expatriates and highly educated international employees most; how organizations can attract, motivate and retain them in the long run. She is especially interested in the study of the social exchange of intangible rewards or returns between organizations and their international assignees, as well as the use of total rewards. She has authored and coauthored articles published in international academic journals such as *The International Journal of Human Resource Management* (IJHRM) and *Cross-Cultural Management Journal* (CCM) and book chapters.

Dr. Vlad Vaiman is Associate Dean and Professor of International Management at the School of Management of California Lutheran University and is a visiting professor at several premier universities around the world. Dr. Vaiman has published three very successful books on managing talent in organizations as well as a number of academic and practitioner-oriented articles in the fields of TM and IHRM. His work has appeared in top academic journals including *Academy of Management Learning & Education, Human Resource Management, International Journal of Human Resource Management*, and others. He is a cofounder and Editor-in-Chief of the *European Journal of International Management* (EJIM), an ISI-indexed publication.

Prof. Charles M. Vance is a professor of Management and Human Resources at Loyola Marymount University in Los Angeles, where he has taught at executive, MBA, and undergraduate levels. He has had considerable experience as a consultant in training and curriculum development and broader TM applications for many corporations and nonprofit organizations in North and South America, Asia, and Europe. He has held U.S. Fulbright teaching and research appointments in Austria and China and has guest lectured at several schools. He is the author of three books and numerous scholarly publications and is on the editorial board of several journals.

Dr. Olivier Wurtz (olivier.wurtz@uwasa.fi) is an assistant professor at the Department of Management of the University of Vaasa (Finland). Olivier earned his Ph.D. in International Human Resource Management at HEC Paris in 2012. His research interests include global work experiences, work–life balance, coping, and cross-cultural management. He previously worked as a marketing manager for Procter & Gamble and L'Oreal. He does research with French multinational corporations.

Ms. Manoela Ziebell de Oliveira completed her undergraduate (2007) and her Masters (2010) in Psychology at the Universidade Federal do Rio Grande do Sul. She is currently a doctoral student at the same university. Currently, Manoela works as a career consultant and researcher. Her main research topics are career development, career transitions, voluntary turnover, high performers, contemporary careers, and career guidance.

Index

A
Arab, 197, 198, 201–209, 211, 279

B
Brazil, 8, 19, 25, 67, 113, 123–138, 184,
   217, 280
BRIC/ BRICS, 67, 123, 126, 184, 217

C
Career capital development
   brain circulation, 149–150
   brain drain, 109, 149–150, 187, 193, 194,
      201–203, 212
   brain gain, 109, 147–150
   brain waste, 67, 68, 87, 89
China, 8, 12, 55, 67, 68, 123, 126, 141–156,
   171, 184, 188, 217, 281
Context
   cultural context, 25, 98
   regionalcountry business characteristics,
      186
   socio-cultural changes, 232
   socio-economic factors, 115

E
Emerging economies, 12, 67, 108, 187, 194,
   217, 232
Expatriation
   international assignment, 10, 11, 45, 71,
      161, 229, 230, 237, 242, 243, 246,
      251–253, 255, 257, 259
   international assignment management, 48,
      79, 162, 252, 281
   repatriate retention, 30

repatriation, 228, 243, 245, 247, 252, 253,
   256, 257, 260–262
retention strategies, 75
self-Initiated expatriation, 252, 279, 280
strategic planning, 34, 59, 253, 254, 258

F
Finland, 10, 11, 49, 51, 56, 237–248,
   279–281
France, 7, 68, 80, 84, 85, 88, 89, 132, 135, 136,
   163, 184, 257, 279, 280, 282, 284

G
GCC countries, 201, 202, 206, 207, 211
Global talent
   adaptability, 45, 46, 109, 131–133, 142,
      226, 277
   cultural intelligence, 6, 65–76, 90, 94, 222,
      273, 280
   flexibility, 8, 32, 101, 125, 130, 133,
      136–138, 226, 245, 259
   innovation, 162, 167
   international experience, 60, 70–71, 75,
      90, 227, 233, 239, 241, 246, 256, 268,
      274, 275
   mind-set, 117
Global talent management
   definition, 3, 6, 18, 44, 65, 66, 80, 81, 94,
      108, 126, 199–201, 219, 270
   governmental policies, 10, 144, 147, 202,
      211, 212
   localization policies, 160, 161
   nationalization policies, 198, 207, 209–211
Global workforce
   global careerists, 10, 11, 81, 89, 161, 163,
      166, 168, 237–248, 284

Made in the USA
Middletown, DE
10 March 2019